# Family Careers

## Developmental Change in Families

# Family Careers

## Developmental Change in Families

**JOAN ALDOUS**
University of Notre Dame

**JOHN WILEY & SONS**
New York   Santa Barbara   Chicester   Brisbane   Toronto

*Library of Congress Cataloging in Publication Data:*

Aldous, Joan.
  Family careers.

  Includes index.
  1.  Family.  I.  Title.
QH728.A5        301.42        77-15043
ISBN 0-471-02046-X

Printed in the United States of America

10  9  8  7  6  5  4  3  2

To the memory of my parents
Alfred Evan Aldous
Coral Kerr Aldous

# Preface

This book is about the changes in families from the time they are formed until they are dissolved. It is directed to students who wish to gain a better understanding of families over time—either to do research, to live better family careers of their own, or both. Practitioners who deal with families directly, or indirectly through the help they provide individual family members, should also find the book useful.

For this developmental analysis of families, we will look at the participation of individual members in the marital, parent-child, and sibling roles within the family as a unit. A conceptual framework of how the family develops will supply the analytical "tools" for our endeavor.

The first part of the book is devoted to explaining this framework. It begins with a discussion of "concepts" and "conceptual frameworks" and illustrates them with examples specifically from the framework of family development. The next four chapters examine in detail the important concepts of the family development framework, for which Appendix A provides a glossary of terms.

Once the family development approach is understood, the reader is ready to apply its concepts. The second part of the book contains this application. Here the best available research findings provide a basis for discussing family and positional careers. The discussion focuses in turn on the marital, on the parent-child, and on the sibling subsystems. A chart inserted between the first and second parts of the book indicates the timing and intersection of events in careers both inside and outside the family. The interdependence of these careers—marital, parental, sibling, educational, and occupational—is then discussed in the chapters that follow.

This plan of organization enables the reader to acquire a perspective on change as it occurs over time in the careers in each family subsystem. At the same time, she or he will see the intertwining and interdependence of occurrences in the subsystems as well as in the schools and workplaces that help to shape the career of the family as a unit.

Readers who prefer to examine all the family subsystems at one particular stage can do so by combining chapters in the subsystem sections that cover the same period. They can read Chapters 7 and 11, for example, to get a picture of the child-bearing period and Chapters 8 to 13 for the child-rearing years. Chapters 10 and 15 cover relations between aged parents and their children and grandchildren. Because of the dearth of material on the sibling career, there is only one chapter devoted to it, but this chapter can be divided to fit an organization by stages.

The final chapter of the book contains an assessment of the family development framework. A consideration of the kinds of research that demonstrate the framework's special contribution to family knowledge appears here as does a brief summary of the important points of the book. There is also a discussion of how practitioners can apply the framework. The chapter concludes with a consideration of family development scholars' present activities in the light of future possibilities, a fitting ending for a work concerned with change over extended periods of time.

Joan Aldous

Notre Dame, Indiana
March 29, 1977

# Acknowledgements

It is fashionable in some quarters today to have had an unhappy childhood in which parents were in conflict with each other and with their children. My family life while I was growing up makes me quite out of style. My father, a Professor of Agronomy at what was then Kansas State College, delighted in his family. A special treat was when he would take me along to his experimental plots where he inspected the various strains of grass he was trying to improve. (He was the only person I have known whose doctoral thesis was written before he began his official Ph.D. training). A strain of grass now bears his name, a tribute to his pioneering work on pasture grasses, and I like to think my own interest in research goes back to those pleasant excursions. His sudden death just as he was experiencing the joy of applying his research findings to the drought-fighting activities of the newly established United States Soil Conservation Service was my first experience of great loss.

That this blow was softened by a host of warm memories is due to the indomitable spirit of my mother. Only recently have I come to appreciate what his death must have meant to her, for theirs was a genuinely happy marriage. They used to joke that their only quarrels occurred on moving days, and certainly my remembrance of family arguments is limited to my own disagreements with my sister. Having to support two daughters as well as to make a life of her own, my mother set off for New York City and obtained her master's degree from Columbia Teachers College during that institution's heyday. She returned to a position in the Department of Family and Child Development at Kansas State University where she taught a generation of home economics students about marriage relations and the development and guidance of youth, the latter a course she inaugurated and applied in our own family.

Through her example and that of her friends, it was clear to me that women could lead happy lives writing, doing research, teaching, and travelling as well as being wives and mothers. Consequently, I have never had any difficulty in visualizing women competently engaged in a whole cornucopia of roles.

It should be apparent from all this that I am hopelessly outdated, having been blessed with a family background that continues to comfort me even though my parents are now both gone. I like to think that they would find this book a suitable tribute and in my mother's case an addition to her knowledge as a family scholar.

Over the years, I have incurred intellectual in addition to sentimental debts. Reuben Hill, my thesis advisor, friend, and former university colleague, introduced me to the family development perspective and has been an unfailing source of ideas and support. His influence on this book is reflected in its organization, its content, and along with Martin Stanford's careful editing its readibility. In the early stages of the book's writing, other help came from long discussions with Jan Trost, who forced me to deal with some of the perspective's shortcomings. Paul C. Glick provided the most up-to-date material available on the demography of family development or put me in touch with people who could.

Penny Baron, when I was privileged to have her as a teaching assistant, urged me to turn my lecture notes into a book. In that form, she argued, students could discuss the issues rather than listen to their presentation. To get me started on the writing, she co-authored one of the first drafts of Chapter I. Thus, she bears some of the responsibility—or as I have sometimes thought in the decade since its inception, the blame—for this book. A succession of able teaching assistants who followed Dr. Baron have given me the benefit of their criticisms and comments on various earlier versions. They include Kathy Auerbach, Gary Sponaugle, and Stephen Jorgensen, who, in addition, compiled the glossary. A special thanks goes to David Klein, former student, research assistant, and now valued colleague, for his suggestions and enthusiastic support during various difficult writing periods. Also, numerous students have let me benefit from their thoughts, as I tried out portions of the working manuscript in classes over the years.

The fact that the book was eventually completed results from the favorable intellectual and personnel climate of the Sociological Research Institute of the Catholic University of Leuven, and to its Director, Professor Wilfried Dumon. His counsel and assistances on matters large and small made the work of writing possible. Professor Karel Dobbelaere's assurance that authors did finish books kept me writing during times of discouragement. And Director Marietta De Vos of the University Center for Women Students saw that I enjoyed congenial living arrangements without which no words could have been put on paper.

The difficult job of translating rough drafts into typed copy has been accomplished by a number of skillful persons including Vera Broos and Irene Hinojosa; and Daniel Valdez and Fred Duplain carefully drew charts and found and checked references. Finally, there are several people who at various times in my life assisted me in ways that enabled me to write the book. Leone Kell showed me the intellectual excitement in studying families, and Dorothy H. Funk, Mildred Webb, and Paul M. Arnesen made it physically possible.

This list of acknowledgments is a long one, but so are my debts. Because of the kind of persons they are, it has been a pleasure to remember them, and all the others who in one way or another made this book possible.

J.A.

Notre Dame, Indiana

# Contents

**The Sibling Career**

**Overview**

# Family Careers

## Developmental Change in Families

# Part 1

## The conceptual framework

# Concepts and conceptual frameworks

To begin our study of family development, let us examine a short case history, that of the Jones family. Their description indicates the kind of information students of the family are concerned with. We all know families like the Joneses. They are the kind of family that keeps countries going. They pay their taxes, obey the law, and are active in the various organizations that make community life livable and put bread and butter on the nation's tables. If the school needs someone to explain a proposed sex education program to parents, Principal Mary Piatrowski thinks first of Ed Jones. And the fellows in the dispatcher's office on the seven-to-three shift at Macroglomerate International see Ed as the natural person to complain to the so-and-sos-in-charge about the state of the washrooms. He's a good worker, and the guys upstairs listen when he gets mad.

Chris Jones is check-out cashier at a local supermarket so they can make their house payment and put away something for the kids' college. (Chris Junior keeps talking about being a lawyer like the woman on her favorite TV serial, and she has the grades to be the first Jones to go to college.) Chris remains active in community concerns despite occupational and family demands. There is the matter of serving as financial officer for the church, a "first" for a woman, although Chris is quick to say she's no women's libber, just a fair-play partisan. She also did some telephoning to get out the vote at the last election for one of the political parties and was so busy working she almost didn't get to vote herself.

Meanwhile, back at 301 North Sample when the front door is closed and everyone is home, the Joneses have their share of the worries and disappointments that come with family living, along with the satisfactions that contribute to the family's durability as an institution. Sixteen-year-old Chris Junior, or Tina as she insists on being called, is a credit to her parents and aside from irritating her father by needling him to help out more around the house is seldom a source of worry. She has gotten over her earlier rivalry with her younger brothers, Harry and Eddie, and has managed to stay away from the fast crowd at high school who are supposedly into drugs and "going all the way" in the backseats of cars. Harry, though, continues to be a problem. He seems never to have made new friends after the family moved four years ago into their present three-bedroom rambler in a different school district. He doesn't like his teachers and has been known to skip school. And at least twice that his parents know of, he has had too much beer, which he is too young to drink according to both state law and parental rules. There is also his friendship with the girl next door whose clothes, according to Chris, are too tight and morals too loose.

Tina vacillates between being Harry's severest critic and, when he and his father are arguing, his staunchest advocate. Ed never was much for physical punishment, especially since he's seen how it doesn't do any good. Like Chris, he's relied on scolding, but now that Harry is older it seems nothing "works"—loss of privileges, reasoning, or yelling.

Young Eddie, however, although an "accident," is a joy to everyone. Too young at eight to have to face worldly temptations, he accepts tolerantly Harry's supervision in his parent's absence, perhaps because Harry is clearly so fond of him. In fact, Harry and Tina please their parents (and themselves) by taking Eddie to various events, educational and otherwise, and the parents continue to hope that some of their daughter's ambition will rub off on their older son. According to the birth certificates, there's only a 14-month difference between eleventh-grader Harry and twelfth-grader Tina, but in maturity they're several years apart.

As for the parents' private lives, in the bedroom it isn't so good as it once was; occasionally Chris wonders about those young secretaries in the front office. And, although quickly dismissing such thoughts as disloyal, Chris has seen her world lose some of its taken-for-granted character since several of their best friends got divorced. Ed accepts the lack of excitement in their marriage as something that comes with middle age. His attention is focused on the discrepancy between income and outgo, a worry that overshadows his content with the reassuring routines of television, community affairs, and an occasional night out with Chris.

What are we to make of all this? Family development, the subject of this book, is one approach to studying the Joneses and other families. Its focus is on the characteristics of families over the period of their existence, beginning with the couple's cohabitation and ending with the death of family members, or with their departure into other family units. The time perspective of the concepts that constitute the framework of family development includes a systematic analysis of the changes that members of a family can expect throughout its existence. This approach sets family development apart from those frameworks that analyze the family primarily as it exists at one point in time. Thus, in analyzing what is going on in the Jones family, we will try to see how the content and timing of past events in individual and family histories affect present interaction patterns among the family's members. Such potentially disruptive events can be a residential move to a different school district, the wife-mother's return to outside employment, the anticipated future departure of the daughter-sister after her graduation from high school, or any one of innumerable others.

The distinctiveness of the family development framework, thus comes from the responses and concepts that compose it. This book is devoted to presenting these concepts and to showing how they can be applied in analyzing family behaviors. Because the knowledge of any subject is so dependent upon concepts, let us examine the intellectual tools we propose to use and the context in which we propose to use them.

## CONCEPTS AND THEIR CHARACTERISTICS

Each object or event that we experience has a particular set of characteristics such as size, shape, or color. Some of these characteristics are similar to those of other objects or events, and some are not. Concepts result from the abstracting of common elements from a host of particular occurrences we perceive in the world. Those similarities that a concept points to as its own are differentiated from those of other concepts by a meaningful label, either a word or phrase.

The selective perspective that a concept provides thus enables the individual to organize and to rely on centers of meaning from the flux of sensations impinging upon him. Concepts give stability to existence and simplify its complexity by indicating the common elements in experiences. Without concepts, it would be difficult to communicate, let alone to think in the first place.

The word "family," for example, refers to a concept that abstracts from a large variety of different groups certain similarities that families share. These similarities consist of the following: membership based on mutual consent, blood, or adoption; group properties usually including common residence; and certain functions such as socialization and procreation that the groups perform for their members and for society. The concept of family points to these similarities and ignores characteristics that differentiate family groups from one another such as composition or authority patterns. Because the concept of the family exists we can focus, for example, on the similarities among such seemingly diverse phenomena as a group composed of a woman, her daughter, and her daughter's son; of a young man and women living together in a consensual union; and of a three-generation household consisting of grandparents, parents, and a son and his wife.

In addition to simplifying our experiential world, concepts enable us to accomplish other cognitive tasks.[1] The categories they supply are our means for identifying objects and events in the world. Once we have learned the shared properties of families, for example, we do not have to ask each time we see several people whether it is a family or not. Knowing the concept, we know the defining properties it abstracts. We possess, therefore, guides to appropriate and inappropriate actions with respect to families.

Concepts also have properties that enable us to relate categories of events. The concepts of marriage, parenthood, and critical role transition, for example, can all be related. Getting married and having a child are both critical role transition events, because they signal new behavioral demands and new relationships. These concepts taken together give us more information than each concept looked at separately. As a group, concepts help us perceive patterns in the phenomena we experience by creating a "vocabulary" of thought and communication. They provide the cognitive organization that enables

---

[1] This paragraph draws heavily on Bruner, Goodnow, and Austin (1956)

us to learn from experience, to identify current events, to behave appropriately, and to study systematically such phenomena as the family.

The conceptual lenses through which we view the world, however, filter out those characteristics not pointed to by our conceptual vocabulary. Our choice of family development concepts thus focuses our attention on changes in family groups from the time these groups are first formed until they dissolve. These concepts touch only incidentally on the formative events that punctuate historical time. This is not to say that wars, depressions, or inflation periods do not affect family development. They do, of course, but their occurrence is not predictable as are the more homely events of committing oneself to marriage, of bearing and nurturing children, of entering school, of leaving home, and of adjusting to retirement. These expectable happenings in the lives of families will be our concern.

**Evaluating Concepts**
Nietzsche was quite correct in remarking that there is no "immaculate perception." Any object can be classified in more than one way, and no single point of view or classification is "natural" or inherent in the nature of the world. In organizing an experience or subject matter, we thus select concepts for their usefulness to the purpose at hand. In our case, we wish to study those characteristics of families that stand out sharply when perceived through concepts of family development. To enable us to accomplish these goals, the concepts we introduce for scientific discourse must meet certain standards that concepts in day-to day use need not. We shall examine three such standards in some detail. These include (1) clarity; (2) scope; and (3) systemic coherence (Phillips, 1966: 32–35).

The *clarity* of a concept has to do with the sharpness of its limits. The concept's definition should be so unambiguous and precise that different people at different times can agree on what phenomena are similar enough to be assigned the word label of that particular concept. In order to illustrate differences in conceptual clarity, let us examine the following definitions of a *small group* and a *family*.

> *Small group*  that group of persons in which it is possible for each member to affect every other member reciprocally and directly.
>
> *Family*  any group whose members are related to one another by marriage, birth, or adoption.

Now the concept of a small group is fairly clear. If we know what a group is, we can generally agree on what groups are included in the concept "small group." We have only to determine whether the members can see and hear each other.

The concept "family," on the other hand, is not so clear as that of "small group." The definition above fails to give us much aid in deciding how we are to classify those extended kinship households that are found in other cultures and that may include several married couples and their children living in the same household. Do we classify them as one family or as several? Or, to take an example from our own society, suppose we have a small group that consists of a mother, a father, their own two children, and a foster child who has not been legally adopted. Is this third child a member of the family or not? And what about married couples without children? Are they families, or do they become so only after children arrive?

Clarity, accordingly, is an important property of a scientific concept. If a concept is not clear, we do not know exactly what we are talking about when we use it, nor are we sure what other persons are referring to when they use the concept.

Clarity is related to the ease of "operationalizing" a concept. Can one express it in terms of observable events? Some concepts lack clarity partly because they are hard to translate into concrete terms. For an example, let us take the concept of "family development task," a concept that links the demands that each family member makes on the family as a unit with the requirements of governmental, educational, and other societal agencies. It has been defined as a "growth responsibility that arises at or about a certain period in the life of a family, full achievement of which leads to satisfaction and success with later tasks, while failure leads to unhappiness in the family, disapproval by society and difficulty with later family developmental tasks" (Duvall, 1971: 150). This concept's lack of clarity as defined is associated with its abstractness. We have to operationalize a number of other terms in order to define them. Terms such as "certain period," "successful achievement," and "disapproval by the society," in turn, are difficult to translate into observable events. Different observers can disagree as to what constitutes "successful achievement," and they may not even agree as to what constitutes "growth responsibility."

With concepts, we also face the problem of what events to include in their definition. It is not only a question of having to decide at what point phenomena become dissimilar enough to be defined as belonging to another concept. As scientific inquiry proceeds, new issues appear that demand redefinitions of old concepts to sharpen their focus on a part of experience (Kaplan, 1964: 62–71). The meaning of these concepts is modified as our idea of what constitutes the "standard case" of a concept changes. Thus, the concept of family may be undergoing change as it becomes common to include as families not only married couples with children, but also unions without children, and unattached single persons who share a residence and play family roles. With this change goes a change in our notion of what is the "standard family."

The second criteria scholars use in evaluating concepts is their *scope*. The scope of a concept refers to the range of phenomena that it includes. For instance, the concept, "small group," has much broader scope than does the concept, "family." All families are small groups, but there are many small groups that are not families. Scientists attempt to develop concepts of broad scope, since they link together and point up the commonalities in a variety of seemingly different phenomena.

The *systemic coherence* of a concept is a third standard for evaluating the usefulness of concepts. It has to do with how many other concepts can be linked meaningfully to a single concept. Systemic concepts are often interdefined and embedded in a "nest" of concepts. The concept, husband, for example, groups together all males having a certain status usually acquired through the wedding ceremony. But, in addition, the individuals so grouped share many other characteristics. We can predict, among other things, that in most societies they will hold some occupation that makes them the primary family breadwinner; that they will, accordingly, have somewhat more power than other family members; and that they will represent the family in relation to other groups. The concept "husband" thus classes together individuals sharing characteristics other than marital status. Husband is a systemic concept because it suggests or points to other linked concepts having to do with role behaviors, economic activities, interaction patterns, and power relations (Hempel, 1952: 53).

Color of hair is not a systemic concept insofar as family analysis is concerned. To know that persons have the same hair color does not enable us to predict that they also share a series of other similar characteristics having implications for family behavior.

## SYSTEMIC CONCEPTS AND CONCEPTUAL FRAMEWORKS

Now that we have some understanding of what we mean by the systemic quality of concepts, we can begin discussing conceptual frameworks and, specifically, the family development framework. Investigators attempting to analyze some phenomena like the family necessarily use concepts. Those that are systemic suggest other concepts useful in the analysis. If they are new, the investigators will have to specify and give them a label. Conceptual frameworks are composed of concepts that, taken together, give us some sort of unified picture of the subject matter with which the concepts are concerned. Thus conceptual frameworks can be thought of as clusters of concepts whose integrative strength derives from the phenomena they categorize.

To provide knowledge of conceptual frameworks and their development, the systemic concepts of position and role can serve as good examples. A *position* consists of a certain location in social groups to which are assigned a collection of rights and duties (Bates, 1956). Examples of positions would be the positions of husband-father, wife-mother, daughter-sister, and brother-son in the family group. The concept of position is linked to the concept *role*, a concept that categorizes the behaviors appropriate to realizing the rights and duties tied to a particular position (Linton, 1936: 113–131). A family position, therefore, is composed of various roles. Thus the husband-father position generally includes among other roles those of breadwinner, sex partner, disciplinarian, teacher, and companion. Each role in turn consists of a set of *norms*, norms being behavioral expectations that set off one role from another. The role of breadwinner, for example, contains as one norm that a certain proportion of the earnings should go to the family. These concepts—norm, role, and position—are defined in terms of each other, and interdefinition is one of the principal characteristics of conceptual frameworks.

### Role concepts in the Family Development Framework

Let us see how the family development framework incorporates role concepts. Using the time dimension that distinguishes the family development framework, Deutscher (1959) created the concept of *role sequence.* It includes the behavioral changes in the content of a role over time. Take the father's role of teacher as shown in Figure 1-1. When children are young, a father does less teaching of values and skills than he will when the child is older and has the cognitive and motor abilities to accomplish more advanced learning tasks. The role of teacher persists at least as long as there are children in the home, but its behavioral specifications change, making it an example of a role sequence.

*Role cluster*, another concept derived from role that we owe to Deutscher (1959), refers to the total complement of roles and their associated norms that make up a social position during any one stage

**Figure 1-1 Roles, role sequences, and role clusters in the positional careers of fathers.**

| Role Cluster at Time 1 | Role Cluster at Time 2 | Role Cluster at Time 3 |
|---|---|---|
| *Role I:* Teacher | *Role I:* Teacher | *Role I:* Teacher |
| *Norms:* F is expected to help baby son become aware of his physical abilities. | *Norms:* F is expected to teach pre-school son behavior needed to enter school. | *Norms:* F is expected to teach school-aged son more complicated skills and tasks, to teach him values of the larger society and the behavior they require. |
| *Role Behavior:* F shows baby son interesting objects, helps him mold and manipulate objects, talks to him, and responds to the sounds he makes. | *Role Behavior:* F teaches his pre-school son simple skills as buttoning his coat and reads to him to teach him to sit still and to listen to new ideas. | *Role Behavior:* F takes an interest in son's school activities, shows him how to do tasks like mowing the lawn, takes him to sports events, and tells him how to behave there and why. |

Role Sequence

| | | |
|---|---|---|
| *Role II:* Disciplinarian | *Role II:* Disciplinarian | *Role II:* Disciplinarian |
| *Norms:* F is expected to keep baby son from harming himself or others, to avoid rewarding him for undesirable behavior. | *Norms:* F is expected to prevent his child from engaging in undesirable behavior and to correct him when he does engage in it. | *Norms:* F is expected to provide his school-aged son with a set of rules to guide his behavior and to guarantee that he follow them by using appropriate sanctions. |
| *Role Behavior:* F removes baby son from danger, prevents him from pulling on lamp cords, and ignores him when he cries for no apparent reason. | *Role Behavior:* F warns his pre-school son not to bite his sister and spanks him when he does it anyway. | *Role Behavior:* F explains to school-aged son why he must take out the trash and deprives him of TV privileges when he does not obey. |

Role Sequence

| | | |
|---|---|---|
| *Role III:* Affection Giver | *Role III:* Affection Giver | *Role III:* Affection Giver |
| *Norms:* F is expected to give warmth and affection to his baby son. | *Norms:* F is expected to give his son attention and display positive affection. | *Norms:* F is expected to give son support, to convey positive affection, and to give approval. |
| *Role Behavior:* F holds and cuddles baby son. | *Role Behavior:* F asks his pre-school son about his activities; tells him he's proud of him; roughhouses with him; candy, and other tokens brings him small toys, when he comes home from work. | *Role Behavior:* F gives support to son when he has problems, is understanding even when son is in error, and shows son he enjoys his company. |

of a family life-span. As Figure 1-1 shows, the husband-father position at any one time may contain, among others, the roles of teacher, disciplinarian, and affection given. When viewed over time, a position such as that of a husband-father can be thought of as a changing sequence of role clusters, and this sequence can be termed a *positional career* (Farber, 1961). A person in the husband-father position in Figure 1-1 changes his behaviors as teacher, disciplinarian, and affection giver as time passes; later, he adds the role of companion and drops that of disciplinarian. All these additions, subtractions, and role modifications make up the positional career.

Farber (1961) then used the concept of positional career as a basis for characterizing the family as a set of mutually contingent careers. By this term he meant that the events in the life-course of individual family members, summarized in their school history, employment, and, in the case of young adults, departure from home to marry and to have children of their own, all affect others in the family. These multiple family "career lines and their timetables and synchronization" (Elder, 1975: 178), which together compose what Rodgers (1964: 266) calls the *family career*, constitute the major focus of this book.

The concepts of role sequence, role cluster, and positional career are interrelated to and interdefined with the concepts of role, norm, and position from which they stem. Thus, when given a time dimension, the idea of role cluster suggests the need of the concept of positional career just as the concepts of role, when viewed from a temporal perspective, gives rise to the concept of role sequence.

It is this quality of mutual implication that makes the family development vocabulary of concepts a framework. In this instance, it is possible to see how the framework itself, once it is recognized and used, self-consciously, engenders new concepts. Because of its scope, clarity and systemic coherence, the concept of role is found in other frameworks. But the focus on expected change in the family, which differentiates family development from other approaches, has created a need for new concepts that simultaneously incorporate the concept of role and that point up change explicitly. As a result, individuals working with the family development framework have produced such terms as "role sequence" and "positional career" that, by naming and defining phenomena, become part of the conceptual structure for increasing our understanding of the family.

**Conceptual Frameworks in Family Analysis**
In assessing research studies on the family, Hill and Hansen (1960) examined the work of researchers and writers to discover what sets of

assumptions underlay their conceptual frameworks. At the time, Hill was heavily involved in the construction of the family development approach and, after having revised a text in the symbolic interaction tradition (Waller, 1951), he was keenly aware of the similarities and differences in concepts from one approach to the other. This awareness made him eager to discover conceptual affiliations in the work of other scholars.

In their search of the literature, Hill and Hansen were able to distinguish five essentially sociological frameworks, each of which possessed a grouping of concepts that produced a different view of the family. Each centered on the family as a group, or on its marital, sibling and parent-child subgroups, rather than on individual family members. The frameworks Hill and Hansen identified were the following: (1) (symbolic) interactional; (2) structure-functional; (3) situational; (4) institutional; and (5) developmental.[2] A decade later, Broderick (1971) argued that a good case can be made for eliminating the situational and institutional approaches. According to Stryker (1964), the concepts and insights derived from the situational framework can be incorporated in most instances into the interactional framework. The institutional approach as delineated by Sirjamaki (1964) emphasized a methodology based on cross-cultural or historical comparisons rather than on concepts unique to itself. Family scholars also restricted their use of the frameworks to the developmental, structure-functional, and interactional according to the research and theory survey of Klein and others (1969).

More recently, a conflict perspective on family life has appeared. Higher divorce rates and the women's rights movement as well as the revelation of the extent of child abuse and marital violence have led some scholars to focus on the consequences of power discrepancies and the management of conflict in family interaction (Gillespie, 1971; Straus, 1974). Characterized by concepts like oppression, exploitation, and alienation, which are drawn from the theories of Karl Marx (Morgan, 1975), the perspective based on conflict points to the "darker side" of family life.

To provide some basis for comparison of the family development framework, we will examine briefly two other frameworks—the inter-

---

[2] To these, Nye and Berardo (1966: 6–7), drawing from disciplines other than sociology, added six others where there appeared to be a "substantial body of concepts" useful in studying the family and a "distinctive set of assumptions concerning the individual, society, and family relationships." The additional frameworks were the psychoanalytic, economic, anthropological, social psychological, religious, and legal.

actional and the structured-functional. Here are Hill and Hansen's descriptions of these frameworks.

The Interactional Approach. *An interactional conception of the family takes these lines: The family is a unit of interacting persons, each occupying a position(s) within the family to which a number of roles are assigned, i.e., the individual perceives norms or role expectations held individually or collectively by other family members for his attributes and behavior. In a given situation an individual defines these role expectations primarily in view of their source (reference group) and of his own self-conception. Then he role-plays. Most immediately the family is studied through analysis of overt interacts (interaction of role-playing family members) cast in this structure. . . . Thus the hundreds of studies it has stimulated have focused on the internal aspects of the family but neglected consideration of the family as an entity in relation to the community or collateral associations.*

*Substantively, in addition to role analysis, the framework has focused on such problems as status and inter-status relations, which become the basis for authority patterns and initiative taking; processes of communication, conflict, problem solving, decision making, and stress reaction; and other aspects of family interaction and interactive processes from dating to divorce. . . .*

The Structure-Functional Approach. *The functionalist might conceive of the family as one of many components of the complete social system (society) and as best studied for the functions it performs in society. Internally, the family itself is composed of individuals who are best studied through their status-role bundles and who are significant for their functions in the maintenance of the family system and, ultimately, of the social system. Individuals contribute to the boundary maintenance of the system either by acting in response to demands of the structure or by acting under the constraint of the structure. . . .*

*The scope of the functional approach to the family is broad. . . . The framework thus encompasses the interplay between (1) the family and collateral systems like the school, the occupational world, and the market place, and (2) the transactions between the family and the smaller subgroups of the husband-wife dyad, the sibling cliques, and the individual personality systems of family members. . . .*

*The individual family member is viewed more as a reactive bundle of statuses and roles than as an active, action-initiating person; similarly, the family is viewed more as a passively adapting element of the system than as an agent of change. (Hill and Hansen, 1960: 302–304)*

As Hill and Hansen note, there is an overlap of concepts in the frameworks although each framework contains some concepts peculiar to itself. Thus, each framework is different from the others because, apart from utilizing some of the same concepts, each organizes its concepts in a different way. The concept of role, for example, is found in the symbolic interaction, the structure-function, and the family development frameworks. Only the family development framework, however, contains such concepts as "role sequence" and "positional career." Thus while the family development framework borrows some concepts from other approaches, it brings them together in a different overall context. Consequently, the concept of role is given a time perspective because of concepts like *role sequence* and *positional career* with which it is associated. (See Hill and Rodgers (1964) for an earlier discussion of family development concepts.)

The use of any conceptual framework always involves a set of underlying assumptions. These assumptions indicate what the framework takes for granted about the phenomena to which it is applied. Assumptions make specific the bonds linking the concepts in a framework. Each of the frameworks used to study the family has its own set of assumptions, though some of them overlap at certain points. Some assumptions of the family development framework are:[3]

1.  Family behavior is the sum of past experience of family members as incorporated in the present as well as in their goals and expectations for the future.
2.  Families develop and change over time in similar and consistent ways.
3.  Humans not only initiate actions as they mature and interact with others but also they react to environmental pressures.
4.  The family and its members must perform certain time-specific tasks set by themselves and by persons in the broader society.
5.  In a social setting, the individual is the basic autonomous unit.

Note how these assumptions differ from those of the structure-functional framework as applied to the family:

1.  Social conduct is best analyzed as it contributes to the functions and requirements of a society.

---

[3] The assumptions in the discussion that follows were chosen to highlight the differences between the frameworks. They deirve only in part from the work of Hill and Hansen (1960) and that of Nye and Berardo (1966).

2.  The family performs at least one of these societal functions while meeting family needs.
3.  As a social system, the family tends toward stability.
4.  Family behaviors are largely determined by norms.
5.  A social human is basically one who is thoroughly conditioned by the social system in which he or she lives; autonomous action is rare and asocial.

The assumptions of the interaction approach are the last we will list:

1.  Family behaviors are affected more by intrafamilial factors than by societal norms.
2.  Social conduct results from the social milieu, particularly its symbolic context as reflected in communication.
3.  The basic autonomous unit is the active individual in interaction with others who are present either symbolically or actually.

Frameworks in the family area differ not only in their assumptions and in the concepts utilized but also in their scope. In general, the less specific the concepts contained in a framework, the broader the scope of the framework as a whole. Although the assumptions listed above are predicated on the family being the phenomenon to be analyzed, the concepts in the structure-function and interaction frameworks are abstract enough to be applied to many kinds of sociological phenomena. Because the concepts of family development are chosen specifically for studying the family, this framework is probably less applicable to the study of other types of groups. Its focus on change over time, however, has implications for other collectivities, and some of its concepts are of broad enough scope to be useful in group analysis.

What one looks at in studying families depends upon the conceptual framework he or she uses. Symbolic interactionists, as interactionists are often called, concentrate on processes within the family mediated by communication. Parent-child socialization, power maneuvers, and love relationships receive high priority. To take the Jones family, whose description began this chapter, as an example, a symbolic interactionist would look at how Chris and Ed are bringing up their children in terms of what they talk to them about, when and how they discipline them, and how much love they show their daughter and two sons. For structure-functionalists, the subjects of interest are what families do to sustain and to socialize new members so that society may continue. Interchanges between families and other societal units like economic and educational agencies necessarily take on importance. The effects of workplace and school life on the Jones family would be of special interest from this perspective. Family development scholars might well be concerned with many of the same issues as their symbolic interactionist and structural-functionalist colleagues. They differ, however, by analyzing these issues within the context of expectable change over time in family careers, such as the children's school progress and the eventual retirement of Ed and Chris.

Just as the frameworks differ in how they focus on families so too does the logic of the research design their exponents employ. Symbolic interactionists may very well turn to in-depth studies of a small number of families. Through a series of interviews with family members and observations of each of the families, they strive to gain an understanding of the kinds of interaction patterns that characterize the family (Turner, 1970; Kantor and Lehr, 1975; Laslett and Rapoport, 1975; Aldous, 1977). In contrast, structural-functionalists tend to find "one-shot" interviews with members of many families that meet certain basic criteria. They can then generalize their findings about responses in certain kinds of families as they are triggered by societal events in the larger population. Given the same monetary resources, scholars operating in the family development tradition, however, try ideally to obtain measures of family behavior over a period of time in a longitudinal as opposed to a cross-sectional design. In this fashion, they try to perceive and describe family change even at the cost of being confined to smaller sample sizes (Hill and Rodger, 1964).[4]

None of these approaches is right or wrong. Nor does any single framework offer a complete picture of family life. As the approaches differ, so do they complement each other in the sense that they offer alternative viewpoints on families, for phenomena left out of one framework are pointed up in another.

## CONCEPTS, PROPOSITIONS, AND HYPOTHESES

As is true in other areas of sociology, most family analysis is concerned with description. But the systemic qualities of the concepts in a framework, the qualities that have suggested other related concepts to scholars, also permit the framework to serve as an intellectual tool for going beyond description to explanation. Once a phenomenon is con-

---

[4] Chapter 17 contains a discussion of some of the research designs used in family development research.

ceptualized scholars can begin to relate certain of its properties to those of other phenomena by stating these relationships in propositions. A *proposition* is a statement that affirms something to be true about two or more aspects of phenomena which are earlier pointed to by concepts. Propositions provide us with more information than do concepts. For example, in the previous discussion of the concept "husband," the statement asserted that persons in the family position of husband were generally the chief breadwinners and for that reason had somewhat more power in shaping family decisions. This description of the characteristics of husbands suggests the following proposition. "The larger the proportion of the family income that the husband contributes, the greater will be his power in the family." This proposition relates the concept of husband to concepts of breadwinner and of power, and it gives us more information than do any of the concepts alone.

Systemic concepts, by pointing to other concepts, give rise to propositions. We can then test how valid propositions are in reporting on reality. When propositions are translated into operational terms, they are often called hypotheses, that is, they point to reality by claiming that "If x is present in a certain way under certain conditions, then y will also be present in a certain way, etc." Propositions as propositions, on the other hand, tend to be used after all the evidence is in and the proofs fully tested, when it is time to formulate theory from many well-confirmed hypotheses.

A good example of the process of developing and testing hypotheses from propositions and concepts is found in the work of Zelditch (1955) and Aronoff and Crano (1975). Zelditch took the concept of role differentiation from the structure-functional framework and related it to the concept of gender in the following hypothesis.

*If a nuclear family consists . . . of the male adult, female adult and their immediate children, the male adult will play the role of instrumental leader and the female adult will play the role of expressive leader (Zelditch, 1955: 315).*

This hypothesis states that the concepts of gender and role differentiation are associated so that individuals of a given gender play a certain type of role. The concept, role differentiation, classified roles into the categories of instrumental roles and expressive roles just as gender refers to the classification of people into males and females.

The concepts in this hypothesis illustrate several characteristics we have mentioned. Role differentiation is clear, but it cannot be defined directly in observational terms. Thus Zelditch must "translate" the abstract terms of instrumental and expressive roles, the divisions of role differentiation he uses, into concrete observable behaviors in order to examine whether the resultant hypothesis is consistent with reality. Accordingly, he defines the concepts in terms that apply particularly to the family rather than to all small groups. With regard to instrumental roles, he looks for evidence concerning who is "leader of the hunt," or "boss manager of the farm," and who is the final authority and executor of discipline, punishment, and control over the children in the family. He examines expressive roles through evidence of such behaviors as mediation resolving disputes, consoling, loving, and indulging (Zelditch, 1955: 138). The concepts, so defined, are now clear enough that others not only can understand what he is talking about but also can replicate his study to check its accuracy. In addition, the concepts in the proposition are broad enough in scope to encompass behaviors of urban Protestant Americans and those, say, of Asian Buddhist peasants so that the common elements underlying these observable differences can be identified and classified.

Zelditch examined data for 56 nonindustrialized societies in various parts of the world where ethnographic reports provided the evidence necessary for testing his hypothesis. Although relevant evidence generally supported this hypothesis, critics have argued from the perspective of the interaction framework that persons interacting in families rarely maintain completely separate roles. Wife-mothers organize household activities and are active in economic activities outside the home. Husband-fathers maintain the morale of their wives and their children through affection giving and active interaction in resolving family disputes. Moreover, as we shall see in the second portion of this book, men's expressive behaviors turn out to be of major importance for the marital satisfaction of couples in the later stages of the family life.

Aronoff and Crano (1975) in the light of these criticisms of the Zelditch proposition subjected it to a more rigorous empirical test. They had the advantage of detailed information that had become available on other societies since the earlier study appeared. Thus they were able to look at the dependence of 862 societies on the subsistence activities of gathering, hunting, fishing, animal husbandry, and agriculture, and the degree to which men and women were separately engaged in these activities. Aronoff and Crano (1975: 17) found that women made a substantial contribution to the subsistence level of these societies, which are distributed in all areas of the world. Role sharing rather than role differentiation characterizes instrumental activities among families in nonindustrialized societies. The fact that this conclusion can be generalized to highly industrialized societies will be documented in succeeding chapters.

The research on this proposition indicates how knowledge accumulates over time. Once a proposition has been developed, placed in operational form, and tested, others can examine it. The role differentiation proposition was clear enough that scholars who were reasoning from other perspectives on families could challenge it. Yet, without Zelditch's original work, which stressed the relation of role differentiation to gender, we would not now have the knowledge we do on the distribution of instrumental task performance in families. Similar systematic research going beyond the work of Zelditch on expressive activities is now underway by other investigators.

Because conceptual frameworks bring together concepts with systemic qualities, they can give rise to propositions and, perhaps eventually, to theories. A *theory* is a set of related propositions, some of which are derived from others and some of which have received empirical support. Theory guides research in at least two ways: it suggests new propositions and hypotheses; it highlights research findings, so that their contribution to existing bodies of knowledge appears. Theory is thus an important part of the scientific endeavor.

At the present time, the family development framework, like the structure-function and the symbolic interaction frameworks, is not a theory. The concepts of each framework, even though they make us clearly aware of certain aspects of family behaviors, have not been joined into sets of related propositions. Throughout this book, we will assess the varying degrees of research support given to propositions based on family development concepts. At the outset, however, let it be understood that additional propositions are still necessary to fill the gaps in our knowledge as is a master codifier to collect and integrate the resultant propositions according to their relationship, validity, and derivation (Aldous, 1970). Only then will family development become a theory.

## SUMMARY

In this chapter, we examined concepts and conceptual frameworks in some detail. By organizing experience, concepts point out similarities in seemingly disparate events and aid us in identifying phenomena, in suggesting appropriate behavior, and in relating events. Clarity, scope, and the quality of systemic coherence provide criteria for evaluating the usefulness of concepts in analyzing phenomena. In addition, the power of concepts to suggest other concepts leads to conceptual frameworks, which are groups of concepts centered upon some phenomena to which they all relate.

The terms "position" and "role" provide good examples of systemic concepts that, when given a time dimension, suggest concepts specific to the family development framework. Characteristically, these derived concepts—role sequence, role cluster, and positional career—are interdefined and suggest each other.

Since concepts exclude objects and events outside their particular focus, the chapter has compared the family development framework with the family focus provided by the interaction and structure-function frameworks. In the family development framework, the perspective of time highlights predictable changes in the family throughout its existence, a perspective not shared by the other approaches.

Because conceptual frameworks constitute schemes for classifying related phenomena, they also suggest how concepts can be joined into propositions or hypotheses. Research then leads to the refining, revising, or rejecting of hypotheses. Theories, in turn, are composed of propositions and hypotheses as yet not disproven by empirical tests.

The remainder of this book will be devoted to documenting the family development approach. Its concepts will permit us to describe systematically families and the ways families change over time. Study of family development concepts and the research in which they have been used will alert us to numerous propositions. These propositions that state the relationships existing among phenomena as delimited by specific concepts tell us why, as well as what, is going on within the family. Frameworks and their associated concepts thus constitute powerful descriptive devices for family analysis while pointing the way to the propositions and theories of a mature science.

# REFERENCES

Aldous, Joan, "Strategies for Developing Family Theory," *Journal of Marriage and the Family*, 1970, 33, 250–257.

Aldous, Joan, "Family Interaction Patterns," in Alex Inkeles, James Coleman, and Neil Smelser, eds., *Annual Review of Sociology III*. Palo Alto, Ca.: Annual Review Press, 1977, 105–135.

Aronoff, Joe and William D. Crano, "A Re-Examination of the Cross-Cultural Principles of Task Segregation and Sex Role Differentiation in the Family," *American Sociological Review*, 1975, 40, 12–20.

Bates, Frederick I., "Position, Role and Status," *Social Forces*, 1956, 34, 313–321.

Broderick, Carlfred B., "Beyond the Five Conceptual Frameworks: A Decade of Development in Family Theory," *Journal of Marriage and the Family*, 1971, 33, 139–159.

Bruner, Jerome S., Jacqueline J. Goodnow, and George A. Austin, *A Study of Thinking.* New York: John Wiley, 1956.

Deutscher, Irwin, *Married Life in the Middle Years.* Kansas City, Mo.: Community Studies, 1959.

Duvall, Evelyn M., *Family Development.* Philadelphia: J. B. Lippincott, 1971.

Elder Glen J., Jr., "Age Differentiation and the Life Course," in Alex Inkeles, James Coleman, and Neil Smelser, eds., *Annual Review of Sociology I.* Palo Alto, Ca.: Annual Review Press, 1975, 175–190.

Farber, Bernard, "The Family as a Set of Mutually Contingent Careers," in Nelson Foote, ed., *Household Decision-Making.* New York: New York University Press, 1961, 276–297.

Gillespie, D. L., "Who Has the Power? The Marital Struggle," *Journal of Marriage and the Family*, 1971, 33, 445–458.

Hempel, Carl G., "Fundamentals of Concept Formulation in Empirical Science," *International Encyclopedia of Unified Science*, II, no. 7, Chicago: University of Chicago Press, 1952.

Hill, Reuben and Donald A. Hansen, "The Identification of Conceptual Frameworks Utilized in Family Study," *Marriage and Family Living*, 1960, 22, 299–311. Copyright 1960 by National Council on Family Relations.

Hill, Reuben and Roy H. Rodgers, "The Developmental Approach," in Harold T. Christensen, *Handbook of Marriage and the Family.* Chicago: Rand McNally, 1964, 171–211.

Kantor, David and William Lehr, *Inside the Family: Toward a Theory of Family Process.* New York: Harper Colophon Books, 1975.

Kaplan, Abraham, *The Conduct of Inquiry.* San Francisco: Chandler, 1964.

Klein, John, Gene Calvert, Neal Garland, and Margaret Polomo, "Pilgrims Progress I: Recent Developments in Family Theory," *Journal of Marriage and the Family*, 1969, 31, 677–687.

Laslett, Barbara and Rhona Rapoport, "Collaborative Interviewing and Interactive Research," *Journal of Marriage and the Family*, 1975, 37, 968–977.

Linton, Ralph, *The Study of Man.* New York: Appleton-Century, 1936.

Morgan, D. H. J., *Social Theory and the Family.* London: Routledge & Kegan Paul, 1975.

Nye, Ivan F. and Feliz Berardo, *Emerging Conceptual Frameworks in Family Analysis.* New York: Macmillan, 1966.

Phillips, Bernard S., *Social Research: Strategy and Tactics.* New York: Macmillan, 1966.

Rodgers, Roy, "Toward a Theory of Family Development," *Journal of Marriage and the Family*, 1964, 26, 262–270.

Sirjamaki, John, "The Institutional Approach," in H. T. Christensen, ed.,

*Handbook of Marriage and the Family.* Chicago: Rand McNally, 1964, 33–50.

Straus, Murray A., "Leveling, Civility and Violence in the Family," *Journal of Marriage and the Family*, 1974, 36, 13–29.

Stryker, Sheldon, "The Interactional and Situational Approaches," in H. T. Christensen, ed., *Handbook of Marriage and the Family.* Chicago: Rand McNally, 1964, 125–170.

Turner, Ralph H., *Family Interaction.* New York: John Wiley, 1970.

Waller, Willard, *The Family, A Dynamic Interpretation*, Revised by Reuben Hill. New York: Dyden Press, 1951.

Zelditch, Morris Jr., "Role Differentiation in the Nuclear Family: A Comparative Study," in Talcott Parsons and Robert F. Bales, *Family, Socialization and Interaction.* Glencoe, Ill.: Free Press, 1955, 307–352.

# 2

# The family as a social system

With this chapter we begin our systematic discussion of the important concepts that make up the family development framework. We shall first examine the family as a unit. The concepts in this analysis will point up one of the central issues in the family development approach: how the family maintains itself as an entity despite its continuous change. The discussion will center on the family as a social system. The presentation here will draw upon the insights of modern systems theory, which incorporates ideas from communication, technology, and cybernetics. This approach is also consistent with the underlying assumptions of the framework detailed in the previous chapter. The schema of the system is compatible with the assumptions that the individual initiates activity as well as reacts to that of others and that the family as a task-performing group encounters a series of expected changes over its lifetime.

A system can be defined as "a complex of elements or components directly or indirectly related in a causal network, such that each component is related to at least some others in a more or less stable way within any particular period of time" (Buckley, 1967: 41). The family clearly can be subsumed under this definition of system (Hill, 1971; Speer, 1970). Its systemic characteristics are as follows: (1) The positions occupied by family members, the elements of the family system, are to varying degrees *interdependent.* (2) The family also through *selective boundary maintenance* constitutes a unit. (3) The family *modifies its structure* of interaction networks. (4) The family in order to continue is a *task performance group* meeting the demands of other societal agencies as well as those of its members. The following discussion treats each of these characteristics in detail.

## FAMILY INTERDEPENDENCIES

Let us begin with the elements of the family system that are its positions. Positions specific to the family are husband-father, wife-mother, son-brother, and daughter-sister. These positions are filled by individuals who in their interaction with other family members create the structure that makes the family a system. In some societies, however, the *joint family* is the household unit for more affluent groups at various stages in the family life cycle. In India, for example, the son brings his bride home, and the couple lives with his parents through the arrival of the first children. The son and his wife only establish their own household when the son is educated and doing well enough in his occupation to afford a separate household (Gore, 1965). Also, in a heavy majority of the world's societies surveyed by Murdock (1967), 720 out of 857 recognize polygamy rather than monogamy as the ideal form of marriage. Even in our own country, where the nuclear family is normative, a sizable segment of families lack some nuclear family positions at any one time. For example, in 1976 a parental position was lacking in the family of about 20 percent of all children 18 years of age and younger primarily because of divorce and desertion. The husband-father position was vacant for 15.8 percent of all children, and there was no one in the wife-mother position in the families of 1.2 percent of children. A remaining three percent were living with neither parent (U.S. Bureau of the Census, 1977). And, since about six percent of all couples in which the women were born in the 1930s and 1940s will not have children, the family positions husband-father and wife-mother

---

[1] According to the nuclear family table of organization, there were "outsiders" present in the five percent of households that had a grandparent present, or in the two percent of homes where one or more uncles or aunts were residents (Clausen, 1966: 6).

will remain unfilled (Carter and Glick, 1976: 145).[1] The discussion in this book, however, will most often concern nuclear families, although family development concepts have been applied to other family forms (Marioka, 1967).

Our rationale for utilizing the nuclear family focus is that in all societies from historic times to the present, this family form has been the most common domestic group. Lack of organizational skills and economic resources set limits on the number of joint families that exist (Levy, 1965; Burch, 1967). Pologyny and polyandry are constrained by the sex ratio, and high divorce rates are associated with high remarriage rates.[2]

Because the family is a system, family members are not only affected by their interactions with others but they are constantly playing the role of interested third party. The behavior of one member to another can affect other third parties not originally involved. For example, when five-year old Michael misbehaves, seven-year old Colleen runs to tell her father. He hears Colleen's side of the story and calls for Michael's version. He lectures Michael about his wrongdoing and sends him to his room. Michael cries, which upsets his mother. She remains upset about the crying and about the punishment. This causes tension between husband and wife. Colleen comes to her mother with a request, but she is still too upset about Michael to pay attention to Colleen. Colleen goes away feeling rejected. Thus the effects of interaction between two family members spread throughout the system.

It is well to point out that the interdependency discussed here and illustrated in the example includes more than *role complementarity*. The latter concept refers to such situations as when a husband in his role as breadwinner depends upon his wife in her role as housekeeper to maintain his lodging and see that he is fed, and she in turn is dependent on him for income. The situation could be reversed with his wife as the wage earner, and the husband as the housekeeper, but in both cases the parties are mutually dependent.

Our concept of interdependence, however, is of broader scope, covering specific behaviors of family members that influence others as well as their physical and emotional dependencies. In addition, our

[2] The U.S. divorce rate is one of the highest in the world. It was 32 per 1000 married women 14 to 44 years old based on the years 1972–1974. But the remarriage rate for divorced and widowed persons, in general, is substantially higher than for never-married persons of comparable ages. For example, in the years 1972–1974, of those divorced and widowed women 14 to 54 years old, each year 151 per 1000 on the average remarried, as compared with 103 per 1000 for never-married women 14 to 44 years old (Norton and Glick, 1976).

concept does not presuppose that the behaviors mesh, as is the case with role complementarity. As the property of a system, interdependence signifies both conflict and cooperation, as shown in the above example. In similar fashion, the family's emotional interdependency, the feelings of love and liking along with the occasional feelings of hatred and loathing that galvanize family interchanges, are encompassed in our concept since these emotions generate interaction.

In applying this thinking to the family, it is apparent that variation in degree of dependency of one family member on another is related to the stage of the family life cycle. As children grow older, their ties to siblings and to parents attenuate as their interests in the views of peers and older persons they meet in nonfamily situations become stronger. They disengage from one set of ties while committing themselves to the obligations of nonfamily groups. The type of disengagement from family influence appears to be related to parental treatment. A set of related studies on parent-adolescent relations showed that when parental warmth was high, even youths of college age retained parental values although they were in conflict with values from the peer counterculture. High-school youths also reported such families to be those in which they felt able most often to express their "authentic" selves. Friends took on importance when parents were not warm (Thomas, et al., 1974: 42).

Marital interdependencies also vary over time. If one uses power in family decision making as an operational indicator of the dependence of family members on one member, the dependency of wives on husbands appears to be greatest during the family stages when there are preschool children. Women are constrained by family demands, so that they are less apt to have outside employment and are economically dependent. Men, accordingly, being more autonomous, possess the means to demand that wives and children conform to their decisions. But "the power of the husband decreases as a function of age of husband, as well as age of wife" (Centers, Raven, and Rodrigues, 1971: 273), with the power of husbands at a low point when couples are over 70.[3] As time goes on, women's greater social resources of kin and

---

[3] Centers, Raven, and Rodrigues (1971), as well as Blood and Wolfe (1960), did find a brief upturn in men's power in the 60–69 age years. Neither research group has an explanation for this resurgence. We might speculate that it has something to do with the higher male mortality rates which become apparent when spouses are in their sixties. Norton (1974) predicts that the median age for wives born from 1930–1939 at the time the first spouse dies will be 64.4. Since most husbands are more apt to die before wives, their "scarcity" value supplemented by their relatively high preretirement

friends, coupled with the lesser demands of growing children, allow them to look outside marriage for satisfaction (Lowenthal and Haven, 1968). Husbands, however, as their work responsibilities lessen and are eventually cut off by retirement, lose job associates and so look to the marital relation for meeting sociability needs.

**Family subsystems**

The interdependencies of family members vary in degree as well as in time. Not all family members are equally caught up in family interchanges. As Gouldner points out (1959), position occupants can develop relationship patterns that satisfy their needs and enable them to be less affected by other family members. Thus between some family positions interchanges are so built-in that they constitute subsystems in the family. These are *paired positions* whose associated behaviors presuppose the existence of the other position. A man, for example, cannot occupy the position of husband unless there is someone in the position of wife.

The nuclear family operates with a limited number of paired positions as detailed in Figure 2-1. Each of these subsystems can become independent to the degree that the individuals isolate themselves from the influence of the broader family unit. They can serve as coalitions to wrest concessions and to force changes in other family members. This practice is legitimated for husband and wife in both conservative and liberal family ideologies. Traditionalists admonish them to maintain a united front in socializing children, and radicals warn the couple to beware of the children's threat to the affection bond. But children too can play the coalition game. Irish (1964) points out that siblings seek

**Figure 2-1   Paired Positions In the Family.**

| | | |
|---|---|---|
| I. | The Marital Relation: | Husband-wife |
| II. | Sibling Relations: | Brother-sister |
| | | Sister-sister |
| | | Brother-brother |
| III. | Parent-Child Relations: | Father-daughter |
| | | Father-son |
| | | Mother-daughter |
| | | Mother-son |

incomes may serve to increase the importance of husbands and thus power in the eyes of their wives. Husbands' after-retirement companionship and physical dependence on their usually younger wives could produce the lessened husband power found in elderly couples.

from each other the comfort and understanding that indifferent or uncomprehending parents fail to provide, thereby lessening their emotional dependency on parents and increasing their own power. Parents are adept at using a divide-and-conquer strategy, but general protest from all the children rather than complaint from a single child is more difficult to handle.

The marital, parent-child, and sibling subsystems are able to maintain varying degrees of insulation from one another. Events in one subsystem are not immediately or always felt in the others. Children can be unaware of marital happenings, as parents can be ignorant of goings on among siblings. The presence of subsystem differentiation within the family system suggests that the analogy of a threshold rather than a ripple effect is appropriate for considering family interdependencies. Only role changes reaching a certain threshold of magnitude will influence all family positions rather than each change in a subsystem eventually rippling out to affect others in varying ways (Hill, 1976).

The analysis in the second half of this book traces expectable changes in families over time through the subsystems considered one at a time. This strategy enables the discussion to focus on a more manageable number of positions while the interdependencies of the subsystems can be examined from their different perspectives.

**Interdependence and Change**
The variation of interdependencies among family members can be a source of change in the family. The strategy of closing ranks and excluding members appears whenever individuals become too autonomous of the family. Into this class fall such diverse cases as men away on military service; adolescents departing for school, job, or marriage; spouses preparing for divorce or separation; and individuals who are acute alcoholics. Through choice or exigency, they have all cut family commitments. With maturing adolescents, disaffected spouses, and other potential dropouts, family members may attempt initially to modify behaviors and expectations that are sources of friction. If these strategies prove ineffective or the departure is inevitable, then the role responsibilities of the recalcitrant or absent member must be assumed by others. Younger siblings take over the home tasks of departing adolescents, wives go to work outside the family to offset the failure of alcoholic husband-fathers to provide funds (Jackson, 1956), and relatives provide emotional support and assistance when husband-fathers are absent, as in the difficult cases of prisoners of war in the recent war in Viet Nam (McCubbin et al., 1975).

On the other hand, the family may attempt to retain its unity and reinvolve the independent member in its network. And the member can then use his relative freedom to press for reorganization of the relationships. He may demand greater voice in decisions before he agrees to rejoin the family system. Least effective of the strategies is the use of force as a means to reinvolve the member in family affairs. Listen to George Wade, an 18-year-old black who ran away from home because of his stepfather's treatment. He explained why to a sociologist, Charles S. Johnson.

*I just couldn't get along with him. He made me do a lot of work and I couldn't get my hands on any money and I needed clothes. He was mean, too. He'd fuss at me, whip me, and make me do a heap of work. One day he started to whip me, and I left. Mama didn't want me to leave but she couldn't stop me then (Johnson, 1941: 62).*

## SELECTIVE BOUNDARY MAINTENANCE

Family members may vary in the degree to which they are interdependent, but certain characteristics possessed by all families contribute to their identity as a family unit. A change of residence immediately sets new physical boundaries about the newly formed family in the highly industrialized societies of the western world. But retention of the same residence for a long period continues to establish the family as an entity despite its changes over time. Kinship terminology also creates boundaries. There are many alternate terms for the actors in family positions, as the following brief catalogue suggests: hubby, the mister, the missus, dad, mum, mommy, daddy, pop, sis, the kid brother, the old lady, the old man. As Schneider and Homans (1955: 1204) note, however, these terms—and the formal ones of father, mother, husband, wife, sister, and brother—are limited to nuclear family members and do not refer to outside kindred. In societies in which extended family relatives are more important, the child may use the same term in addressing the father and the father's brothers and another common term in addressing the mother and the mother's sisters. The child is thus not taught to set these relatives apart from the parents through terms of address, though the child recognizes differences in his or her rights in, and obligations to, relatives and to parents.

Families themselves through their interaction tend to set boundaries. The Bible admonishes the new husband and wife to foresake all others, and this pattern is supported in western societies by the love for each other which a couple is expected to develop prior to marriage. The romantic sentiments that establish the initial solidarity of a couple are supplemented by shared values and expectations that develop after marriage. These grow out of interdependencies based on mutual responsibilities for sexual relations, child care, and physical maintenance.

The more family members develop a common perspective on events, the more these situational definitions will set them apart. Families create their own histories, first by living through happenings, and then by developing their own interpretations of them. The reason why Jane Rose flunked high-school algebra the first time, the Roses will tell you, was because she insisted on being leading lady in the high-school play. Mr. Valdez, Jane's teacher, has a different version, which has to do with Jane's lack of ability, a version never recognized by the Roses. Family members also set boundaries when they come home, close the door, and as it were, "take off" their public selves. The privileged nature of family life, the intimacies shared only by family members—Mother cooking in her slip, Dad's talking through the open bathroom door— all appear during the repeated and lengthy periods of family interaction. Common mispronunciations, colorful swear words, expressions that carry over from past family experiences and symbolize them, remind the outsider as well as the family member that he is, indeed, one of the Roses with all their distinctive traits and tastes.

Finally, the prescribed, unchanging procedures that are the "right" way to greet Sunday morning, or to spend Thanksgiving, and that are subsumed under the concept "ritual" also contribute to a family's solidarity and also to its maintenance as an entity despite change (Bossard and Boll, 1950). Rituals bring family members together to interact in habitual ways. These ways reaffirm their solidarity, since the family members "know" the proper procedures. Performing these rituals also demonstrates the distinctive identity of the family and the common values shared by family members.

Insofar as family solidarity is strong, household members not found in the nuclear family table of organization are viewed in our society as outsiders. Their norms and values, to the extent that they differ from the family's own, are resented and resisted as threats to the family's accepted ways. Parents may fear loss of power in decision making with respect to child rearing when grandparents are present. Children also can feel jealous of stepsiblings or of friends and relatives with whom they compete for the time and affection of parents. All these persons are not part of the normal roster of the nuclear family. George Wade, who was quoted above, might not have run away from home if his own mother and not his stepfather had been punitive to him.

## Family Interdependency and Boundary Maintenance

Because of variations in family interdependencies, the permeability of family boundaries also varies. In a provocative study of London, Bott (1957; 1971) has documented how the density of the sociability networks of husband and wife affect their interdependency. She uses the concept *close-knit social networks* to refer to an individual's friendship group in which the members are mutually acquainted. Individuals entering marriage with such networks, particularly when these friends are of the same sex as the individual (Harris, 1969), do not need to seek emotional and marital support from the spouse. They can turn to their social networks for counsel and aid with household problems. Because everyone knows everyone else there, frequent meetings occur with pressure to develop and adhere to common values of mutual assistance. Bott found that couples with close-knit social networks tend to follow the traditional pattern of "segregated conjugal role organization" in which there is a clear-cut division of labor, that is, little sharing of tasks and little interdependency.

Contrast the openness of family boundaries under the close-knit social network situation and its associated but separate worlds of leisure, work, and affection for wife and for husband to those of couples possessing *loose-knit networks*. In these cases the members of the sociability groups of husband and wife are not mutually acquainted. They all know one or both spouses but not each other. There is no consensus of values setting norms for the reciprocal exchange of services and support. Husband and wife are thus more dependent upon each other for help and comfort. In some cases, although not all (Aldous and Straus, 1966; Udry and Hall, 1965), such couples develop a "joint conjugal role organization" in which both work together, or interchangeably, at child care, housekeeping, and other family tasks. Leisure times are shared. The mutual interchange of affection and services, and the shared activities, generate common values, with little influence of competing values from the social networks. For such couples, social networks with their casual friendship ties are complemented by the closed boundaries of the family organization.

The openness of the family to friends and kin can weaken family solidarity. The pattern of closed social networks is more common among the less geographically mobile, lower-class families, and it may contribute to their greater proneness to divorce and desertion (Cohen and Hodges, 1963). Each spouse retains close ties to kin, former schoolmates, and work associates as a sort of insurance system for financial or housing aid in times of crisis. To give up these ties for conjugal interdependencies is to court disaster since the probability of the partner's being able to assist, when funds are low, is less than that of the collectivity of several persons in the network.

An increasing number of persons, however, are beginning to write that family boundary maintenance, even if it contributes to present family solidarity, may in the long run be harmful. Mead (1971), for example, argues that families need to have more people around for help in emergencies, for companions, and for role models. Moore (1958) emphasizes the problem of socialization for occupational roles in today's nuclear family and the need for outside contacts. The loss of economic functions has weakened the basis for the authority of fathers, while mothers, who are still often isolated from external affairs, have difficulties in serving as appropriate role models.

The mutual matching of husband and wife in phase of development necessary for their continued marital happiness might be encouraged, according to Foote (1956), by selective opening of boundaries to sources of new ideas. In order to go beyond the shared interests and information inventory that created the initial sociability and sentiment that led to the uniting of a couple, there must be mutual ability to adapt to the range of situations and of relationships that appear after marriage. Otherwise, one partner is liable to "outgrow" the other with resultant mismatching. Contacts outside the family can provide the information and support needed to get individuals to try new roles whether they are taking on a new occupation, entering politics, or joining a weekly bowling club. And the wise spouse, husband as well as wife, serves as guide to new opportunities and as constructive critic to encourage and to set standards for new role performances. Each also works to develop shared interests to keep the marriage vital. Friendships with persons of both sexes can also contribute to the viability of the husband-wife relation by providing the input of new ideas, the release of family tensions, and the prevention of boredom. Paradoxically, therefore, maintenance of the comfortable predictability of marital interdependencies may demand a number of other meaningful relationships. The normative restriction of intimacies of the body to the spouse, one theologian has written (Hobbs, 1970), can be less important to marital satisfaction than intellectual sharing. Couples with ideas to share require inputs from outsiders.

Although the boundary maintenance characteristics of the family may thus suggest that the family is a closed system, the family is not self-sufficient. Families are always involved in transactions with outsiders. As in the past, families welcome the services and contacts provided by kindred, especially in times of crisis. Kinsmen cross family boundaries with less challenge than most other outsiders, but at all times the family has been selectivity open to nonmembers. The counsel and comfort of religious functionaries has traditionally been important in family life. And, since the nineteenth century, families experience the influence of school teachers operating through their contacts with children.

More demanding, but perhaps less willingly accepted, are transactions with the world of the job. Its time and energy demands on men, women, and adolescents determine meal and leisure time schedules as well as needs for child-care facilities. Lack of job security creates the financial problems that underlie marital and parent-child conflict in working and lower-class families (Rubin, 1976). Large corporations regularly shift their middle-management personnel to plant sites about the country and reportedly promote those men whose wives conform to corporation standards of entertaining and getting along with people (Whyte, 1951). Families of academicians, too, are accustomed to breaking friendship ties as men and women move upward in professional rank through judicious changes in university affiliation. Professionals and men who manage may find their occupational roles more salient than their family roles. In these cases, families are co-opted to serve career interests, and wife-mothers must assume major responsibility for the family. If employed wives have to leave stimulating jobs because of the priority of the husband's occupational success, the competing occupational demands can strain marital ties.

Even though all families are open to external influences, they vary in the degree to which these influences have been ones of the family's own choice and in the degree to which the external influences operate. The effects of historical events like wars, depressions, and periods of inflation affect all families regardless of the strength of their boundaries. But the more affluent have a greater range of occupational choices, less fear of unemployment, more flexibility in working hours, and less supervision. The affluent can also keep policemen, welfare workers, and bill collectors away, through expensive legal talent if necessary. Power to choose a residential area is correlated with power to choose friends and kin contacts and to control those of one's children. Thus, the greater the affluence of a family, the greater their selectivity of boundary maintenance; the less the affluence of a family, the less their selectivity of boundary maintenance. This difference is exemplified in an affluent couple's choosing a counseling specialist for marital or parental problems before they get out of control, while an impoverished couple in like difficulties has little choice aside from an assigned welfare worker or an emergency police team; it must live through periods of heightened conflict, see the family unit destroyed, or both.

A summary of the discussion of selective boundary maintenance points up the paradoxical nature of the concept. Separate residences, kinship terminology, shared experiences and intimacies, and periodic rituals encourage families to set boundaries. At the same time, there are breaches in the boundaries occurring from the family's choice or from the coercion generated by external agencies. The influence of these external agencies is particularly great on those family members who are less involved in the interdependencies of the family. External agencies also determine the family's income and thereby the ease with which it lives. But family members also use external contacts to supply the resources that make for heightened interaction within the family, resources that bring with them boundary-setting results.

## ADAPTABILITY TO CHANGE AND CHANGE INITIATION

The third characteristic of the family as a system is its adaptability to internal and external change. The nuclear family system is perhaps more subject to organizational instability than other organizations because of its rapidly changing age composition and frequently changing plurality patterns. Its leaders are two relatively inexperienced amateurs in the roles of spouse and parent. They must work with a succession of followers having few skills and lacking in judgment under conditions that appear never to remain stable enough, long enough, to allow for organization. The family has hardly established one set of relations based on mutual, normative expectations and agreements when some child begins demanding a reinterpretation of the rights and duties built into his roles. Yet, despite these disruptive factors, which are part of its standard operating procedures, the family somehow, in a majority of cases, manages to maintain the structured interaction patterns that enable it to continue as an entity. There is enough continuity in many areas of behavior to give it the stability and the conservative quality observers often association with the family.

The varying interdependencies of family members and the web of relationships maintained with outsiders provide a never-ending flow of information to the family with respect to the demands of its members and of its physical and social environments (Speer, 1970). The transmission of information from outsiders and family members has been conceptualized as *feedback processes* in systems theory. Families must not only develop communication patterns to receive and transmit information, but they must also develop patterns for interpreting their meaning for the family in relation to its goals. Family members, in Buckley's (1967) terms, "map" the environmental changes through comparing where they are with respect to goals as compared with where they want to be. One family may have the goal of being able to meet food and housing needs before the next paycheck is due. Another family may be concerned with saving for their children's college education and seeing that the secondary school grades of their children are good enough to admit them to a college of their choice. A third family may have as its goal the development of each person's capacities within the constraints of shared family responsibilities. The comparison of task performance with goals may result in a "mismatch" between information and family goals. At this point, family members will either change their goals or, if they have a set of behaviors to choose from, institute changes in their behaviors to enable the family better to attain environmental goals or to conform to demands of family members.

## Negative Feedback
Traditionally in systems theory, these operations have been thought of in terms of negative feedback. Systems were conceptualized in organic terms as having only limited repertoires of responses to adapt to change. The emphasis was on homeostasis or relative stability. Such an approach sees families as changing over time through an accumulation of small changes. If the changes were minor enough, therefore, the family's primary response, if it mismatched information, could be seen as countering deviations from structural patterns, a negative feedback process.

A description of a negative feedback process might take the following sequence.

1.  The family as a system of interdependent actors has developed in the course of time a network of interaction patterns in conformity to shared norms. Through these patterns, it performs the tasks that enable it to meet family and individual goals and to fulfill the requirements of society.
2.  Since a family is not a closed system, its members participate in other groups, such as those at work and at school. Because of these contacts and the different role definitions resulting from maturational changes, not all family members are satisfied with the existing structure of interaction in the family.
3.  The dissatisfied members of a family make different demands, which are supported by pressures from outside agencies such as teachers, peers, and employers.

4.   Attempts to accommodate the new demands to existing patterns prove inadequate, and conflict and tension result.
5.   The family makes use of a number of techniques to handle the conflict situation. These include avoiding the problem, expressing emotion with regard to it, and trying to coerce recalcitrant members into conformity with existing patterns.
6.   If these strategies are not successful, the family modifies its normative expectations and the behaviors they govern. The changes feed back upon and affect other interaction behaviors.
7.   As the new behaviors are repeated, they become patterned and produce another tentative equilibrium in the family system.

**Positive Feedback**
Yet the family as a stable system in which change is slow to occur and limited in its extent is clearly not an accurate characterization. The behavioral changes—one might also say upheavals—that accompany the life course events of marriage, the arrival of the first child, his or her entry into school, and final departure from home suggest what Maruyama (1963) calls "positive feedback." Instead of keeping the family's changes within a narrow range set by existing value limits, the family at times can create or innovate. The family can initiate change, not simply react to it.

The signals from outsiders or family members indicate a mismatch with current family goals, but when the family initiates change, unlike situations in cases of negative feedback, there is no attempt to smother the deviation. The family sets in motion processes of *morphogenesis.* This concept borrowed from biology refers to the development of the individual from embryo to adult and means "form- or structure-changing process." The family tries new behaviors, and explores alternate goals so that there is a clear divergence from old ways and values. The information inputs are then matched with new family structures. When there is a "fit," the family's search for new structures ceases. The family must have the characteristic of "ultrastability" (Cadwallader, 1959) to be able to leave established patterns and to develop new ones while still maintaining its identity.

Why should families initiate positive feedback processes instead of modifying existing structures? We shall see in a later chapter how changes of personnel, of school, and of occupation serve as criteria for demarcating periods in the life cycle of a family. These periods are theoretically dissimilar enough that one must use the morphogenesis concept to explain what accounts for the observed differences in behavior. For example, the arrival of each new child and his eventual departure when an adult disrupt existing interaction patterns and force new strategies to reach family goals, which may also undergo change as the family changes composition. Pressures resulting from actions in outside agencies such as job changes or a spouse's retirement also bring now demands that disrupt old behaviors of the members. The formation of a new family unit is a third occurrence requiring fundamental modification in the relations of the husband and wife.

Families can develop "anticipatory norms," norms that encourage them to anticipate change inside and outside the family. With expectancies of change and sufficient lead time to cope with coming variations, families can do a better job of developing new ways or new goals. Such families also are readier to explore structure modification that will enhance abilities of members to meet their own and family goals. These "experimental families" exercise tolerance for deviation from accepted ways and reward new behaviors that promise payoffs for other family members as well as for the innovating person.

During the period of flux when the family is innovating new ways, family members may consciously utilize various "safety valves" to lessen the pressures arising from conflicting behavioral expectations. Having a night out with the "boys" or "girls," packing the children off to visit mother, or letting Joey have the car for the high school football game, are all strategies that permit time for thinking or for taking a "breathing period" while an idea incubates.

The greater the variety of information the family possesses, the greater its ability to adapt to change or to initiate it. The system's properties of selective boundary maintenance and of interdependency are critical here. Attempts to handle pressures for change innovatively depend on the family's base of information. Extrafamilial contacts that tap a variety of class, occupational, religious, and ethnic groups increase the range of information input.

The communication network in the family thus determines the processing of the information. If the family members are organized into marital, sibling, or parent-child subsystems with little interchange, only a limited portion of the family's total information input is available for processing into ideas for coping with its problems. Moreover, such families are organized neither to receive signals from members or outsiders nor to analyze these communications for their information on the current state of the family. Discords can fester and misunderstandings mount if communication barriers prevent the flow of information and feelings to and from all family members.

Suggestive evidence concerning the importance of extrafamilial contacts and intrafamilial interdependencies comes from a series of laboratory studies of family problem solving. The families in the research had to adapt to unannounced changes in the rules of a game they were playing when they were penalized for previously successful actions. The family members, father, mother, and early adolescent, were pressing hard to develop new behavior structures that would enable them to triumph over the scores of other family triads. In this situation the negative effect of restricted communication networks was apparent. Families did less well when children did not present their observations, criticisms, and ideas to parents (Straus, 1968). In a second and similar study the most successful families were those with two contrasting organization forms. In the first type, the three family members exchanged suggestions on possible strategies for playing the game. One person then, usually the father, evaluated the information and came to a decision about the best interaction strategy, which the family then carried out. The second organization centered on the father as the source of information, but the mother and son were then active in the evaluating and decision-making stages (Tallman and Miller, 1970). Both types of family organization possessed open communication channels among the members at one or more stages of the problem-solving sequence.

The studies also showed that middle-class families usually do better than working-class families. Presumably, the greater education of middle-class parents, their greater adherence to equalitarian values, and their approval of the children's demands for autonomy, all encourage a wider range of information input and more interdependence in its processing. Children as well as wives contribute to the solutions so that the husband-fathers do not have to bear the burden of problem solving alone. Middle-class families also have the monetary and information resources that permit them to be experimental families, to plan for and to initiate change.[4]

---

[4] Class is measured in a number of different ways in the various researches reviewed in this volume. In general, references to working-class families refer to families in which the principal wage earner is steadily employed in a manual occupation with accompanying prestige as a function of associated income and education. Examples of such occupations would be a machine operator or a truck driver. Lower-class families are those in which wage earners are sporadically employed in occupations such as those of construction laborer or household help. Middle-class families are those in which the wage earners are in occupations requiring work with ideas, persons, or papers. If a differentiation is made between upper-middle and lower-middle class families, the researcher has generally distinguished between professionals such as doctors, lawyers, and managers of large businesses and the group of salesmen and clerical employees. Upper-class families are less dependent upon wage earners

To summarize this discussion of the family's change characteristics, the family sets goals for itself that enable it to meet the individual demands of members and the requirements of external agencies. The family, then, through its selective maintenance of boundaries and its properties of interdependency collects information to see whether or not there is a match between its current condition and the tasks it must perform to meet its goals. When a mismatch exists, the family institutes feedback processes. These are either negative, in which case change is minimized; or they are positive, in which case interactional changes of structure occur. Through these feedback processes the family adapts to change and sets it in motion.

## THE FAMILY AS A TASK PERFORMANCE GROUP

In assessing how well they are meeting their goals, families examine how well members are performing certain tasks. The tasks are based on members' needs, and their accomplishment enables the members to perform their family roles, to reach family goals, and to meet the requirements of societal agencies. Such agencies, therefore, have a direct interest in the family's task performance. Families are able to maintain selective boundary maintenance according to their own standards, provided they are able to accomplish the following tasks.[5]

1.  Physical maintenance of family members
2.  Socialization of family members for roles in the family and other groups
3.  Maintenance of family members' motivation to perform familial and other roles
4.  Maintenance of social control within the family and between family members and outsiders

---

for income. Their wealth comes from investments and is particularly prestigious if it is inherited from previous generations. The occupations adult family members hold may be the same as those of middle-class persons, but the presence of wealth and a name known in the community for several generations are distinguishing characteristics. Luther B. Otto (1975) provides a useful commentary on class measures in family research.

[5] A number of social scientists have made lists of functions that families must perform for their own and society's continuance. The list of tasks presented here stems from Bennett and Tumin (1948: 49).

5.    Addition of family members through adoption or reproduction and their release when mature

Physical maintenance is a good task with which to begin a discussion of the tasks families perform. This task encompasses the cooking and housekeeping chores that keep family members sufficiently clothed, sheltered, and fed so they can perform roles both inside and outside the family. This task involves critical exchanges with economic agencies in which family members work in return for wages to buy consumer goods. Since members have little control over these agencies, whether they are employed or not depends to a high degree on events in the broader society.

When the family is unable to perform this task, it seeks assistance; or governmental welfare agencies intervene. At such times, families often fail in boundary maintenance attempts. Welfare regulations may require family actions such as disclosure of finances, canvassing of aid from kin, or the employment of family members in available but undesirable jobs—actions that families not subject to welfare would reject as "invasions of privacy."

A sizable number of families in the United States are still not able to fulfill the physical maintenance task for their offspring. Although from 1959–1974 the number of families defined as impoverished dropped from 18.5 to 9.2 percent of the population, the number of school-aged children, comprised 31 percent of the poverty population compared with only 24 percent of the general population (U.S. Department of Health, Education, and Welfare, 1976).

The family's ability to fulfill its physical maintenance task critically affects its performance of other tasks. Divorce rates, which are higher among the poor, indicate the corrosive effects of poverty on morale maintenance. Strained finances and unhappy family relations also lead to the premature release of adolescents from the family and their entrance into marriage. The early formation of family units in the younger generation short-circuits the socialization process into family and occupational roles. School dropout rates are higher for youths from poor families so that job opportunities are not commensurate with their newly acquired family responsibilities (Aldous and Hill, 1969).

The task of social control refers to the attempts of family members to avoid the disruption of established behavioral patterns and the destruction of property and person. The intimate and enduring qualities of family interaction, coupled with the sheer length of time spent at home, means that emotions can run high. In addition, the younger generation may not know the behaviors required for the family's continued functioning. Thus the family has to establish some methods of social control. Whenever formal control agencies intervene to quiet violent domestic quarrels or to adjudicate youthful misdeeds, the family is failing to some extent as a source of social controls.

Parental discipline and rewards not only socialize children into new ways of behavior but are social control devices. The review of discipline studies by Thomas and associates (1974) indicates the influence parental practices have on social control. Parents who set a variety of restrictions and insist that children conform to them, but who are also warm, tend to have children who are obedient and minimally aggressive. Youths from such homes were least likely to accept such counterculture values as drug use and disengagement from society. Low restrictiveness coupled with parental hostility is associated with children who are aggressive, noncompliant, and delinquent and who have low self-esteem. Such children are most likely to create control problems for parents and outsiders. Low restrictiveness and high warmth, however, seems to be related to children's being friendly, creative, independent, and aggressive in peer groups. The aggressiveness of these children, at least in preschools, is accepted by their age-mates, which is not true of the aggressive behavior of children from hostile, low restrictive homes. Finally, children from high restrictive, hostile homes are withdrawn, quarrel with their peers, and show self-aggression. Adolescents with restrictive, hostile parents are more likely to take on the values of outsiders, specifically the hippy youth culture. Thus, children who have trouble getting along with peers and who engage in activities that lead to encounters with the police seem to come disproportionately from homes where parents are hostile.

The findings point up the importance of the maintenance of morale among family members if they are to perform roles inside and outside the family. Mutual interchanges encourage customary role performance, but at times of low energy levels or conflicting demands—and without a heavy infusion of positive sentiments—individuals may not live up to role expectations. In learning new behaviors demanded by himself, the family, or external agencies, an individual requires sympathetic urging to get started and patient understanding when learning proves difficult. At such times, the application of praise and affection by others, when coupled with their insistence on the value of the learning, keeps the individual going. The more autonomous a person is in the family, and the stronger the ties with outsiders, the more central is the task's fulfillment if the family wishes him or her to remain a member. Other societal agencies, like schools, law enforcement units, and business firms, are dependent on the family to keep people in good enough physical and mental condition to perform a daily round of activities, which are all too often demeaning and lacking in intrinsic rewards.

Families also socialize adults in various roles. Only after a couple cohabits does it learn many roles and marital behaviors; which may be performed behind closed doors (Hill and Aldous, 1969). Even when husband and wife interact as spouses in front of children, the latter are only observers and not participants. After marriage, each spouse serves as model and teacher for the other, and this socialization extends beyond that of family roles. Rehearsals for job interviews, discussions of occupational problems, and decisions to start new careers and preparations for them, can all occur in the family.

The family, too, is the source of the antimaterialist values of student activists who demand environmental upgrading, equal opportunities for all, and wider participation in governmental decision making (Kenniston, 1967). True, some exponents reject current forms of the family, but even in the communes and collectives, which they establish in order to live according to the values and behaviors that set them apart, they perform family roles whose content derives from their parental families.

Addition of new members through reproduction formerly was a task critical to the continuance of society. Today, however, when overpopulation rather than lack of numbers threatens the existence of humankind, this task is less central. In fact, the high evaluation placed on motherhood and the pressure for its attainment among women can be viewed as dangerous survivals of an earlier era.[6] If the welfare of society depends increasingly on fewer women having fewer children, tremendous changes in the family's performance of the socialization task must occur.

### Learning Gender Behavior

But children by the time they are in primary school have acquired a stereotyped notion of what constitutes male and female roles. Whether children come from low- or middle-income homes (Kagan and Lemkin, 1966), girls and boys alike see men as decision makers and breadwinners, and women as nurturant persons responsible for house and child care. These findings are consistent, and all the more remarkable

---

[6] In developed countries, too many people means rising food costs, increased pollution, and higher taxes to ameliorate the problems of overpopulation. In developing countries, too many people means malnutrition and famine. In 1975, as many as 800 million of the world's people were suffering from lack of food, and the world population had passed the four billion mark, twice what it was in 1930. It was expected to double again by the first decade of the next century (Anonymous, 1975:1).

since they appear even when some children's experiences run counter to gender role stereotypes. Children from father-absent families necessarily see their mothers performing so-called male roles. Yet studies of father-absent and father-present families in the United States and Japan found no difference in children's perceptions of adult behavior (Aldous and Kamiko, 1972). Thus from an early age, girls stake their futures on motherhood despite growing societal concern about population problems. At the present time of effective contraceptives when the number and timing of children can be determined by couples, the limited portion of the family cycle when children are at home means that women have many years when they have lost their occupations as mothers.[7]

**Task Performance over the Family Life Cycle**
The importance of the various tasks waxes and wanes over the family life cycle and so does the difficulty of fulfilling them. Physical maintenance is especially problematical during the child-bearing and retirement years. Families with young children often drop from two incomes to one as wives stop working and the husband's earnings, despite increasing expenses, are not yet at their peak. After retirement, the drop in income and its erosion through inflation means that over one-fifth of all families in which the wage earner is over 65 are in poverty (U.S. Bureau of the Census, 1975).[8]

Families with adolescents may be most concerned with the social control task. Youths are increasingly independent of family control networks but families are still held responsible by community agencies for their young people's behavior. And with the increasing emphasis on youth as a moratorium period, this is the time when individuals either "try out" new behaviors and roles or "try to live up to" the ideals they have been taught in home and church. Drug experimentation and marching in demonstrations can lead to police investigations and harassment with the resultant possible problems of legal costs and prison records.

The social control task ties into the tasks of socialization and release of mature adults. Where the young person has long been a part of the

---

[7] For women born in the 1950s, it is estimated they will have about 13 years after their last child leaves home, when their median age is 52, before their marriage is dissolved by their own or their spouse's death (Glick, 1977).

[8] Of families with female heads 65 and over, 28.4 percent were in poverty in 1974. The comparable figure for men was 14.6 percent (U.S. Bureau of the Census, 1975).

family's communication network, his parents and sibs have had time to become acquainted with his thinking to influence it and be influenced by it. This two-way socialization increases the likelihood that parents will know what to expect from their children. Yet when youths engage in what parents see as sexual adventures, many parents may still be surprised and disappointed.

Maintaining the morale of family members is critical, since parents must somehow keep up their spirits despite precipitous mood changes of adolescents. At times they are eager to assert their independence, and at others they seek emotional support in their decision-making attempts.

## SUMMARY

The first family characteristic discussed in this chapter was that of the interdependencies of family members. For the couple subsystem, interdependency based on sentiment is highest during the newlywed period before the erosion of the conjugal bond brought about by the cares of earning a living and the competition from the parent-child subsystem. After an initial period of heavy parent-child interdependency, external agencies begin supplementing family efforts as children prepare to leave the family. The conjugal couple is then left alone to rediscover each other or to drift apart if the common interests or complementary skills that create interdependency are lacking.

Selective boundary maintenance, the second characteristic, indicates that even as families attempt to set themselves apart, they welcome or must accept the influence of outsiders. The latter often make their presence felt through those least involved in the network of family interdependencies, the disaffected and those ready to establish new family units. Family boundaries are most problematical when a new family is formed and when its progeny begin to leave.

The family is able to preserve itself as an entity only through its capacity to counter or to amplify changes. The events that lead to family formation, the addition of members—their passage through the educational system and their eventual departure—all require the family to change existing interaction patterns to accommodate new personnel, to fill in the gaps left by those who have gone, or to meet the changing demands of its members and of society. Families can also have norms that lead them to anticipate the need to change so they can plan for and try out new divisions of labor, different power relations, and varied communication patterns.

Finally, the family as a system sets goals and performs tasks to reach them that enable its members to maintain their daily activities and the family to continue as a group. Some tasks such as physical maintenance are monitored by societal agencies that will attempt to set in motion morphogenetic processes when the family's present organization is not fulfilling these tasks. If these tasks are carried out effectively, the family has the resources to elaborate morale maintenance and socialization tasks, to anticipate change, and to set additional goals for itself. Physical maintenance and social control are less problematic in the middle years when children's socialization is largely completed and the couple relation has "shaken down" to an enduring bond. More stormy for morale maintenance are the initial years of marriage when couples are exploring whether they can continue as a couple. Such problems can be exacerbated by low finances with individuals just beginning jobs and women stopping work at the onset of childbearing. Whether or not a family can prepare for change and institute a morphogenetic process to deal with it is particularly apparent when adolescents demand changes in family interdependencies. Their orderly release into the adult world depends upon the family fulfilling socialization, morale maintenance tasks, and physical maintenance tasks.

It should be apparent from this summary and the chapter discussion that properties of systems are interrelated. Each property affects the others and is affected by them. Task accomplishment is affected by external influences that cross the family boundaries. These influences ease or complicate task performance; they demand or discourage change. Whether or not tasks can be performed according to the usual interdependency patterns depends on the demands made by external contacts and by family members. And mutual interdependencies determine how tasks are performed and how external influences affect family members.

# REFERENCES

Aldous, Joan and Reuben Hill, "Breaking the Poverty Cycle: Strategic Points for Intervention," *Social Work*, 1969, 14, 3–12.

Aldous, Joan and Takeji Kamiko, "A Cross-National Study of the Effects of Father-Absence: Japan and the United States," in Marvin Sussman and Betty Cogswell, eds., *Cross-National Family Research*. Leiden: E. J. Brill, 1972, 86–101.

Aldous, Joan and Murray A. Straus, "Social Networks and Conjugal Roles: A Test of Bott's Hypothesis," *Social Forces*, 1966, 44, 576–580.

Anonymous, "The Growing Crisis," *War on Hunger: Report from the Agency on International Development*, 1975, 9, 1–8.

Bennett, John W. and Melvin Tumin, *Social Life*. New York: Alfred A. Knopf, 1948.

Blood, Robert O. and Donald M. Wolfe, *Husbands and Wives: The Dynamics of Married Living*. New York: Free Press, 1960.

Bossard, James H. S. and Eleanor S. Boll, *Ritual in Family Living*. Philadelphia: University of Pennsylvania Press, 1950.

Bott, Elizabeth, *Family and Roles, Norms, and External Relationships in Ordinary Urban Families*. London: Tavistock, 1957.

Bott, Elizabeth, *Family and Roles, Norms, and External Relationships in Ordinary Urban Families*, Second Edition. New York: Free Press, 1971.

Buckley, Walter, *Sociology and Modern Systems Theory*. Englewood Cliffs, N.J.: Prentice-Hall, 1967.

Burch, Thomas K., "The Size and Structure of Families: A Comparative Analysis of Census Data," *American Sociological Review*, 1967, 32, 347–363.

Cadwallader, Mervyn, L., "The Cybernetic Analysis of Change in Complex Social Organizations," *American Journal of Sociology*, 1959, 65, 154–157.

Carter, Hugh and Paul C. Glick, *Marriage and Divorce: A Social and Economic Study*. Cambridge, Mass.: Harvard University Press, 1976.

Centers, Richard, Bertram H. Raven, and Aroldo Rodrigues, "Conjugal Power Structure: A Re-Examination," *American Sociological Review*, 1971, 36, 264–278.

Clausen, John, "Family Structure, Socialization and Personality," in Lois W. Hoffman and Martin L. Hoffman, eds., *Review of Child Development II*. New York: Russell Sage, 1966, 1–54.

Cohen, Albert K. and Harold M. Hodges, Jr., "Characteristics of the Lower-Blue-Collar Class," *Social Problems*, 1963, 10, 303–334.

Foote, Nelson, "Matching of Husband and Wife in Phases of Development," *Transactions of the Third World Congress of Sociology*, IV, 1956, 24–34.

Glick, Paul C., "Updating the Life Cycle of the Family," *Journal of Marriage and the Family*, 1977, 39, 5–13.

Gore, M. S., "The Traditional Indian Family," in Meyer F. Nimkoff, ed., *Comparative Family Systems*. Boston: Houghton Mifflin, 1965, 209–231.

Gouldner, Alvin, "Reciprocity and Autonomy in Functional Theory," in Llewellyn Gross, ed., *Symposium on Sociological Theory*. Evanston, Ill.: Row, Peterson, 1959, pp. 241–270.

Harris, C. C., *The Family*. London: Allen & Unwin, 1969.

Hill, Reuben, "Modern Systems Theory and the Family," *Social Information*, 1971, 10, pp. 7–26.

Hill, Reuben, "Social Theory and Family Development," in Jean Cuisenier and Martine Segalin, eds., *The Family Life Cycle in European Societies*. The Hague: Mouton, 1976.

Hill, Reuben and Joan Aldous, "Socialization for Marriage and Parenthood: The Transition to Adulthood," in David Goslin, ed., *Handbook of Socialization, Theory and Research*. Chicago: Rand McNally, 1969, 885–950.

Hobbs, Edward, "An Alternate Model from a Theological Perspective," in Herbert A. Otto, ed., *The Family in Search of a Future*. N.Y.: Appleton-Century-Crofts, 1970, pp. 25–42.

Irish, Donald P. "Sibling Interaction: A Neglected Aspect in Family Life Research," *Social Forces*, 1964, 42, 279–288.

Jackson, Joan K., "The Adjustment of the Family to Alcoholism," *Marriage and Family Living*, 1956, 18, 361–369.

Johnson, Charles S., *Growing Up in the Black Belt: Negro Youth in the Rural South*. Washington, D.C.: American Council on Education, 1941.

Kagan, Jerome and Judith Lemkin, "The Child's Differential Perception of Parental Attributes," *Journal of Abnormal and Social Psychology*, 1966, 4, 87–91.

Kenniston, Kenneth, "The Sources of Student Dissent," *Journal of Social Issues*, 1967, 23, 108–137.

Levy, Marion J., "Aspects of the Analysis of Family Structure," in Ansley J. Coale, Lloyd A. Fallers, Marion J. Levy, Jr., David M. Schneider, and Silvan S. Tomkins, *Aspects of the Analysis of Family Structure*. Princeton: Princeton University Press, 1965, 40–63.

Lowenthal, Marjorie F. and Clayton Haven, "Interaction and Adaption: Intimacy as a Critical Variable," *American Sociological Review*, 1968, 33, 20–30.

McCubbin, Hamilton D., Barbara B. Dahl, Gary R. Lester, and Beverly A. Ross, "The Returned Prisoner of War: Factors in Family Reintegration," *Journal of Marriage and the Family*, 1975, 37, 471–478.

Marioka, Kiyomi, "Life Cycle: Patterns in Japan, China and the United States," *Journal of Marriage and the Family*, 1967, 29, 595–606.

Maruyama, Magoroh, "The Second Cybernetics: Deviation-Amplifying Mutual Causal Processes," *American Scientist*, 1963, 51, 164–179.

Mead, Margaret, "Future Family," *Transaction*, 1971, 8, 50–53.

Moore, Barringston, "Thoughts on the Future of the Family," *Political Power and Social Theory*. Cambridge, Mass.: Harvard University Press, 1958, 160–178.

Murdock, George P., "Ethnographic Atlas: A Summary," *Ethnology*, 1967, 6, 109–236.

Norton, Arthur J., "The Family Life-Cycle Updated: Components and Uses," in Robert Winch and Graham Spanier, eds., *Selected Studies in Marriage and the Family*. New York: Holt, Rinehart and Winston, 1974, 162–170.

Norton, Arthur J. and Paul C. Glick, "Marital Instability: Past, Present, and Future," *Journal of Social Issues*, 1976, 32, 6–7.

Otto, Luther B., "Class and Status in Family Research," *Journal of Marriage and the Family*, 1975, 37, 315–332.

Rubin, Lillian B., *Worlds of Pain: Life in the Working-Class Family*. New York: Basic Books, 1976.

Schneider, David M. and George C. Homans, "Kingship Terminology and the American Kinship System," *American Anthropologist*, 1955, 57, 1194–1208.

Speer, David C., "Family Systems: Morphostasis and Morphogenesis or Is Homeostasis Enough?" *Family Process*, 1970, 9, 259–278.

Straus, Murray A., "Communication, Creativity, and Problem-Solving Ability of Middle-and-Working-Class Families in Three Societies," *American Journal of Sociology*, 1968, 73, 417–30.

Tallman, Irving and Gary Miller, "Class Differences in Family Problem Solving: The Effects of Language Style, Hierarchical Structure, and Role Expectations," Paper presented before the Annual Meeting, American Sociological Association, 1970.

Thomas, Darwin, Viktor Gecas, Andrew Weigert, and Elizabeth Rooney, *Family Socialization and the Adolescent: Determinants of Self-Concept, Conformity, Religiosity and Countercultural Values.* Lexington, Mass: D. C. Heath, 1974.

Udry, J. Richard and Mary Hall, "Marital Role Segregation and Social Networks in Middle-Class, Middle-Aged Couples," *Journal of Marriage and the Family*, 1965, 27, 392–395.

U.S. Bureau of the Census, *Current Population Reports*, Series P-20, No. 198, "Characteristics of the Low-Income Population: 1973," U.S. Government Printing Office, Washington, D.C., 1975.

U.S. Bureau of the Census, *Current Population Reports*, Series P-20, No. 306, "Marital Status and Living Arrangements: March 1976," U.S. Government Printing Office, Washington, D.C., 1977.

U.S. Department of Health, Education, and Welfare, "The Measure of Poverty: A Report to Congress as Mandated by the Education Amendments of 1974," U.S. Government Printing Office, Washington, D.C., Apirl, 1976.

Whyte, Wililam H., "Corporation and the Wife," *Fortune*, 1951, 44, 109–111.

# 3

# The making of family roles within family composition constraints

The concept of social system described in the previous chapter permitted us to view the family as a unit. In the present chapter, we will go into the family unit and look at the interactions of family members. We will be concerned with the relatively enduring behavior interchanges or structures that arise from the roles family members play. We will examine how people "make" their roles—given certain family constraints—as well as how pressures from other family members keep an individual performing these roles.

The concept, structure, refers to the enduring interrelationships that join the elements of the family. A structural element, in turn, consists of the social positions that are found in all social organizations of a particular type, regardless of the personal characteristics of the organization's members. In the nuclear family, these structural elements consist of the positions of husband-father, wife-mother, son-brother, and daughter-sister.

The occupants of family positions are related to one another by a network of enduring interaction patterns. Some of these structures develop from the family members' attempts to fulfill family tasks and individual goals.

All make family life more predictable. Members know what to expect of each other, a great necessity in the close emotional quarters of the family. This chapter will begin with a discussion of family composition variables that set limits on interaction patterns regardless of the individual characteristics of family members. These variables include family size, its age, and sex composition. The discussion will then shift to the roles performed by incumbents of family positions and how their content is created within structural constraints.

## FAMILY COMPOSITION VARIABLES

### Family Size

The first demographic factor to be considered is family size. Family size determines the number of family positions, the number of structural elements, which in turn determines the number of interpersonal relationships that can develop between the members. At any one point in time, these plurality patterns of a family are based on the number of members and the resultant number of possible interpersonal relationships. For example, the effect of the number of family members on the number of two-person dyadic relations is demonstrated by the formula in Figure 3-1.

The family begins with two members, husband and wife, and so one interpersonal relation. The addition of a child results in two more interpersonal relations, though the number of units was increased by only one. Similarly, the addition of one more member to a three person family adds three more dyadic relations. Since each new family member results in a disproportionate increase in the number of interpersonal relations, the coming of children increases the complexity of family life. There are myriad possibilities for misunderstood children and family conflict arising from the simultaneous addition of a number of new role relations. Although the presence of a new member does not insure that other family members will always interact with her or him, particularly

**Figure 3-1.    Formula for determining the number of two-person relationships in the family.**

$$\frac{Y^2 - Y}{2}$$

$X$ = the number of personal interrelationships
$Y$ = the number of persons in the family

Source: Bossard and Boll, 1956: 77.

in [...] edy once re[...] that he was 10 years
old [...] aware of his brothe[...]t's existence), one
can a[...] the interdependent family system each person's
presenc[...] has an effect on the others.

The effe[...] family behavior of sheer number of structural elements
and the resu[...] number of interaction patterns was a primary interest
of the sociolog[...] J. [...] Bossard. In an exploratory study of 100 families having at least six children, he found several interaction patterns
that distinguished t[...] large family system. There tended to be high
emphasis on organization and leadership. Set patterns developed to
get things done. Each member had his particular task to perform, hence
the family was highly interdependent. Discipline emphasized conformity to family patterns and cooperation in accomplishing family tasks.
Parents lacked time to give individual attention to children, and siblings
served as parental surrogates. Under these circumstances, family members were less demanding and less possessive in their relations to one
another than was true in smaller families (Bossard and Boll, 1956).

These findings were supported in a study a decade later with a sample of white seventh graders in central North Carolina, a sample that
was large enough to allow analyses according to the social class of the
families. Working-class girls in large families, defined as having four or
more children, perceived their fathers more often as authoritarian, and
both parents as more given to physical punishment, more controlling,
less communicative, and less praising than working-class girls from
smaller families. Family size had comparatively little effect on the child-
rearing practices of middle-class parents of girls. The authors explain
the differential effect of large family size on girls in the middle class as
compared with those in the working class as due to the greater anxiety
by working-class families to maintain the respectability of their girls.
Middle-class boys in large families saw parents as more controlling,
more punishing, and less communicative than boys from the same class
in smaller families. When all children in the family are boys, similar
findings appear for large lower-class families.

Verbal behavior in children is also affected by family size. Only children and children in small families have more opportunity to interact
with their parents and so more quickly learn adult vocabulary. In large
families, contacts with adults are often more restricted; consequently,
children have fewer opportunities to acquire adult speech habits. This
"retardation in the child's verbal development" explains in part (Nisbet,
1961) the general negative relation between family size and intelligence test scores. Family size thus influences behavior patterns regardless of the individual characteristics of the family members.

## Age and Gender Composition

Like family size, which determines the number of family plurality patterns, the demographic elements of age and sex affect family structure. Age and gender have much to do with prescribing roles as labor is divided and power apportioned in the family. When children are young, parents must assume responsibility for family task performance, just as when women are pregnant some tasks are reallocated to husbands. Moreover, few parents leave many decisions to the young to make, even if the parents are highly committed to a democratic ideology.

The age categories a society chooses to make salient vary with the culture, and the associated behavioral expectations do not necessarily depend on maturational changes or biological capacities. Our own society tends to differentiate the period from birth to primary school age into just two categories, for example, the infant and the preschooler. The Balinese people, however, make finer divisions within this period. They distinguish the three categories of the lap baby, the knee baby, and the yard baby. A lap baby, like a child in our age grade of infant, is seen as relatively passive and helpless. The knee baby can walk but is expected to remain close to the mother and to compete with the lap baby for her attention. The yard child, although old enough to run about and to have "major responsibility" in the care of a lap baby, is still considered too young to leave home and to play with peers (Mead, 1954, 173). In our society, in contrast, children of four and five years of age rarely serve as sole babysitters for younger children. They are encouraged to play with others, however, and to become less dependent upon their families.

Our own and other industrial societies are increasingly organized and operated by those of middle age. Those under 14 are no longer counted in the labor force, and the participation rates of 16 to 19 year olds are declining (Riley, 1971). At the other end of the age continuum, retirement at 65 is becoming compulsory, and some agencies set an even earlier age. As a result, the period of playing leisure or student roles without job responsibilities is lengthening for the young and the old, another example of cultural definitions of age roles.

Gender and age roles, with their attached normative prescriptions as to how the actors must behave, are what Linton called *ascriptive roles.* The actor is assigned *ascriptive roles* by virtue of some characteristic he possesses and over which he has no control, such as his age or sex. *Achieved roles*, on the other hand, are acquired by the individual's own efforts. Since the individual is destined for certain ascribed roles because of birth, he can receive intensive training to insure that the roles will be performed adequately. In rapidly changing societies, however, role requirements are subject to flux since specific behaviors cannot be built into ascribed roles when the recruitment of occupants is not assured. As a result, task performance is due more to achieved roles.

In our society today, role ascription, particularly on the basis of gender, plays a less important part in family role assignments. Although husband-fathers and wife-mothers often perform different tasks in the family, their task division may vary from gender role stereotypes, depending on the different abilities of the marriage partners. Couples can reverse the traditional roles with wives making financial decisions and husbands mediating family conflicts, or they can share breadwinner and child-care roles.

There is good evidence, as Chapter 1 showed, to discredit the idea of a universal allocation of particular roles in families based on gender. If socialization is to occur in the parent-child subsystem, parents have to play both expressive (nurturant) roles and instrumental (demanding) roles. The child learns instrumental roles from a parent only if the parent also is expressive enough to make it rewarding for the child to learn work skills. Moreover, a role ascription based on gender in the family is true only of societies that encourage role rigidity in their members. Our society is quite the opposite, its members valuing highly the ability to play a wide range of roles and to switch them quickly in the face of exigencies (Slater, 1961). Moreover, in the marital subsystem, more satisfactory relations tend to exist when there is no social-emotional specialization. Highly satisfied couples in a sample of urban, middle-class families, reported more socially supportive activities and more marital communication than low-satisfied couples. To maintain high morale, wives as well as husbands need a spouse to reciprocate and to sustain an expressive relation unless the emotional support is available elsewhere (Levinger, 1964), as was true of couples like those discussed in the previous chapter, who have close-knit social networks (Bott, 1971).

**Positional Elements and Role Performance**
An examination of family roles as they are affected by structural variables is a good introduction to a detailed consideration of positions, roles, and norms discussed in Chapter 1. Figure 3-2 presents examples of these concepts in terms of the family.

The wife-mother position for example is made up of such roles as provider, sexual partner, confidant, and affection giver. Certain norms

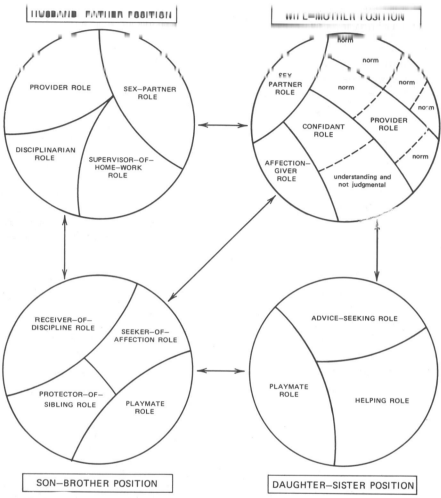

**Figure 3-2  The relations of family positions, roles, and norms.** *Source:* **adapted from Bates, 1956: 314, Fig. 2, and 318, Fig. 3.**

exist for each of these roles that set limits on how the actor should behave, as the mother's being understanding and not judgmental when she is receiving confidences from her daughter.

What creates family structures are the relationships between position incumbents. Husband roles presuppose wife roles, just as parent roles presuppose child roles. To be more specific, the father role of disciplinarian cannot be activated unless there is an actor in the role of receiver of discipline as shown in Figure 3-2. To preserve the interdependence of the family system, some pairs of roles may be lacking. In our society, where family solidarity is heavily dependent upon the husband-wife relation, we have already noted that relations with persons outside the nuclear family unit can constitute a threat to the family's continuance. Norms proscribe that relations crossing nuclear family lines will be secondary to those within the family. But more important insofar as role relations are concerned, are kin roles, which are often discretionary or even lacking in order to prevent marital conflict. This is more often the case with son roles in the husband-father position than daughter roles in the wife-mother position. Relatives often assist women to play family roles, the usual focus of their role repertoire. Men's ties with kin, however, can compete with the demands of wife and children for the time and energy men reserve from occupational responsibilities, and so lead to conflict between relatives and family (Duvall, 1954).

Role relations within the family indicate why vacant family roles must be reallocated, and why the network of family relations changes as a result. When the wife-mother is in the hospital with a new baby, for example, an older child may assume some of her roles. Because the child is fulfilling new roles with their attached responsibilities, he or she expects to interact with the father in ways to which he is often unaccustomed. The son, in his new role as purchaser of groceries, for example, may be in conflict with the father, because the father as provider of funds does not permit the son the range of choice in purchases the latter feels appropriate for the role of purchasing agent. The father has not yet accepted as normative the behaviors appropriate to the new role of the son.

## Role-Making and Role Behaviors

The above example should remind us that the content of the roles people play are increasingly the result of improvisation rather than that of rigidly prescribed norms. Ascriptive roles are decreasing, and people lack a prepared, consistent script in performing roles that must be achieved. Instead, individuals learn general normative guides to role performances but the exigencies of the situation tend to determine specific behaviors. These guides enable the role performer to relate to others in a situation but only in a tentative fashion. Each assesses the other's role on the basis of behaviors actually displayed and on that of behaviors predictable by imaginatively assuming the other's position. The correctness of the judgment on which each actor stakes his or her behavior is confirmed or denied by the other person's response. Under these circumstances, Turner's (1962) concept of ''role making'' rather than "norm playing," seems a more appropriate concept to describe role performance. Within broad normative limits, a wide range of behaviors will be accepted as appropriate to a particular role. Individual behaviors, if they prove appropriate to the individual and his associates are repeated often enough to become role expectations. Interaction patterns are based on individuals' conformity to these expectations. Interaction patterns are accordingly improvised by the actors with patterning developing out of habituation rather than initial normative prescriptions (Aldous, 1974: 232).

What implication does this role-making perspective hold for family analysis? This perspective suggests that we look for the interactional structure of the family to come primarily out of the day-to-day getting along of family members, within the limits set by family composition constraints and norms deriving from class, religious, or ethnic subcultures. Under these circumstances, who does what around the house, or even who makes the decisions, is not automatically set by societal norms. Family interaction patterns begin through improvisation, and then as persons find them satisfactory for getting things done with a minimum of effort, the patterns become normative. The members are committed to existing arrangements that developed from the original improvised role interactions.

Studies of family power structures suggest how families improvise roles by meeting situational needs rather than by conforming to class values. Within lower- and middle-class families, the power structure is generally contrary to expressed values. Families in which husband and wife have some college education subscribe to an egalitarian ideology that places high value on shared decision making. In actual practice, husbands tend to have more power (Blood and Wolfe, 1960; Centers, Raven, and Rodrigues, 1971). In contrast, working-class couples more often accept the value that husbands should be dominant. Yet within this class, husbands appear to have less power in practice than in middle-class families with their equality values.

The reason for the failure to conform to value prescriptions may lie in their vagueness. Neither set of class values clearly specify which decisions should be shared and which left to husbands. Within the resultant area of freedom from norms, husband and wife are left to develop their own arrangements in line with their respective resources.

More working- and lower-class women are employed outside the home during the early years of marriage to supplement the income of husbands just entering their work-life careers. It is particularly likely when husbands have yearly incomes below $5,000, or close to the poverty line for families of four (Bronfenbrenner, 1975: 9). Wives work because they have to and their economic contributions constitute an important portion of the family income. Wives thereby possess the means to influence financial decisions.

In middle-class households, however, husbands' incomes and occupational prestige clearly surpass those of most working wives. Husbands earn most of the money, and their occupations are often of a type to give them expertise qualities. Husbands, accordingly, have more say-so in purchasing decisions or decisions where money is involved. But when a family lacks all presetting of roles, husband and wife can jockey for roles to be defined in terms compatible to each as well as to the other. Role expectations are subject to "role bargains" (Goode, 1960), and patterns that fail to meet one party's value standards become subject to renegotiation. In the family, age changes, peer influences, and demands from school and occupation can, as we indicated earlier, render existing role bargains unsatisfactory. Commitment to the status quo weakens as maturing junior members seek more decision-making power or a reallocation of tasks better suited to their changing identities. At this point, the old rewards or punishments for performing or not performing according to previously established role expectations, as well as threats of enforcement efforts by third parties, are no longer sufficient to prevent the individual from instituting new behaviors.

Periods when members try out different behaviors, see other's reactions, and maintain or modify the actions are recurrent throughout the family cycle in which changing needs lead members to remake their roles and encourage family morphogenesis to occur. Between these predictable and critical periods of role transition, some of which usher in new family stages, role behaviors "shake down" into the habitual interaction patterns that turn families into functioning social systems.

### Role Conformity and Family Social Control
The idea of role making alternating with behaviors appropriate for normatively prescribed roles raises the issue of role conformity. The task of social control that insures a predictable social order to families and societies, is a critical issue in sociology. One answer to the problem is that of role reciprocity. When there is role reciprocity, each party in the relation has rights and duties. Each role actor receives something from, and gives something to, the other. Role reciprocity is based on exchange, so that failures to reciprocate rights can be sanctioned immediately. The aggrieved party can simply stop recognizing rights until duties are met.

Because family relations endure longer than those in most other groups, members do not keep accounts concerning what they have received from one member in exchange for what they have given him or her. Not only are older members supposed to act in accordance with the value that some self-sacrifice is required for family welfare, but rewards can come from members other than those whose rights a person has fulfilled. Marital partners during the child-rearing period, for example, are particularly important as a source of comfort just because children are unable to reciprocate the many services they receive. This family practice of members providing services for one and receiving rewards from another is a source of family solidarity as well as a means of family control (cf. Ekeh, 1974: 206).

Another family control that makes for predictable role performances is the inculcation of rules and values by parents while socializing their children. Parents can ensure reciprocity by establishing norms of family relations which children internalize. Such norms also affect how many rights family members have and the timing of their fulfillment. In family life, women are often at the end of the line insofar as rights are concerned. The survival of families certainly depends upon their members putting the welfare of others before individual interests in cases of conflict, but women are increasingly questioning the norm that makes them the primary upholders of the value, "family first." With this questioning has come the opening of new family areas to role making as spouses negotiate interaction arrangements in which both men and women interact less in terms of ascribed rights than in terms of mutual responsibilities.

A third factor that enables families to accomplish their social control task involves other concerned individuals who may intervene to sanction the behavior of one party in the role relation. To take an example, the man in the husband-father position may be performing the teacher role with regard to his son who needs help with his arithmetic. The son's active role is that of playmate, not the role of student. In the interaction process, it quickly becomes apparent that the range of behaviors each is expecting, and has prepared to articulate his behavior with, is not emerging. One or the other will have to modify his behavior or the interaction cannot continue. The father can sanction the boy through a brief explanation of why study is necessary now, or a short command to get down to business with a promised reward of play after study. The wife-mother, however, may intervene and tell the father that the child has had a long day at school and would probably learn more about arithmetic after the father and son play together a bit. Because of the third party's intervention, the father performs the role of companion and waits until after dinner to open the arithmetic book.

All these conformity pressures are particularly potent in the family. Family expectations that delimit interaction patterns are among the first norms children internalize through socialization. And the sanctions of other family members are effective, because the members are dependent upon each other for emotional support or physical maintenance. If internal sanctions and those of others directly involved in the relation are not effective, another family member is apt to apply pressure if the interaction deadlock is causing conflict. Failure in one role obligation has negative implications for role performance in other family relationships; thus the self-interest of other family members dictates intervention. The mother's intervention in the above example stems from her knowledge that if the child is forced to activate the student role, his fatigue may make him too irritable to eat his dinner. The father also may concede to his wife's wishes knowing, if he does not, she may be loath to help him get ready for a fishing trip the next day. Finally, as Goode (1960) notes in his discussion of factors encouraging conformity to role expectations, their role as socializers requires parents to serve as examples of good behavior. As a result, they may fill requirements they are attempting to make normative for their children, so that the children with whom they interact will "follow their model."

## Conformity and Change

Conformity contributes to the maintenance of a family's current role relations. Patterned ways become habitual and require little conscious thought and energy to continue. Yet, paradoxically, conformity to any set of role relations may result in family morphogenesis.

Conformity of one family member to another family member's expectations can lead to less rather than more gratification for the conforming person. The latter may come to take these actions for granted and give fewer rewards. Under such circumstances, the wife may try harder to please her husband with more tasty meals, better budgeting, or larger contributions to family finances. But eventually the cost of obtaining gratification becomes too high in time and energy, and at this point the wife stops conforming to her husband's expectations. The classic complaint, "you don't appreciate me," with other verbal and nonverbal sanctions often follow, until the husband institutes a higher level of rewards. Nonconformity may be necessary at times to keep role relations going (Gouldner, 1970).

As Turner (1970: 34) perceptively points out, each family member who goes beyond his obligations in fulfilling family responsibilities places other family members in his debt. The role of family martyr, which wife-mothers sometimes play, may well result from the normative

expectation referred to earlier, namely, that women place "family interests first." Overfulfillment of family obligations can be one way of actu-
alizing this value as well as a strategy for gaining one's rights through
playing upon the guilt feelings of those less scrupulous in performing
family duties. Conformity, therefore, can create tension and eventually
conflict, as can dissent and nonconformity to role performance expectations. The resulting conflict can reinvigorate the system by encouraging family change.

The possibility of nonconformity also forces family members to be
sensitive to each other's actions. This sensitivity springing from uncertainty about the behavior of others brings us back to our initial discussion of role making with its emphasis on the tenuous quality and
changing nature of interrelations. When families must develop their own
role agreements and look largely to their own members to enforce
them, interpersonal sensitivity becomes essential for the role monitor-
ing and role modifying that enable the family system to endure through
periods of change and through periods of stability.

# INTERACTION STRUCTURES

The discussion has centered thus far on patterns implicitly growing out
of dyadic role relations. Let us now turn to interaction structures involving all family members. Here the discussion will cover patterns of
power, communication, and affection as they are most critical for the
family's performing its tasks and accomplishing its goals.

## Power Structure

Power can be defined as the probability that one person will be able to
exert his will despite resistance from others (Weber, 1947). Such a
structure is activated when decisions must be made concerning the
allocation of resources and the division of tasks to keep the family fed
and clothed and the residence maintained.

Raven, Centers, and Rodrigues (1975) have examined the basis of
power in the conjugal subsystem, and how it changes over time. They
had a representative cross-section of married individuals from the
urban population of the United States give their reasons for conforming
to requests of their spouses. The respondents were offered the following reasons to choose among: (1) *Coercive power*—unless there is
conformity and the request is granted, the spouse will say or do something unpleasant; (2) *Reward power*—as a result of conformity, the

spouse will do or say something pleasant; (3) *Expert power*—the spouse knows what is best in this instance for the individual to do; (4) *Referent power*—since they are members of the same family, spouses should agree; (5) *Legitimate power*—because the spouse has a right to make the request, the husband or wife should conform.[1] Note that the use of love as a power base is conspicuously absent, unless one subsumes it under reward power.

Wives conform more often, the study shows, because they feel their husbands have superior expertise. Husbands are much more likely to give referent power as the basis of their being influenced than to concede that their wives have greater expertise. Older persons, however, less often attribute expert influence to spouses while referent power increases with age. And few respondents conform because of possible coercion or rewards. Role reciprocity, this study suggests, depends more upon mutual respect of the spouses and their desire for a continuance of the relation than upon specific sanctions. Marriages survive the stress of time through maintaining solidarity, and this is reflected in the increasing importance of referent power (Raven, Centers, and Rodrigues, 1975: 224).

Figure 3-3 illustrates several possible structures of family power. In only one, the horizontal structure, is power not asymmetrical. The

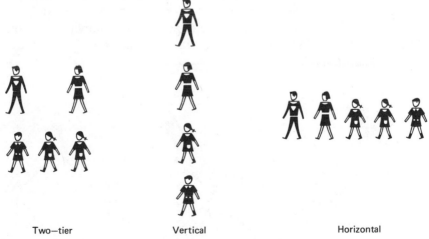

|  |  |  |
|---|---|---|
| Two—tier | Vertical | Horizontal |

**Figure 3-3 Family power structuers.**

[1] The labels of the power bases did not appear in the alternatives the interviewers gave the respondents.

vertical arrangement is reminiscent of the armed forces table of organization in which everyone but the top commander is under the control of someone. The two-tier system permits intracohort solidarity but emphasizes intergenerational power differences.

These power differences affect and are affected by the communication structure. Children may try to keep information from parents whose control is irksome. But parents, because they possess power, can demand that children keep them informed.

**Communication Structure**

The communication interaction patterns can be analyzed in terms of the following: (1) Are all family members in direct communication? (2) Is the communication two-way, or does one person always initiate the conversation? (3) Are the communication channels open, or are there areas of family life that are not discussed? A diagram of the communication structure of a family shows the location of positions that serve as communication centers and points out those positions in which occupants are isolates or one-way communicators. This structure, like the power structure, can vary according to the topic of communication.

Figure 3-4 gives some different family communication patterns. In the *switchboard* arrangement, everyone is joined by communication channels. In the *wheel* arrangement, one family member, often the mother, keeps family members in touch. The *gap* structure indicates that there are communication barriers among the family members. These barriers suggest that the peripheral members may soon be outside the family boundaries.

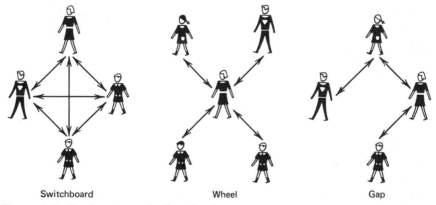

| Switchboard | Wheel | Gap |

**Figure 3-4 Family communication structures.**

Communication through speech or nonverbal gestures can serve several purposes (Rausch, Goodrich, and Campbell, 1963: 376–377). The first has to do with providing others with information as to one's knowledge and intentions. In transactions with others, such shared communications can be the means for clearing up family misunderstandings and conflicts about such issues as children's outside activities and the division of family income. Family problems arising from unexpected happenings external to the family such as higher taxes, job layoffs, or the illness of aging relatives can all be dealt with through such communication.

A second purpose of communication is to underline the solidarity of the persons in communication, to point up their closeness and separateness from others. This boundary-setting function assists the family in establishing its identity and its feeling of distinctiveness from other groups. Casual remarks that point up the "peculiar" ways of outsiders, amused glances that indicate a shared perspective on the opinions of friends, and the surprised reports that describe the idiosyncrasies of neighbors all serve this function.

This second purpose blends into a third—the communication of feelings. The affective aspect of communication is particularly important in "role-making" families where persons must work out agreements not only about task allocation and performance content but also about family goals and ways family members work together. To work out relatively stable division of labor and power patterns, individuals must know the sentiments of the other actors toward their roles in the family drama. Even though each member works out the content of his role in conjunction with others, the expectations generated in others "sets" that role content as final for the time being. Communication still permits a family member to modify his role so it will suit her or him better, while informing others of the feelings that led to the additional role making. The others, in turn, can express satisfaction or dissatisfaction about the proposed new arrangements. Even couples who do little experimenting with role assignment or role content can use communication of feelings to prevent the buildup of irritations and misunderstandings that can lead to deep-seated family conflicts.

Communication, however, does not always lead to increased family solidarity. Telling others of one's negative feelings, supplying information concerning irreconcilable differences, or raising unsolvable issues can lead to family conflicts. Thus parents and children who fail to agree on premarital, courtship behaviors or spouses who let their consumer needs outstrip their finances are well advised to remain silent in the interest of family harmony.

## Affection Structure

One form of communication that is often overlooked is that of affection
There is much variation among families in the amount of love members
have for one another. High separation and divorce rates indicate that
the sentimental bond that is supposed to join husband and wife is often
brittle. Sibling rivalry and parent-child conflict also show that a family's affection structure can be problematical.

The ways and amount of affection families display vary depending
upon the ethnic backgrounds of the spouses and the age and sex of
the children. The English and German peoples are reputed to be much
more reserved in their expression of emotion than the French and
Italian, and this carries over to the display of affection, through words
or touch. Touching another person, as Jourard points out (1966), is
the last step in reducing distance between people. Touching conveys
information to the individual in a form he cannot overlook, whether it
be disapproval, hatred, affection, or good will. With a touch, parents
punish children, wives arouse husbands to love, and family members
soothe each other.

In Europe, and especially England, Montagu (1971) reports the
higher the class, the less there is of tactility. There is some evidence
on mother-child relations that shows class differences to be the reverse in the United States. Members of the middle and upper classes
appear to give their children more attention than do the lower classes
(Montagu, 1971: 261). The reason for this American difference may lie
in the greater social mobility of individuals. Being upwardly mobile,
they turn to child guidance authorities, whose counsel is heeded by
the more highly educated. These authorities encourage parents to give
children tender, loving care.

The study of mother-child relations that produced these findings was
of the tactile experience of children from infancy to four and a half
years of age in working-class, middle-class, and upper-class families.
Clay (1966) as reported in Montagu (1971) observed 45 mother-child
pairs with 20 boys and 27 girls on public, country club, and private
beaches. She noted the average tactile contacts by age of child and
class for one hour of observation. The higher the class, the more the
contacts and the longer the duration of the contacts. The age of the
child, however, was a critical factor, with touch playing less of a role
in the mother-child affection pattern as the child became older. Contrary to what one might expect, however, the nonwalkers from two to
fourteen months received less touching than did the just-walking tod-
dlers from fourteen months to two years. As Montagu states (1971:

242), this is a most striking finding, given the manifest needs of the infant. The explanation seems to lie in the toddler's need for reassurance from the mother that he will be safe in his beginning forays away from her and so his greater affectionate attachment. Clay also found that mothers showed more affection to their little girls than to their little boys.

Males seem to be handicapped in growing up in the family in their more limited opportunities to communicate through skin contacts. Boys, as compared with girls, have less contact with their mothers' bodies, both touching and being touched, and this is also true of tactile contacts with their fathers. This carries over to adulthood when fathers less often hold children and so miss the exchange of pleasure-giving sensory experiences that are expressions of affection (Montagu, 1971: 272). In addition, men are burdened by gender-role expectations that put a premium on not expressing emotions. This is particularly true of father-son relations or male friendships, in which gestures of affection are limited to handshaking or backslapping. Other tactile behaviors are often labeled in this society as effeminate or indications of homosexuality.

The sexual relation between husband and wife, with the tactile pleasures of touching, stroking, and rubbing it incorporates in lovemaking, takes on added significance for men. For some it may be the only relation in which they feel comfortable displaying affection. The unashamed kisses, hugs, and handclasps that married couples engage in indicate not only mutual affection but contribute to the marital bond and are particularly important for husbands.

The affection structure of a family, however, is not only reflected in "touching relations" but also in the choices members make in seeking verbal comfort from other family members in times of adversity. The sensitivity to other's pleasures as shown in little attentions such as gifts of candy to the member with a "sweet tooth," cooking someone's favorite dish, or relieving "mom" of the dinner dishes also suggests who is particularly fond of whom. The use of endearment terms is an additional indicator.

As the family experiences the various expectable events that mark off family stages, its patterns of seeking and giving affection change. The adolescent aware of growing sexual capacities looks increasingly to someone of the opposite gender outside the family to fulfill her or his affectional needs. These needs help instigate and support the formation of new family units. Children's feelings for their parents change qualitatively as they move from being dependents to independent heads of their own families. Spousal relations too change as the raptures of early marriage mellow into the multitudinous interdependencies that undergird the mature union.

Figure 3-5 shows possible affection structures. In the cloverleaf pattern, family members are equally close. The mother is the center of family affection in the satellite arrangement while in the isolate pattern, one family member does not participate in the affection giving structure.

The distribution and amount of love in a family is influential in its continuance over time. Love is a means for achieving reconciliation of family members in cases of conflict. Affection cushions the ups and downs of family existence, makes the daily routine more agreeable, and underlies family boundary maintenance.

The affection-giving structure is related to that of communication and power. Those who are the center of attention have power to give rewards of affection and also receive much information. If they are young, however, they do not know how to use their power for long-term purposes, and the communications they receive are of little importance.

## THE INTERRELATION OF INTERACTION STRUCTURES

Communication, power, and affection structures are interdependent. To demonstrate this and to analyze them in greater detail, the concepts and discussion of Basil Bernstein (1970) are useful. He relates power and communication structures through the concepts of position-oriented and person-oriented families and of restricted and elaborated language codes, a language code being the "principle which regulates the selection and organization of speech events" (Bernstein, 1970: 30).

Isolate                    Cloverleaf                    Satellite

**Figure 3-5    Family affection structures.**

In defining his category of *restricted language code*, he refers to the example of long-time married couples' communications. Such couples in conversation resort to a sort of oral shorthand. A narrow range of words provides the staple of conversation, because common assumptions, values, and experiences preclude the necessity for verbal specification. Restricted codes arise out of subcultures or cultures where common life produces a social solidarity in which the "we" is more important than the "I." The language gap is between sharers and non-sharers of the core.

Persons who communicate by using an *elaborated language code*, as you would expect from the label, utilize a wide range of vocabulary and sentence structures that are flexibly organized. The speaker focuses upon the auditor as a person having different experiences and tries to select words and to place them into sentence structures that will bring understanding to the auditor. Elaborated codes are necessarily person-oriented. They arise when persons who lack a universe of shared meanings attempt to communicate. The culture or subculture emphasizes the "I" over the "we" of the group.

With this summary of Bernstein's communication distinctions, it is now possible to relate them to family types and power structures. Roles in positional families tend to be ascriptive, based on the age and gender status of the member and not on the basis of his or her individual characteristics. Socialization is unilateral from parents and other elders to children with accompanying one-way communication channels. The children have two-way communication channels with their peers who serve as role models and information sources in matters adults do not concern themselves with. In the vertical power structure, parents' control of children is less oriented to the person and verbally explained than based on parental force or on their appeals to norms that regulate the status of children. Parents are central in the power structure on the basis of age status. The attendant factor of gender makes the husband-father the final authority.

Here are some examples Bernstein (1970) gives of social control statements in positional families along with the status they refer to.

*"You should be able to tie your shoes at your age."* (age-status role)

*"Little boys don't cry."* (gender-status role)

*"Don't speak to your father like that."* (age-relation role)

Role in the person-oriented system are allocated on the basis of achievement, not on ascription according to age and gender. Communication lines are two-way in a switchboard structure. Children socialize parents as well as being socialized by them, since parents are sensitive to their children's individual characteristics. In such families, elaborated linguistic codes are essential for parents and children to explain their role-making attempts. Social control through the two-tier power structure tends to be verbal and to take into account the particular characteristics of the culprit. Parents are power figures because of greater experience. As their competencies increase, the power structure becomes more horizontal in character. Appeals to the child might take the following form:

*"Try tying your shoes once more. You remember yesterday you could do it the third time, and you were so pleased."*
*"Sit down in your seat as you are too tall for the woman in back to see over."*

Family conflicts will have different outcomes in the two types of families with their varied communication channels, associated language codes, and power structures. In person-oriented families, challenges to the rules do not threaten the authority of the rule giver. He has not relied on his position as an older person to enforce the rules. The two-way communication channels joining him and the youth have also permitted the youth to voice any disagreements so that role modifications can be made when the youth demands them.

By contrast, objections to rules in position-oriented families may result in the adolescent's rejecting the parents' authority, since it was on the basis of their formal status as older persons that they initiated the rules. Instead of continuing to belong to the "we group" of their value community, he or she can be driven by the conflict to move into another community where in time a shared background instills its own restricted language code.

So far, we have not related Bernstein's family typology to affection structure. He says little on this matter except to write of the greater use of gestures and touch to convey emotions in position-oriented families. This seems to indicate that pats, hugs, kisses, cuddling, and other physical demonstrations of affection are greater in position families. The emphasis on role assignment based on status, however, suggests that males consider expressions of affection for other males, even including their own sons, as at best effeminate, and at worst an indicators of homosexuality. The expressive roles of affection giver and comforter are left largely to girls and women. Children, accordingly, turn to mothers in times of distress or for affection. This tendency is accentuated by the father's position as an authority figure. As rule giver and disciplinarian he may gain respect, but as an authority he is seldom loved. This is particularly true when one-way communication in a wheel structure permits him to make pronouncements but to escape complaints and demands for explanations from the less powerful.

Person-oriented families are not limited in showing affection by considerations of age and sex. Whether the heavy emphasis on individual differences, coupled with an elaborated language code to bridge these differences, leads to an emphasis on verbal rather than on "touch" forms of affection display remains an open question. One can hypothesize that person-oriented families, with their greater dependence on role making, perform affection-giving or affection-receiving roles more often than do position-oriented families. Change is easier in the person-oriented families because affection is used to soften confrontations and misunderstandings while new roles are made and new interaction patterns developed.

The classification of person-oriented families and position-oriented families in reality is not a clear-cut dichotomy. Parent-child communication channels are not always open in person-oriented families nor always closed in position-oriented families. Nor is access to power invariably based on status claims in the latter families. It is also true that the clipped, terse language of the restricted code is used under usual circumstances by all families to save time and energy. Persons in positional families, however, have more difficulty communicating in terms of an elaborated code. Interpersonal sensitivity may be present, but the associated necessity for "getting through" to the listener in all his uniqueness is lacking in families that assign roles and rules according to age and gender categories.

## Class and Family Type

Bernstein predicts positional families are more often found among working-class families who are long-time residents of communities composed of like-minded families. In these closely integrated communities, common norms and values are passed on from one generation to the next, intragroup marriage rates are high, and a restricted speech code is usually sufficient for communication. Families that are residentially mobile, or that have parents who deal with "outsiders" from different backgrounds, shift more toward personal control forms and to more individualized uses of language with increasingly open channels of communication.

Working-class girls, particularly older girls, are also more likely to use elaborated codes. They often play mothering roles in the family along with their sibling roles. They must be able to interchange the roles of controller of siblings, mediator between parents and sibs, and companion to sibs. In their parental surrogate roles, they are more dependent upon elaborated, person-oriented control tactics than on coercive measures, because their age and sex status give them little power. They are also less involved than boys in the kind of group-centered peer activities that foster restrictive codes.

Because of geographical and social mobility, middle-class families tend to be interpersonally sensitive. Communication channels are two-way between parents and children, and power structures are not inevitably and always parent centered. Their emphasis on the separateness of individuals is compatible with and generated by role making as against conformity to traditional role prescriptions.

These assertions of Bernstein fit with the research results reported in an earlier chapter on class differences in problem solving and also with research on class differences in the importance of age and sex status for role assignments. Lower-class persons are more constrained by ascribed roles based on age and sex than are those of other classes. A segregated conjugal role organization is not uncommon in such families.[2] For the lower-lower class person, particularly, such a concern is consistent with his or her own social position. Being poor often rests on ascribed roles having to do with race or physical or mental characteristics. Disproportionately represented in the poverty ranks are blacks, because of job discrimination, and the aged, because of retirement policies and health.[3] Since persons in middle-class families are more often able to enter esteemed achieved roles, there appears to be less emphasis on age and sex differences in family role assignments.[4]

---

[2] One study of 257 families in three urban centers showed that 72 percent of lower-lower-class black and white families have a segregated conjugal role relationship as compared with no middle-class couples and 23 and 36 percent respectively of the white and black upper-lower class families (Rainwater, 1965: 32; Bott, 1971). The working-class and middle-class couples tended to have a division of labor in which more roles were shared or interchangeable.

[3] The rate of poverty among white persons in 1971 was 10 percent. It was 33 percent for blacks (Chilman, 1975: 49). Poverty is defined, most conservatively, as an income below $4137, for a nonfarm family of four. Two-thirds of families having incomes, under $4000 were families with female heads (Bronfenbrenner, 1975: 10).

[4] In discussions about class differences, family composition differences, and the other factors used to explain family behaviors, keep in mind that there is always overlap in the groups delineated by the factor in question. Some middle-class families on income, husbands' occupations, and other measures display behaviors we have described as lower class. Working-class families, as judged by the same measures, can be middle class in behavior. Group differences indicate tendencies not divisions among the groups.

## SUMMARY

In this chapter, we have tried to present a picture of the elements of the family and the interrelations that enable the family to hang together. We began the chapter with an analysis of some of the constraints placed on family functioning by its size, and by its age and sex composition. An analysis of roles and role relations followed, with a description of the process of the actor's "making up roles" rather than performing them according to normative patterns. We then faced the problem of why people conform to role expectations. The chapter closed with a consideration of three of the structural networks that enable the family to fulfill its tasks. To illustrate the patterns of power, communication, and affection, we discussed Bernstein's (1970) concepts of person- and position-oriented families and restricted and elaborated language codes.

The chapter attempted to put to use in a new context the concepts of the family as a system examined in the previous chapter. The interdependence of family members continues to be a central concern, with much attention paid to role reciprocity as a means for establishing family interaction structures. As a changing entity, the family is conceptualized in terms of role making in contrast to a more static approach based on normative behavior. How families organize to perform tasks is suggested by their power, communication, and affection structures. Selective boundary maintenance is of less central importance, although occasionally there are problems in setting boundaries to be observed by kin.

We shall continue to make apparent in future chapters how the concepts of one chapter are related to those of earlier ones. In spite of differences in content focus in these introductory chapters, we are striving for a maximum of conceptual integration.

## REFERENCES

Aldous, Joan, "The Making of Family Roles and Family Change," *Family Coordinator*, 1974, 23, 231-235.

Bates, Frederick, L., "Position, Role and Status," *Social Forces*, 1956, 34, 313–321. Copyright © The University of North Carolina Press.

Bernstein, Basil, "A Sociolinguistic Approach to Socialization: With Some Reference to Educability," in Frederick Williams, *Language and Poverty: Perspectives on a Theme.* Chicago: Markham, 1970, 25–61.

Blood, Robert, O., and Donald M. Wolfe, *Husbands and Wives: The Dynamics of Married Living.* New York: Free Press, 1960.

Bossard, James H. S. and Eleanor S. Boll, *The Large Family System: An Original Study in the Sociology of Family Behavior.* Philadelphia: University of Pennsylvania Press, 1956.

Bott, Elizabeth, *Family and Social Network: Roles, Norms, and External Rela-tionships in Ordinary Urban Families.* New York: Free Press, 1971.

Bronfenbrenner, Urie, The Challenge of Social Change to Public Policy and Developmental Research," Paper presented at the Meeting of the Society for Research in Child Development, 1975.

Centers, Richard, Bertram H. Ravan, and Aroldo Rodrigues, "Conjugal Power Structure: A Re-examination," *American Sociological Review*, 1971, 36, 264–278.

Chilman, Catherine S., "Families in Poverty in the Early 1970's: Rates, Associated Factors, Some Implications," *Journal of Marriage and the Family,* 1975, 37, 49–60.

Clay, Vidal, S., "The Effect of Culture on Mother-Child Tactile Communication" Unpublished doctoral dissertation, New York; Teacher's College: Columbia University, 1966, cited in Ashley Montagu *Touching: The Human Significance of the Skin.* New York: Columbia University Press, 1971.

Duvall, Evelyn M., *In-Laws: Pro and Con*, New York: Association Press, 1954.

Ekeh, Peter P., *Social Exchange Theory: The Two Traditions.* Cambridge, Mass.: Harvard University Press, 1974.

Elder, Glen, H. and Charles E. Bowerman, "Family Structure and Child Rearing Patterns: The Effects of Family Size and Sex Composition," *American Sociological Review*, 1963, 28, 891–905.

Goode, William, J., "Norm Commitment and Conformity to Role-Status Obligations," *American Journal of Sociology*, 1960, 66, 246–258.

Gouldner, Alvin, *The Coming Crisis in Western Sociology.* New York: Basic Books, 1970.

Jourard, Sydney, "An Exploratory Study of Body-Accessibility," *British Journal of Sociology and Clinical Psychology*, 1966, 5, 221–231.

Levinger, George, "Task and Social Behavior in Marriage," *Sociometry*, 1964, 27, 433–448.

Mead, Margaret, "Age Patterning in Personality Development," in William E. Martin and Celia B. Stendler, eds., *Readings in Child Development.* New York: Harcourt, Brace and World, 1954, 170–176.

Montagu, Ashley, *Touching: The Human Significance of the Skin.* New York: Columbia University Press, 1971.

Nisbet, John, "Family Environment and Intelligence," In A. H. Halsey, Jean Floud, and C. Arnold Anderson, eds., *Education, Economy and Society.* New York: Free Press, 1961, 273–287.

Rainwater, Lee, *Family Design: Marital Sexuality, Family Size, and Contracepting.* Chicago: Aldine Press, 1965.

Raush, Harold L., Wells Goodrich, and John D. Campbell, "Adaptation to the First Years of Marriage," *Psychiatry*, 1963, 26, 368–380.

Raven, Bertram H., Richard Centers, and Aroldo Rodriguez, "The Bases of Conjugal Power," in Ronald F. Cromwell and David H. Olson, eds., *Power in Families.* New York: Halstead Press, 1975, 217–232.

Riley, Matilda, W., "Social Gerontology and the Age Stratification of Society," *The Gerontologist*, 1971, 11, 79–87.

Slater, Philip, "Parental Role Differentiation," *American Journal of Sociology*, 1961, 67, 296–311.

Turner, Ralph, H., *Family Interaction*. New York: John Wiley, 1970.

Turner, Ralph, H., "Role-Taking: Process vs. Conformity," in Arnold M. Rose, ed., *Human Behavior and Social Process*. Boston: Houghton Mifflin, 1962, 20–40.

Weber, Max, *The Theory of Social and Economic Organization*. New York: Free Press, 1947.

# The family career as a means for analyzing systematic change

This chapter introduced concepts that constitute the "development" aspect of the family development framework and thus distinguish it from other ways of viewing families. The changes emphasized in this framework are those expectable occurrences that large numbers of families experience with the passage of time. Since some of the concepts relating to family development bear the same labels as those used by developmental psychologists to characterize the development of individuals, we must be alert to their different meanings when used in the context of the family development framework.

The family, unlike the individual, is not an organism. Its existence depends on family members fulfilling various family tasks and continuing willingly in the family group. Because members interact and are interdependent, the roles they play are shaped by the expectations of others in the family. These interactions and their outcomes, which define a family, are different from individual actions and their consequences when considered alone. Thus we can study family changes either as products of specific interactions between individual members or as group outcomes that restructure the family.

The first of the concepts that is useful in analyzing family change can be labeled family career, or family cycle, a more common term. This concept emphasizes the existence of family units from their inceptions to their dissolutions. Family development analysis is often labeled family cycle analysis. If we view the nuclear family as beginning with the couple relation and adding the parent-child and sibling sybsystems when a couple has children, the use of the term "cycle" is not inappropriate. The end of the existence of each family sees the same persons present as at its beginning, since both spouses now live beyond the period of their children's departure from home. A cycle, however, refers to a repeated sequence of events (Feldman and Feldman, 1975; Rodgers, 1964). Family existence over time does not constitute a cycle in this sense since obviously an aging couple does not repeat the events of a newlywed couple. For this reason, we prefer the term, family career (Rodgers, 1964), which was discussed in Chapter 1 in connection with positional career. We retain the term family cycle for occasional use because of its present widespread acceptance as a label for the family development approach.

The concept of *stage* will enable us to analyze the time periods through which families exist. A stage is a division within the lifetime of a family that is distinctive enough from those that precede and follow it to constitute a separate period. It presupposes qualitative changes so readily discernible that earlier interaction patterns cluster together in clear distinction from later phenomena. Unless this sort of segregation occurs in portions of a developmental process, it makes little sense to use the concept of stage (Flavell; 1963).

The use of the term "stage" indicates that the framework does not specifically handle short episodes encompassing a limited number of interactions. These changes are caught up in the concepts of role making discussed in the last chapter and role sequence, which we indicated (Chapter 1) refers to changes in the content of a role over time. The family career stages cover sizeable time spans, and although one stage shades into the other, there are breaks or discontinuities between them that give each stage its distinctive character. The changes in family organization that occur with each new stage are fundamental enough to comprise a morphogenesis of the family.

Families in the same stage face similar problems in fulfilling the tasks that keep them operating. These problems differ from those of previous stages and require different family interaction patterns to meet them. There are similarities in the content of the roles and role clusters of members of families in the same stage. It is this commonality that makes the family developmental approach, and its emphasis on stage analysis of the family career, useful in understanding families. Family careers are continuous, however, and an arbitrary element enters all schemes for dividing family careers. And, unlike developmental stages of an organism, family stages are not invariant or irreversible (Rodgers; 1962). For this reason, I shall use the terms "category," "period," and "stage" interchangeably to signify that family stages do not have the properties usually associated with stages of growth.

### Role Transitions Introduce Family Stages

To determine where to make stage divisions, the concept of critical role transition, introduced by Rapoport (1964), is helpful. These transitions mark discontinuities sufficiently great in the behaviors of individuals to cause family morphogenesis. Note that the concept *critical role transition point*, refers to individuals while *morphogenesis*, and *stage* refer to families. Change comes from individual family members who, by interacting with other family members, force sufficient modification in behavior patterns that we can say family morphogenesis has occurred.

Although the label, critical role transition point, suggests a specific event delineating a new family stage, in actuality, "point" covers a variable period of time. New patterns are not established immediately just as old ways do not cease all at once. There is a greater or lesser period when families flounder, search for, and try out new ways before "settling" into new behavior patterns.

The role transition points introduce stages and mark discontinuities in behaviors that are normal for individuals and for groups at certain intervals of their existence. It is these intervals or points that allow us to demarcate family stages. In most societies, getting married, having children, seeing mature children setting up new conjugal units, and coping with a spouse's dying, constitute such critical role transition points in the positional careers of family members. Regardless of how much prior expectation, preparation, and role rehearsal there may have been for these and similar critical changes, the individuals and groups affected encounter the experience with some uncertainty. This is particularly true in our own society where social change has been rapid, and where traditional role prescriptions have been questioned. This opens the way for making new roles as individuals encounter these critical role transitions.

Critical role transition points may also be characterized as "points of no return." Other people redefine individuals so that once they have passed the transition point they are never the same. Even divorce, for example, cannot restore the never-married status to individuals. Once married, the woman loses for all times her culturally defined virginal

status, and the man cannot again regain the position of never-married
bachelor (Rapoport and Rapoport 1964: 42)

These role transitions can be used to delineate the family career
stages, because a number of family members are directly involved
and because those not directly experiencing the role transition are
soon involved because of the interdependence of all family members.
Family members interact in new social contexts as a result of the role
change. They have different expectations of the persons taking on
the new roles, who in turn make different demands of the others as a
result of changes in self-concepts brought about by the new roles.
When the family is in a new stage, the roles in each family position,
which make up the role cluster of that position, are significantly
changed. Thus the *role complex* of the family, which consists of the
role clusters of all the family members at any one point in time
(Rodgers, 1964: 266), tends to be qualitatively different at each stage
in the family career. Indeed, one definition of family stage is that of
"a marked change in the family's role complex."

Take getting married, as an example of a critical role transition point.
The new spouses have moved from the son or daughter positions of
the families of orientation—in which they grew up—to spousal positions in the new family of procreation—which they create by their
marriage. Morphogenesis occurs in the couple relation. New living
arrangements on a neolocal basis and new relational patterns differentiate the social context of marriage from what went before. Parents
and sibs must cope with changes in affection patterns and in living
arrangements.

The behavior structures of new couples must also develop to accomplish marital tasks. Previous arrangements of interaction are no longer
sufficient, and every couple has to initiate morphogenetic processes.
Couple interaction is tentative, as spouses grope for new solutions and
experience conflicting expectations. Communication and power patterns have to be worked out so mutual socialization into marital roles
can occur. Work arrangements within the home and the demands of
the occupational structure must be integrated to facilitate tasks of
physical maintenance.

Getting married as a critical role transition point for demarcating a
family stage has to do with events in the positional career of persons
in the family. The roles of individuals in work life and schooling also
contain critical role transition points for the individual. Occupational
changes—job demotion, job promotion, and job termination—represent such points in work life. In the educational career, entry into and
graduation from school at various levels can be critical role transition

points. The individual involved in these family-member, work-life, and educational careers has to synchronize their demands, just as the various career demands of other members have to be reconciled within the family as it develops over time. Accordingly, information on these multiple careers must be taken into account in establishing family stages as well as in understanding the lives of individuals (Elder, 1975).

## DIVIDING THE FAMILY CAREER

In this century a number of researchers have examined families by using a developmental perspective. Since individuals in their own life-courses face a number of critical role transitions, researchers have had to make a choice of which to use in distinguishing different stages. To do so, they have looked for those transitions that large numbers of people can expect to experience in areas of interest to them. Consequently, their stage schemes have categorized together families whose common characteristics provided answers to the researchers' questions.

Early studies utilizing the family lifetime concept were largely the product of rural sociologists (Sorokin, Zimmerman, and Galpin, 1931; Loomis 1936) whose focus, following the work of the English researcher Rowntree (1906), was on how changes in family size and composition affected the economic status of families. Their concern with family finances reflected the high unemployment years of the 1930s in which they did their research. The first stage they singled out was that of the childless family whose finances are adequate but low, as are those of adults in their first jobs. In the next stage, the growing family stage, the married couple experiences financial difficulties as children arrive and must be reared. There are fewer financial problems in the contracting family stage that follows. Children become earners, or they leave home. The final stage is that of the aging family. With no family breadwinner, finances are once again low.

The concern with the nuclear family's ties to the economy continued to influence persons working with the family development framework. Consumer buying studies (Lansing and Kish, 1957) and research-based policy statements on the optimal family stage for governmental financial assistance (Aldous and Hill, 1969) are examples.

The main focus of family development analysis, however, has been on significant changes in the internal organization of married couples who at some time in their marriages are engaged in bearing and rearing children. Let us examine the stage classification of Duvall and Hill

(1948) which has been widely used by family scholars to analyze intrafamilial change in nuclear families.

## Duvall and Hill's Stage Criteria

The criteria Duvall and Hill (1948) first suggested for establishing stages were three in number: (1) changes in the number of members in the family; (2) developmental stages of the oldest child; and (3) retirement status of the husband-father. These criteria all take into account the influence of events in the occupational and educational careers of family members as well as changes in marital and parental careers that put strain on customary interaction patterns.

The first criterion refers to changes that come with the establishment of the couple relation and the arrival and departure of children. Earlier, we saw some of the changes that marriage brings, and there is a sizable literature on the family morphogenesis that occurs with the first baby's arrival in the way of changes in conjugal sex relations, in housekeeping schedules, and in consumption patterns. When children leave home, research also shows that wives and husbands develop different relationship patterns to compensate for the vacant roles in the interaction structures. Figure 4-1 identifies stages based on the criteria of changes in the family's plurality patterns.

The second criterion has to do with the role transition points arising from the age and the school career placement of the oldest child. This criterion gives us the stages shown in Figure 4-2.

**Figure 4-1. Family stages based on the plurality criterion.**

1. Establishment Stage
2. Expanding Stage—Addition of first child to arrival of last child
3. Stable Stage—Period of child rearing until first child leaves home[a]
4. Contracting Stage—Period of children's leaving home until last child has gone[a]
5. Couple Alone Stage

[a] Note that the period when youths leave one family can be juxtaposed to the establishment stage of another family unit. The member who leaves his family of orientation often does so to form his family of procreation. As with the other criteria, the literature on the changes these different stages bring will be discussed in future chapters.

**Figure 4-2. Family stages based on the age and school placement of the oldest child.**

1. Family with Infant, 0–2 years of age
2. Family with Preschool Child, 3–5 years of age
3. Family with School-Aged Child, 6–12 years of age
4. Family with Adolescent, 13–20 years of age
5. Family with Young Adult, 21 years of age to the leaving of this child

At all these stages, Duvall and Hill (1948) believed that role pre-scriptions by age levels, which are coupled in some cases with bio-logical changes, produce critical role transitions and lead to family morphogenesis. As the child experiences the critical role transition point of school entry, for example, parents not only must conform to school scheduling demands but must accept the influence of a teacher and of peers on their child's thinking and behavior. Parents have to modify expectations, to re-allocate role tasks, and to modify activities in response to the child's demands for greater autonomy (Klein and Ross, 1958).

The third stage criterion of Duvall and Hill (1948) is based on changes in the family resulting from the occupational retirement and the ending of the work-life career of the wage earner. This role transi-tion point serves to divide the period after children leave home into the middle and aging phases of a couple's life, the aging period lasting from retirement until the death of one spouse. The critical role transi-tion point of job retirement of a husband, a wife, or both ushers in sharp changes. Lower income affects consumer patterns. More time at home for a couple brings changes in leisure activities and redivi-sions of labor for household tasks. The stages of the family life cycle when all three criteria are used can be seen in Figure 4-3.

### An Evaluation and Choice of Stage Criteria

Because family members are involved in multiple careers in multiple locations, it is difficult to establish stage classifications that do not obscure critical role transitions of at least one family member. Thus Rodgers (1962) found in a test of the Duvall and Hill criteria that after 21 years of marriage, some couples, who had married children, also had infants. This finding should emphasize that no stage classifica-tions are completely satisfactory. Such classifications are only guides to family career changes of interest to the user, and the families cate-

**Figure 4-3. Nuclear family stages based on the Duvall and Hill criteria.**

| | | |
|---|---|---|
| Stage | I | Establishment Stage |
| Stage | II | Families with Infants |
| Stage | III | Families with Preschool Children |
| Stage | IV | Families with School Children |
| Stage | V | Families with Adolescents |
| Stage | VI | Families with Young Adults |
| Stage | VII | Families in the Middle Years (postparental) |

Source: Duvall, 1971: 106–107.

gorized together may well differ on other characteristics of interest
to other scholars

In this book, the Duvall and Hill stage classification, with some modi
fications, will serve as our guide for the analysis of family careers. We
will use the school entrance of the oldest child rather than chronological
age as a stage criterion. School placement seems more useful for our
purpose of studying changes in family interaction patterns since school
careers vary in their age chronologies at entrance and exit points.
Some children attend "preschools" and others continue their education
past the legal school-leaving age. The oldest child's school progress,
however, often coincides with changes in the work careers of parents.
He serves as a role model for younger siblings in their educational
careers and introduces parents to the expectations school personnel
have for the progress of children through school. Younger children's
school transitions, therefore, can constitute, although they need not, a
repetition of events to which parents were introduced by their oldest
child. (See Rodgers, 1962, for a classification in which the youngest
child's development as well as the oldest child's is taken into account.)

Thus the criteria of plurality patterns, the school placement of the
oldest child, and the discontinuance of the work careers of the couple
will set off the stages we will use in our analyses. These criteria produce a classification (Fig. 4-4) that differs from Duvall and Hill's by
eliminating their stage of "Family with Preschool Children."

## STAGE ANALYSIS OF FAMILY CAREERS

Family stage is one of the few concepts in the family development
framework that can be tied to observables; hence its definition is relatively clear. More importantly, the stages of the family life cycle permit
the practitioner or researcher to gain some idea of the particular vulner-
abilities of a family, or families, by knowing the stage they are in. In
some stages, the child and the parental developmental tasks ushered

**Figure 4-4. Nuclear family stages.**

| | | |
|---|---|---|
| Stage | I | Newly Established Couple |
| Stage | II | Childbearing |
| Stage | III | Families with School Children |
| Stage | IV | Families with Secondary School Children |
| Stage | V | Families with Young Adults |
| Stage | VI | Families in the Middle Years |
| Stage | VII | Aging Families |

in with the new family stage are more complementary than at other times. Thus, in the role complex of the family with secondary school children, positional role clusters seem not to be synchronized well. The demands of youths for greater freedom from family rules and responsibilities can create difficulties with parents fearful of losing control. Sibling relations too may deteriorate in these years as adolescents turn to peers for values and counsel.

Besides the fact that the individual tasks of family members are not synchronized in some stages, the demands made on the family's resources at some stages peak at the same time as do the obligations of extrafamilial careers. The childbearing years are such periods for many husband-fathers. The financial drain resulting from the growing family comes before the period of top earnings for men and at a time when women may still be out of the labor market because of child-care responsibilities. At the same time, the occupational demands on white-collar men, who are struggling to advance their positions, lower the energy and time resources they have for their families. If wives are employed—and an increasing number of them are at this period—they often expect their husbands to share household tasks. Marital disenchantment becomes pronounced during these deficit periods because of the high potential for financial problems and conflict over the household division of labor (Spanier, Lewis, and Cole, 1975).

In contrast to these periods of high family vulnerability are the resource buildup times of the establishment couples before children arrive and the financial recovery later in the middle years after the children have left. During the establishment phase, both spouses have incomes, the relationship has not yet lost the charm of newness, and no child-care responsibilities threaten the priority of the marital dyad. By the middle years, the financial burden of children has decreased and wives are back in the labor force in large enough numbers to usher in something of a "financial recovery" period. If the spouses have not become irremediably estranged as a result of the hectic child-rearing years, there is the possibility of an increase in marital satisfaction (Rollins and Cannon, 1974).

Thus the concept of stage in family career analysis has systemic properties. It enables us to make predictions about the behaviors of families, behaviors that hold for a majority of families despite class, ethnic, religious, or other differences. By knowing what stage of the family life cycle a family is in, we have well-grounded expectations concerning the relative income level, the propensity of a wife to work outside the home, the level of marital satisfaction, and the degree of parent-child conflict, to mention only a few aspects.

## Historical Changes in Family Careers

An examination of differences in the timing of critical family role transitions can tell us how influential various periods will be in the family
career. A graphic demonstration of the effect of these differences
comes from data on women living at three different historical periods
of ever-married women born during the decades of the 1880s, 1920s,
and 1950s (Glick, 1977), and a sample of Quaker wives born before
1786 whose family careers were roughly similar to those of their con-
temporaries (Wells, 1971). A study of Table 4-1 indicates great changes
over the centuries in the timetables of family events. Time at marriage
was about the same during the late eighteenth and mid-twentieth centuries, although the nineteenth century women were somewhat older.
But in all three centuries, the first child usually arrived within the first
two years in most families.

At this point the similarity ends, as differences in fertility patterns
over the centuries drastically changed the length of the childbearing
periods. The period between the birth of the first and last child has a
median length of 9.7 years for women born in the twentieth century.
For the Quaker wives of the eighteenth century, it was 17.4 years. As a
consequence, these women and their husbands spent longer periods
in the child-rearing stages. The wives had a median age of 60.2 when
their last child left home. This fact coupled with earlier mortality rates—
69 percent of the Quaker marriages were of shorter duration than the

Table 4-1
**Median Age of Wives at Stages of the Life Cycle of the Family**

| Stage of the Life Cycle of the Family | Wives born before 1786[a] (U.S. Quakers) | Wives born 1880–1889[b] (U.S.) | Wives born 1920–1929[b] (U.S.) | Wives born 1950–1959[b] (U.S.) |
|---|---|---|---|---|
| A. Age at first marriage | 20.5 | 21.4 | 20.7 | 21.2 |
| B. Age at birth of last child | 37.9 | 32.9 | 31.5 | 29.6 |
| C. Age at marriage of last child | 60.2 | 55.4 | 53.2 | 52.3 |
| D. Age at death of first spouse to die | 50.9 | 57.0 | 64.4 | 65.2 |

[a] Modification of Wells, 1971: 281, Table 1; [b] Glick, 1977: 6, Table 1. Stages are based
on data for once-married mothers instead of ever-married wives. Ages for events
beginning with birth of last child for recent cohorts are for projections based on the
ages at childbearing completion of older cohorts of women in the light of the experiences of the younger cohorts.

child-rearing period—meant that the period of family life coincided with the bearing and rearing of children.[1] There was no child-free stage of the family. The median length of marriage was 30.4 years so that the youngest child rarely had two parents when he reached his majority. The widow or widower of the eighteenth century could expect to take care of children for a median period of 4.3 years after the death of her or his spouse.

In contrast, the twentieth-century wives with their shorter childbearing spans would be 52 when their children had all left home. They could expect some 12 additional years of marriage. For the first time in history, this century has seen family life add a stage to marriage that begins when the last child becomes independent. The median length of marriage has increased to 43.6 years, and the child-rearing period, as we have seen, has been shortened. The importance of the marital career has thus increased as couples spend longer periods of their life together alone.

The threat of death to family stability in the colonial period has been replaced in the present era by divorce. Children today, therefore, are much more likely to have a stepparent and a parent in the same parental position than were Quaker children of the eighteenth century.

## The Careers of NonNuclear Families

The stages that guide our family development study refer to nuclear families, but variation in existing household units indicates the need for criteria to analyze other types of family careers. First of all, a small percentage of people spend their lives as single persons, and this percentage is becoming somewhat larger. The percentages were around four to five percent for cohorts coming of age after World War II but may reach six to seven percent for women born in the 1950s. Of those who do marry, not all will have children. For the four percent of married women born in the 1940s and 1950s who will not have children (Glick, 1977), there will be no stages in their family life-span involving the presence of children.[2]

The family life cycle can also be affected by divorce or death of

---

[1] Massachusetts records from the seventeenth century suggest life spans similar to our own (Demos, 1970, Greven, 1970). People, however, appear to have died younger in the eighteenth century (Greven, 1970).

[2] Marriage rates as well as fertility rates have fallen in the 1970s (Glick, 1975), but until the cohorts coming of age in these years are older, it is impossible to determine what the final rates of singlehood and childlessness will be.

upouuuu uuriiiy iiiu uuriy yuuiiu ui iiiuiiiiyii. i ii iiiiiiiii iiiiiii iiii iii i iiii yiaaii
uld lii 1970, 5.5 peiueiil weie uivuiueu witli tliu fiyuiu fui bluuli iiiuii
being 10.0 poroont. It woo 8.0 poroont for whito womon and 10.4
poroont for blaoli womon. When it oamo to boing widowod, 0.6 poroont
ul wliile iiieii lii llie saine ayeu yiuup, aiid less lliaii uiie peiueiil lui
black men 2.1 percent of white women and 11.1 percent of black
women had lost a spouse through death (U.S. Bureau of the Census,
1977: 9–10, Table 1).[3]

Thus for one reason or another, a sizable number of families do not
negotiate the life cycle in its entirety or with a full complement of family positions. According to the stage guides discussed above, couples
who remain childless go in undifferentiated fashion from the establishment stage to the aging period, clearly an unrealistic assumption. The
stages are also applicable only to the widowed prior to the dissolution of the couple relation. It is possible, however, for investigators
interested in these nonnuclear family types to prepare more appropriate classifications using available research. We shall attempt to demonstrate this possibility with divorced women who have children.

The analysis of variations in family composition has already documented the likelihood of divorce in the current era. By the mid 1970s,
the divorce rate was 32 per 1000 married women under 45 years of
age and was continuing to rise (Norton and Glick, 1976; 6, Table 1).
The estimates are that of women 27 to 31 years of age in 1971, 25 to
29 percent will experience a divorce and about 5 to 10 percent will be
involved in two divorces (Glick and Norton, 1973: 308), with many of
these divorces affecting children. In 1973, for example, an estimated
one million children were involved in divorces and annulments with
the mean number of children under 18 years of age per divorce being
1.17 (U.S. National Center for Health Statistics, 1975).[4]

---

[3] The percentage differences between men and women due to divorce and widowhood
reflect the younger age at which women marry. Accordingly, they have a longer period
than men to file for divorce or to lose a spouse than do men of the same age. Women
also live longer, so there are more of them surviving to be counted as single at
advanced ages.

[4] "In 1973, the number of children under 18 years of age whose parents divorced was
an estimated 1,079,000," the second year that more than one million children were
involved in divorce. This 1973 estimate nearly doubled the estimate of a decade earlier
(562,000 in 1963). In spite of the pronounced increase in the number of children
affected by divorce, the average number of children continued to decline: 1.17 per
divorce decree in 1973 compared with a maximum of 1.36 in 1964. "In 1973, 40 percent of divorcing couples had no children under 18 years of age; 25 percent had one
child; 19 percent, two children; and 15 percent had three children or more" (U.S.
National Center for Health Statistics, 1975: 1).

The criteria we have used to develop a stage classification for single-parent families consist of women's work-life careers, their marital status, and the school careers of their children. According to this classification, the student trying to do a phase analysis of the divorced woman and her family would use the stage criteria for nuclear families prior to the divorce with the critical transition point of deciding to divorce or to accept divorce as terminating the first period. The loss of the husband-father demands considerable family morphogenesis to develop new patterns of power, communication, and affection. Child-rearing patterns are disrupted and, in the initial period of divorce, parents are less affectionate and more inconsistent in their discipline, although they make fewer maturity demands. Sociability networks are dismembered, and women miss the intimacy and sexual relations of the marital relation (Hetherington, Cox and Cox, 1976).

The difficulty divorced women have to fulfill the physical maintenance tasks suggests that the housewife's obtaining a job marks the second critical role transition point. Most men do not provide support for their children or their wives after divorce. Only 14 percent of wives questioned in a 1975 national poll reported receiving alimony (National Commission on the Observance of International Women's Year 1976: 229), and a majority of judges in a national survey awarded "less than 35 percent" of husbands' incomes to their former wives and families.

Husbands generally fail to provide even these amounts. In the late 1960s, only 38 percent of ex-husbands in Wisconsin, for example, were in full compliance with divorce decrees (Brandwein, Brown, and Fox, 1974: 401). Thus the median income in 1973 for intact families with at least one child under six was $12,000, far higher than the median income of $3600 for single-parent, mother-headed families with one child, and the $9500 median income of the approximately one percent of single-parent households with children under six headed by men (Bronfenbrenner, 1975: 6, 12). As a consequence, the woman's obtaining employment will generally mean an increase in level of living, unless her earnings go largely for child-care expenses.[5]

The mother's employment results in new family physical maintenance

---

[5] The median years of marriage for women with one child who divorce is 5.4, and it is 9.2 for women with two children (U.S. National Center for Health Statistics, 1975: 19, Table N). Assuming that the first child is born within the second year of marriage and the next child within the fourth or fifth year after marriage, the employed mother initially after her divorce is likely still to have preschool children for whom to arrange care in her absence. Institutional day care as opposed to baby-sitting arrangements costs about $2000 a year, Chilman (1975: 56) estimates, or about half the yearly earnings of women in lower socioeconomic groups.

arrangements, since she now has less time and energy for such activi
ties. Relationships with young children especially will have to be re
structured. An emphasis initially on affection giving instead of an
insistence on conforming to socialization demands is necessary to
maintain the morale of children upset by the change in household
routines. If they were fond of their father, their unhappiness at his
absence may increase their sensitivity to the mother's departure from
home for shop or office. But the opportunities offered by the work pace
for performing the provider role, as well as for seeing people and making friends, can provide a boost to the mother's self-esteem that will
enable her to give the children the needed extra nurturance.

Remarriage constitutes another possible guide to family career
change. As the divorce rate goes up, so does the remarriage rate. The
remarriage rate per 1000 widowed and divorced women, 14 to 54 years
of age, was 151 in 1972–1974 as compared with 133 per 1000 in 1960–
1962, with divorced women more apt to remarry than widows at every
age (Norton and Glick, 1976). It is even possible to estimate the amount
of time women who remarry will spend in the state of divorce. The
median number of years that characterize women under 70 as divorcées
is 3.1 years (Glick and Norton, 1971: 310, Table 3). Given the figures
we already have on the likely preschool ages of children of women
who divorce, this time period means that when they remarry their
children will be in primary school or about to enter it.

The new interaction structures that have to be developed to incorporate a husband-father replacement within the family boundaries make
high morphogenesis demands on family members. The wife-mother
reinstitutes lover and companionship roles in the marital relation, roles
that will provide the morale support she needs to deal with possible
stress in the parent-child relations.

The primary school years make high demands on parents to teach
children how to behave in the presence of peers and adults. Children,
however, may view a new man around the house as an intruder and
see his attempts at father roles as usurpations of authority. Even if the
stepfather does not perform the disciplinarian and rule-giver role but
plays only the companion role, children may see him, for a time at
least, as a competitor. This can indeed be the case if the husband is
interested only in his marital career with resultant conflict and heartache
for mother and child alike.

The merger of two, one-parent family units can lead to even greater
disruption in established power, communication and affection-giving
patterns. New "sibling" relations as well as marital and parent-child
associations must be encompassed within the boundaries of the new

family union. During the transition period, competition for attention and feelings of neglect are constant threats to the morale of the family members. After the critical role transition period of remarriage occurs, the family development scholar can utilize the nuclear family stages as guides in analyses of women who have been divorced.

The progress of children through school marks off phases for the analyses of families when women do not remarry. As for the years after the children have left school and home, work-life events for the employed women may signal critical role transition points. For women not in the labor force, changes in social network contacts caused by the loss of aging parents or residential moves may serve this purpose. Because there is virtually no research on the family life of unmarried persons in the middle and later years, whether divorcées, widows, or single persons, these transitions constitute only educated guesses.

Figure 4-5 contains the stages we have defined tentatively for families of divorced women who do not remarry. The mother's remarriage is a critical role transition not delineated in this figure since the applicable nuclear family stages can be reintroduced as guides. Note too that the school-career transition of the children depend upon their placement at the time of the divorce, assumed here to be primary school on the basis of the evidence presented. Stage II would be absent for families in which women were in the labor force before their divorce. School careers substitute as critical transition points for women who are already employed or who do not enter the labor force.

## SUMMARY

This chapter has introduced the concepts that give the family development framework its perspective of change. Because the family career can be divided into stages suited to the interests of an investigator who

**Figure 4-5. Stages for single-parent families of divorced women.**

| | |
|---|---|
| Stage I | Establishment of the Single-Parent Family |
| Stage II | Women Institute or Reinstitute Their Work-Life Career |
| Stage III | Women with Adolescents |
| Stage IV | Women with Young Adults |
| Stage V | Women in the Middle Years |
| Stage VI | The Retirement of Women from Work-Life Career or Responsibilities for Parents. |

is studying family change, we first discussed critical role transition points and family morphogenesis. By emphasizing positional careers and the interlocking of family work life and school life events for individuals, the periods we demarcated can tell us a number of things about the internal interactions of families as affected by members' extrafamilial careers.

Our attempt to develop a classification of families headed by divorced women indicates the dependence of stage classification on the investigator's purposes. Thus the stage classification to be used in this book may not be appropriate for all the types of the nuclear family that one may encounter. Yet it serves to suggest the periods, problems, and behaviors that most nuclear families are liable to experience. The stage guides provide a backdrop as well as a standard for judging family change. Occurrences such as war separations, unemployment periods, and school leavings may introduce new stages to families not demarcated in the present classification. Investigators of these issues will necessarily utilize different stage guides. But the importance of these different transition points for family functioning can be evaluated in terms of the expectable events emphasized in the present classification.

# REFERENCES

Aldous, Joan and Reuben Hill, "Breaking the Poverty Cycle," *Social Work,* 1969, 3–12.

Brandwein, Ruth A., Carol A. Brown, and Elizabeth Maury Fox, "Women and Children Last: The Social Situation of Divorced Mothers and Their Families," *Journal of Marriage and the Family,* 1974, 36, 498–514.

Bronfenbrenner, Uria, "The Challenge of Public Change to Public Policy and Developmental Research," Paper presented at the Meeting of the Society for Research in Child Development, Denver, Colorado, 1975.

Chilman, Catherine B., "Families in Poverty in the Early 1970's: Rates, Associated Factors, Some Implications," *Journal of Marriage and the Family,* 1975, 37, 49–60.

Demos, John, *A Little Commonwealth: Family Life in Plymouth Colony.* New York: Oxford University Press, 1970.

Duvall, Evelyn Millis, and Reuben Hill, cochairmen. "Report of the Committee on the Dynamics of Family Interaction," prepared at the request of the National Conference on Family Life, Washington, D.C., 1948, mimeographed.

Duvall, Evelyn M., *Family Development.* Philadelphia: J. P. Lippincott, 1971.

Elder, Glen H., J. "Age Differentiation and the Life Course," in Alex Inkeles,

James Coleman, and Neil Smelser, eds., *Annual Review of Sociology*, 1975, 1, 165–190.

Feldman, Harold and Margaret Feldman, "The Family Life Cycle; Some Suggestions for Recycling," *Journal of Marriage and the Family*, 1975, 37, 277–284.

Flavell, John, H., *The Developmental Psychology of Jean Piagot*. New York: D. Nostrand, 1963.

Glick, Paul, C., "A Demographer Looks at American Families," *Journal of Marriage and the Family*, 1975, 37, 15–26.

Glick, Paul C. and Arthur J. Norton, "Frequency, Duration and Probability of Marriage and Divorce," *Journal of Marriage and the Family*, 1971, 33, 307–317.

Glick, Paul C., "Updating the Life Cycle of the Family," *Journal of Marriage and the Family*, 1977, 39, 5–13.

Glick, Paul, C. and Arthur J. Norton, "Perspective on the Recent Upturn in Divorce and Remarriage," *Demography*, 1973, 10, 301–314.

Greven, Philip, T., *Four Generations: Population, Land, and Family in Colonial Andover, Massachusetts*. Ithaca, N.Y.: Cornell University Press, 1970.

Hetherington, E. Mavis, Martha Cox, and Roger Cox, "Divorced Fathers," *Family Coordinator*, 1976, 25, 417–428.

Klein, Donald C. and Ann Ross, "Kindergarten Entry: A Study of Role Transition," in Morris Krugman, ed., *Orthopsychiatry and the School*. New York: American Orthopsychiatric Association, 1958, 60–69.

Lansing, J. B. and Leslie Kish, "Family Life Cycle as an Independent Variable," *American Sociological Review*, 1957, 22, 512–519.

Loomis, Charles, P., "The Study of the Life Cycle of Families," *Rural Sociology*, 1936, 1, 180–199.

National Commission on the Observance of International Women's Year, ". . . To Form a More Perfect Union . . . Justice for American Women," Washington, D.C.: U.S. Government Printing Office, 1976.

Norton, Arthur, J., and Paul C. Glick, "Marital Instability, Present and Future," *Journal of Social Issues*, 1976, 32, 5–20.

Rapoport, Rhona, "Transition From Engagement to Marriage," *Acta Sociologica*, 1964, 8, 36–55.

Rapoport, Rhona and Robert Rapoport, "New Light on the Honeymoon," *Human Relations*, 1964, 17, 35–56.

Rodgers, Roy, *Improvements in the Construction and Analysis of Family Life Cycle Categories*. Kalamazoo, Michigan: Western Michigan University, 1962.

Rodgers, Roy, "Toward a Theory of Family Development," *Journal of Marriage and the Family*, 1964, 26, 262–270.

Rollins, Boyd C. and Kenneth L. Cannon, "Marital Satisfaction over the Family Life Cycle: A Reevaluation," *Journal of Marriage and the Family*, 1974, 36, 271–283.

Rowntree, B. S., *Poverty: A Study of Town Life*. London: Macmillan, 1906.

Sorokin, Pitirim A., Carle C. Zimmerman, and C. J. Galpin, *A Systematic*

*Source Book in Rural Sociology, II.* Minneapolis, University of Minnesota Press, 1931.

Spanier, Graham B., Robert A. Lewis and Charles L. Cole, "Marital Adjustment over the Family Cycle: The Issue of Curvilinearity," *Journal of Marriage and the Family*, 1975, 37, 263–275.

U.S. Bureau of the Census, *Current Population Reports Series P–20*, no. 306 "Marital Status and Living Arrangements: March, 1976," U.S. Government Printing Office, Washington, D.C., 1977.

U.S. National Center for Health Statistics, "Vital Statistics Report: Summary Report, Final Divorce Statistics, 1973," U.S. Department of Health, Education, and Welfare, Vol. 24, No. 4, July 7, 1975.

Wells, Robert V., "Demographic Change and the Life Cycle of American Families from the Eighteenth to the Twentieth Centuries," *Journal of Interdisciplinary History*, 1971, 2, 273–282. By permission of the M.I.T. Press, Cambridge, Mass.

# 5

# The developmental task concept

The developmental task concept takes its place along with the concepts of family career, critical role transition, and stage discussed in the previous chapter and with those of positional career and family career defined in the first chapter. All play key parts in the family development framework in analyzing expectable changes in families. In the present chapter we examine the developmental task concept in its varying definitions—as applicable to the family and to the individual—and in the multiple functions in the family development framework. Its relations to other concepts that deal with the phenomena of change in the family are also covered as are research studies that operationalize the concept and test its assumptions.

## THE INDIVIDUAL DEVELOPMENTAL TASK

The concept of the developmental task received its first definitive statement from Robert J. Havighurst, who used it to study individuals. According to him, an *individual developmental task* is a "task which arises at or about a certain period in the life of an individual, successful achievement of which leads to his happiness and to success with later tasks, while failure leads to unhappiness in the individual, disapproval by the society and difficulty with later tasks" (Havighurst, 1953: 2).[1] There are certain features of the definition worth noting. The use of the term, "task" indicates the active part played by an individual, whose intellectual, physical, and cognitive characteristics mediate the external and internal demands that he/she experiences. The task is something the *individual* must accomplish. The outcome is not something that will occur without the individual's active participation. The concept is, accordingly, consistent with the assumption of the family development framework that the individual in the social setting is the basic unit. In addition, the concept of the developmental task embraces individual and group levels of analysis by focusing on an individual's decision to undertake tasks set by societal norms as they are interpreted for and urged on that individual by his or her associates.

An individual takes on a developmental task in roughly the following way. Through associations with others and their expectations, through self-discoveries of changing capacities, and through observations made by others, an individual forms a new sense of self-awareness—a modified self-identity. She or he now perceives different potentialities in the present situation, potentialities previously overlooked or beyond imagining. Such an individual now feels ready to take on a developmental task, to try to learn new ways of coping with the situation. The steps outlined in Figure 5-1 illustrate this process.

The concept of the developmental task and its emphasis on timing relates to another assumption in the family development framework. This is the assumption that humans initiate actions because of their maturational and social development as well as their reactions to environmental pressures. There are, as Neugarten (1968) points out, biological and social clocks that mark off a temporal framework for

---

[1] The terms "happiness" and "unhappiness" in the definition that links "success" in fulfilling a developmental task with "happiness" and "failure" with "unhappiness" present several difficulties. Happiness and unhappiness are ephemeral subjective states that are highly dependent upon situational factors and cultural definitions. One has only to note in this connection that a noisy, crowded, smoky room is usually associated with happiness when defined as the setting of a party. When the same sort of situation is defined as a work setting, the participants often associate it with fatigue and boredom. What is defined as happiness incorporates a personal value judgment. An outsider's judgment of happiness or unhappiness may not be the same as the judgment of the group members themselves if the outsider and the group have different aspirations and values.

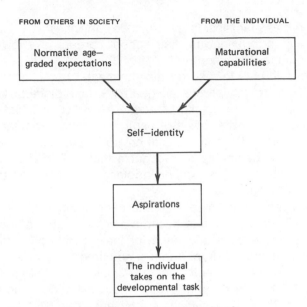

**Figure 5-1    Sources of the individual developmental task.**

behavioral changes. In the early years of life, the internal thrust that leads to developmental task learnings stems in large part from physical maturation, for example, a child learning to walk. Still later, at puberty, bodily changes contribute to changes in self-identity and so to a youth's aspirations within the context of cultural definitions given by his or her social group.

To discover the importance of biological timing, let us turn to data from the Oakland Growth Study, a longitudinal research on a cohort of individuals begun at the time a group of adolescents entered junior high in the early 1930s. Early-maturing boys, with their greater athletic ability than late-maturing boys, developed more self-confidence and a greater sense of being competent. At 16, they appeared to observers to be more "relaxed, matter-of-fact and poised" than the late-maturers. By the time they were 33, their scores on personality tests suggested conformity to such conventional societal values as being sociable, making a good impression, and taking responsibility. In contrast, late-maturing boys, who had experienced more self-doubt and fitted less smoothly into the high prestige extracurricular activities of the high-school world, showed at the age of 33 more sensitivity to others on such tests as well as greater possibilities for originality. Girls who matured early attracted the attention of older boys and were under pressure to begin going out with them. Particularly if the girls were from working-class families, these cross-sex activities and relationships impaired their performance in their school careers and lowered their school aspirations (Clausen, 1973: 160-170).

The internal thrusts to take on developmental tasks, although originally based on growth processes geared to a biological time table, shift their emphasis to a social timetable as individuals enter school. The individuals act on the basis of aspirations and expectancies arising from their interactions in a social environment. And developmental psychologists are beginning to recognize that individuals continue to change in qualitative ways beyond adolescence, perhaps throughout the life course (Chandler, 1975).

Just as biological clocks set the time periods when a child is ready to learn to walk, to read, and to become a sex partner, so social clocks prescribe the proper time sequence for leaving school, getting a job, marrying, and having children. And just as parents are aware of a child being "on schedule" or "off schedule" with the biologically timed events of learning to talk and to control the elimination of body wastes, so men and women know whether they are "early," "late," or "on time" with the social timetables of occupational and family careers (Neugarten, 1968: 143).

The features of the developmental task concept that have to do with an individual's initiating action according to a certain time schedule relate the concept to the work on cognition by the famous developmental psychologist, Jean Piaget. In Piaget's view, children accommodate to new and different aspects of the environment at the time their existing cognitive structures are sufficiently advanced that they can handle the information. As the receiving and processing of information proceed, cognitive structures become modified so they can assimilate different kinds of environmental information, which in turn lead to further modifications and accommodations (Flavell, 1963: 50). In any situation, individuals utilize their existing perceptual observations, which are in equilibrium when some sort of balance or stability exists between internal and external events. At such times, individuals interpret events in terms of their existing sets of values or behaviors. When individuals cannot overlook the lack of fit between their perceptions of events and their expectations of outcomes, disequilibrium occurs and forces modifications of the existing cognitive structures (Hunt, 1969). Whether or not individuals modify their cognitive organization of meanings and ideas that give structure to their interpretation and understanding of events, they are forced to be active agents in confronting their social and physical environments.

The feature of time enters Piaget's approach when he posits critical periods in the maturation of an individual. These are times when particular environmental encounters are maximally productive in an individual's acquiring advanced thought and behavior structures. If a child is fortunate with respect to reading, for example, he or she will experience the convergence of the following factors on the same time schedule: demands by the social group that reading begin; maturing cognitive capacities that permit reading; and strong desires to become a successful reader.

**The Influence of Associates**

Although the developmental task points up the individual in the situation, the concept also indicates the influence of others in task accomplishment. Social time clocks are set by others and the socialization pressures of parents to keep their children on schedule reflect the interdependence of family members.

A child's sense of accomplishment in fulfilling a task successfully and sense of failure in not doing so are specifically included in the developmental task concept. The urging of significant others that a child take on the task and their responses to signs of progress, although only suggested in the definition, can be critical. By encouraging a child who decides to learn, or by scolding and punishing a child who refuses, they exert a strong influence on the feelings and behavior of children.

Figure 5-2 provides lists of developmental tasks for individuals of different ages in 10 behavioral categories. Since the perspective is not that of the individual in family roles, the dovetailing of the tasks of family members is not apparent. What is clear, however, is that these tasks do not exist in isolation. As an example, take the task of an older adolescent in the area of developing a conscience. According to Figure 5-2, an adolescent must learn that practices and principles do not always conform and how to deal with this knowledge in a responsible manner. In complementary fashion, Figure 5-2 shows that mature individuals face the task of maintaining their integrity in the light of violations of principles of honesty and fair dealing while seeing that their children conform to these same moral codes.

The tasks in both cases call for a coming to terms with reality. Parents have the thankless task of convincing their adolescents that moral principles are worth working for in politics, work life, and the family although all will fail to meet the standards at some time. The idealism of the young will be tempered by the experience of the mature, while the incipient cynicism of the mature will be counteracted by the high

**Figure 5-2.** Developmental tasks in ten categories of behavior of the individual from birth to death.

| Task Category | Infancy (birth to 1 or 2) | Early Childhood (2–3 to 5–6–7) | Late Childhood (5–6–7 to pubescence) | Early Adolescence (pubescence to puberty) | Late Adolescence (puberty to early maturity) | Maturity (early-late active adulthood) | Aging (beyond powers of adulthood through senility) |
|---|---|---|---|---|---|---|---|
| I Achieving an appropriate dependence-independence pattern. | 1. Establishing oneself as a very dependent being. 2. Beginning the establishment of self-awareness. | Adjusting to less private attention; becoming independent physically while remaining strongly dependent emotionally. | Freeing oneself from primary identification with adults. | Establishing one's independence from adults in all areas of behavior. | Establishing oneself as an independent individual in an adult manner. | 1. Learning to be interdependent—now leaning on, now succoring others, as need arises. 2. Assisting one's children to become gradually independent and autonomous beings. | Accepting gracefully and comfortably the help needed from others as powers fail and dependence becomes necessary. |
| II Achieving an appropriate giving-receiving pattern of affection. | Developing a feeling for affection. | 1. Developing the ability to give affection. 2. Learning to share affection. | Learning to give as much love as one receives: forming friendships with peers. | Accepting oneself as a worthwhile person worthy of love. | Building a strong mutual affection bond with a possible marriage partner. | 1. Building a strong, maintaining a strong and mutually satisfying partner relationship. 2. Establishing affectional bonds with one's children and grandchildren. 3. Meeting wisely the new need for affection of one's own aging parents. 4. Cultivating meaningful warm friendships with members of one's own generation. | Facing loss of one's spouse and finding some satisfactory sources of affection previously received from the mate. Learning new affectional roles with own children, now mature adults. Establishing ongoing, satisfying affectional patterns with grandchildren and other members of the extended family. |

| | | | | | | | |
|---|---|---|---|---|---|---|---|
| III Relating to changing social groups. | 1. Becoming aware of the alive as against the inanimate, and the familiar as against the unfamiliar. 2. Developing rudimentary social interaction. | 1. Beginning to develop the ability to interact with age-mates. 2. Adjusting in the family to expectations it has for the child as a member of the family group. | 1. Clarifying the adult world as over against the child's world. 2. Establishing peer groups and learning to belong. | Behaving according to a shifting peer code. | Adopting an adult-patterned set of stable social values. | 1. Keeping a reasonable balance activities in the various social, service, political, and community groups and causes that make demands upon adults. 2. Establishing and maintaining mutually satisfactory relationships with the in-law families of spouse and married children. | Choosing and maintaining ongoing social activities and functions appropriate to health, energy, and interests. |
| IV Developing a conscience. | Beginning to adjust to the expectations of others. | 1. Developing the ability to take directions and to be obedient in the presence of authority. 2. Developing the ability to be obedient in the absence of authority where conscience substitutes for authority. | Learning more rules and developing true morality. | | Learning to verbalize contradictions in moral codes, as well as discrepancies between principle and practice, and resolving these problems in a responsible manner. | 1. Coming to terms with the violations of moral codes in the larger as well as in the more intimate social scene, and developing some constructive philosophy and method of operation. 2. Helping children to adjust to the expectations of others and to conform to the moral demands of the culture. | Maintaining a sense of moral integrity in the face of disillusionments in life's hopes and dreams. |

**Figure 5-2. Developmental tasks in ten categories of behavior of the individual from birth to death.**

| | | | | | | |
|---|---|---|---|---|---|---|
| V Learning one's psychosocio-biological sex role. | Learning to identify with male adult and female adult role models. | Beginning to identify with one's social contemporaries of the same sex. | 1. Strong identification with one's own sex mates. 2. Learning one's role in heterosexual relationships. | 1. Exploring possibilities for a future mate and acquiring partner "desirability." 2. Choosing an occupation. 3. Preparing to accept one's future role in manhood or womanhood as a responsible citizen of the larger community. | 1. Learning to be a competent husband or wife and building a satisfactory marriage. 2. Carrying a socially adequate role as citizen and worker in the community. 3. Becoming a good parent and grandparent if children arrive. | 1. Learning to live on a retirement income. 2. Being a good companion to an aging spouse. 3. Meeting bereavement of spouse adequately. |
| VI Accepting and adjusting to a changing body. | 1. Adjusting to adult feeding demands. 2. Adjusting to adult cleanliness demands. 3. Adjusting to adult attitudes toward genital manipulation. | 1. Adjusting to expectations resulting from one's improving muscular abilities. 2. Developing sex modesty. | 1. Reorganizing one's thoughts and feelings about oneself in the face of significant bodily changes and their concomitants. 2. Accepting the reality of one's appearance. | Learning appropriate outlets for sexual drives. | 1. Making a good sex adjustment within marriage. 2. Establishing healthful routines of eating, resting, working, playing within the pressures of the adult world. | Making a good adjustment to failing powers as aging diminishes strength and abilities. |
| VII Managing a changing body and learning new motor patterns. | 1. Developing physiological equilibrium. 2. Developing eye-hand coordination. 3. Establishing satisfactory rhythms of rest and activity. | 1. Developing large muscle control. 2. Learning to coordinate large muscles and small muscles. | Refining and elaborating skill in the use of small muscles. | Controlling and using a "new" body. | Learning the new motor skills involved in housekeeping, gardening, sports, and other activities expected of adults in the community. | Adapting interests and activities to reserves of vitality and energy of the aging body. |

| | | | | | | |
|---|---|---|---|---|---|---|
| VIII Learning to understand and control the physical world. | Exploring the physical world. | Meeting adult expectations for restrictive exploration and manipulation of an expanding environment. | Learning more realistic ways of studying and controlling the physical world. | | Gaining intelligent understanding of new horizons of medicine and science sufficient for personal well-being and social competence. | Mastering new awareness and methods of dealing with physical surroundings as an individual with occasional or permanent disabilities. |
| IX Developing an appropriate symbol system and conceptual abilities. | 1. Developing preverbal communication. 2. Developing verbal communication. 3. Rudimentary concept formation. | 1. Improving one's use of the symbol system. 2. Enormous increase in conceptual patterns. | 1. Learning to use language actually to exchange ideas or to influence one's hearers. 2. Beginning understanding of real causal relations. 3. Making finer conceptual distinctions and thinking reflectively. | 1. Using language to express and to clarify more complex concepts. Achieving the level of reasoning of which one is capable. | Mastering technical symbol systems involved in income tax, social security, complex financial dealings, and other contexts familiar to Western man. | Keeping mentally alert and effective as long as is possible through the later years. |
| X Relating oneself to the cosmos. | Developing a genuine, though uncritical, notion about one's place in the cosmos. | Developing a scientific approach. | | Formulating a workable belief and value system. | 1. Formulating and implementing a rational philosophy of life on the basis of adult experience. 2. Cultivating a satisfactory religious climate in the home as the spiritual soil for development of family members. | Preparing for eventual and inevitable cessation of life by building a set of beliefs that one can live and die with in peace. |

Source: An elaboration of Caroline Tryon and Jesse W. Lilienthal III, "Guideposts in Child Growth and Development." *NEA Journal*, 1950, 39, 189.

hopes of the young. In both instances, pressures from one side and the other force moral standards and lead to their maintenance in an imperfect world.

# THE FAMILY DEVELOPMENTAL TASK

### A Definition
In this chapter we have been talking thus far about the individual and the developmental task concept; let us now turn to the family and the developmental task concept. This concept joins the responsibilities that all societies place upon families to the demands members make of families in order to accomplish their individual developmental tasks. A family developmental task can be conceptualized as any one of the family functions reputedly necessary for its continuance at a particular stage. These functions listed and discussed in Chapter 2 are:

1.  Physical maintenance of family members.
2.  Socialization of family members for roles in the family and other groups.
3.  Maintenance of family members' motivation to perform family and other roles.
4.  Maintenance of social control within the family and between family members and outsiders.
5.  Addition of family members through adoption or reproduction and their release when mature.

The family developmental concept gives content to the various stages of the family's life-span, whereas the individual developmental task relates to the life course of the individual. Within the time covered by a given family stage, family members may take on a variety of individual developmental tasks. In contrast, these tasks remain nominally the same from one stage to another (with the exception of the addition and release of family members) although their content differs as the demands of family members and of community representatives change.

One can view family developmental tasks somewhat as follows. To continue as a unit, the family as a group must meet minimal task performance standards satisfactory to its members and to the broader society. As individual members acquire new aspirations through experiences with work associates, schoolmates, and other family members, and as each faces new expectations from these associates, he or she makes different demands on other family members. These demands constitute internal pressures on the family to change. The family also receives pressures from the broader society to conform to certain minimal standards of civic responsibility. These pressures from the broader community vary according to the family's age composition. The school entry of the oldest child, for example, introduces a new family stage, in part because school personnel now share the socialization function with parents and siblings. They expect the child to have acquired in his family training the control of physical functions and the willingness to pay attention to adults that classroom learning presupposes. If children in their school careers do not do well in class or make it hard for others to learn through disruptive activities, school personnel will eventually contact parents to obtain their cooperation in improving the child's school performance.

As the discussion on boundary maintenance in Chapter 2 showed, the family acquires an identity and community reputation for meeting standards of task performance, in their socialization efforts and in their assistance with the efforts of the school. This identity affects the way families conform to community expectations and the way expectations themselves are shaped for a given family. Thus some young children lose out in school, because teachers have found that parents were not concerned with school achievements of older siblings. This kind of family reputation can lead busy teachers to expend their greatest efforts on children of families reported to be more interested in education. Figure 5-3 shows how family developmental tasks at a particular

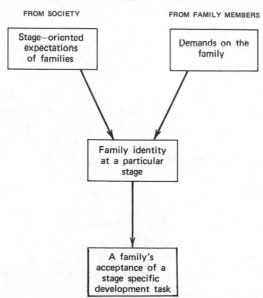

**Figure 5-3    Sources of the family developmental task.**

time arise from the conjunction of pressures from members and from
external groups. Family members will attempt to accomplish these tasks
in ways consistent with the family's values and reputation in the
community.

## Limited Linkages

There is nothing in the definition of family development task that relates
its degree of accomplishment specifically to task performance in later
stages of a family's lifetime. The discussion of the concept of stage in
the previous chapter did indicate, however, that family role performance
at one stage can narrow the family's behavioral options at the next.
And one of the assumptions of the family development framework listed
in Chapter 1 is that families must perform certain time-specific tasks
set by their members or the broader society. Magrabi and Marshall
(1965: 456), in a thought-provoking analysis of the developmental task
concept, deal specifically with this phenomenon of *limited linkage*, as
we prefer to label it. The style of life according to which families eat,
take shelter, clothe themselves, socialize their members, maintain one
another's motivation, and preserve some sort of social order at any one
stage sets limits on their alternatives in these same areas at the next
stage. For example, families with one-way, wheel-type communication
patterns and vertical power structures at the primary-school stage can
have difficulty at the next stage establishing person-oriented, two-way
communication patterns and achieving more egalitarian power structures, despite the pressures for change from adolescent members and
the expectations of outsiders that adolescents should have more part
in family decision making.

Magrabi and Marshall argue that within any family stage, there will
be variation in the mastery of family tasks as judged by family members and outsiders. As a family moves from one stage to another,
it encounters pressures for change in the content of the family developmental task performance. The level the family attains in task performance depends in part on the demands of the new stage, in part
on the continuing effects of past performance.

Let us look at the argument as expressed in Magrabi and Marshall's
(1965: 456) chart shown in Figure 5-4. This type of chart is sometimes
called a "directed graph" or "game-tree model," because there is a
branching of lines from an initial starting point or "root." This starting
point in Figure 5-4 is *1*. It is doubtful, however, that anyone but a dedi-
cated scholar of the family would see Figure 5-4 as looking much like
a tree. The numbers in the graph—*1,2,3*—indicate a family's position

**Figure 5-4** **Linkage of accomplishments of family developmental tasks from one stage to the next.** *Source:* **modification of a chart in Magrabi and Marshall, 1965: 456.**

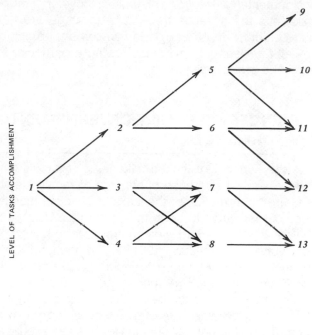

at a particular stage according to their overall performance on the family developmental tasks. In Figure 5-4, the family proceeds from position *1*, which represents the family's overall task accomplishment level at stage *A*, to one of the succeeding three alternatives available at stage *B*. These alternatives are *2, 3,* or *4*. The family's performance on the family developmental tasks at stage *A* limited it, therefore, to three options. Similarly, the family's performance on the changing content of its tasks as a group at stage *B* limits the alternatives at stage *C.* From position *2*, family members have two options of task performance, *5* or *6*, but families at position *3* or *4* have no alternatives. An earlier position, therefore, can prevent a family's arriving in some later position. For example, positions *9* and *10* can only be reached from position *5* at stage *C.* Note also that the level of task performance at *4* (stage *B*) predetermines the outcome at stage *D* (Magrabi and Marshall, 1965: 456).

According to the chart, therefore, stage positions on family developmental task performance are linked selectively. The performance of family developmental tasks at one stage sets limits on their performance in the next. Thus the linkages from stage to stage are not complete. A particular combination of task performances at one stage cannot be attained by all families, but only those having a particular level of task performance at a previous stage.

## CONSEQUENCES OF FAMILY DEVELOPMENTAL TASK PERFORMANCE

To illustrate the concept of limited linkage, let us review a study that shows how the task performance of addition of family members affects a family's future performance of the tasks of physical maintenance and maintenance of motivation to perform family roles. Using a representative sample of white, married women from Detroit, who had a first, second, or fourth birth in July, 1961, Freedman and Combs (1966) related the timing of childbearing to income and economic asset accumulation. They found that the longer the interval between marriage and the first or the last birth, the better the couple's economic position. This relation held even when adjustment was made for such alternate explanations of the findings as duration of marriage, education of the husband, and religious affiliation of the wife. Families in which the wife was premaritally pregnant were particularly disadvantaged economically.

Maintenance of motivation to perform family roles appeared also to be affected by the timing of first pregnancies. At each birth parity, women who took longest to have a child reported "fewer pregnancies are coming 'too soon' compared with those with the shortest birth intervals" (Freedman and Coombs, 1966; 639). Such feelings presumably have an adverse influence on a woman's willingness to perform the various duties of infant caretaker. Thus the way a couple times its births sets limits on future physical maintenance abilities as well as on motivational factors. This research, therefore, supplies supporting evidence for Magrabi and Marshall's hypothesis that past success or failure in family developmental task performance constrains future performance.

### The Relation of Individual and Family Developmental Tasks
By viewing the family development tasks in terms of functional requirements specified according to the stage of the family cycle, the family

development task can be related to the individual developmental task concept. We have already suggested that the family can be viewed as a set of the intercontingent (interdependent) careers of its members (Farber, 1961). These careers are composed of the changing role clusters of the incumbents of the various family positions. The individual's behaviors that constitute his role performance initially were individual developmental tasks. The individual has to be able to accomplish many of these tasks in order to fulfill his family roles. Family developmental tasks help make possible individual task accomplishment, which in turn enables the family to fulfill its tasks.

To see the relation between family developmental task accomplishment and individual developmental task performance, we can look at research done by H. W. Smith (1973). Smith's data are relevant to the family developmental task of socialization as it changes over time to encourage and allow for the increasing abilities of children to take on individual developmental tasks. Let us look particularly at those in Figure 5-2 having to do with group relations, conscience development, and symbol use. The data come from observations of groups of five persons having the same gender and the same median age. The all-white groups were chosen randomly from persons enrolled in Catholic schools and a Catholic college and came from working-class and lower-middle-class backgrounds. The median ages in the various groups were 5, 6, 8, 10, 13, 16, and 20 with four groups at each median age, equally divided as to sex composition. Each group had to come to an agreement on what the members saw in a Rorschach "inkblot" card and create a group story. There was one card for each of the first three sessions and two for the fourth session.

The relevant findings have to do with differences in interaction behaviors in the different age groups. There were no significant gender differences in the development of group interaction skills. The first finding, one of no particular surprise to persons who know children, is that children of six and younger did not make good group members. Group interaction patterns were slow in developing because these children's behaviors were less predictable than older children's from one session to another. Their difficulty in interacting with peers was also shown by their failure to acknowledge others, to indicate an understanding of other's behavior, or to give suggestions (Smith, 1973: 545–547).

What do these findings suggest for families trying to socialize children of these early school ages? If we can generalize from peer groups to groups with mixed age compositions, it appears that for primary-school youngsters, parent-child or sibling instruction should be more effective than rule teaching when the family is all together.

The children's instability of behavior and possible failure to recognize gradations of authority among parents and older sibs demand patient repetition of rules by socializing agents as well as clear demarcation of authority among them. Family socialization attempts will then dovetail with the children's developmental tasks of learning to recognize authority as well as to meet behavioral expectations as members of the family group.

As the children accomplish these group interactional tasks, the family's socialization task becomes easier. Even older children, however, do not make good peer group members. Children between the ages of 5 and 10 devoted more time to social and emotional behaviors than to accomplishing the work of their groups. As might be expected from the large emotional content of their group behaviors, primary-school children asked less often for the opinions of other group members. The older the children, however, the better able were they to indicate their appreciation of contributions by other group members (Smith, 1973: 547). As a consequence, they may react more graciously to socialization pressures from parents and siblings to conform to family routines. These pressures, in turn, can encourage the child to take on the individual developmental task of using language symbols instead of emotion to influence others and thereby increase her or his ability to get along with peers.

When children reach adolescence, they must learn to evaluate changing peer codes and to express ideas and reactions verbally. As Figure 5-2 shows, their abilities to function in groups, both with peers and family members, also increase. Past family socialization efforts that encourage individual development pay off as youths begin to function effectively in groups. Concentration on task performance as a group becomes common among 13-year-olds along with the ability of youths to assume the role of the other, even when a parent is trying to encourage or discourage some particular behavior. The ability to work productively in a group is also shown by attempts to answer peer questions in detail and by decreases in negative reactions and negative statements (Smith, 1973: 551). By adolescence, youths thus acquire interaction skills that permit them to accomplish peer-centered developmental tasks. Family conflicts may well increase, however, as adolescents are exposed to increased behavioral alternatives in their widening explorations of the world beyond the family. But the Smith study suggests that individual development at the same time reaches a point where family socialization efforts based on reasoning can elicit "reasonable" responses from youths. The Smith research also suggests that parents of children of different ages must use a mix of socialization techniques in their role sequences of rule giver and disciplinarian, a mix that encourages each child's individual task accomplishment, and with it the family's as well.

## DEVELOPMENTAL TASK RESEARCH ISSUES

So much for the definitions of developmental task concepts, but how do we determine *what* constitutes a developmental task and *what* underlying assumptions give it validity? The present section examines research on the conceptualization of the tasks with these two questions in mind. Let us begin our analysis with the individual developmental task.

Havighurst (1956: 216) describes three procedures for discovering and defining individual developmental tasks. One is based on observing homogenous age groups and deciding for each age group what they are working at. Another consists of asking people what their concerns and interests are, on the assumption that they are aware of developmental needs and can discuss them. The final procedure is for the social scientist to be introspective about his own personal career and to define the developmental tasks he sees himself taking on.

The lists of tasks obtained by such procedures have in common those tasks set by biological time schedules. In making the lists, individuals who belonged to the same social groups are also subject to the same social time schedules sanctioned by the group, although such schedules may differ for individuals belonging to other groups. A third component of such lists are those tasks the individual himself chooses without external urging.

An example of a task set by societal pressure is that of choosing an occupation. Most social groups expect the married man with children to have a job that will enable him to establish and maintain some sort of economic standard of living. If he fails to accept an available job and his wife is not employed, he will experience social disapproval and the possible suffering of his loved ones. Whether an individual decides to take on such civic responsibilities as participating in party caucuses where nominees are endorsed or to trudge door to door and distribute political literature is more a matter of personal choice affected by one's friends, job orientation, and historical climate than either task is of societal pressures. Failure to accomplish the task of "good citizen"—however one defines it in a broad range of behavior—brings little negative reaction; and there are usually few positive rewards aside from the inner satisfaction of having helped to make democracy work. In like fashion, there are also few external pressures to encourage the middle-aged adult to expand his leisure time interests in preparation for the long days of retirement.

At the present time, there is a lack of research evidence on what constitute age-graded tasks in different class and ethnic groups. For that reason, we are limited to lists such as Figure 5-2 contains, lists of maturationally based tasks and of educated judgments of researchers on other types of tasks.

We do have some research on the assumptions of developmental task concepts. One of these assumptions is that good achievement on a developmental task at one period is followed by good achievement on similar tasks at subsequent periods. Havighurst, who did much to sketch out the concept, was able to subject this assumption to empirical test in a study of 10-year-old children born in 1933 in a small midwestern town of some 7000 inhabitants. In addition, he tested the following hypotheses derived from the developmental task definition.

1.  Good achievement on a developmental task tends to be associated with good achievement on other tasks at the same age.
2.  In a minority of cases, good achievement on one developmental task may be used to compensate for poor achievement on other tasks.

A group of 30 girls and boys, all white and equally divided as to gender, were studied for a period of seven years. The study method was to define developmental tasks in terms of the behavior of boys and girls and then to rate each child on his accomplishment of the tasks at ages 10, 13, and 16. Only with such a longitudinal research design is it possible to observe "progress or regress" in the process over time (Rubin and Levenger, 1974: 336). The five tasks were the following: (1) learning an appropriate sex role; (2) developing conscience, morality, and a set of values; (3) getting along with age mates; (4) developing emotional independence; and (5) developing intellectual skills (Havighurst, 1953: 289–290).

The findings provided some support for the assumption underlying the task concept of one of the hypotheses listed above (Havighurst, 1953: 320–322). The assumption concerning the "carry-over" of degree of achievement of a task at one period to the same or similar tasks at subsequent periods was supported.[2] As one might expect, however,

---

[2] The close parallels of the hypothesis to the Magrabi and Marshall formulation for families shown in Figure 5-4 is noteworthy.

there was more of a break between the ages of 10 and 13, which covers the period of puberty changes, than between the ages of 13 and 16.[3] The first hypothesis tested predicted that at any one time good or poor achievement on one development task would be associated with good or poor achievement on other tasks.[4] The task of getting along with peers was most closely related to other tasks, particularly to the intellectual skills task and to the development of conscience task. Development of conscience also was related fairly closely to other tasks. The emotional independence task showed the lowest relationship to the other tasks. Although the correlational data cannot tell us the causal relationships, we can speculate that positive peer relations may derive from the sensitivity to others indicated in conscience development. Peer relations, in turn, can influence the degree to which the individual sees himself as a competent person able to handle classroom tasks.

The prediction that good achievement on one task for some individuals may compensate for poor achievement on another received scant support. The intercorrelations of tasks were high enough, as reported in the results on the test of the previous hypothesis, to suggest that the number of compensators "in this group must be quite small" (Havighurst, 1953: 322). Instead, the level of task achievement in one area tended to be associated with the same level of task accomplishment in other areas.

The Havighurst research also assessed the importance of task accomplishment at a particular point in time, one of the components of the definition of the individual development task concept. It appeared that preadolescent learnings where there was some carry-over of tasks from one age to another did affect later adolescent task performance. The exception was the sex identity task where changes in the normative expectations of others associated with the onset of puberty created role discontinuities. Havighurst (1952: 31), however, has pointed out that there is a difference between tasks in which there are particular moments when the individual is ready to learn, as with maturational tasks, such as learning to walk and talk, and tasks that recur over a long period, such as the task of getting along with one's peers.

[3] The average correlation of each of the five tasks from age 10 to 13 was .78; from age 13 to 16, it was .92; and from age 10 to 16, .70. Learning an appropriate sex role was an exception. The average correlation of performance at age 10 and age 13 was .61; at age 13 and age 16, .84; and age 10 and age 16, .42.

[4] Product-moment correlation coefficients for each pair of developmental tasks at each age level showed a consistently high relationships (correlations of .60 or higher) for five pairs of tasks, and a consistent but lower relationship (correlations of .37 to .51) for three pairs. Two pairs varied in the degree of relationship from age to age.

Havighurst believes that these latter tasks, which involve role sequences, are better learned when they first become salient to the individual. He suggests, however, that delay in learning to get along with one's age-mates, for example, although it may lead to an unhappy adolescence need not have serious permanent consequences. The more mobile adult has greater opportunity to search out persons with similar interests, particularly since the age range of adult friendship possibilities is less restricted than those of the young.

Havighurst's analysis also suggests that the changing content of the tasks in a role sequence lacking a maturational foundation prevents their accomplishment once and for all. Getting along with one's peers, to continue with the previous example, is a task whose learning demands recur over the entire life cycle, just as does engaging in an occupation once the individual achieves economic independence. The group of which the individual is a member—whether family, social clique, or work detail—determines the sequence of tasks that must be taken on as well as the stage when the learning becomes critical for social approval and self-esteem.

A questionnaire study of age-appropriate behavior in a group suggests that timing emphasis varies according to a member's age. Middle-aged (33–55) and elderly (65+) persons in the middle class sample were more apt to "place constraints upon adult behavior in terms of age appropriateness" than were young adults. The young adults, aged 20 to 29, especially young men, were less apt to see harmful consequences from being "off-schedule" in accomplishing such life events as having children or moving to be near one's married children. Thus these young adults, who still may be facing the tasks associated with these events, are less demanding than the middle-aged and elderly that individuals accomplish a developmental task within a limited time period (Neugarten, 1968).

The limited research available, therefore, suggests that for group-prescribed developmental tasks there is a varying period for learning as well as fixed sequence in which tasks should be learned. The consequences of not meeting these timing schedules would seem to depend upon the age and social class of the individual's associates.

## Operationalizing the Family Developmental Task Concept

To see what correspondence, if any, exists between definitions of the family developmental task and phenomena in the empirical world, Ferguson undertook his doctoral research (1971). He used Rollins's marital role inventory with a sample of 195 middle-class Mormon couples in all stages of the family life cycle. The behaviors covered in the inventory were designed to fall into six functional areas. Five of them bear similarities to the list of tasks we have hypothesized as having to be fulfilled by families at each stage of the family life cycle. Let us examine each of the tasks in terms of one of the several role behaviors he used to gauge their fulfillment.

1.  **Physical Maintenance.** Role behavior—*care for all family members when ill.*

    Nursing behaviors constitute an important segment of familiar role clusters when children are young and liable to sudden incapacitating illnesses and again at the end of the family life cycle when the spouses are approaching death. But being solicitous of the family member who is not well, deciding if a doctor's advice is necessary, and seeing that the individual follows a regimen for recovery are activities family members must perform throughout the life cycle.

2.  **Addition of family members through adoption or reproduction and their release when mature.** Role behavior—*use birth-control techniques when children are not desired.*

    This role behavior, which is critical to family planning in the childbearing years, can be the task of either spouse. The increasing number of vasectomies indicates that husbands too can take responsibility for implementing a decision to have no more children. Of the 6.8 million couples choosing sterilization as their birth control method in 1975, about 3 million husbands and 3.8 million wives were sterilized. Although 24 percent of couples planning to have no more children placed the responsibility upon the wife using the pill, 43 percent of these couples chose sterilization, up from 31.9 percent in a comparable 1973 national representative sample. The oral contraceptive, however, continues to be the most widely chosen contraceptive method among couples of childbearing age who have not yet decided to close out their families (Westoff and Jones, 1977). For women who experience "side-effects" from oral contraceptives and fear other female techniques will not be effective, their husbands' use of contraceptives not only accomplishes the family planning task but also contributes to marital morale maintenance.

3.  **Maintenace of the motivation of family members to perform family and other roles.** Role behavior—*determine friends and relatives to visit and with whom to maintain close relations.*

    The need for emotional support from outsiders to supplement the warmth and affection of family members is particularly apparent at periods when one stage is ending and another beginning. The critical role transition points of getting married, having children, and seeing them leave home to start their own families are all occasions when the support of others is needed. The form this support takes can vary. At the getting married stage, the assurances of outsiders to the young couple and their parents that things are going as can be expected can be comforting. More concrete forms of assistance coupled with praise at task accomplishments can mean much to new parents. At the stage when the home is empty of young people, encouragement from friends and kin can ease the lonely feelings some parents experience.

4.  **Socialization of family members for roles in the family and other groups.** Role behavior—*try to get improvement in family members by giving them reminders of personal responsibilities.*

    The behaviors that family members encourage in one another change along with the family's age composition. The socialization responsibilities are heaviest for parents during the early child-rearing periods. Once the children go off to school, however, even parents who attempt to maintain a high level of control find themselves exposed to new ideas and different ways. By the time children have reached adolescence, socialization becomes even more clearly a mutual task of all family members.

5.  **Maintenance of social control within the family and between family members and outsiders.** Role behavior—*do most of the talking when you and your spouse discuss marital problems.*

    Conflict is endemic in the close quarters of the family. In part, it results from the changing demands of members taking on new developmental tasks, whether independently or at the behest of others. Even when the age expectations of others are instrumental in initiating new task learning, these others may still be unprepared to accommodate readily to every learner's increasing competence. Parents of adolescents must be particularly skilled at resolving conflict or able to live with it and the many issues generated by the demands of youths for independence.[5]

In his research, Ferguson asked subjects how they would feel if their spouses performed these and other behaviors in the marital roles inventory for varying percentages of the time. He also asked them to state their perceptions of the actual performances of these roles by their

---

[5] Ferguson's sixth area, production and distribution of goods and services, is encompassed in our physical maintenance category.

spouses. When their responses were factor analyzed to see what items grouped together, those items in the areas of socialization of children and maintenance of morale did indeed form separate factors. The physical maintenance area also formed one factor but included items from other areas.[6] There was also a factor Ferguson terms "emotional nurturance" on the basis of the associated role behaviors that seem to be related to what we term maintenance of motivation in family members, just as the function we call maintenance of social control incorporates the factors he labels "external integration" and "coercive control."

Ferguson found temporal variations in the performance of the role behaviors grouped together in the factor analysis. We expect to find such variations in task performances, since the definition of family developmental task specifies task content as varying according to family stage, even though the tasks themselves remain the same from one period to another. Ferguson found, for example, a good deal of change over the family stages in how the family accomplished physical care of the home and family. The participation of wives in this task was lowest in the initial marriage stage when there were no children. Their participation was at its highest point when the oldest child was younger than 30 months or was in primary school. Husbands were least active in household care when children were leaving home. They were most active in carrying out the physical maintenance task after retirement. This same pattern for husbands was also true of their emotional nurturance behavior. They performed these morale maintenance activities least often when children were leaving home and were most nurturant after retirement.

## USES OF THE DEVELOPMENTAL TASK CONCEPTS

### The Bridging Function

The developmental task concept in the family development conceptual framework serves two uses—one of bridging different levels of analysis and another of explaining change. As a bridging concept, it spans the

---

[6] The results from this study suggest that there may be more family developmental tasks than rational considerations would suggest (Ferguson, 1971: 75). The items from the Rollins's role inventory appeared to group themselves into ten factors, although some factors could be subsumed under our postulated family development tasks.

individual and the societal levels of analysis. Figure 5-1 and Figure 5-3 display this bridging function in graphic form. In the case of the individual developmental task, the unit of analysis is the person, while in the case of the family developmental task, the unit of analysis is the family. For both the individual and the family, the developmental task points up the interaction of extraindividual and extrafamilial requirements and expectations with intraindividual and intrafamilial demands and requirements in instigating behavior. In the individual, these needs and demands initially have a biological foundation. As the individual grows, behavior in a given situation becomes both a response to the requirements of significant others to perform particular roles and a response to the individual's own needs and aspirations to interact with others and to accept social norms. In the use of the family developmental task, the concept links the requirements that governmental, educational, and other groups set for the family as a group, and the demands that each family member makes on the rest of the family.

**The Change Function**
The second function served by the developmental task concept is to explain why there are changes in the family over its life-span. We have already noted that the arrival and departure of children, the demands of school and occupation, and the variable compositions of the family and the ages of its members lead to family change. The developmental task concept allows us to be more specific about changes in individual behaviors that lead to family morphogenesis. It also suggests that families within a stage continue to experience pressures to change. The concept does this through its bifocal view of two sources of change in the behavior of an individual: (1) changes of role expectations that coincide with the aging process of the individual; (2) changes of the individual's aspirations and demands. The family development task concept adds to these two sources the changing societal demands on the family as a unit and the changing set of demands placed on individual family members. All these factors can bring about changes in the behaviors that individuals and families display.

# SUMMARY

What does a candid assessment of the developmental task concepts reveal? On the criterion of scope, the concepts score high. The individual developmental task refers to a large number of learned behaviors that can be found over the life course of an individual. The family developmental task concept also points to recurring tasks during family lifetimes.

Some empirical evidence supports several propositions associated with both the individual and the family developmental task concepts. Consistent with the proposition that the levels of task accomplishment by an individual are related at different times is the finding that the performance level of certain tasks at preadolescence seem to be related positively to the individual's task performances at adolescence. Also, performance on one task by a preadolescent or adolescent seems to be related positively to the performance of other tasks by the same individual at the same stage. Aside from certain maturationally based tasks, however, the optimal timing of task learning appears to be determined by the age-related role expectations of the learner's associates. Culture also seems to have much to do with what tasks the individual attempts to accomplish, although adequate research evidence is lacking on this point.

The existence of several of the postulated developmental tasks appeared in the findings of the Ferguson study (1971). The way these tasks are performed also varies over the family stages as may be expected, given changing demands on the family from society and from family members. There is also research evidence that family developmental task performance at one stage affects the adequacy of task performance at subsequent stages.

The concepts of individual and family developmental tasks also possess systemic qualities. The individual developmental task links age-role expectations and the concepts of timing as differentiated on social and biological clocks, to use Neugarten's (1968) felicitous terms. This concept also implies that individuals may go beyond societal and biological demands to define tasks for which they set the achievement standards. This idea, in turn, ties into *role making*, since role behaviors are composed of task performances. Taking on tasks in anticipation of role changes, suggests *role transitions* that herald stage changes and resulting *family morphogenesis*. The family developmental task, too, has systemic qualities. It has given rise to the concept of limited linkages across stages of task performance (Magrabi and Marshall, 1965) and to that of the influence of individual members and of the community on family change.

The developmental task concept, however, lacks clarity. There are several lists of tasks, including the one of Tryon and Lilienthal (1959), which is the basis of Figure 5-2 in this chapter. Unfortunately, these lists do not always coincide. Until someone actually investigates the variability of age-graded tasks by class and by ethnic group, questions concerning the validity of such lists will continue.

The research reviewed here, however, does indicate that, consistent with the definition of individual developmental task, the accomplishment level at one age period appears to be related to the level of accomplishment at a later period. Although there is continuity in the level of accomplishment in the tasks contained in a role sequence, task performance level at one stage does not always generalize to performance of a different task at another stage. If the individual becomes too content with his task accomplishments at one stage, he may have difficulty undertaking different tasks at another period.

Similar issues are also applicable to families. The fact that family members as well as family composition changes over time enables a family to accomplish some family tasks as a unit despite failures at an earlier period. More research is needed to discover those tasks that fit the Magrabi and Marshall (1965) linkage hypothesis. The changes in family members during the family career also suggests investigation of those tasks that families can accomplish despite their failures at earlier periods.

Apart from research questions waiting to be answered, the concepts we have examined alert us to changes in family behavior that can be examined descriptively and mapped for variability over time. As these concepts are put to increasing use, their meaning in terms of observable phenomena should become clearer; if they do not, they will be replaced by other, more fruitful concepts.

# REFERENCES

Chandler, Michael, "Social Cognition and Life-Span Approaches to the Study of Child Development," in P. B. Baltes, ed., *Implications of Life-Span Developmental Psychology for Theory and Research in Child Development*. Unpublished symposium manuscript, College of Human Development, Pennsylvania State University, 1975.

Clausen, John A., "The Life Course of Individuals," in Matilda White Riley, Marilyn Johnson, and Anne Foner, eds., *Aging and Society: A Sociology of Age Stratification*. New York: Russell Sage, 1972, 457–514.

Farber, Bernard, "The Family as a Set of Mutually Contingent Careers," in Nelson Foote, ed., *Consumer Behavior: Models of Household Decision-Making*. New York: New York University Press, 1961, 276–297.

Ferguson, Hall G., "Performance of Marital Roles over Stages of the Family Life Cycle," Unpublished doctoral dissertation, Provo, Utah: Brigham Young University, 1971.

Flavell, John H., *The Developmental Psychology of Jean Piaget.* Princeton, N.J.: D. Van Nostrand, 1963.

Freedman, Ronald and Lolagene Coombs, "Childspacing and Family Economic Position," *American Sociological Review*, 1966, 31, 631–648.

Havighurst, Robert J., *Human Development and Education.* New York: Longmans, Green, 1953.

Havighurst, Robert J., "Research on the Developmental Task Concept," *The School Review*, 1956, 64, 215–223.

Hunt, J. McV., "The Impact and Limitations of the Giant of Developmental Psychology," in David Elkind and John H. Flavell, eds., *Studies in Cognitive Development: Essays in Honor of Jean Piaget.* New York: Oxford University Press, 1969.

Magrabi, Frances M. and William H. Marshall, "Family Developmental Tasks: A Research Model," *Journal of Marriage and the Family*, 1965, 27, 454–461. Copyright 1965 by National Council on Family Relations.

Neugarten, Bernice L., "Adult Personality—Toward a Psychology of the Life Cycle," in Bernice L. Neugarten, ed., *Middle Age and Aging.* Chicago: University of Chicago Press, 1968, 137–147.

Rubin, Zick and George Levenger, "Theory and Data Badly Mated: A Critique of Murstein's SVR and Lewis' PDF Models of Mate Selection," *Journal of Marriage and the Family*, 1974, 36, 226–231.

Smith, H. W., "Some Developmental Interpersonal Dynamics Through Childhood," *American Sociological Review*, 1973, 38, 543–552.

Tryon, Caroline and Jesse W. Lilienthal III, "Child Growth and Development," *National Education Association Journal*, 1950, 39, 188–189.

Westoff, Charles F. and Elise F. Jones, "Contraception and Sterilization in the United States, 1965–1975," *Family Planning Perspectives*, 1977, 9, 153–157.

# Part 2

# Analyzing family development through subsystem careers

The discussion of major concepts in the family development framework is complete. We are now ready to utilize them to examine expectable changes in families over time. Our analysis will focus on the careers individuals have in the marital, parent-child, and sibling subsystems of the family. By focusing on one subsystem at a time, the task of studying family dynamics becomes more manageable. At the same time, the interdependence of family subsystems require that the discussion of each subsystem take into account the other subsystems.

The careers that individuals follow in the various family subsystems, in work life, and in school are graphically portrayed in Table 6/17-1. This table demonstrates how changes in one career are related to changes in other careers so that critical role transition points in particular careers mark off family stages.

The timing element in these changes is the individual's life course indicated at the left-hand side of the table. Events in the careers are arranged according to the median age of their occurrence in women's lives in the United States. By adding approximately three years to the age shown for a particular family career event—as

# The Timing and Intersection of Human Careers in Individual Life-Course Perspective

| Age of Individual | Marital Career[a] | Parental Career | Sibling Career | Educational Career | Occupational Career Men | Occupational Career Women |
|---|---|---|---|---|---|---|
| 2 | | | | | | |
| 3 | | | Begins | | | |
| 4 | | | Competition for parental attention | | | |
| 5 | | | | Begins | | |
| 7 | | | Oldest child provides role model | | | |
| 12 | | | Sibling socialization may conflict with parental socialization in peer relation and sexual behavior | Entrance to secondary education | | |
| 16 | | | | Legal Requirement for Schooling ends | | |
| 18 | | | Sibling relations become voluntary | Entrance into college | Begins | |
| 21 | Marriage | | | | | |
| 22 | | Birth of first child | | Graduation from college or university | | Begins |

**The Timing and Intersection of Human Careers in Individual Life-Course Perspective**

| Age | Marital / Conjugal | Parental | Sibling | Educational | Occupational | Labor Force |
|---|---|---|---|---|---|---|
| 23 | Conjugal roles more segregated; Power structure more husband centered | | | | High job-time demands | May leave labor force |
| 29 | Separation of spousal interests | Increasing time demands for socialization task | Sibling relations complete with marital and parental responsibilities | | | |
| 30 | Lessening of marital satisfaction | Birth of last child | | | Decreasing job satisfaction | |
| 32 | | | | | | |
| 33 | | | | | | |
| 35 | | Increasing financial demands | | | | |
| 36 | | Greatest feelings of inadequacy in parental roles | | Reentry of women into college or university | | |
| 37 | Lowest point in marital satisfaction | | | | Peaking of income for lower white-collar, semiskilled and unskilled workers | |
| 43 | | Marriage of first child | Sibling contacts decline with loss of parents | | | Reentry into labor force |
| 44 | | | | | | |

Table 6/17-1

## The Timing and Intersection of Human Careers in Individual Life-Course Perspective

| Age | | | |
|---|---|---|---|
| 46 | | Children establish boundaries around their family units | |
| | | Addition of grandparent roles | Peaking of income for professionals, managers, ar_ skilled worke_ |
| 48 | Return to couple relation | | |
| 51 | Increase in marital satisfaction | | |
| 52 | | Marriage of last child | |
| 53 | | | |
| 54 | Increase in need for companionship | Sibling contacts are again important | |
| 60 | Parents turn to children for counsel and help | | |
| 65 | Death of one spouse | | Retirement |
| 70 | | | Fetire_ent |

Sources: Blood and Wolfe, 1960; Glick, 1977; Oppenheimer, 1974; and Wilensky, 1961.

[a] Events are timed according to women's careers. For men, the events occur approximately two to three years later.

for example, median years of age at marriage—you will have the comparable ages for men. Table 6/17-1 with its multiple career perspective points up career interdependencies that may be obscured in the discussions of particular stages in the various family subsystems. Thus heavy responsibilities in the parental career are associated with changes in marital career structures and with declines in marital satisfaction. The inclusion of the occupational and educational careers also reminds us that events in the outer world have effects within the family, and vice versa. When children enter school, for example, many women reenter the labor market.

Even with the bare-bones approach of the table, one can gain some idea of the joys and sorrows of family life. The parental career, for example, begins with a child's heavy nurturance demands, which necessarily infringe upon the marital career. But at the end of the parental career, role reversal occurs, and the once active parents now turn to their children for nurturance. Although the following chapters add content to the events labelled in Table 6/17-1, the table is worth referring to for a clear, overall perspective of family development.

# REFERENCES

Blood, Robert O., Jr., and Donald M. Wolfe, *Husbands and Wives: The Dynamics of Married Living*. Glencoe, Ill.: Free Press, 1960.

Glick, Paul C., "Updating the Family Life Cycle," *Journal of Marriage and Family Living*, 1977, 39, 5–13.

Oppenheimer, Valerie Kincade, "The Life-Cycle Squeeze: The Interaction of Men's Occupational and Family Life Cycles," *Demography*, 1974, 11, 227–245.

Wilensky, Harold L., "Life Cycle, Work Situation and Participation in Formal Associations," in Robert W. Kleemeier, ed., *Aging and Leisure*. New York: Oxford University Press, 1961, 213–242.

# The Marital Career

# 6

# The establishment of the husband-wife relationship

In beginning an examination of the family over its life cycle the conventional subsystem to choose is the marital couple. The great majority of new family units are formed by a man and woman cohabiting over a period of time with the approval of society, that is, as a consequence of a couple's going through some conventional ceremony of marriage. And, even if the couple adds children to their unit, eventually the children will grow up and leave the couple alone again. It is thus with the husband-wife dyad, which like sibling relationships, generally represents ties between members of the same generation, that we will start our analysis.

The critical role transition point of marriage represents the socially recognized initiation of the marital career. The marital status involves a separation from what went before. New roles are added to the individual's role cluster; the content of continuing role sequences is modified; new interpersonal relationships in the couple role complex develop; and former sociability ties are altered or disappear. As a consequence of these beginnings and the separation from the past they represent, the act of marriage initiates a new family stage. John P. Marquand in his novel

*Women and Thomas Harrow* (1958: 465), well describes this irrevocable break with the past. He writes "one might marry again and again, but in the strictest sense one was only married once."

## GETTING MARRIED

How is it that a particular man and woman come to make such an important decision, a decision that supposedly commits them to a lasting relationship? Novelists and song writers as well as sociologists have all addressed themselves to this question, but here we shall concentrate on what the latter have to say about the process. Kerkhoff and Davis (1962), by observing "seriously attached" couples for some six months, posited the operation of a filtering process for those men and women who made progress toward marriage. As we would expect in a developmental process, limited linkages in the kinds of interaction episodes led to greater commitment among the couples. Value consensus—similarity in interests or home background—appeared to enable couples who had not known each other for long periods to become better acquainted. Longer term couples made progress when they held similar attitudes and values. The meeting of each others' needs—a need for complementarity—was the filtering factor that seemed important in furthering the relation of those couples who went together longest. Dyads who lacked such qualities more often failed to develop greater commitment or dropped the relation altogether. In other words, these pairings were filtered out of the mate selection process.

Times change, however, and a more recent investigation with a similar sample of college couples (Levinger, Senn, and Jergensen, 1970: 441–442) resulted in a somewhat different perspective on the process of mate selection. Couples, indeed, probably do go through a process of discovery. After the initial encounter, however, the disclosure and discovery of less visible traits in the partners leads to a "co-orientation." If the pair relation is to continue to develop, individuals must have more "emotional investment and behavior coordination." Couple relationships seem to progress more quickly than in the past since the individuals involved now put more emphasis on attachment and joint activities. Instead of partner similarity being the critical factor in the courtship process that leads to marriage, it is the construction of a "pair community."

This interpretation of how couples decide to marry is congenial to the traditional belief that mutual attraction determines the decision. But social pressures and unexpected parenthood, as well as events in the occupational and educational careers of individuals, may be more important than sentiment as "escalators" and "turning points" in the development of the pair relation (Bolton, 1961). Parents and peers, for example, help construct the boundaries that establish the identity of the pair unit. By joining the names of the individuals in conversations instead of speaking of them separately and by including the two in activities as a pair rather than as individuals, these parents and peers help construct the very unity that makes them outsiders to the courting couple. Graduating from high school or college or getting a job are specific events that can also lead one or both partners to hasten the process leading to a decision to marry.

Less benign circumstances can play a part, as when pervasive poverty in the parental home and parental strictness lead young people to see marriage not only as an escape but also as a means for attaining independence (Rubin, 1976: 56–57). And, in some cases, persons rush into marriage hastened by premarital pregnancies. Under such circumstances, the filtering process preceding getting married which allows persons to avoid courtship escalators until the couple relation is more firmly established or to break off the relation completely is short circuited.

When there is premature timing of the marital and parental careers, marriage serves not as an escape from parents and poverty but a trap for younger and older generations alike. One interview study of a representative sample of New Orleans women between the ages of 15 and 45, for example, showed that early marriage among whites was associated with living with relatives and with being lower class. Among blacks, however, it was not the timing of marriage, but the early timing of pregnancy that differentiated those living with relatives. Those who conceived and delivered the first child out of wedlock were more apt to live in extended families. Families with "such a rapid generational turnover barely have time to get over the economic drain of raising one generation" before they have to take on the problems of "supporting a growing set of grandchildren followed by the problems of supporting declining parents" (Fischer, Beasley, and Harter, 1968: 299). This "telescoping" of generations precludes the economic recuperation of families in the middle years that later timing of marriage and parenthood makes possible.

## CONSTRAINTS ON MARRIAGE

### Timing Factors in Women's Getting Married

Most social groups still perceive family roles as the proper focus of the lives of women, and too many still view single women as failures both in their duty to society and in their own self-fulfillment. The pervasive norm of getting married becomes translated into social time in terms of expected age for marriage. With 21.3 being the approximate median age at which women marry at the present—for men it is 23.8 years— a young woman who is not yet married at 25 may spend sleepless nights worrying about being single (U.S. Bureau of the Census, 1977: 1, Table A).

To get at some of the effects of a couple's timing on their "ever after" period, let us examine the retrospective reports of a representative sample of the cohort of white women born between 1925 and 1929, supplemented by data from a more recent cohort of white, married women born between 1940 and 1943. For the cohort of women who came of marriageable age during World War II, there was a speed-up in the timing of marital career events. The 31 percent who married before age 19, could be considered the "early"-marriers with the "average" timing group—45 percent of the cohort—marrying between 19 and 23 years of age. The "late"-marriers were the 24 percent of women who waited until they were 22, hardly an advanced age from today's later marital timetable perspective (Elder and Rockwell, 1976: 34).

The life histories of these women indicate that marrying late may be the " 'optimum' or 'right' time if one is interested in maximizing marital and educational prospects" (Elder, 1972: 20). Women who married early had been least able to fulfill their intellectual abilities through educational attainment. Over half (56.3 percent) of them as opposed to 18.5 percent of the women marrying at the average age had not completed high school. And the later the timing of marriage, the greater the proportion of women who gained class status in marriage. This was not only true for women with some college education but for high school graduates as well.

The decision to marry for these "young" brides appeared to be more the result of unpleasantness in their parental families than the attractions of the marital state. They were more often lower class and came from broken families with large number of siblings, with this relationship between low family status and early marriage even more pronounced among women born in the early 1940s (Elder and Rockwell, 1976: 39).

But women who waited beyond the usual age to marry were more likely to challenge convention and to marry younger men. Among the college educated, where this phenomenon was particularly pronounced, 40 percent who married late as compared to four percent of those marrying at the average time had younger husbands. Apparently, these higher achieving women compensated for the diminishing pool of eligible bachelors in their own or older age groups by dipping into the pool of younger men.

Women who rejected the norm that wives should be younger than husbands, however, had the satisfaction of partners who even though younger were more apt to have equalled the number of their wives' years in college. This was true of half (52 percent) of the women who married younger men as contrasted with 30 percent of college educated women who married similar or older aged men (Elder and Rockwell, 1976: 43).

### Income Level and Men's Marriage Rates
It would be untrue, however, to give the impression that only women experience societal constraints with respect to marriage. These constraints for women operate to set up certain age norms as to the proper time to marry. Men also are affected by timing pressures, but the greatest constraints operate to keep them from marrying at all. We are referring here to the influence of the occupational career, specifically earned income, on getting married. By and large, men still experience normative pressure to be the primary family breadwinner. This expectation is reflected in census figures, which show that the lower the income, the higher the percentage of males who are single (U.S. Census Bureau, 1972). The relation holds within racial, age, and, generally, within occupational and educational groups. This means that for a particular occupation or education level, as income rises so usually does the percentage of men marrying. Education and occupation, therefore, appear to affect men's marrying indirectly, through their effect on income.

The timing factor of age plays a part within the limits set by income. As men get past 24, regardless of income level, their marriage rate drops (Cutright, 1970; 636, Table 6; U.S. Census Bureau, 1972). The effect of age, however, is not so great as that of income in determining marriage rates for men.

The fact that societal norms with respect to age roles and the amount of income earned have such large effects on the timing of marriage reminds us that family events cannot be explained only in terms of personality and the interactions of family members. Societal forces can obliterate the most solid family boundaries and prevent individuals from having a chance to demonstrate their job skills. Thus Cutright [illegible] productivity is high, to industries where demand is strong and profits are high, to jobs with strong unions etc." with resultant high wages has little to do with individual characteristics such as educational achievement or interpersonal skills, but much to do with where men live and what companies are hiring.

**Parental Influences on Marriage Timing**
As noted earlier, parents, too, can be thought of as an extracouple factor who interpret and enforce, along with peer groups, group norms in the getting-married process. The influence of these parental families is ˌusually more immediate and apparent than societal constraints, which in the long run may have greater effect.

In their review of the literature on socialization for marriage, Hill and Aldous (1960: 890) note that the initial motivation to marry, especially for men whose occupations can provide a socially approved alternate commitment, is influenced by the degree of parental marital happiness. And, in his previously discussed analysis of longitudinal data concerning women born in the 1920's, Elder (1970: 20) documents how family influences channel this motivation to marry into the timing of the ceremony. For those women marrying before the age of 20, the period of adolescence appeared to be quickened with a "rapid convergence on traditional marital status roles." These women found early marriage congenial because of parental example, heightened domestic interests, early heterosexual involvement and limited educational opportunities as a result of economic deprivation. In contrast to this group of early-marriers, those who married past the age of 23 experienced a prolonged adolescence, because of family constraints on social independence and restricted contacts with men.

**Consequences of Timing**
You will remember that late-marriers had more education than their early marrying peers. They also more often had husbands with higher median incomes. As a result they tended to terminate their occupational careers after the birth of children or never to have been employed after marriage. Early-marriers more often worked outside the home during their families' childbearing and childrearing periods presumably because of economic need, for they had their children earlier, had more of them and had husbands with lower median incomes. They

also experienced more divorces than those who married later—four times as many (Elder and Rockwell, 1976: 44, 46–47).

These early-marrieds' lives of diminished educational opportunities, lengthened working lives and higher exposure to divorce affected the family career timetables they wanted their own daughters to follow. Eighty-six percent of them wanted their daughters to marry later. The later-marrieds (58 percent), however, preferred their daughters to marry at the same age as they, and 10.6 percent wanted them to marry even later. Only for those who had married after age 25, did their timing seem too late for optimal parental careers. Three-fourths of them felt earlier marriages would be better. As for those women who had married at the average time, the split was about half and half between those favoring their daughters keeping to the same marital timetable, and those women wanting their daughters to delay their marriages. None favored an earlier marriage than their own (Elder and Rockwell, 1976: 49).

The restrictive linkage of task accomplishments associated with early marriage is also shown in the Detroit survey discussed in the chapter on development tasks where "the lower the current income level, the more likely the marriage occurred at an early age and that the children were born early in the marriage (Freedman and Coombs, 1966: 636). It appears even more clearly in a longitudinal study of 37 couples who had married while both partners were still enrolled in high school (DeLissovoy, 1973), whose results are supported by Furstenberg's (1976) longitudinal study of 306 black and white unmarried adolescents who became parents and a group of their classmates who did not. The former couples were first contacted within three months of marriage and were approached again 30 to 38 months later. There appeared to be growing dissatisfaction as time went on. Finances, scarce initially, continued to be a problem. No couples were completely dependent on public assistance, an improvement from the 13 on welfare and 31 receiving surplus food at the time of the first interviews. Parental help, however, continued to be important. Physical maintenance task accomplishment remained a matter of survival, and not management of resources but lack of them led to conflict.

The couples were beginning to develop the separate interests based on ascribed gender roles that tend to characterize the families of manual and farm workers from which they came. Joint churchgoing among these couples had been one source of morale maintenance. The accomplishment of this task was lowered, however, because the husbands continued their separate leisure time activities with friends.

Wives were left alone. Sexual relations were also a problem at this
early period: in the view of the wives, sexual intercourse was too fre
quent; in the view of the husbands, too infrequent.

Interviews and ratings at the second time period showed a loss of
joint church activities, coupled with a continuation of men's separate
contacts with male friends. Women now appeared to be resigned to
the situation rather than irritated by it. They were busy taking care of
at least one baby. Both in adjustment and in frequency, there was also
a "marked decrease" in the couples' sexual satisfaction, which was
previously not very high. (DeLissovoy, 1973: 250). The coming of children, which had been looked forward to by these couples—three-
fourths of whom were premaritally pregnant—proved disappointing.
The responsibilities and irritations that babies can cause in financially
hard-pressd families fed back upon and led to further deterioration
in marital relations.

Wives in particular were enmeshed in problems issuing from poor
timing and continuing, inadequate family task performance. The stigma
still associated with premarital pregnancy fell primarily upon the
woman. These wives felt they had been "dropped" by their friends.
Along with 57 percent of the men, two-thirds of them also lost school
contacts by withdrawing from high school. In addition, it was the wives
who had to care for and socialize the new babies and attempt to keep
house on a limited budget, while largely isolated from friendly peers.

## DEVELOPMENTAL TASKS OF THE
## GETTING-MARRIED PERIOD

Since mate selection in our society is left largely to the individual, the
couple relation has quite clearly developed prior to marriage. In her
analysis of marriage as a critical role transition point, Rapoport (1962),
has divided the getting-married period into three phases: (1) the period
of commitment to marry, signaled conventionally by the engagement
and ending with the weddiing; (2) the period of the honeymoon; and
(3) the early marriage period set arbitrarily at the first three months
after the wedding. She has hypothesized that the level of accomplishment of certain individual and couple tasks in the first two periods will
limit future task accomplishment of the new family unit. Let us examine her description of these tasks in some detail.

According to Rapoport (1962: 74), the two parties must take on
three individual developmental tasks in order to cope with the transi-

tion from engagement to marriage. The first of these tasks is preparation to take over marital roles.

In the past the "job descriptions" of marital roles were pretty much set by group norms. For males, particularly, societal norms demanded that they be able to perform the breadwinner role, as indicated by work plans, assessments of the couple's financial requirements, and strategies for fulfilling them. Normative requirements for women were that they be able to keep the house, to know how to cook and to clean. Today, role assignments are not so rigidly based on gender, and couples can do more role making. But whether or not both members of the engaged couples plan to work and whether or not they plan to handle the household management chores on an equal basis, the couple will have to negotiate some sort of division of labor.

The second of the individual tasks that the engaged persons must accomplish prior to marriage is, Rapoport believes, that of boundary maintenance. The solidarity of the new couple relation must be established, and competing interpersonal ties modified. Unless these ties can be accommodated to the priority demands of the marriage, a fertile area for marital conflict exists.

In addition to modifying close extramarital ties and developing the skills to perform marital roles, the engaged parties must be able to shift their gratifications from those satisfactory to each in his or her unmarried state to those satisfactory to both. Men sometimes define this task in terms of loss of freedom while women see it as giving up the flattering attentions inherent in courtship behavior. In either case, the individual has to accomplish the task of changing from a "single-minded" to an "other-oriented" perspective.

Besides the individual tasks, there are also couple tasks to be performed during the engagement period analogous to family development tasks. The task of physical maintenance, for example, seems to incorporate Rapoport's engagement task of creating mutually agreeable work and decision-making patterns, as well as planning for the events of the wedding, the honeymoon (if there is one), and the early months of marriage. The task of developing a satisfactory pattern of family planning is similar to the family task of recruitment of members, just as Rapoport's tasks of establishing a couple identity, a satisfactory relation with friends and relatives, and a pair communication pattern are consistent with the family task of maintenance of order in the family and in its relation with outsiders. Finally, the task of maintenance of motivation to perform family roles is analogous to the engaged couple's task of developing a mutually satisfactory sexual adjustment (Rapoport, 1962: 76).

For the honeymoon phase in the transition period of getting married, Rapoport and Rapoport (1964; 43–47) have hypothesized two individual and two couple developmental tasks that must be accomplished for the well-being of the marital couple. The individual tasks are developing a competence to engage in sexual relations with one's partner and developing some facility for living in intimate association with him or her. Both of these tasks concern behaviors that are not a part of the couple's experience in their respective families of orientation. The behaviors also bring into play emotions and feelings concerning one's adequacy as a sexual being and one's security as a separate entity. In a society where many groups place a high premium on sexual enjoyment but at the same time emphasize autonomy and individual development, fears and anxieties can make difficult the accomplishment of these two tasks. The man's fears of impotence, joined by the woman's fears of not being able to satisfy her mate, affect the couple's sexual feeling for one another, their sexual performance, and the place sex will hold in the marriage. The sexual act with its physical union symbolizes the loss of privacy and autonomy that is demanded for the close quarters of day-to-day couple existence in which the individual must give up some independence in order to take into account the other's needs.

These individual tasks of sexual competence and intimate living complement the couple tasks of developing sexual relations that are mutually satisfactory and shared experiences that are mutually agreeable. The honeymoon, presumably, provides the couple with a salubrious setting, the time, and the societal sanction to engage in explorations of each other's body and mind. These experiences can provide the emotional boost that will encourage the couple to take on the more homely roles bound up in marital living. In times of future stress, this period also can supply reassuring memories that husband and wife are joined by bonds of shared pleasure as well as by the more pedestrian interdependencies of work and children.

To assess her limited-linkage assumption, namely, that couples' performance on the tasks she hypothesized as necessary for the engagement and honeymoon phases of getting married would indeed affect their situation a year later, Rapoport (unpublished manuscript) did an exploratory study of seven middle-class student couples. The couples were interviewed jointly and separately four times during the engagement period, with the last interview coming immediately before the wedding. Further interviews came as soon as possible after the honeymoon, three months later, and a year later. Despite the similarity of the couples, Rapoport and her associates were able to discriminate a range of accomplishment from "relatively 'high' " (two couples) to "relatively 'low' " (two couples), with three couples judged to be in between.

For her purposes, Rapoport used test scores as her measures of task accomplishment outcomes. Strictly speaking, however, she notes that the term "outcome" is a misnomer, since it is an arbitrary point in an ongoing process and will itself have effects on future events in the process. The measures tapped the following: (1) the partners' psychosomatic functioning; (2) the difference between their role performance and their spouses' expectation; (3) the degree to which the partners met each other's needs; and (4) their marital happiness.

The score patterns on the outcome measures were consistent with the limited-linkage task formulation. "Better" outcomes appeared among the high task accomplishers. Although the sample is too small for the findings to be conclusive, they are consistent with the hypothesis that the level of developmental task accomplishment in the period before and just after the couple's establishing a new family unit is related to later individual and couple functioning.

These tasks of the getting married period need not be accomplished, however, within the confines of engagement and honeymoon as was true of the conventionally oriented couples Rapoport studied. Many couples do not take honeymoons just as many couples do not leave sexual relations until after the wedding ceremony. Thus the tasks, Rapoport posits, are handled at different times relative to the wedding ceremony by different couples.

More youths, for example, are now engaging in premarital intercourse than formerly. Zelnik and Kantner's (1977) national survey of never married women showed that 55 percent had had sexual intercourse by the time they were 19. (See Baldwin, 1976). Twenty years earlier, Kinsey (1953) reported that in his convenience sample of women less than half that percentage of women, 20 percent in fact, had had sexual intercourse before they were 20 years old. Inasmuch as many women reporting premarital coitus experience it with a fiancé or steady boy friend (Christensen and Gregg, 1970), the tasks associated with establishing sexual compatibility are occurring before marriage for these couples. And when this is the case, or when finances are a problem, couples are less likely to see the need for the ritualized departure of the honeymoon to establish identity as a couple.

We should also not overlook individuals who choose to cohabit without benefit of clerical or civil ceremony. Data from a representative, national sample of 2500 Selective Service registrants showed that 18 percent of these young men, 20 to 30 years of age, had lived for at least six months at some time with a woman. Of these men, 65 percent had cohabited with just one partner. And at the time the men were interviewed, just five percent of them were cohabiting. Thus, this information indicates that as far as "serious heterosexual relationship" are concerned, "most young men in the United States are conventional" (Clayton and Voss, 1977: 282).[1]

## MARITAL ROLES AND ROLE MAKING

Once a couple has started cohabiting on a permanent basis, the man and woman must establish the set of relationships that will enable them to accomplish the family tasks specific to this stage. The roles they perform may be developed either by a role-making process or by following normative prescriptions.

To take the role-making process first, when marital roles grow out of the couple's interaction, the couple has to work out what the task solutions are to be rather than to follow customary ways (Raush, Goodrich, and Campbell, 1963: 372). The man and woman in the role-making case can discuss what each wants to do based on her or his expressed desires. The woman may want to escape the food preparer and housekeeper roles and concentrate on her occupational role. The decisions on role assignment and role content will involve couple negotiation in which resources of expertise, ability to punish refusals or reward concessions, and appeals to the other's affection will all be brought into play. The wife, for example, may point out the husband's cooking experience in an officer's club in the army as an indication of his greater expertise. The husband may counter that his well-paying job, with its payoffs for her in the form of luxuries her salary cannot provide, leaves him too tired and too preoccupied to cook. The possibilities of conflict are everpresent. A judgment, moreover, as to the effectiveness of task coping depends not alone on the task performance, but also on the process of working out the roles with the gratifications and clashes involved.

When individuals follow normatively prescribed roles, their effectiveness depends on earlier socialization in these roles. The role demands

---

[1] There is a greater tendency for blacks than whites to cohabit. Twenty-nine percent of black respondents had ever cohabited for at least six months compared with 16 percent of the whites. At the time the men were interviewed, eight percent of blacks and four percent of whites were cohabiting (Clayton and Voss, 1977: 282).

may not coincide with the individual's desires or abilities, and she or he may be poorly trained. Since the individual must perform a preset role, ineffective coping will be manifest primarily in an intrapersonal rather than interpersonal struggle. Anxiety and unhappiness can appear along with repression and denial. The wife who expects to fulfill traditional household roles may have had little training in her parental home. She experiences a period of stress as she learns to cook from a book, does the laundry and irons, and keeps the house clean (Rausch, Goodrich, and Campbell, 1963: 372).

Role making, as we noted in an earlier chapter, permits greater freedom for personal and couple development and gives the couple a greater potential for adapting to change as well as creating it. On the other hand, the less stable family structures that result from role making may create confusion and heighten conflict by broadening the range of alternative behaviors. It is also true that role prescriptions allow the individual free run within these constraints. Role making permits the actor to develop his or her own role content in consultation with the partner. But this interaction enables the partner to have a voice in the role performance of the actor that can infringe on his or her autonomy (Raush, Goodrich, and Campbell, 1963: 380).

Let us look at what research shows us about the kinds of couples that are more apt to engage in role making as opposed to those who follow prescribed roles after marriage. The discussion of selective boundary maintenance suggests that role makers would be couples whose friends do not know one another. Couples entering marriage with close-knit social networks, where everyone knows everyone else, tend to develop segregated conjugal role organizations. Friends and kin can assist with support and instruction so that each spouse can perform traditional gender-based family roles. The linked sociability group can also exert concerted pressure to ensure that the couple conforms to their normative prescriptions (Bott, 1971).

This research of Bott is consistent with the findings of a study of 50 white middle-class couples interviewed in their fourth month of marriage. Goodrich, Ryder, and Raush (1968: 388–389) found that the most common marital type minimized boundary maintenance and centered on close relations with one of the parental families usually in association with an active social life with friends. These couples had a nonemotional style of communication, with husbands who anticipated fatherhood to an unusual degree but were relatively uninterested in sexual expression. There are accordingly some suggestions that these peer- and parent-oriented couples in the early months of marriage were still caught up in the parent-child subsystem while planning their own parental careers. Couples who had cut themselves off from their families were more interested in the marital career and role making. They were concerned with their sexual experience and not with their prospects in providing child care.

Not only ties with parents and peers, as Bott suggests, but also men's unhappiness in the parental home, as Goodrich, Ryder, and Rauch (1968: 388) reported, is associated with acceptance of traditional marital roles. Men describing troubled childhoods tended to marry maternal, home-centered wives who expressed little interest in an occupation outside the home. Their husbands, however, seemed to be "single-mindedly" concerned with their work and to be little involved in household concerns. The reported data from wives having unhappy childhoods showed them to be in conflict with their husbands over housekeeping matters and to have trouble getting along with their in-laws. Unlike the men, the women were less able to escape the performance of family roles. But with unhappy childhoods and unhappy marriages they appeared to find little satisfaction in playing the traditional roles of housekeeper and kinkeeper.

In her exploratory study of intergenerational changes in conjugal authority patterns in the families of 37 middle- and working-class college students, Ingersoll (1948) also found that home backgrounds affected the marital role performance. Role making to set up joint decision-making power structures occurred when the partners experienced different power patterns while growing up. If, however, both came from families with the same joint matricentric or patricentric patterns, they followed those role prescriptions in their own marriages without working out different arrangements.

The flexibility in conjugal organization that role making brings about is encouraged by changes in the broader society. As Lopata (1971: 149) points out, new consumer goods have made housekeeping quite different for many women from what they observed or were taught as children. Convenience foods, standardized recipes, a wide concern with health foods and gourmet cookery made easy are examples in the area of food preparation.

Less-educated and less-travelled elders who transmit the traditional expectations lose prestige. Only 35 percent of the housewives surveyed in the Chicago area, mentioned their mothers as sources of information on carrying out homemaker roles. An additional nine percent mentioned "home" and four percent other relatives. As a consequence, women are less constrained by customary ways and more ready to experiment with household tasks and this experimentation can carry over to role assignment.

## Conflict Management Among Newlyweds

All couples, whether they engage in role making or accept traditional spousal roles, find themselves disagreeing. The patterns of conflict management that couples establish who do not divorce because of their conflicts appear to carry over to future family stages (Raush et al., 1974). These patterns clearly demonstrate, moreover, the couple's systemlike character. Observation of a group of 48, white, middle-class newlyweds in situations designed to elicit conflict showed that what one partner said clearly influenced the response of the other. And the response was likely to be of a similar type. If one spouse made an emotional statement or a coercive statement, the other was likely to reply in kind. Thus conflicts could escalate; although among couples committed to the continuance of their marriages, there did appear to be ways of getting off such an escalator. When conflict reached a pitch at which one partner uttered a rejection statement, the other did not reply in kind. The couples thereby escaped from a potentially destructive conflict cycle.

There were definite differences, however, in the conflict sequences of the more happily married couples as contrasted with those having trouble getting along. The happily married couples tended to resort to rejecting and coercive statements much less than other couples who preferred instead to provide information about the issue causing the disagreement or to suggest a solution. The husbands of the happier couples were also more likely than other husbands or even their own wives to initiate peace-making statements. In contrast, the statements of the discordant couples spiraled quickly into power struggles in which neither one listened to the other and in which both resorted to destructive personal attacks. In contrast, the happier coupels who engaged in conflict were sensitive to each other's feelings and more concerned about their interpersonal relationship remaining positive than the outcome of any conflict interchange.

Those couples who preferred to avoid confrontations over disagreements appeared to be as happy as those who talked their conflicts out, "given the context of continuing positive affection" (Raush et al., 1974: 106). In the long run, however, their relative lack of tolerance for conflict may cause difficulties as disagreements fester and their existence cannot be overlooked (Raush et al., 1974: 174).

A study by Cutler and Dyer (1965) sheds some light on the strategies that husbands and wives who are in the initial stages of marriage see themselves as using in conflict situations. Sixty student couples reported separately how they responded to their spouse's violations of their behavioral expectations in various areas of marriage. Differences arising from ascribed gender characteristics appeared. Here, husbands perceived themselves as more often utilizing a no action, wait-and-see strategy as a first reaction. Wives, however, saw themselves as handling husbands' transgressions by communicating their displeasure openly or by talking about the situation.

When it came to a spouse's reactions to these strategies, husbands more than wives believed their spouses behaved negatively. Even though husbands reported taking no action initially when their expectations were violated, their wives apparently sensed the displeasure, and in the husbands' views, they did not respond in a way that made for an adjustment. In addition, open communication in which feelings were expressed did not always clear the air. Almost half of the non-adjustive reactions of men and women resulted from open communication. Since women are more apt to express their emotions, one may speculate that such open communication may seem inappropriate and even threatening to men, who are more accustomed to hiding their feelings. Perhaps, also, what is perceived as open communication to the individual speaking may be interpreted as criticism by the spouse. On the other hand, when the wives in the study reacted negatively to their husbands' behavior, husbands in about half the instances then acted in a way leading to adjustment.

The husbands and wives also differed in the areas in which they reported spousal behaviors they did not like. Wives six times more often than husbands mentioned how little time their spouses spent at home. Continuing the picture of wives' interest in the home, they also were more exercised about violations in the care of the home. Husbands differentiated their strategies according to area. They talked openly about things that their wives did counter to their expectations in the area of finances. Where sexual intercourse was concerned, however, the husbands, perhaps unused to discussing such matters, adopted a wait-and-see strategy in handling spousal transgressions (Cutler and Dyer, 1965: 198).

## A BALANCE SHEET ON THE ESTABLISHMENT STAGE OF MARRIAGE

Depending upon the couple, the early stage of marriage can be both the best of times and the worst of times. Tables 6-1, 6-2, and 6-3 document this statement with a rough assessment of family resources and couple satisfactions and dissatisfactions over the family life cycle.

Table 6-1

**The Family's Vulnerability to Stress Owing to Deficits in Expressive Resources**[a]

| | Family Stage | | | | | | |
|---|---|---|---|---|---|---|---|
| Deficit | Establish-ment | Child-bearing | School-age Children | Adoles-cents | Launch-ing | Post-parental | Aging |
| Incidence of divorce and separation[b] | 5 | 3 | 2 | 2 | 1 | 1 | 1 |
| Degree of marital dissatisfaction[c] | 1 | 1 | 2 | 3 | 5 | 4 | 5 |
| Dissatisfaction with love[d] | 1 | 1 | 2 | 3 | 5 | 3 | 4 |
| Dissatisfaction with companionship[e] | 1 | 2 | 3 | 4 | 5 | 3 | 4 |
| Lack of marital communication[f] | 1 | 2 | 5 | 4 | 3 | 2 | 2 |
| Segregation of marital roles[g] | 1 | 2 | 2 | 3 | 5 | 4 | 5 |
| Husband's alienation from home tasks[h] | 1 | 2 | 5 | 5 | 5 | 3 | 3 |
| Wife's failure to share problems with husband[i] | 1 | 3 | 4 | 5 | 5 | 4 | 5 |
| Total vulnerability score | 12 | 16 | 25 | 29 | 34 | 22 | 29 |
| Duration of marriage (in years) | 0–1 | 2–7 | 8–14 | 15–21 | 22–29 | 30–43 | 44–50 |
| Husband's age | 22 | 24–30 | 31–37 | 38–44 | 45–52 | 53–65 | 66–72 |

Source: Aldous and Hill "Breaking the Poverty Cycle" 1969: p. 7.

[a] The scores range from least vulnerable (1) to most vulnerable (5).

[b] Thomas P. Monahan, "When Couples Part," *American Sociological Review*, Vol. 27, No. 5 (October 1962), Table 1, p. 630.

[c] Robert O. Blood, Jr., and Donald M. Wolfe, *Husbands and Wives: The Dynamics of Married Living* (Glencoe, Ill.: Free Press, 1960), p. 265.

[d] Ibid., p. 232.

[e] Ibid., p. 156.

[f] Harold Feldman, *Development of the Husband-Wife Relationship* (Ithaca, N.Y.: Department of Child Development and Family Relationships, Cornell University, 1964) p. 126. (Mimeographed.)

[g] Ibid., p. 70.

[h] Ibid., p. 71.

[i] Ibid., p. 188.

Table 6-2

## The Family's Vulnerability to Stress Owing to the Insufficiency of Instrumental Resources[a]

| Deficit | Family Stage | | | | | | |
|---|---|---|---|---|---|---|---|
| | Establish-ment | Child-bearing | School age Children | Adoles-cents | Launch-ing | Post parental | Aging |
| Income per member[b] | 5 | 4 | 4 | 3 | 3 | 1 | 5 |
| Size of family[c] | 1 | 4 | 5 | 5 | 3 | 1 | 1 |
| Adequacy of housing[d] | 4 | 5 | 4 | 3 | 3 | 2 | 2 |
| Medical expenses[e] | 1 | 4 | 5 | 3 | 2 | 2 | 5 |
| Family debts[f] | 2 | 5 | 5 | 4 | 3 | 1 | 1 |
| Job changes[g] | 5 | 5 | 3 | 3 | 2 | 2 | 1 |
| Wife in labor force supplementing income[h] | 1 | 5 | 4 | 3 | 2 | 3 | 5 |
| Total vulnerability score | 19 | 32 | 30 | 24 | 18 | 12 | 20 |
| Duration of marriage (in years) | 0–1 | 2–7 | 8–14 | 15–21 | 22–29 | 30–43 | 44–50 |
| Husband's age | 22 | 24–30 | 31–37 | 38–44 | 45–52 | 53–65 | 66–72 |

Source: Aldous and Hill "Breaking the Poverty Cycle" 1969: p. 8.
[a] The scores range from least vulnerable (1) to most vulnerable (5).
[b] Paul C. Glick and Robert Parke, Jr., "New Approaches in Studying the Life Cycle of the Family," Demography (1965), pp. 187–202.
[c] Reuben Hill and Nelson Foote, Household Inventory Changes Among Three Generations of Minneapolis Families (New York: General Electric Co., 1962), Chart 2.
[d] Nelson Foote et al., Housing Choices and Housing Constraints (New York: McGraw-Hill Book Co., 1960), Table 19, p. 99.
[e] John B. Lansing and James N. Morgan, "Consumer Finances Over the Life Cycle," in Lincoln Clark, ed., The Life Cycle and Consumer Behavior (New York: New York University Press, 1955), p. 49.
[f] Ibid., p. 44.
[g] Hill and Foote, op. cit., Chart 4.
[h] Robert O. Blood, Jr., and Donald M. Wolfe, Husbands and Wives: The Dynamics of Married Living (Glencoe, Ill.: Free Press, 1960), p. 98.

Although income is low in the beginning stage, so are family debts, and wives are most apt to be providing supplementary income. Satisfaction with marriage, love, and companionship are high, husbands are involved in household matters, communication between husband and wife is good, and wives feel free to share their problems with their spouses.

But divorce is also most common at this time. The highest number of marriages break during the first two to three years of marriage

Table 6-3

**The Family's Vulnerability to Stress Owing to Dissatisfaction with Instrumental Resources[a]**

| Evaluation | Family Stage | | | | | | |
|---|---|---|---|---|---|---|---|
| | Establish-ment | Child-bearing | School-age Children | Adoles-cents | Launch-ing | Post-parental | Aging |
| Satisfaction with level of living[b] | 1 | 3 | 4 | 4 | 3 | 5 | 2 |
| Satisfaction with job[c] | 1 | 3 | 5 | 5 | 3 | 1 | 1 |
| Disagreements over money[d] | 1 | 5 | 4 | 4 | 4 | 4 | 3 |
| Worries about financial cost of children[e] | 1 | 3 | 5 | 2 | 4 | 2 | 1 |
| Total vulnerability score | 4 | 14 | 18 | 15 | 14 | 12 | 7 |
| Duration of marriage (in years) | 0–1 | 2–7 | 8–14 | 15–21 | 22–29 | 30–43 | 44–50 |
| Husband's age | 22 | 24–30 | 31–37 | 38–44 | 45–52 | 53–65 | 66–72 |

Source: Aldous and Hill "Breaking the Poverty Cycle" 1969: p. 8.
[a] The scores range from least vulnerable (1) to most vulnerable (5).
[b] Robert O. Blood, Jr., and Donald M. Wolfe, *Husbands and Wives: The Dynamics of Married Living* (Glencoe, Ill.: Free Press, 1960), p. 112.
[c] Haorld L. Wilensky, "Life Cycle, Work Situation and Participation in Formal Associations," in Robert W. Kleemeier, ed., *Aging and Leisure* (New York: Oxford University Press, 1961), pp. 228–229.
[d] Blood and Wolfe, op. cit., p. 247.
[e] Ibid., p. 143.

(U.S. Bureau of the Census, 1976: 8). The probabilities of divorce are higher for those who marry young, have a low income, and have children soon after marriage (Norton and Glick, 1976). Within 20 years after first marriage, for example, the Census Bureau (1971: 3) found in 1967 that 28 percent of men who married before the age of 22 were divorced, as compared with 13 percent of men who married later. Much the same percentage differences characterized women. Of those marrying before the age of 20, 27 percent were divorced. Fourteen percent of women who married after this date experienced divorce. And the chances of divorce were twice as high among men who had low earnings. There were eight divorces per 1000 married men who made less than $8000 yearly and four per 1000 married men with incomes of $8000 and over. Finally, women having children in the first two years of marriage had an average divorce rate of 24 per 1000 married women. The rate for those whose children arrived after this period was 12 per 1000 married women.

An early report on middle class couples married an average of 20 years indicates the problems that are particularly pronounced in low-income and early-married groups. Sexual relations and decisions on how to spend money were tasks that took the longest time for couples to arrange satisfactorily. In fact, about a tenth of the 409 couples in the sample had not yet reached an agreeable sex pattern and were still unhappy over monetary matters (Landis, 1947). Low incomes and the arrival of children soon after marriage would exacerbate these pervasive marital problems, and both characteristics are disproportionately found among early-marriers. For example, the individual developmental task delineated by Rapoport (1964) of learning to participate in an appropriate sexual relation with one's partner would be jeopardized by the "too early" timing of childbirth. Lack of income also makes difficult the accomplishment of the family development task of physical maintenance.

**Reentering Marriage**

In some respects first marriages that end in divorce can be viewed as socialization experiences. About five-sixths of all divorced men and three-fourths of divorced women eventually remarry, on the average within three years of their divorce, thereby indicating their continued faith in the institution of marriage (Glick, 1977). Here again, however, timing plays a part. The older the individual is and the longer he or she has been divorced, the less the probability of remarriage. The lower the income among men and the greater the number of children among women, the lower also the remarriage rate. Thus traditional roles, breadwinner for men, child care for women, affect remarriage opportunities. But second marriages, unlike the first time around, do not represent complete discontinuity with the past. The participants have had "on-the-job" training for marital careers and so presumably can do better the second time.

The evidence on how much persons learn from this prior experience as reflected in the happiness and stability of their second marriages is not overly encouraging. Although the reported marital happiness of ever-divorced and never-divorced couples respondents in representative national samples of white persons shows no "very substantial differences," the existing differences do favor the never-divorced. And for women, the differences are statistically significant (Glenn and Weaver, 1977: 335). Moreover, while at most 15 percent of women 30 to 60 years of age in 1975 who had ever married had been divorced after a remarriage, these figures may eventually increase along with the rise in first divorce rates. Thus, estimates of the eventual first divorce rates for married women 26 to 50 years of age in 1975, range from 24 percent to 38 percent with the higher rates appearing among younger women. As for those women who remarry, the estimate of divorce for the same aged women, range from 23 percent to 44 percent (U.S. Bureau of the Census, 1976; 6, Table G).

The phenomenon of limited linkages seems to constrain the carry-over to the new marriage of whatever skills have been learned in the previous. The dissolved first marriage for many who divorce and re-marry serves as a reminder that marriages can be broken. Divorce, then, becomes a conscious alternative to conflict management when marriages fail to run smoothly, and couples who are in remarriages appear more often to resort to it.

# REFERENCES

Aldous, Joan and Reuben Hill, "Breaking the Poverty Cycle," *Social Work,* 1969, 14, 3–12. Reprinted with permission of the National Association of Social Workers.

Baldwin, Wendy H., "Adolescent Pregnancy and Child Bearing: Growing Concerns for Americans," *Population Bulletin,* Vol. 31, No. 2 (Population Reference Bureau, Inc., Washington, D.C., 1976).

Blood, Robert O., Jr. and Donald M. Wolfe, *Husbands and Wives: The Dynamics of Married Living.* Glencoe, Ill.: Free Press, 1960.

Bolton, Charles D., "Mate Selection as the Development of a Relationship," *Marriage and Family Living,* 1961, 23, 234–240.

Bott, Elizabeth, *Family and Social Network: Roles, Norms and External Relationships in Ordinary Urban Families.* New York: Free Press, 1971.

Christensen, Harold and Christina F. Gregg, "Changing Sex Norms in America and Scandinavia," *Journal of Marriage and the Family,* 1970, 32, 616–627.

Clayton, Richard R. and Harwin L. Voss, "Shacking Up: Cohabitation in the 1970's," *Journal of Marriage and the Family,* 1977, 39, 273–283.

Cutler, Beverly and William G. Dyer, "Initial Adjustment Processes in Young Married Couples," *Social Forces,* 1965, 44, 195–201.

Cutright, Phillips, "Income and Family Events: Getting Married," *Journal of Marriage and the Family,* 1970, 18, 3–24.

DeLissovoy, Vladimir, "High School Marriages: A Longitudina Study," *Journal of Marriage and the Family,* 1973, 35, 245–255.

Elder, Glen H., "Role Orientations, Marital Age and Life Patterns in Adulthood," *Merrill-Palmer Quarterly,* 1972, 18, 3–24.

Elder, Glen H., and Richard C. Rockwell, "Marital Timing in Women's Life Patterns," Journal of Family History, 1976, 1, 34 44.

Feldman, Harold, Development of the Husband Wife Relationship. Ithaca New York Department of Child Development and Family Relationships Cornell University, 1964.

Fischer, Anne, Joseph D. Deasley, and Ouri L. Harton, "The Occurrence of the Extended Family at the Origin of the Family of Procreation: A Developmental Approach to Negro Family Structure," *Journal of Marriage and the Family*, 1968, 30, 290–300.

Foote, Nelson, Janet Abu-Lughod, Mary Mix Foley, and Louis Winnick, *Housing Choices and Housing Constraints.* New York: McGraw Hill Book Co., 1960.

Freedman, Ronald and Lolagene Coombs, "Childspacing and Family Economic Position," *American Sociological Review*, 1966, 31, 631–648.

Furstenberg, Jr., Frank, *Unplanned Parenthood: The Social Consequences of Teenage Childbearing.* New York: Free Press, 1976.

Glenn, Norval D. and Charles N. Weaver, "The Marital Happiness of Remarried Divorced Persons," *Journal of Marriage and the Family*, 1977, 39, 331–337.

Glick, Paul C., "A Demographer Looks at American Families," *Journal of Marriage and the Family*, 1975, 37, 15–26.

Glick, Paul C., and Robert Parke, Jr., "New Approaches in Studying the Life Cycle of the Family," *Demography*, 1965, 2, 187–202.

Goodrich, Wells, Robert G. Ryder and H. L. Rausch, "Patterns of Newlywed Marriage," *Journal of Marriage and the Family*, 1968, 30, 383–391.

Hill, Reuben and Joan Aldous, "Socialization for Marriage and Parenthood," in David A. Goslin, ed., *Handbook of Socialization: Theory and Research*, Chicago: Rand McNally, 1969, 885–950.

Hill, Reuben and Nelson Foote, *Household Inventory Changes Among Three Generations of Minneapolis Families,* New York: General Electric, 1962.

Ingersoll, Hazel, "A Study of the Transmission of Authority Patterns in the Family," *Genetic Psychology Monographs*, 1948, 38, 225–303.

Kerkhoff, Alan C. and Keith E. Daivs, "Value Consensus and Need Complementarity in Mate Selection," *American Sociological Review*, 1962, 27, 295–303.

Kinsey, A. C., W. B. Pomeroy, C. E. Martin, and P. H. Gebhard, *Sexual Behavior in the Human Female.* Philadelphia: Saunders, 1953.

Landis, Judson, T., "Adjustment After Marriage," *Marriage and Family Living,* 1947, 19, 32–34.

Lansing, John B., and James N. Morgan, "Consumer Finances over the Life Cycle," in Lincoln Clark, ed., *The Life Cycle and Consumer Behavior.* New York: New York University Press, 1955.

Levinger, George, David J. Senn, and Bruce W. Jergensen, "Progress Toward Permanence in Courtship: A Test of the Kerkhoff-Davis Hypotheses," *Sociometry*, 1970, 33, 427–443.

Lopata, Helena Z., *Occupation: Housewife*. New York: Oxford University Press, 1971.
Marquand, John Phillips, *Women and Thomas Harrow*. Boston: Little, Brown, 1958.
Monahan, Thomas, P., "When Couples Part," *American Sociological Review,* 1962, 27, 625–633.
Rapoport, Rhona and Robert Rapoport, "New Light on the Honeymoon," *Human Relations*, 1964, 17, 35–50.
Rapoport, Rhona, "Normal Crisis, Family Structure and Mental Health," *Family Process*, 1962, 2, 68–80.
Rapoport, Rhona, unpublished manuscript.
Rausch, H. L., W. A. Barry, R. K. Hertel, and M. A. Swain, *Communication, Conflict, and Marriage*. San Francisco: Jossey-Bass, 1974.
Raush, H. L., Wells Goodrich, and J. D. Campbell, "Adaptation to the First Years of Marriage, *Psychiatry*, 1963, 26, 368–380.
Rubin, Llililan B., *Worlds of Pain: Life in the Working Class Family*. New York: Basic Books, 1976.
U.S. Bureau of the Census, 1970, Census of Population, Vol. II, LIC, "Marital Status," U.S. Government Printing Office, Washington, D.C., 1972.
U.S. Bureau of the Census, Current Population Reports, Series P-20, No. 306, "Marital Status and Living Arrangements: March 1976," U.S. Govern-Printing Office, Washington, D.C., 1977.
U.S. Bureau of the Census, Current Population Reports, Series P-20, No. 297, "Number, Timing and Duration of Marriages and Divorces in the United States: June 1975," U.S. Government Printing Office, Washington, D.C., 1976.
U.S. Bureau of the Census, Current Population Reports, Series P-20, No. 223, "Social and Economic Variations in Marriage, Divorce and Remarriage: 1967," U.S. Government Printing Office, Washington, D.C., 1971.
Wilensky, Harold L., "Life Cycle, Work Situation and Participation in Formal Associations," in Robert W. Kleemeier, ed., *Aging and Leisure*. New York: Oxford University Press, 1961, 213–242.
Zelnik, Melvin, and John F. Kantner, "Sexual and Contraceptive Experience of Young Unmarried Women in the United States, 1976 and 1971," *Family Planning Perspectives*, 1977, 9, 55–71.

# 7

# The impact of parenthood on marital roles

A number of social scientists are prepared to argue that it is parenthood rather than marriage that marks the individual's entrance into adult status (Hill and Aldous, 1969: 923; Rossi, 1968: 32). Because of the increased educational requirements for occupational careers, many couples are entering marriage before husbands can play the traditional role of breadwinner. Instead, working wives alone play this role, or if they are also still in school, parental families or governmental agencies may subsidize the new family unit. The coming of children, however, on the average two years after marriage, forces the couple to take on the domestic responsibilities that go with being adults.

Entering the parenthood career, therefore, represents a more serious critical role transition point than does marriage. The choice of a mate and the decision to marry tend to be relatively voluntary decisions within the constraints of timing and income described earlier. Parenthood, in contrast, may not be the consequence of a voluntary act but the unanticipated effect of sexual intercourse recreative and not procreative in intent (Rossi, 1968: 30). This difference is expressed in customary terminology. One "decides" to get married, a purposeful action, but one becomes a parent, a more passive status.

An unplanned pregnancy can, in fact, be one of the constraints forcing a decision to marry. The first pregnancy occurs on the average in the first two years of marriage (Glick, 1977), but Freedman and Coombs (1966) found 30 percent of their representative sample of white wives in Detroit were premaritally pregnant. With the rise in the rate of premarital intercourse in recent years—a study of junior and senior high school students in Michigan showed 16 percent of the students to be sexually active in 1970 as compared with 22 percent three years later (Baldwin, 1976)—a number of couples with unplanned pregnancies will continue to choose marriage from the alternatives of abortion, placing the child for adoption, or the mother alone keeping the child.[1]

Since unplanned pregnancies can occur both before and after marriage, there is a greater probability of unwanted pregnancies than of marriages. Marriages, moreover, can be dissolved by divorce or separation. Parenthood, in contrast, is irrevocable. Unless the child is given for adoption, a practice normatively discouraged for all but unwed mothers, there is no way of escaping parental responsibilities. As Rossi (1968: 32) reminds us, "we can have ex-spouses and ex-jobs but not ex-children."

## THE PREGNANCY PERIOD

From the birth of the child to the time the last child leaves home, parental roles compete with marital roles for temporal and emotional priority. Pregnancy itself profoundly affects a couple's sexual relation, a form of marital union bearing directly on couple morale maintenance. Masters and Johnson (1966) have done much to illuminate this neglected area. They were able to question both partners of 79 middle-class married couples in separate interviews. Wives gave information toward the end of the second month, again at the sixth month, and finally during the eighth month of pregnancy. There was a postpartum interview with both spouses in the third month after delivery.

---

[1] Only one third of adolescent women having coitus use contraceptives although some 70 percent worry about it (Sorensen, 1973). Many of the nonusers believe they know the safe period for intercourse although they display a lack of understanding between sex and reproduction (Baldwin, 1976).

Eroticism and effectiveness of sexual performance in the early stage of pregnancy were closely related to parity. Of the 43 women pregnant for the first time, 33 reported loss of interest in coitus and less effectiveness in performance during the first trimester of pregnancy. The 68 women who had given birth before reported little change in sexual interest and performance during this period. The second trimester produced a heightening of eroticism and sexual performance among the women regardless of parity.

In marked contrast was the third trimester. Physical symptoms and medical advice led to lessened sexual activity or to continence. Three-fourths of the women who reached this period (77 of 101) had doctors who proscribed intercourse for from one to three months before delivery. Some women reported that sleepiness, backache, and abdominal discomfort contributed to their losing interest in intercourse, while exhausting demands from children and their own physical discomfort lessened the sexual desire of women who already had children.

Even after the women had given birth, about one-half of the women (47 of 101) reported low levels of eroticism as late as the third postpartum month. Thus, for a large proportion of the couples, there was almost a six months' semimoratorium on sexual relations, with concomitant strains placed on the marital relation. Fatigue, weakness, pain with attempted intercourse, and fear of permanent harm from too early resumption of coitus were some of the physical reasons wives listed for their low interest in intercourse. Although most medical authorities at the time of the study discouraged intercourse for six weeks after birth, married women who experienced high sexual tension or were attempting to satisfy their husbands started intercourse within three weeks of delivery.

The information from the husbands largely complemented what their wives said. Thirty-one of the 79 men reported a slow decrease of sexual activity beginning at the end of the second or the beginning of the third trimester of pregnancy. They gave no consistent reason aside from fear of harming the fetus. Only five mentioned the displeasing physical appearance of their wives as a reason, although two more mentioned their wives' lack of personal cleanliness as a factor.

Despite the importance of coitus to couple morale it appeared in the Masters and Johnson study (1966) that doctors were not doing a good job explaining their orders for sexual continence to the husbands of the pregnant women. More men whose wives were medically prohibited from intercourse prior to confinement did not understand the reasons, were not sure the doctor had given the order, or wished that the doctor had explained the situation to them as well as to their wives,

than reported understanding the prohibition. And all the husbands expressed concern as to how quickly sexual relations could be reinstituted
after wives gave birth although they did not wish to endanger their
wives' physiological recovery or to create feelings of repugnance. The
prevailing lack of knowledge concerning sexual matters also added to
their difficulties. Despite their high general level of education, they had
no information concerning women's postpartum physical or psychological condition.

## Implications of Pregnancy and Birth for Marital Relations

The pregnancy period and the immediate postbirth period have definite
effects on the marital career, effects that are not always positive. The
discontinuance of the sexual act that symbolizes the unique relation
as well as the cohesiveness of the marital couple removes one powerful
means for fulfilling the couple task of maintaining each other's morale
for the performance of family roles. Its absence can also threaten the
couple's performance of the social control task. To the man who is
used to and enjoys regular coitus, sexual abstinence presents a real
hardship, and he may seek satisfaction outside his marriage. Thus
twelve husbands in the Masters and Johnson (1966) sample sought
extramarital release throughout the continent time, as did an additional
six during the postpartum continent period.

That wives were aware and worried about this problem was shown
by the voiced concern of 68 of the 77 wives whose doctors had prescribed sexual continence. Forty-nine reported making deliberate attempts to satisfy their husbands during this period. Whether or not the
husband seeks relief outside of his marriage, pregnancy can serve to
frustrate his sexual needs and serve as a potential cause for marital
conflict.

Additional evidence of the strain pregnancy places on marriages
appears in the responses of 400 first-time parents. While the couples
engaged in sexual intercourse an average of three times per week at
midpregnancy, in the last month of pregnancy it occurred about once
every other week. There was an associated decline in marital satisfaction during the pregnancy period when the couples compared it
with their memories of the prior period, with the decline being significantly greater for husbands than for wives. During the first month after
the birth of the baby, these couples had intercourse at least once, but
even by the fifth week the predelivery rate was not reached. This rate
of three times a week had been reinstituted only when the infant was
five months old (Meyerowitz and Feldman, 1967).

Because of these facts, Masters and Johnson (1966: 167) strongly urged doctors to approach the problem of coitus during the third trimester of pregnancy and the postpartum period individually. Moreover, they should encourage the desire of wives to engage in intercourse as soon as physically possible after giving birth. For women who seek a longer period of continence, the doctor can attempt to dispel fears and, above all, see to it that there exists some sort of mutual understanding between husband and wife.

Certainly one advantage that today's couples possess in reestablishing sexual relations after pregnancy is effective contraceptives. The addition of family members can be orderly, so the fear of an unplanned pregnancy, "too soon" after the current baby's arrival, need no longer make the resumption of intercourse an unpleasant duty for wives.

Many husbands, however, show increased solicitude toward their pregnant wives, not only in their restraint in engaging in sexual intercourse, but also in their performing more household tasks. Among couples expecting their first child and childless couples who were married during the same period and asked to respond as if they were expecting, Feldman (1971) found that during the pregnancy period husbands helped more than during nonpregnancy periods with physical maintenance responsibilities. The household division of labor is modified with husbands doing more of the "heavy" work. Nurturance also occupies a more prominent place in their role hierarchy. They take care of their wives instead of the customary reverse pattern. Husbands, in fact, were more willing to do household tasks customarily done by women, than wives were to have husbands do them. The couples in which the wives were pregnant were more romantic and at the same time more realistic about possible money problems and lack of ability to cope with parenthood than were childless couples who were asked to imagine themselves as expectant parents.

## HUSBANDS AND WIVES AS FATHERS AND MOTHERS

There have been a number of studies testing LeMaster's thesis (1957) that, though normal and expected, the transition to parenthood constitutes a "crisis" for the marital relation. Particularly among middle-class couples who tend to be concerned about the quality of their marital careers, the parent-child subsystem can compete with the marital subsystem for resources of time, nurturance, and affection giving. The exclusive pair relation that has developed through the courtship and early-married days is disrupted by the baby, forcing a reorganization into a three-person group system. But, as Simmel (1950: 145–169) hypothesized around the turn of the century, triads are inherently unstable, tending to split into a coalition and an isolate. When power is unequally distributed in a triad, small-group laboratory research shows the weakest member in the triad tends to become part of the coalition (Freilich, 1964). As applied to parents with a firstborn, this finding suggests that the child and one parent, usually the maternal caretaker, will be pitted against the other parent thereby destroying the marital subsystem. Bernard Shaw (1913) has expressed such an outcome through one of his characters who says, "There is no reason why a mother should not have male society. What she clearly should not have is a husband."

Whether the data come from Dyer's (1963) convenience sample of 32 middle-class, first-time parental couples, or from Russell's (1974) representative urban sample of 296 couples who became parents for the first time, the parental career does appear to create problems for the marital subsystem. Women particularly are anxious about the potential competition between marital and maternal roles. The women in Dyer's sample specifically mentioned fears of neglecting their husbands because of the demands of the baby. The women Russell studied worried about being emotionally upset and their poor physical appearance, factors probably tied to marital concerns. In both samples, women complained of exhaustion, fatigue and loss of sleep, and inability to keep up with housework. They also worried about being able to be competent mothers while at the same time they resented being tied down.

Men too complained about loss of sleep and about adjusting to new responsibilities and routines. They were also anxious about upset schedules, presumably because of their ignorance of the time and work babies require. In addition, men worried about finances as wives gave up outside employment to care for the new arrival.

Most couples negotiate the transition period when they take on parental roles with no great sense of crisis (Hobbs and Cole, 1976). Those who do seem to have prepared themselves for parenthood are also ready for a change requiring system morphogenesis. Factors that are operative in these cases include the cohesiveness of the marital bond before the child's arrival so that couple morale is high and the child's conception being planned along with having resources to meet attendant financial requirements. Couples who make the transition successfully have also had time to work out mutually satisfactory marital arrangements, since they have been married for some time, at least three years Dyer found. Husband or wife have also taken a preparation for marriage course, so they have some prior knowledge of what impact the baby's arrival will have on their family organization (Dyer, 1963: 198).

Consistent with the evidence that the stronger the marital bond, the higher the morale and the fewer the manifestations of parenthood crisis is a finding of Russell (1972: 40). There was less crisis in her city sample when husbands got up at night with the baby. The concern for the wife's well-being that this activity represents helps to maintain good marital relations while developing the common interest in the child that strengthens rather than splinters the marital bond. And both Dyer (1963) and Russell (1972) found current high marital adjustment related to fewer parenthood difficulties. The causal relation between the two factors is unclear, but Russell's research did suggest that the more time the couple had alone together in the evening, with presumably a focus on conjugal relations, the fewer the parenthood complaints.

These results indicate that the accomplishment of the family development task of morale maintenance in the beginning stage of marriage is linked to how threatening parenthood is to the marital relation. If couples have a communication structure characterized by a way of conversing that results in agreement and the smoothing over of conflict, they are more apt to be effective family planners and to be more satisfied with their marriage (Russell, 1972: 16). Taking pleasure from each other and planning the birth for an optimal period in the couple's relation eases the difficulties of parenthood.

**The Conjugal Role Organization**
The morphogenesis initiated by couples who take on parental roles is particularly pronounced in their division of labor and power patterns. The family development tasks of physical maintenance and socialization loom so large that women often drop out of the labor market to stay home and care for their young infants. A survey of 1300 families from a variety of socioeconomic backgrounds living in Syracuse, New York, in 1967–1968 shows just how much difference children make in housework.[2] It required on an average 6.3 hours a day for husbands and wives with no children, but jumped almost 50 percent to 9.1 mean hours a day for couples with one child (Walker, 1971).

Women continue to carry the overwhelming responsibility for physi-

[2] The survey provided information on the following tasks: (1) all house-care, car, and yard maintenance; (2) all food preparation and meal cleanup work; (3) all clothing care such as washing and ironing; (4) care of family members; and (5) shopping, bill paying, and record keeping.

cal maintenance, whether or not they are employed outside the home and regardless of the women's rights movement. Take the average number of hours per day family members should be physical and other care of each other. When the youngest child was no more than one year of age, the nonemployed wife spent 0.0 hours per day in such work. Her husband spent 0.7 hours in the same activities. Among employed women, the average number of hours wives spent in such activities per day was 2.7, reflecting her commitment outside the home. Although the husbands of these employed women did help more than the husbands of women who were not employed—the help of the former averaging 1.1 hours a day—the additional time did not bring the husband-wife total to the time of couples with nonemployed wives (Walker, 1971).

As household demands and the marital division of labor change with the coming of children, so may the marital power balance. Blood and Wolfe's interviews with a representative sample of wives in the Detroit and surrounding area showed that their husbands' power increased during the childbearing and child-rearing years with declines, however, in later years. Blood and Wolfe interpreted the findings as being due to wives' withdrawal from the labor market and resulting financial dependence on their husbands (Blood and Wolfe, 1960: 43). A survey that obtained data from a representative sample of husbands and wives in Los Angeles also showed husbands' power to be highest during the first four years of marriage (Centers, Raven, and Rodrigues, 1971: 273). This period would cover the initial childbearing years when presumably, women are still getting used to their new responsibilities.

The coming of children, therefore, affects the position of the wife-mother disproportionately. The addition of maternal roles is conventionally associated with the discontinuance of occupational role sequences at least temporarily. Other extrafamilial roles are also curtailed or eliminated as women bear the brunt of child-rearing responsibilities.

## MARITAL SATISFACTION AND THE COMING OF CHILDREN

All changes brought by parenthood in the lives of wives, and to a lesser extent in those of husbands, affect marital satisfaction. Some of the most useful information we have about the coming of children and marital satisfaction is that from Feldman (1971). Using a longitudinal research design, he compared three groups of couples at three different points in time. One group, the primiparas, had their first child during the study's duration. The couples completed questionnaires when the wife was five months pregnant, when the first child was about five weeks old, and when the same child was about five months old. The second group of couples completed questionnaires at the same intervals but had no children. The third group contacted at the same times were having their second child. This ingenious study thus provides comparisons among the childless, those having their first child and those having more than one child. Because the couples in the childless and in the primipara groups had been married on an average the same number of years, the study also permits us to draw some conclusions about the effect of children on the marital relation.

In general, the findings support the parenthood studies just discussed. Couples who had entered the parental career were less satisfied with marriage than they were before the child was born (Feldman, 1971: 116). This decline was not universal, however, so let us examine the varying marital arrangements of new parents who did and did not become less happy with their marital relationship. Couples whose marital satisfaction went up with the arrival of the first child were those characterized by a segregated marital role organization, to use the concept of Bott (1971) discussed earlier in connection with the family's selective maintenance of boundaries.

These couples talked with each other less, turned less often to each other for help, and were less emotional toward the spouse in times of conflict than were new parents who were less satisfied with marriage. The former couples appeared to be less dependent upon each other for satisfaction of affectional needs. The type of marital role organization they possessed is consistent with such an interpretation. Their traditional beliefs that husbands should not perform household tasks supported a segregated type of conjugal organization. The wives also seemed to view motherhood as the fruition of their family careers. They placed high value on such maternal role behaviors as preference for breast feeding, concern about the child's crying, and "being child centered in plans for feeding" (Feldman, 1971: 117). The marital career being of lesser importance, therefore, would compete less with the parental career.

Interestingly enough, however, these same women also viewed children as a means for moving to a less-segregated mode of marital role organization and to one stressing conjugal activities. Their increased marital satisfaction was associated with the expectation that their husbands would help out with nurturant tasks, such as changing diapers, calming the baby when he/she cried, and putting it to sleep as well as caring for the child when the mother was gone.

On the other hand, the wife already in a joint marital arrangement before the birth of the child apparently saw her new maternal roles as interfering with this marital organization. Instead of involving the husband in the family, the baby cut into the time she had to devote to carrying on activities already shared with her husband. Thus marital satisfaction went down.

Both the more-satisfied and less-satisfied wives, therefore, preferred marital interdependency based on shared activities and an affection and communication structure encouraging intimacy. They sought to change the separation of marital roles for performing family developmental tasks that drew them and their husbands apart, whether the separation existed before the baby's arrival or was the result of the neonate's arrival.

Attitudes toward pregnancy as well as type of marital role organization also played a part in marital satisfaction after the baby came. If the wife while pregnant was unhappy about her appearance, felt uncomfortable in public, and compared her present appearance unfavorably with that before pregnancy, she was apt to be happier with her marriage after her delivery. These feelings, which may be associated with problems in sexual relations during pregnancy, presumably would improve after the baby's arrival (Feldman, 1971: 110).

Comparison of the couples having their first child with those couples married the same general time but still without children showed why there was an overall tendency to associate having a baby with lesser marital happiness. New parents had less time for each other. Sexual relations suffered since the wives worried about intercourse and about their husbands being less satisfied.

There were, however, some perceived, positive personality changes associated with parenthood. Husbands seemed less selfish, and wives were less moody, less selfish, and less easily angered in their spouses' views. Husbands, however, also were rated as having a lowered sense of humor and wives more often seemed nervous and unhappy. The wives with five-month-old babies recognized the infants' threat to the marital relation. When speaking of their greater marital happiness before pregnancy, these mothers were unable to express their feelings about the change to their husbands. Conversations were more about the wives' interests, presumably house and child care, but potential conflicts centering on money, husbands' jobs, and the couples' parents also increased. The new parents, as compared with the childless, also put a greater emphasis on emotional and financial security and, to counteract the upsurge of family responsibilities, developed their own interests. The power structure became more asymmetrical among the primiparas, with husbands making more decisions.

That the changes parenthood brings tend to exercise a negative effect on marital satisfaction even after child-care routines are established is suggested by the experience of 112 couples in the metropolitan area of Washington, D.C. Those with a child were less happy after becoming parents than those who remained childless. The mostly middle-class couples who were interviewed after three to four months of marriage and then one to two years later were compared on their marital satisfaction and sense of being loved by their spouses at the two periods. Both husbands and wives who were new parents showed statistically significant greater drops in marital satisfaction, and wives in the sense of being loved, than did couples without children (Ryder, 1973: 605).

### The Second Child
What about the effects of the arrival of the second child on marital satisfaction? One might argue that having had the experience of the first child's coming, couples could minimize possible negative effects of the second child's arrival through initiation of positive feedback processes. Feldman (1971: 120) found, however, when comparing his primipara and multipara groups that "there appeared to be an even greater negative effect for the multipara." The lowered marital satisfaction was associated with a lowering of sexual satisfaction, less satisfaction with the home, perceived negative personality change in spouse, and more conversations having to do with instrumental matters than sentiments and emotions. At the same time, the couples expressed more concern for the child and warmth toward it. Thus the family developmental task accomplishment of morale maintenance was dependent on the parent-child relation since marital intimacy appeared to lessen.

# SUMMARY

The parental career brings satisfaction, but the new roles can displace or eliminate some marital role sequences. Wives, particularly, have less time to devote to marital activities. Even if they expect husbands to be drawn more into the family orbit through sharing parental roles, the role making of this division of labor may not feed back and increase marital intimacy. Husbands, tired from job and parental activities and worried about increased financial problems, can have less energy to devote to wives.

Sexual relations, for example, an important component of the affection structure, seem to be less fulfilling as more children come. Thus many husbands and wives find satisfaction in parental activities with marital intimacy assuming a less central place in family life.


# REFERENCES

Baldwin, Wendy H., "Adolescent Pregnancy and Childbearing—Growing Concerns for Americans," *Population Bulletin*, Vol. 31, No. 2 (Population Reference Bureau Inc., Washington, D.C., 1976).

Blood, Robert O. and Donald M. Wolfe. *Husbands and Wives*. Glencoe, Ill.: Free Press, 1960.

Bott, Elizabeth, *Family and Social Network: Roles, Norms and External Relationships in Ordinary Urban Families*. New York: Free Press, 1971.

Centers, Richard, Bertram H. Raven, and Aroldo Rodrigues. "Conjugal Power Structure: A Re-Examination," *American Sociological Review*, 1971, 36, 264-278.

Dyer, Everett D., "Parenthood as Crisis: A Re-Study," *Marriage and Family Living*, 1963, 25, 196–201.

Feldman, Harold, "The Effects of Children on the Family," in Andrée Michel, ed., *Family Issues of Employed Women in Europe and America*. Leiden: E. G. Brill, 1971, 107–125.

Freedman, Ronald and Lolagene Coombs, "Childspacing and Family Economic Position," *American Sociological Review*, 1966, 631–648.

Freilich, Morris, "The Natural Trends in Kinship and Complex Systems," *American Sociological Review*, 1964, 29, 529–540.

Glick, Paul C., "Updating the Family Life Cycle," *Journal of Marriage and the Family*, 1977, 39, 5–13.

Hill, Reuben and Joan Aldous, "Socialization for Marriage and Parenthood," in David A. Goslin, ed. *Handbook of Socialization Theory and Research*. Chicago: Rand McNally, 1969, 885–950.

Hobbs, Daniel F., Jr.. and Sue Peck Cole, "Transition to Parenthood: A Decade Replication," *Journal of Marriage and the Family*, 1976, 723–731.

LeMasters, E. E., "Parenthood as Crisis," *Marriage and Family Living*, 1957, 19, 352–355.

Masters, William H. and Virginia E. Johnson, *Human Sexual Response*. Boston: Little, Brown, 1966.

Meyerowitz, Joseph H. and Harold Feldman, "Transition to Parenthood," in Irving M. Cohen, ed., *Family Structure, Dynamics and Therapy*. New York: American Psychiatric Association, 1967, 78–84.

Rossi, Alice S., "Transition to Parenthood," *Journal of Marriage and the Family*, 1968, 30, 26–39.

Russell, Candyce S., "Transition to Parenthood: A Restudy," Unpublished master's thesis, University of Minnesota, 1972.

Russell, Candyce S., "Transition to Parenthood: Problems and Gratifications," *Journal of Marriage and the Family*, 1974, 36, 244–303.

Ryder, Robert G., "Longitudinal Data Relating Marriage Satisfaction and Having A Child," *Journal of Marriage and the Family*, 1973, 35, 604–608.

Shaw, G. B., *Getting Married: A Disquisitory Play*. London: Constable, 1913.

Simmel, Georg, "The Triad," in Kurt H. Wolff, ed., *The Sociology of Georg Simmel. New York*: Free Press, 1950, 145–169.

Sorensen, R. C., *Adolescent Sexuality in Contemporary America, Personal Values and Sexual Behavior Ages 13–19*. New York: World, 1973.

Walker, Kathryn E., "ARS Summary Report of Time Used for Household Work." Ithaca, New York: New York State College of Human Ecology, Cornell University, 1971.

# 8

# The marital relation during the child-rearing years

We are fortunate in having findings from longitudinal studies to highlight factors associated with changes in husband-wife relationships during the years when children are present in the household. To provide some estimate of how much of the change occurring is due to the presence of children and how much is due simply to the passage of time, the discussion includes available comparable data from childless couples, along with relevant material drawn from cross-sectional research. Consistent with the assumptions of such studies that couples of different marriage durations will show similar behaviors despite their experiencing different historical events at different points in the family career, we shall examine cross-sectional findings that are less affected by social upheavals or that appear in studies done at different times. In this fashion, we shall attempt to discover trends over the marital career that appear to hold despite differences in the historical time location of couples.

We are less fortunate in the research findings we can draw upon in this and other chapters on family careers in non-middle-class families. Only fairly recently have family scholars gone beyond the walls of their universities to study families other than those of their students. Thus, prior to the early 1970s, we find few, if any, large-scale studies that use samples other than those of white, middle-class couples. Until more research is done with a broader range of families, we are trying, in a sense, to put together a jigsaw puzzle in which many of the key pieces are missing. Indeed, many of them have yet to be cut.

## MARRIAGE ADJUSTMENT IN THE EARLY AND MIDDLE YEARS OF MARRIAGE

Tables 6-1, 6-2, and 6-3, which provide a useful summary of how the middle years of marriage compare with other years on a number of indicators, should be studied carefully. Let us begin our discussion here, however, by examining the course of marital satisfaction as well as various conjugal interaction patterns during the child-rearing years relying on a landmark longitudinal study for our data. In 1939, when they became engaged, 1000 middle-class, predominantly white, couples were first contacted; later, in their early years of marriage, they completed follow-up questionnaires (Burgess and Wallin, 1953). After they had been married from 16 to 20 years, husbands and wives in 400 couples again filled out questionnaires. Attrition in the sample over time was due to broken engagements, divorce, death, refusals, and lost contacts.[1]

The primary finding of this longitudinal study was that over two-thirds of the couples scored lower in marital adjustment during the middle years of marriage than they had when contacted one to five years after the ceremony. In overall terms, this meant that husbands and wives were living less comfortably with one another.[2]

There was a decrease in consensus on such important issues as child rearing, finances, and relations with in-laws among couples scoring lower in marital satisfaction. The couples' power structure became more vertical. Less couple consensus among the less satisfied was accompanied by declines in equality of decision making. Only among

---

[1] The various investigators who have worked with these data do not give a breakdown of the relative contribution of the various causes to sample loss.

[2] Paris and Luckey (1966) studied a sample of 80 middle-class couples who had been identified in their seventh year of marriage as the 40 most-satisfied and 40 least-satisfied couples with marriage. They, too, found a net decline in marital satisfaction among all the couples when they were contacted again during their thirteenth year of marriage.

those couples in which both partners decreased in dominance was marital satisfaction at least sustained, if not enhanced, from the early to the later years of marriage.

But while the less-satisfied couples were diverging in activities and power to more traditional conjugal role arrangements, their ideas as to what should occur in marriage, ironically, were growing less traditional. As compared with the early years of marriage, they were less apt to adhere to the values of husband domination. Because the couples' power structures were at odds with their sense of the way things should be, these structures contributed to lesser marital adjustment.

There were indications of a lower level of morale maintenance accomplishment. Along with the decrease in shared values among the less-satisfied couples went a loss of intimacy, with accompanying "real regrets" and reports of loneliness (Pineo, 1961: 10). Sexual intercourse was less pleasurable for these wives, who, more than wives in satisfactory marriages, became less sexually responsive in terms of frequency of orgasm (Clark and Wallin, 1965: 195). And despite an increase in the number of felt personality needs of the spouses (Pineo, 1961: 3), the number of annoying personality traits they perceived in their partners decreased (Farber and Blackman, 1956: 600). The growing apart of husbands and wives, therefore, was seemingly not due to personality conflicts but to a growing separation on family issues and interests.

The decreased consensus and increased dominance appears to be associated with a change to a segregated marital organization among couples whose marital adjustment declines from the early years of marriage. Interviews with a representative sample of women living in Detroit and nearby rural counties, showed couples who had been married longer tended to be less satisfied, to specialize more in household task performance, and to perform fewer tasks together.

Role specialization on household tasks also carried over to sociability and to communication, as couples with a marital organization based on role segregation along traditional lines were less companionable in leisure activities and conversation (Blood and Wolfe, 1960).

This separation of couple interests begins soon after a child's arrival. Five months after the birth, first-time parents in Feldman's sample were complaining of unshared leisure time and sexual incompatibility. The communication structure reflected the divergence in interests. The spouses no longer felt free to express their feelings and wives complained of being unable to discuss their husbands' work (Meyerowitz and Feldman, 1967). The power structure also became more vertical with husbands increasing in dominance (Feldman, 1971: 120).

## DIVISIVE INTERESTS IN MARITAL CAREERS

What had gone on among these dissatisfied couples in the middle years of marriage to lead them to adopt a segregated role organization? Developments external to the marital subsystem seem to have a part in the decreased overlap of tasks and interests of husbands and wives. In the middle-class, especially, husbands often became immersed in their occupation, leaving wives to specialize in child care and household upkeep. These preoccupations threaten the solidarity of the marital unit. Occupational demands for the middle-class husband eager to get ahead can offer equally as much competition to the marital relation as do children. Husbands, to be successful, must allocate more hours to work concerns leaving fewer for their families, and the role values they accept in order to be successful—using persons as means rather than ends, being competitive and aggressive rather than cooperative and open to suggestions—are counter to the values families need for task accomplishment (Dizard, 1968: 76).

The separation in interests and activities that middle-class couples experience when the husbands are successful in their occupations appears in both the longitudinal (Dizard, 1968: 57) and cross-sectional studies (Blood and Wolfe, 1960) described earlier. The more the husband earned, the less he did around the house, and the more the wife had to take on. The role segregation in activities among the higher income families was also accompanied by greater husband dominance in decision making. At the same time, wives of high income men tended to be less pleased with their husbands' companionship and showed less marital satisfaction.

Let us now examine the analogous process among wives during the child-rearing years. We have already seen from Feldman's longitudinal study of couples having their first child (1971: 117) that wives, because of child-care responsibilities, tended to become more distant from their husbands, with couples having a joint marital role organization prior to their baby's arrival, more often experiencing a drop in marital satisfaction. We shall now compare childless wives with women playing maternal roles for longer periods on our variables of marital role organization and marital adjustment to determine whether it is either the coming of children or the passing of time that leads to decline in marital adjustment.

Blood and Wolfe (1960: 42) found that childless couples in the various stages of the family career engaged in less household task specialization and maintained more equalitarian power structures than couples with children. Childless wives were also more satisfied with their husbands' companionship. Thus these findings suggest less marital role segregation among the childless. But, lest we underestimate the contribution children can make to morale maintenance particularly for women, childless wives were less happy than wives with children during the years of the various child-rearing stages except at the stage when there were children 19 years of age or older. However, number of children does affect marital happiness. Wives having more than three children were less happy than those with fewer children (Blood and Wolfe, 1960). The former mothers appeared too preoccupied with the parental career to enjoy the marital relation, a finding consistent with the argument that children can serve as a divisive force in the marital relation.[3]

When Feldman (1964) compared couples with children living at home in the Syracuse sample with couples married an equivalent number of years who had never had children, his findings were consistent with the trends already discussed. Children appeared to be associated with lesser marital communication and satisfaction. Couples with children, however, placed a higher value on marriage, particularly on the affection-giving values of being needed and being in love as well as having children rather than having financial security or an orderly home, values that probably had something to do with the couples' assuming parental roles.

The childless, in contrast, were more concerned with getting ahead, cultivating their intellectual capacities, and developing their personal interests, all of which are activities that children would disrupt. The childless were also more involved with their parents, perhaps using them as a substitute for children. Conflict and affection giving between spouses of childless marriages was more direct since the absence of children allowed more open expression of feeling. For, spouses admitted both to slapping each other more and to giving more caresses when they had no children. Thus couples with children may have less marital interaction, but their interests center on the family. The childless have more marital satisfaction, but their interests center on personal development.

---

[3] Farber and Blackman (1956) found in their analysis of the Burgess and Wallin longitudinal study data no clear relation between number of children and marital tension. A couple's adjustment at three years of marriage was a better predictor of their role accommodation in terms of personality complaints at fourteen years. "If there is a relation between marital tension and the number of children," they wrote (1956: 601) "apparently it is a curvilinear one" with couples having either no or four or more cihldren showing the most role tension.

Few researchers have measured parents' marital adjustment and related it directly to their feelings for their children and their treatment of them. Porter (1966) did so using a sample of 43 men and 57 women, all middle class and all with children in the six-to-ten age range. His results provide some additional support for the thesis of the competition between the marital and parental subsystems. Individuals scoring in the highest third on his parental acceptance scale scored less high on marital adjustment than did individuals scoring in the middle third on parental acceptance.

These various studies all point up the existence of limited task linkages. The way couples accomplish tasks at earlier stages sets limits on their current level of task accomplishment. When communication channels cease to be two way, then power relations are no longer horizontal, affection giving declines, and activities become separate; and couples cannot easily reverse these trends. The loss of intimacy may be gradual, but to return to closer relationships requires more role making than many couples are willing to undertake. The resocialization process into different marital role-playing styles takes energy and time away from socializing children. Since the task of morale maintenance can be fulfilled through the joys of parenthood, the press to do something about the decline in marital satisfaction may not exist.

**Gender Roles and Marital Unhappiness**
Neither the husbands' occupational preoccupations nor the coming of children are sufficient, alone or together, to account for the lessening of marital satisfaction during the child-rearing years. The historical changes we are now living through put strain on all marriages. Women and men, have different expectations of marriage because of differences in socialization, and these differences are becoming increasingly apparent with the publicity attending the women's movement (Bernard, 1973). These differences tend to be sharper in working-class couples, because position-oriented socialization is more common in this milieu (Rubin, 1976: 125).

Women taught from childhood to be expressive and concerned with others are seeking more companionship in marriage. Rubin found with the working-class wives she talked to that they are rejecting a segregated conjugal role organization for a joint arrangement in which emotions can be shared along with leisure and household activities. No longer content with demonstrations of affection restricted to intercourse in the marriage bed, they want their husbands to talk about their love and to show it in other ways (Rubin, 1976: 120).

Past socialization that emphasizes gender-role distinctions makes it hard for men to fulfill such expectations. Their self-esteem rests on being rational not emotional, active not passive, and achievers not nurturance givers. In talking with Rubin (1976: 128), working-class men expressed their inability to meet their wives' expectations while confessing their concerns about family and job occurrences, concerns they believed unmanly to reveal to wives or buddies.

But men, too, are making demands that stem from the climate of greater sexual freedom and that women feel inadequate to meet. Women have long been socialized to make distinctions between good women who are not particularly interested in sex and the "other kind" who, like men, know all about it. Thus they complained to Rubin about their husbands' need for sex as well as their husbands' expectations that they have orgasms during intercourse, or that they try oral sex (Rubin, 1976: 144).

These changes in gender-role expectations create marital difficulties not only because of conflicting role expectations but because the conflicts reflect underlying power struggles. Thus wives, awakened to their own sexual feelings, want more from their husbands, but men who have used sex as a symbol of domination no longer enjoy it under conditions of equality (Rubin, 1976).

## THE MATCHING OF COUPLES IN DEVELOPMENT

So far, we have seen the declines in marital satisfaction that occur as time goes on among married couples and some of their causes among middle-class and working-class couples alike. The separation of interests and expectations can be due to changing gender roles or to husbands' work concerns and wives' maternal roles. Nelson Foote (1956) relates this conjugal role segregation and lesser marital adjustment by way of the individual developmental task concept. His thesis, already referred to in Chapter 2, is that husbands' and wives' development is unequal, and this mismatching accounts for their growing apart. Marital interaction, however, can be a means for encouraging spouses to try out novel behaviors and different solutions to recurrent problems. The individual development tasks that the partners voluntarily attempt to accomplish, as a consequence of role making, can lead to new self-concepts and increased self-esteem.

Wives' competencies in the roles of confidante and companion, with their heavy components of support giving, listening, and supplying advice, must be acquired by husbands, so they too can encourage their wives to add to their role clusters through expansion of their activities and interests beyond the family circle (Foote, 1956). The resultant mutual development of husbands and wives and their associated joint concerns help prevent their growing apart.

The positive effects of this mutual development on marital adjustment has been documented. Among the couples in their middle years studied longitudinally, for example, working wives perceived themselves as more in agreement with their husbands than nonworking wives. Another of the findings was that wives with husbands heavily committed to occupational matters had less decline in marital adjustment when they increased their organizational activities as compared to wives who decreased theirs (Dizard, 1968: 58).

Something of the marital interaction that goes on in such situations can be grasped from the Detroit cross-sectional data. Role segregation and unequal power structures are less common in working-wives' households. In order for the cooking, cleaning, laundry, and other physical maintenance tasks to get done, husbands have to supplement the activities of their wives, whose extrafamilial roles leave them less time for family duties. Thus the wife's involvement in the community is complemented by her husband's involvement in family affairs. The couple has a joint role organization with shared roles at home and shared concerns outside, and if "role overload" is avoided, marital satisfaction can result from this couple mutuality.

Indirect evidence also comes from Cuber and Harroff's provocative inquiry (1965: 56) into the marriages of middle-aged men and women in prominent positions in economic, educational, and political organizations of the United States. The interview results showed five configurations of marital behavior. Three—the "devitalized," "passive-congenial," and "conflict-habituated"—clearly reflect low levels of marital satisfaction. The "vital" and "total" marital configurations, however, include couples with "exciting mutuality of feelings and participation together in important life segments," the difference between the two configurations lying in the greater number of shared roles in the total relation.

Are marital adjustment and personal growth associated? The argument of Foote that we discussed earlier utilizes the idea of feedback. Mutual support by husbands and wives, which indicates some degree of marital adjustment, can lead to the taking on of individual developmental tasks leading to personal growth. The matching of husband and wife in personal development, in turn, contributes to marital adjustment. The longitudinal study begun by Burgess and Wallin (1953) had some findings specifically relevant to the Foote argument. There were data on husbands' personal growth scores as well as their marital adjustment scores from the early and the middle years of marriage (Dentler and Pineo, 1960: 48). The data suggest marriage had led to better health, new interests, loss of restlessness, increased ambition, better work, and greater happiness. High marital adjustment over the years, as well as increasing adjustment from the early to the later period, were associated with positive personal growth from initial low levels. Forty-four (65 percent) of 68 husbands, who scored low on personal growth in the initial years of marriage but were in highly successful marriages, increased their personal development. And 49 of the 53 husbands in marriages whose adjustment increased from an initially low level experienced positive personal growth. Positive spousal interaction thus seems to encourage personal development.

The converse did not seem to be true. Persons who had high rates of individual development were not apparently able to take on marital adjustment as a task and failed to succeed in raising it when marital adjustment was low early in marriage. While 15 of 49 husbands with initial low marital adjustment but high personal growth scores showed both high marital adjustment and personal growth in the middle years, 16 were found to have lowered their personal growth to the low level of their marital adjustment. Marital adjustment affected personal growth, therefore, more than the reverse. Moreover, loss in marital adjustment was associated with loss in personal growth in 61 percent of the cases. But increases in personal development occurred without any increase in marital adjustment in 63 percent of such cases (Dentler and Pineo, 1960: 48). Thus, personal growth can occur, as we have seen previously in our discussion of maternal and occupational roles, at the expense of marital roles. Within the context of a supportive couple relation, however, mutual personal development can have positive consequences for the marriage.

It is well to stop at this point in our discussion to sum up what we have said and also to specify the argument. A number of cross-sectional studies (Blood and Wolfe, 1960; Burr, 1970; Rollins and Feldman, 1970; Rollins and Cannon, 1974; and Spanier, Lewis and Cole, 1975) and the Burgess and Wallin longitudinal study (1953) have all shown a decrease in marital adjustment over time whether recently married couples and couples in their middle years of marriage are compared, or whether the same couples are compared in their early and middle periods of marriage. There is some evidence that middle-class couples shift from shared interests and household concerns to segregated activities. Occupational and parental demands appear to account for the shift.

Working-class couples, however, do not experience joint marital role organization to such an extent (Rubin, 1976). From the beginning, their marriages have been more often characterized by a segregated task organization in which roles are assigned according to traditional gender norms. It is among middle class women, who are more apt to expect interaction with husbands in many areas (Lopata, 1971: 136), that one finds resentment at competing responsibilities. Thus middle-class wives with organizational and occupational roles outside the home maintained higher levels of marital adjustment (Dizard, 1968). They chose to engage in outside employment in order to share more of the concerns of their occupationally committed husbands. But national surveys show marital strain when women are employed outside the home through economic necessity, which is more often the case with working-class couples. Husbands report increased conflicts and wives perceive less sociable interaction with their husbands (Orden and Bradburn, 1969; Nye, 1975). Apparently, the shared interests husbands and wives can derive from their outside employment make for greater happiness only when wives want to work and work life is of intrinsic interest, conditions generally lacking in the working-class world.

To summarize, the decline in marital satisfaction associated with a change from joint to segregated marital arrangements occurs among person-oriented couples, who have initially at least experimented with role making. Such couples are disproportionately found among the more educated segment of the middle class. The declines in marital adjustment that working-class couples also appear to experience over the child-present years, therefore, do not stem from a loss of shared activities since rarely were they there in the first place to lose. The coming of children for this group serves as a common interest rather than a divisive force, but the additional expenses and responsibilities children bring can also create conflict particularly in couples hard-pressed for funds. In addition, new expectations coming from the current emphasis in the broader society on greater sexual freedom and women's rights exacerbate differences in families of all classes.

## AFTER DIVORCE

We have been examining what goes on in marriages during the children-present stages and noting the decline in marital satisfaction as well as some of the reasons for the decline. An increasing number of couples are not willing to continue the family career under these circumstances. And so they divorce, but do they then live happily ever after, in a state of singlehood or in another marital career?

The information we have indicates that the role transition to the divorced status is rarely an easy one, even when at least one partner has seen divorce as a solution to an impossible interpersonal situation. The problems the newly divorced face reflect and require morphogenesis whether in the dismembered family unit or in the former spouses themselves. One particularly good study on the after-divorce stage is longitudinal in nature and permits comparisons between middle-class intact and divorced parents of children in the same preschool (Hetherington, Cox, and Cox, 1976). The 48 divorced couples and equal number of married couples were roughly matched as to age, education, and length of marriage. As one would suspect, the greatest amount of role making and of unhappiness in the divorced parents appeared in the two months' period after the decree was granted. Men, particularly, who had always depended on wives for their physical maintenance now had to learn to take care of themselves. Those who had been living in a joint rather than in segregated conjugal organizations were better prepared.

Both spouses, however, had difficulty breaking customary interaction patterns despite the lack of the legal bond. Relations with ex-spouses continued to occupy most of their time and energy, and two-thirds of these interchanges were a continuation of previous patterns involving conflicts. Conflicts were particularly bitter over finances, since the ex-couples had to develop new purchasing patterns to spread the same income over two households instead of one. Men attempted to raise their incomes during the first postdivorce years by working more, a difficult strategy since many reported being unable to work effectively due to emotional problems stemming from the divorce (Hetherington, Cox, and Cox, 1976: 422).

But along with the conflicts, old affection patterns too persisted in this transition period. Six of the 48 couples had sexual intercourse during the first two months after the divorce. And 34 of the women and 29 of the men said that their ex-spouses would be the first persons they would call upon in a crisis (Hetherington, Cox, and Cox, 1976: 424).

The societal legitimation and personal sense of security were lacking in these continuing ties, however, so both men and women desperately sought a new intimate relationship. This search was especially hard for women. At two months postdivorce, married friends were still being supportive, but as time went on these contacts declined, and the decline was especially pronounced for women. The divorced mothers felt trapped in a child's world, although this was less true for employed women who had contacts with co-workers. These opportunities for adult sociability they felt distinctly outweighed any problems they had in overloading parental and occupational roles. (There was no report on women going back to work, a stage transition we hypothesized in Chapter 4 for the careers of one-parent families in which the husband-father position is vacant.) And even two years after the divorce, the social life of the divorced women remained less than that of married women.

Divorced men's social activities, were higher at the end of the first year, than during the initial postdivorce period, although their seeking out of others had declined. Unlike women, men did not feel trapped but they did feel at loose ends and under pressure. But like women men found casual sexual contacts failed to meet their need for intimacy which led them initially to seek out sociability contacts. Many men, however, in contrast to few women, were pleased to be able to have sex with a variety of partners.

An overall assessment of the after-divorce stage indicates that men tend to have less difficulty in renewing broken intimacy patterns. Their incomes and occupations as well as lack of child-custody responsibilities enable them to be more active in the search for friends and lovers (Raschke, 1974). And the satisfaction or frustration of this need for intimacy, which they at one time met in the former marriage, appears to be most related to a divorced person's happiness. Remarriage brought as much happiness to these formerly divorced individuals as couples in continuing marriages enjoyed. The remarrieds' self-esteem and sense of competency with the opposite sex, however, continued lower (Hetherington, Cox, and Cox, 1976: 423).

# REFERENCES

Bernard, Jessie, *The Future of Marriage.* New York: Bantam Books, 1973.

Blood, Robert O., Jr. and Donald M. Wolfe, *Husbands and Wives.* New York: Free Press, 1960.

Burgess, Ernest W. and Paul Wallin, *Engagement and Marriage.* Philadelphia: J. B. Lippincott, 1953.

Burr, Wesley, R., "Satisfaction with Various Aspects of Marriage over the Life Cycle," *Journal of Marriage and The Family*, 1970, 32, 29–37.

Clark, Alexander L. and Paul Wallin, "Women's Sexual Responsiveness and the Duration and Quality of their Marriages," *American Journal of Sociology*, 1965, 71, 187–196.

Cuber, John F. and Peggy B. Harroff, *The Significant Americans.* New York: Appleton-Century-Crofts, 1965.

Dentler, Robert A. and Peter Pineo, "Sexual Adjustment, Marital Adjustment and Personal Growth of Husbands: A Panel Analysis," *Marriage and Family Living*, 1960, 22, 45–48.

Dizard, Jan, *Social Change and the Family*. Chicago: University of Chicago Community and Family Study Center, 1968.

Farber, Bernard and Leonard S. Blackman, "Marital Tensions and Number and Sex of Children," *American Sociological Review*, 1956, 21, 596–601.

Feldman, Harold, *Development of the Husband-Wife Relationship*. Ithaca, New York: Cornell University, 1964.

Feldman, Harold, "The Effects of Children on the Family," in Andree Michel, ed., *Family Issues of Employed Women in Europe and America*. Leiden: E. J. Brill, 1971, 104–125.

Foote, Nelson, "Matching of Husband and Wife in Phases of Development," *Transactions of the Third World Congress of Sociology*, London, International Sociological Society, 1956, 24–34.

Hetherington, E. Mavis, Martha Cox, and Roger Cox, "Divorced Fathers," *Family Coordinator*, 1976, 25, 417–428.

Lopata, Helena Z., *Occupation: Housewife*. New York: Oxford University Press, 1971.

Meyerowltz, Joseph H. and Harold Feldman, "Transition to Parenthood," in Irving M. Cohen, ed., *Family Structure, Dynamics and Therapy*. New York: American Psychiatric Association, 1967.

Nye, F. Ivan, "Husband-Wife Relationships," in Lois W. Hoffman and F. Ivan Nye, eds., *Working Mothers: An Evaluative Review of the Consequences for Wife, Husband, and Child*. San Francisco: Jossey-Bass, 1975, 186–206.

Orden, Susan R. and Norman Bradburn, "Working Wives and Marriage Happiness," *American Journal of Sociology*, 1969, 74, 392–407.

Paris, Bethel L. and Eleanore B. Luckey, "A Longitudinal Study in Marital Satisfaction," *Sociology and Social Research*, 1966, 50, 212–222.

Pineo, Peter C., "Disenchantment in the Later Years of Marriage," *Marriage and Family Living*, 1961, 23, 3–11.

Porter, Blaine M., "The Relationship between Marital Adjustment and Parental Acceptance of Children," *Journal of Home Economics*, 1955, 47, 157–164.

Raschke, Helen J., *Social and Psychological Factors in Voluntary Postmarital Dissolution Adjustment*, Unpublished doctoral dissertation, Minneapolis: University of Minnesota, 1974.

Rollins, Boyd C. and Kenneth L. Cannon, "Marital Satisfaction over the Family Life Cycle: A Reevaluation," *Journal of Marriage and the Family*, 1974, 36, 271–282.

Rollins, Boyd C. and Harold Feldman, "Marital Satisfaction over the Family Life Cycle," *Journal of Marriage and the Family*, 1970, 32, 20–27.

Rubin, Lillian B., *Worlds of Pain: Life in the Working-Class Family*. New York: Basic Books, 1976.

Spanier, Graham B., Robert A. Lewis, and Charles L. Cole, "Marital Adjustment over the Family Life Cycle: The Issue of Curvilinearity," *Journal of Marriage and the Family*, 1975, 37, 263–275.

# The return to the couple relationship

What kind of a critical role transition point is it for husbands and wives when children have left home and they are alone again for the first time in twenty to twenty-five years? It is certainly a normal, expectable event, this postparental period. The postparental label for this period, although misleading—since parent-child relations continue even when children are no longer in residence—does point up the return to "couple blessedness." Parental roles are lost or changed in content and marital interaction patterns again assume importance because children no longer participate in day-to-day family activities. This 12-to-14-year period after the last child leaves and before the occupational retirement or death of one of the spouses is a relatively new period in the family life cycle as Table 4-1 clearly shows. Not only is this period a fairly new one, but lay people and social scientists alike often view it negatively.

These judgments usually center on the changes affecting the wife-mother position. The incumbent of this position supposedly loses a major segment of her role cluster, since she no longer has children at home to nurture. Coupled with this loss of roles is the physiological climacteric marking the end of the woman's capacity to bear children. Outsiders are prone to characterize these events as losses, because maternal roles and the capacity to give birth are seen as central to women's self-identity.

To a lesser extent, students of the period after children leave home see men as undergoing strain. Men, too, are experiencing role change. The impetus for change, however, comes not from family change but from occupational realities. Men are having to accept their present job as the farthest point they are likely to attain on the job trajectory, since promotions or job changes generally go to younger men. Physiological signs of aging also add to men's realization that they no longer have the time, ability, or opportunity to accomplish all they had once planned.

These losses and limitations, whether they affect both or only one spouse, are reflected in a couple's interaction patterns since husband and wife constitute an interdependent interaction unit. They come at a time when husbands and wives, as we have already seen, no longer find so much happiness in being married as they did in the initial stage. Thus couples seem to have good reasons for viewing this period with misgivings.

Since the children's leaving home is a normal turning point in family life, however, it can be prepared for. Although there may be a period of floundering while new behaviors are tried, morphogenesis does occur. With children gone, wives working, and husbands often at the peak of their earning power, couples have financial resources to take advantage of their fewer responsibilities. The tensions that arise when couples no longer are protected by parental roles from interacting as husband and wife can be assuaged by excursions and trips formerly prevented by lack of finances. Sexual relations can become more care-free as the need for contraceptives is gone. Thus the discontinuities in behavior, which the departure of children brings, can result in couples developing more mutually satisfactory relations.

## MARITAL SATISFACTION IN THE MIDDLE YEARS

Longitudinal studies on the period after the children leave are lacking, and the few cross-sectional studies available are often based on small, unrepresentative samples. They do provide us with some evidence for judging the quality of postparental marital life and the factors relating to it.

Increasingly, the findings reveal that the negative side of the period has been overemphasized. Deutscher (1964) was one of the first re-searchers to challenge the prevailing notion that loss of children leads to loss of zest for life. In a study devoted specifically to the postparental period, he found that 22 of the 49 spouses he interviewed defined the stage as "better" than previous stages. As might be expected, given the more drastic change in the role clusters of women, three of the 28 women but none of the 21 men he questioned perceived the post-parental period as "worse" than the preceding family stages.

There was also some tendency for the less well-off in these middle-class samples to define the situation in neutral rather than in positive terms. But the findings generally did not support the thesis that men or women generally perceive the period after the children leave home as difficult. It should be noted, however, that members asked by out-siders to evaluate family matters are apt to give socially desirable answers. For this reason the figures representing those persons who perceive the postchildren era as worse than the previous stages are probably low.

Despite this weakness of the research, Deutscher developed a num-ber of different hypotheses to guide his research, which are well worth summarizing, since they shed light on why couples may not view the stage negatively. One hypothesis postulated a positive relation between satisfaction with the stage and the degree of continuity in role se-quences persons experienced from previous stages. Deutscher was concerned with how much anticipatory socialization or role rehearsal for the children's departure had occurred while the children were still at home. In Deutscher's middle-class sample, however, so many role sequences carried over from the children-present period to the children-absent period that it was impossible to test the hypotheses. The tempo-rary absences of children in college or the armed forces and the occupations that take parents from home are all occasions for indi-viduals to play roles that continue after children leave home for good.

Deutscher (1959) specifically examined the content of these roles, since in a second hypothesis he stated that a positive relation exists between involvement in nonparental roles and satisfaction with the postparental stage. Roles having to do with housekeeping, occupa-tions, voluntary organizations, leisure time, and sociability—in spite of some changes in content—constituted continuing sequences. Women were more caught up than men in roles involving interpersonal skills such as attending informal gatherings, church, and other organizational activities; being grandparents; and caring for aged parents. Men, how-ever, were disproportionately concerned with job roles, hobbies, and weekend recreation (Deutscher, 1959: 30, Table XVI). The more such activities his respondents engaged in, Deutscher discovered (1959: 107, Table XVI), the more positive their evaluation of the postparental period, a finding that substantiated his hypothesis.

Deutscher's final hypothesis (1959: 109) is tied directly to the Dizard thesis of the importance of a joint conjugal relation for marital happiness, which we discussed in the previous chapter. This hypothesis states that couples engaging in mutual activities will define the postparental years more favorably than couples who do not. He found that people more often engaged as couples in weekend recreational activities, in work around the house and yard, and in attending plays and musical events. But organizational activities, informal gatherings, and grandparenting generally remained solo activities. Religious and relaxation roles were about equally divided between solo and joint performances among the couples.

Of the 31 couples of which both spouses were interviewed, 12 reported getting along better since the children had left home. Only three of the remaining 11 perceived a loss in marital satisfaction with their children's leaving. The remaining eight sometimes got along well and sometimes did not, just as in the past. The number of mutual activities, however, was not related to a respondent's judgments of the quality of his or her married life. The understanding and sympathy associated with marriage adjustment could exist even if spouses engaged in separate activities (Deutscher, 1959: 120). These findings, contrary to those reported by Dizard (1968), suggest that by the time children leave, a sense of mutual understanding can compensate for a lack of shared activities. The difference in findings from the two studies may be due to the differences in the socioeconomic composition of the samples. The Dizard sample was composed of upper-middle-class couples of which both spouses placed high value on shared interests and activities. The Deutscher sample, however, also included lower-middle-class couples. They, like working-class couples, may find shared values on household routines and parental and marital roles sufficient to support marital solidarity. After all, Dizard's disenchanted couples appeared to have lost both mutual understanding and activities.

Let us now summarize quickly the research on marital satisfaction after children leave home before focusing on factors related to greater or lesser satisfaction. On the basis of their representative sample from Detroit and an adjoining rural area, Blood and Wolfe (1960: 160, Table 70) state that after the children left, wives' satisfaction with their husbands' companionship was somewhat higher than among wives in the stages with adolescents, or with children over 19 and still at home.

This is an important finding since the women sampled ranked companionship with their husbands as most important in marriage. Satisfaction with love and the marriage did not, however, show an upturn (Blood and Wolfe, 1960; 232 and 265). More recent studies (Rollins and Cannon, 1974; Spanier, Lewis, and Cole, 1975) with cross-sectional samples also suggest that less marital role tension occurs when children are gone as compared with earlier years when children are present. Couples tend to make fewer complaints about each other's personality traits. They have come to see them if not to accept them as part of the predictable aspects of marriage.

## Extrafamilial Factors in Marital Satisfaction

Kin contacts and more disposable income appear to ease the transition to the period when couples are again alone. In one study, whether or not parental roles were particularly important in the spouses' role clusters did not differentiate marital satisfaction in the postchild periods among the working- and middle-class couples (Saunders, 1969: 189). This is a particularly interesting finding since the lives of working-class women, you will remember, tend to be centered on parental roles. Apparently, however, working-class women were happier when they saw children and other relatives often, a finding consistent with the presumed salience of parent roles for them. In contrast, middle-class women were less happy when they had many kin contacts. While such contacts provide leisure time and sociability activities for the working-class women, they meant burdensome requests for help to middle-class women with their wider involvements outside the family.

Working-class couples, particularly the men, more often perceived the postparental period as satisfactory in comparison with earlier periods than did middle-class couples. The relatively greater financial resources the working-class couples could now devote to satisfying consumption desires probably accounts for the class difference, an explanation consistent with the decline in working-class couples' satisfaction caused by the financial burdens of child rearing. Because of higher incomes all along, middle-class couples presumably do not experience such an upgrading in level of living (Saunders, 1969: 190).

## Communication Patterns

Let us now examine the marital relation itself. Communication patterns should be related to definition of the postparental period, since the mutual understanding, which is presumably founded on "switchboard" communication patterns, seems to contribute to heightened satisfaction. It appears, however, that the kind and amount of communication must be specified. Only among the middle-class husbands of the previous sample (Saunders, 1969), was the amount of talking to wives related to more satisfaction, and middle class husbands, although not working class husbands, clearly were less happy the more their wives talked with them (Saunders, 1974).

The content of the communication appeared to be critical. Middle-class husbands and working-class wives and husbands were happier the more information they gave about themselves in their conversations. Middle-class wives were less happy the more they disclosed. The reason for this latter finding may lie in the negative relation between middle-class husbands' happiness with the period and the amount of their spouses' self-disclosure. The husbands, apparently, made their wives aware of their dissatisfaction with such communications.

The relation of communication to a favorable definition of the middle years period can be farther specified by examining spousal understanding or empathy. Regardless of class, wives whose husbands had high empathy with them—as measured by predicting accurately how their wives perceived their own personality characteristics and felt about marital interaction matters—were happier with the period than were wives whose husbands had low empathy. But, the more empathetic wives were with their husbands, the less their own satisfaction (Saunders, 1974).

This finding may be explained by data from the in-depth interviews with the 27 men and 27 women from middle-class and working-class backgrounds. Here the women were shown to be twice as likely to give negative as positive appraisals of their husbands. Husbands, however, were twice as likely to give positive as negative appraisals of their wives. Empathetic wives appear to see more clearly areas of disagreement, although they do not try to modify them (Saunders, 1969).

The conclusion seems to be that communication patterns can be good for marriage if the channels are not overloaded with messages disagreeable to the receiver, and the channels are two-way. Under these circumstances, the understanding is mutual, and both spouses feel the other is at least willing to listen. This seems to be particularly important for wives, perhaps because of the greater discontinuity in roles and role content from the previous period.

### Sexual Relations and Marital Happiness

Popular belief has it that the stage when children have left home is a danger period for husbands. Suddenly aware of waning physiological capacities and the approach of old age, husbands are supposed to seek sex partners outside of marriage to reassure themselves that they are still attractive. Johnson (1968; 1970), one of the few researchers to investigate extramarital involvement, found that at least 12 (25 percent) of his 48 postparental husbands as compared with 8 (14 percent) of his 49 husbands with children about to leave home, had been involved[*] in such affairs. (One-tenth of the wives in both periods gave questionnaire responses indicating experiences). However, when the intervening variable of opportunity for such affairs was added to the analysis, a somewhat different picture appeared. More men (40 percent) in the middle stage than in the previous stage (27 percent) were involved. The proportion of women in the two periods was about the same— 25 percent in the children leaving home period and 29 percent in the middle-years period. Thus men, as compared with women, and men in the middle years of marriage as compared with men whose children are leaving home, seem more vulnerable to extramarital involvement.

The gender difference is further supported by data based on responses to a question concerning desire for having extramarital affairs. While only six percent of the postparental wives and three percent of launching wives expressed an interest in such affairs, one-half the postparental husbands and 46 percent of the launching husbands responded positively (Johnson, 1968: 150). In this sample, therefore, husbands in both periods were equally likely to express a hypothetical interest in having an extramarital affair, but, confirming popular belief, husbands in the middle years of marriage were more likely to take advantage of their opportunities.

The factors related to having extramarital affairs were ones common sense would suggest. Husbands having affairs had lower marital adjustment scores and received less sexual satisfaction in their marriages than did husbands who did not. (The differences were statistically significant.) Wives taking lovers were not clearly differentiated from other wives on these factors (Johnson, 1968: 225).

In spite of evidence confirming the belief that some men old enough to have adult children turn to outsiders for sexual satisfaction, what about intercourse within marriage? To answer this question, let us turn again to the definitive work of Masters and Johnson (1966) for information. They note the Victorian judgment that middle-aged or older women should not be interested in sexual intercourse. From their study of the sexual responses of menopausal and postmenopausal women, they concluded that "the aging human female is fully capable of sexual performance at orgasmic response levels, particularly if she is exposed to regularity of effective sexual stimulation" (Masters and Johnson, 1966: 245).

Supplemental interview data with 152 women, all over 50 years of age, amplify this conclusion. Endocrine changes resulting from natural or surgical causes did not result in any uniform pattern relating to the loss of sex hormones (steroid hormones). Clinical symptoms of menopausal difficulties vary among women. Emotional difficulties such as lack of a sense of well-being and physical discomforts exacerbate or reactivate previous psychological difficulties of sexual origin. Women who have not enjoyed satisfying sexual activity in the past may well see coitus in postmenopausal years as repugnant (Masters and Johnson, 1966: 245), but this is another example of selective linkage between past and present levels of task accomplishment behaviors, in this case that of morale maintenance. Many women who came to maturity before the age of effective contraceptives, or who are unable to use them for religious or financial reasons, welcome the menopause. This is true of one-half of Neugarten's (1970: 244) sample of 100 middle- and working-class women between the ages of 43 and 53. They developed renewed interest in their physical appearance and sexual relations with their husbands. These women, when added to those seeking pregnancy because of fear of loss of procreative capacity, account for the increased sexual activity during the late forties and early fifties, as observers have often found. (See Neugarten, 1970.)

Masters and Johnson (1966: 245) note that the absence of children, which usually coincides with menopause, removes exhausting physical and mental responsibilities from women. The resulting energy reserves can be devoted to sexual activity to the benefit of marital satisfaction. This is particularly true when couples enjoy financial security and, above all, when wives have good relations with their husbands. If there is continued sexual intercourse within the context of a happy marriage, women do not decline in frequency or interest in sexual relations.

For males too, consistency of active sexual activity is the most important factor in the maintenance of effective sexuality. This is true even though there is a "sharp upturn" in sexual inadequacy among men over 50 years of age. Men experiencing a loss of sexual responsiveness report being affected by one or more of the following: (1) boredom with the regular sexual partner; (2) preoccupation with occupational matters; (3) mental or physical fatigue; (4) overindulgence in food or drink; (5) physical and mental infirmities of self or spouse; and (6) fear of performance resulting from any of the other categories (Masters and Johnson, 1966: 262–264).

Categories one and five help explain an older man's interest in extramarital affairs. Impotence resulting from excessive use of alcohol may also lead a man to new sexual partners. If he refrains from drinking excessively, he may well be effective with his new partner. This can add to marital problems. A man may have confidence in his sexual performance with others but be impotent with his wife. Fear of failure may also threaten the regularity of intercourse, with men expressing a lack of interest and women feeling rejected. The understanding and cooperation of both spouses, therefore, is necessary to maintain the regular sexual relations among the middle-aged necessary to preserve an important area of couple mutuality (Masters and Johnson, 1966: 268).

## THE POSTPARENTAL MARITAL YEARS IN PERSPECTIVE

The discussion of this period began with the reasons it is often viewed with alarm among social scientists and lay people alike. The research evidence is more hopeful. Certainly, when couples are specifically asked to compare the present with the past, they do not admit to its being worse. For lower income couples, the period may be the first since the birth of children when they are free of family responsibilities and have the financial resources to enjoy their freedom.

For wives in general, who are presumably more jeopardized by the loss of children in residence than are husbands, this period can be a good one. Menopausal problems are customarily taken in stride, and sexual relations can be even better than in the past. Children continue to be a source of pride and interest (Lowenthal and Chiriboga, 1972: 13), but are no longer associated with the burdens of socialization and physical care. In addition, the loss of child-care roles, even when there is no compensatory gain in community, in occupational, or in marital and kin roles, does not necessarily lead to unhappiness. Neugarten (1970: 83), for example, found life satisfaction uncorrelated with role-change patterns in her sample of middle-aged women. The loss of child-care roles, like physiological changes, are expected events in the family and individual life cycle. In addition, there is no abrupt termination either of roles or of endocrine functions. Being expected, gradual, and normal, these changes can be anticipated and planned for by women. As a result, women as well as men do not necessarily view the leaving of their children as a negative turning point in their lives.

But what about the marital relation? The cross-sectional studies summarized earlier do not always agree, but there is some suggestion that marital satisfaction increases at this time. Couples who do stay together might well be characterized by Feldman's description (1964:

141–142) of postparental partners in his cross-sectional study. "They place the highest values on the conjugal factors in marriage, calmness and companionship," he writes, "and a low value on the more romantic affective factors, indicating that they have come to terms with their marriage as a companionate, more sedentary venture." None of the findings we have reviewed, however, suggest that this companionship is necessarily based on shared activities. The spousal encouragement necessary for the individual to take on new developmental tasks that result in mutual growth seems to be absent. Communication, we have seen, is good as long as it does not reveal irreconcilable differences. Spousal empathy with one's beliefs, however, is important.

The kind of companionship that appears important for couples at this period is one based on shared expectations and values with respect to marital roles. This "normative companionship," as Edgell (1972) calls it, reassures husband and wife that the social reality of perspectives and meanings they have constructed is validated. They are in agreement on what is important in life, how to interpret events, and how one should behave in everyday situations. They can count on one another's behavior to provide the routine order that makes living predictable. The couples are companionable, because they share and maintain together a set of consistent definitions of reality (Berger and Kellner, 1964: 3–4).

An assessment of marital relations after the children leave on the basis of present research indicates that they are more positive than popular belief would predict. There is great continuity with what went on before in the marriage. But this very continuity in the marital career, Saunders suggests (1969: 207), may constitute a tragedy. The limits on family developmental task accomplishment at this stage, which are set by the arrangements of earlier stages, appear to be too narrow to permit a drastic break with the past and construction of a new organization. Too many couples fail to make use of their newly available resources of time and money to take a hard look at personal and marital goals and to fashion roles that are more satisfactory to them as individuals and as couples.

# REFERENCES

Berger, Peter and Hansfried Kellner, "Marriage and the Construction of Reality," *Diogenes*, 1964, 46, 1–24.

Blood, Robert O. and Donald M. Wolfe, *Husbands and Wives: The Dynamics of Married Living*. Glencoe, Ill.: Free Press, 1960.

Deutscher, Irwin, *Married Life in the Middle Years.* Kansas City: Community Studies, 1959.

Deutscher, Irwin, "The Quality of Postparental Life: Definitions of the Situation," *Journal of Marriage and the Family*, 1964, 26, 52–59.

Dizard, Jan, *Social Change and the Family.* Chicago: University of Chicago Community and Family Study Center, 1968.

Edgell, Stephen, "Marriage and the Concept of Companionship," *British Journal of Sociology*, 1972, 23, 452–461.

Feldman, Harold, *Development of the Husband-Wife Relationship.* Ithaca, New York: Department of Child Development and Family Relationships, Cornell University, 1964.

Johnson, Ralph E., Jr. "Extramarital Sexual Intercourse: A Methodological Note," *Journal of Marriage and the Family*, 1970, 32, 279–282.

Johnson, Ralph E. Jr. *Marital Patterns During the Middle Years.* Unpublished doctoral dissertation, Minneapolis: University of Minnesota, 1968.

Lowenthal, Marjorie F. and David Chiriboga, "Transition to the Empty Nest: Crisis, Challenge, or Relief?" *Archives of General Psychiatry*, 1972, 26, 8–14.

Masters, William H. and Virginia E. Johnson, *Human Sexual Response*, Boston: Little, Brown, 1966.

Neugarten, Bernice L., "Dynamics of Transition of Middle Age to Old Age," *Journal of Geriatric Psychology*, 1970, 4, 71–87.

Rollins, Boyd C. and Kenneth L. Cannon, "Marital Satisfaction over the Family Life Cycle: A Reevaluation," *Journal of Marriage and the Family*, 1974, 36, 271–283.

Saunders, LaVell E., "Empathy, Communication, and the Definition of Life Satisfaction in the Postparental Period," *Family Perspective*, 1974, 8, 21–35.

Saunders, LaVell E., *Social Class and the Postparental Perspective.* Unpublished doctoral dissertation, University of Minnesota, 1969.

Spanier, Graham B., Robert A. Lewis, and Charles L. Cole, "Marital Adjustment over the Family Life Cycle. The Issue of Curvilinearity," *Journal of Marriage, and the Family*, 1975, 37, 263–275.

# 10

# The aging couple and the need for companionship

The retirement of one or both spouses from the labor market creates enough of a change in the content of the role clusters of the husband-father and wife-mother positions to constitute a new phase in family life. Changes in the individual that are brought on by aging are symbolized by retirement, which in turn affects his or her functioning in the family and brings about morphogenesis in the couple's interaction patterns. Associations with persons and groups beyond the family boundaries that affect couple relations also change. Retirement thus serves to mark the beginning of the final phase of the family life cycle. Couples who have managed to stay together to this point must face the eventual separation that death will bring. Let us begin our discussion of the aging family with an examination of the changes that retirement reflects and causes.[1]

The first such change has to do with time and its use. The family member who has retired from his or her occupational role automatically has a large block of time now open for other activities. In one survey, there was an increase in the percentage of men reporting leisure time on weekdays from 62 percent among men 45–64 years old to 81 percent among men 65 and over (Riley and Foner,

[1] In the United States, social security payments for males begin at 65, and the proportion of persons gainfully employed beyond this age is decreasing. A third (33.1 percent) of men older than 65 were gainfully employed in 1960, and the 1975 figure is 21.7 percent. Among women, the comparable figures are 10.8 percent in 1960 and 8.3 percent in 1975 (U.S. Bureau of the Census, 1976b: 30–31, Table 18).

1968: 513, Exhibit 17-1) A similar trend appears among women, with 65 percent of women 45–64 years of age having weekday leisure compared to 80 percent among older women.

Much of this free time occurs in the setting of the home, a setting that for men may be devoid of roles associated with a sense of accomplishment or of meaningful expenditure of effort. Moreover, on-the-job friendships are no longer present to fill the gap. The change in time resources is expressed in the following comments of Englishmen about to retire. "I'll miss the fellows at work and the company. I'll be a bit lonely with just the wife and I here," or "I've always sort of preferred men's company, no disrespect to my wife or anything like that" (Crawford, 1971: 259).

Another sharp change has to do with the smaller income available to fulfill physical maintenance tasks and to permit experimenting with new or expanded activities. Pensions resulting from past employment replace the wages received in exchange for labor. Analysis of the mean income in constant dollars of one cohort over time indicates that it drops 15 percent between ages 55–64 and 65–74 (Riley and Foner, 1968: 82). And 18 percent of persons 65 years of age or older had incomes below the poverty line in 1976 (U.S. Senate, 1976).

Death is also more immediately a prospect. There are gender differences in the age at death. Women tend to marry men older than themselves, and men have higher mortality rates.[2] While married men lose their peers through death, married women become widows. Thus 79 percent of men over 65 but only 48 percent of women of comparable age are living with a spouse (U.S. Department of Health, Education, and Welfare, 1975a).

The residential patterns of the elderly, however, remain relatively stable. Elderly couples are less likely than those without spouses to live with children (Riley and Foner, 1968: 170) and are apt to live in the same house they occupied in earlier years of the family life cycle.[3] As a consequence, they tend to have more housing space as measured by rooms per person,[4] although property taxes can add to financial worries.

[2] At 65, men on the average can expect 13.5 more years of living, women 17.5 more years (U.S. Department of Health, Education, and Welfare, 1975b: 9, Table 2; 11, Table, 3).

[3] One fifth of those over 65 in 1975 had moved within the last five years, as compared with 72 percent of those 25 to 29 years of age (U.S. Bureau of the Census, 1975: 6, Table 1).

[4] When children begin leaving home, the proportion of housing units having two or more rooms per persons starts to increase. By age of household head, this proportion

The physiological capacities of the retired continue to follow the trends that are associated with the onset of middle age. Along with decreases in visual and auditory acuity, go decreases in muscular strength. And the percentage of persons reporting having to give up some activities for health reasons increased from 55 percent of those 65 to 69 to 71 percent of those 75 to 79 (Riley and Foner, 1968: Exhibit 6–18). The elderly's greater probability of being in poor health also exacerbates their financial situation. In 1975, the average personal health care bill for persons over age 65 ($1360) was almost four times greater than that for persons under age 65 ($375). (Cooper and McGee, 1971). Public funds, mainly Medicare and Medicaid, paid only two-thirds of the personal health care expenses of the aged in 1975 (U.S. Department of Agriculture, 1976: 17–19).

The physiological balance sheet, however, is not completely in the red. Longitudinal studies of persons over 60 indicate increases in vocabulary, verbal ability, and general information as a result of age. These increases can compensate for a decline in cognitive abilities (Riley and Foner, 1968: 257). Because the present-day elderly were less well educated than younger age cohorts, however, they still appear less wise in comparison to the young than do the elderly in countries where educational opportunities have not increased substantially in the last decades.[5]

When one looks at personality dimensions, the elderly appear to be more careful as well as to be more willing to accommodate to demands of others than younger persons. At the same time, they tend to be introverted rather than extroverted and concerned with their own physical functions and emotions (Riley and Foner, 1968: 278–279). Some of this latter feeling appears in the written comments of a seventy-one-year-old man. "I have finally been fed up with trying to get along with other people's idiosyncracies and have decided it is now their turn to get along, if possible, with some of mine. What's the use of wasting breath saying anything except what you really think?" But if older people are less concerned with achievement values and currying favors,

---

increases from 22 percent among those aged 35 to 44, to 46 percent among those aged 45 to 54, to 83 percent among heads over 65 (Riley and Foner, 1968: Exhibit 6–11).

[5] In 1975, the percentage of persons having eight years or less of schooling among persons 25–29 was 5.8. Among those over 75, it was 59.0 percent. Comparable estimates for those completing high school was 52.7 percent among the younger group and 27.7 percent among the elderly (U.S. Bureau of the Census, 1976a: 9, Table 1).

they do stress the possession of personal qualities like honesty, loyalty, dependability, and religiousness as having to do with goodness in terms of morality (Riley and Foner, 1968. 299).

These personality characteristics are understandable when one examines the retired person's situation. He or she has less energy and finances with which to make good on mistakes, while the increasing threats that old age presents to his or her personal well-being explain the preoccupation with self. Also, the loss of spouses, friends, and kin makes the old person more dependent on the good will of the remaining associates. Thus she or he may give in to another's wishes to avoid conflict or to be free of an issue that seems pointless.

It should be noted, however, that many of the characteristics of the elderly are those advocated by youths seeking a more humanistic society. The elderly are less concerned with making money and manipulating others and more concerned with loving relationships, relaxation, and conservation (Clark and Anderson, 1967: 433). Along with the young, they constitute our largest group of leisure consumers and so can serve as examplars for a people faced with increasing amounts of spare time.

There are class differences, however, in the way people face retirement. In a British study (Crawford, 1971) of 99 couples of which the men were retiring, the middle-class couples proved to be more negative about changes caused by the husbands' loss of occupational roles than did the working-class couples. The work careers of middle-class men generally are more satisfying than those of working-class men in terms of prestige, conditions of employment, and intrinsic interest. The formers' self-identity is more bound up in their occupations, and they have more to lose in retirement. Working-class men are relieved to be quit of the same old routine despite the loss of workmates. Thus only 20 percent of the lower status men and 46 percent of their wives mentioned some unpleasant aspect of retirement when interviewed as compared with 81 percent of the higher status husbands and 93 percent of their wives (Crawford, 1971: 267). The working-class couples were understandably more worried about their loss of income than were the more affluent middle-class couples. Middle-class couples, however, perceived retired men as having no meaningful place in society and so lacking something to do (Crawford, 1971: 268).

As a number of studies have shown (Thompson, 1973; and Streib and Schneider, 1971), it is not necessarily the loss of the worker role that leads to a loss of morale. The retired tend to be less satisfied than the employed because they are older, less able to care for themselves, see themselves as less healthy, and are less well off financially. When the elderly are in good health and have an adequate income, retirement years can be good ones. The rest of this chapter will be devoted to an examination of how the marital relation can contribute to such an outcome.

## MARITAL SATISFACTION IN THE AGING YEARS

When one looks at marital happiness over the family existence, one might speculate that it would be higher in the aging years. Husbands and wives can look to each other for support in the face of an uncertain future. The concept of limited linkage, however, suggests a contrary view. Couples whose interaction brought little satisfaction in previous marital stages are not likely to experience a sudden upsurge in happiness, particularly given the changes in income, physical competencies, and daily activities retirement symbolizes.

Until we have data from longitudinal studies in which the same cohort of couples are followed over their marital careers, it is difficult to give a definitive answer to the question of the marital happiness of elderly couples in comparison with earlier years. The weight of the present evidence shown in Tables 6-1, 6-2, and 6-3 and summarized in Figure 10-1 indicates that elderly couples more often express sentiments of higher marital satisfaction than do couples in the children-present period although, perhaps, somewhat less than couples in the middle years.

On the basis of questionnaires from both spouses in 50 couples of which the wife was over 65 and the children were all gone, Feldman (1965: 143) supports this view. His representative sample of urban middle- and upper-class neighborhoods indicates the "outstanding characteristic" of the elderly group to be the "general feeling of peacefulness and satisfaction with marriage," as compared with that of couples in earlier stages of the family lifetime. Only the early married couples were higher in marital satisfaction, and the elderly were highest of all groups in their satisfaction with the marital career over time. Other studies (Rollins and Cannon, 1974; and Spanier, Lewis, and Cole, 1975), with samples from a broader class range, have also reported modest upturns in marital satisfaction among aging couples, sometimes even as compared with those in the middle years.

Figure 10-1.   Husbands' and Wives' Marital Satisfaction over the Family Career

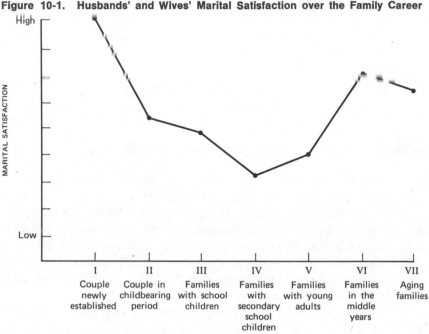

Source: Derived from Blood and Wolfe, 1960; Rollins and Cannon, 1974; Pineo, 1961; and Spanier, Lewis, and Cole, 1975.

## Household Role Allocation

In examining in some detail the dynamics of marital interaction among the aged, one can well begin with changes in family roles. The impact of loss of job activities from the individual's role cluster is greater among men than among women in the present group of aged. Women were less likely to be employed outside the home, and even when employed centered their concerns on the home. As a result, they have more existing role sequences, because their household maintenance activities continue. Men are under greater pressure to modify their self-conception based on the instrumental role of being a good provider or a competent workman to one centered more on family life. If they engage in more activities about the house, the gender-based ascribed differentiation of marital roles between the male's provider responsibilities and the female's homemaking duties necessarily break down.

Unless men's self-conceptions depart from ascribed masculine characteristics, their retirement is a period largely devoid of meaning. That marital role conceptions are related to the morale of older men is shown in the reports of 100 retired couples. The investigator, Lipman

(1960), hypothesized that the men would have had to redefine their view of their social function and marital roles in order to adjust to retirement. The husbands and wives, all over 60, when interviewed separately as to the "most important quality of a good husband" of that age, gave the following categories of responses: (1) shows love, and understanding; (2) is compatible and a good companion; (3) helps wife; and (4) is a good economic provider. The first two categories contained over half the responses of both men and women. They saw older men as possessing primarily expressive roles involving the bestowal of emotional support rather than instrumental roles. Choosing to concentrate on companionship roles as developmental tasks for men, moreover, was associated with higher morale. Those few men who chose the economic provider role as being most important to them were twice as likely to report low morale as men whose responses fell in the other categories (Lipman, 1960: 479). The men still choosing the economic provider role were ignoring the objective reality of their loss of the wage-earner role and avoiding role-making substitute activities.

The discrepancy in matching of individual development (referred to in Chapter 5) during the retirement period can find husbands in the disadvantaged position insofar as things to do are concerned. Although 78 percent of the men and 91 percent of the women reported having plenty to do, almost twice as many men (29 percent) as women (16 percent) reported their spouses had urged them to take on new role activities. This spouse pressure for role making did result in new couple-interaction patterns in the middle-class sample. Husbands took on different activities involving semi-instrumental roles that also provided emotional support for their wives, such as household duties requiring little skill but which could be performed jointly. Three-fourths of the husbands shopped for groceries and other items, and over half cleared the breakfast table, wiped the dishes, and picked up and put away clothes, according to wives' reports. Most of the men did not mind these activities and engaged in them in a "non-competitive, rather compassionate" way. They expressed attitudes ranging from a sense of obligation to real satisfaction with the shared roles. Remarks such as, "It's woman's work and I don't like housework, but I help so the wife is through sooner." And "I'm glad to help. It gives me something to do" were common (Lipman, 1960: 481).

The companionship from shared household activities as well as the common interests these activities create, along with social desirability considerations in reporting to outsiders, may account for the 52 percent of men and 47 percent of women reporting their marriages to be more satisfactory after the husband's retirement. Husbands tended to be more confined when they accepted the legitimacy of their wives expecting assistance in household work (Lipman, 1960: 482). Wives, too, can have difficulty accepting new patterns because at times more, since the new interaction patterns require women to give up their traditional control of homemaking activities. The transition period of role making during which husbands and wives are establishing a division of labor based on role sharing and interchange of roles, therefore, may not be an easy one. Working-class wives, as the English study (Crawford, 1971) referred to earlier suggests, have fewer fears concerning changes in their household roles when husbands retire because the latter are more committed to conventional definitions of men's and women's work. Such husbands are less apt to engage in household activities and to upset the existing segregated conjugal role arrangements. Twice as many wives of nonmanual workers were worried at the prospect of having the husband home all the time. They feared their husbands would perform housekeeping roles leaving them nothing to do, while other wives disliked having to change their daily patterns to permit their husbands to participate in household chores. Still others feared a loss of power with husbands present to inquire as to their comings and goings (Crawford, 1971: 270).

Despite the attendant difficulties, both husbands and wives are happier in the aging period when they emphasize mutual help, companionship, and affection rather than trying to maintain the segregation of daily role activities characteristic of the preretirement period. Women, like men, are more apt to have low morale if they fail to change their usual role patterns. Only 26 percent of the wives in the Lipman study (1960: 483) who gave love and understanding or companionship and compatibility as responses to the question of the most important quality of a good wife had low morale in contrast to 63 percent of the women who mentioned being a good cook or a good housekeeper.

## Marital Companionship

If our previous discussion of role-making activities is correct, we would expect companionship, shared expectations, and an emphasis on two-way communication patterns to characterize spouses who are generally satisfied. A study in Oklahoma of the answers of 408 middle-class husbands and wives, ranging in age from 60 to 89, support this proposition. These persons were satisfied with their marriages. Only five percent rated their marriages as less than "happy" or "very happy." And those who rated their marriages as "very happy" had the highest morale scores while those who perceived their marriages as "unhappy" had the lowest scores (Stinnett, Carter, and Montgomery, 1972: 666,

668). These husbands and wives rated companionship and being able to express true feelings to the spouse as being the most rewarding aspects of marriage. Consistent with their belief in the importance of mutuality in marital satisfaction was the respondents' high rating of affection giving. They listed being in love, compatibility of personalities, and shared interests as the most important factors in achieving marital success. In the same vein, varying proportions of the respondents declared respect, sharing common interests, and effective expression of true feelings to be the three most important characteristics of a successful marriage. Conversely, they rated different values and philosophies of life and lack of shared interests as being most troublesome (Stinnett, Carter, and Montgomery, 1972: 666).

The emphasis on companionship and two-way communication is consistent with a power structure that is horizontal. And husbands' decision-making power, which declines at each succeeding stage from its high point when couples have children of preschool age (four to seven years marriage duration), reaches its lowest point at the aging period (Blood and Wolfe, 1960; and Centers, Raven, and Rodrigues, 1971).

Among some couples, companionship based on shared expectations and shared tasks creates almost a symbiotic relationship. Enfeebled by age, each does what he or she can to keep the couple functioning. The reciprocity is so intimate that a partner cannot usually survive the other's demise both for morale and physical maintenance reasons (Clark and Anderson, 1967).

**Communication Patterns**

The intimate relations ideally found in marriage, so important to the sense of well-being of aged persons, depend heavily on having someone to confide in and talk over problems with (Lowenthal and Haven, 1968: 27). Even without a confidant, the elderly who are still married tend to have higher morale than the widowed. In a sample of 280 urban San Franciscans who were at least 60 years of age, almost half (47%) of those who were married as compared with slightly more than a quarter (27%) of those widowed within the last seven years were satisfied. But with someone to confide in, 65 percent of the married and 55 percent of the widowed had a sense of well-being (Lowenthal and Haven, 1968).

The most interesting finding from the San Francisco study has to do with the identity of the confidant. Among those still married, men of all ages were more likely to report a spouse as confidant than were women. Two times as many women, however, mentioned a child or another relative and were more apt to name a friend. In addition, the class differences in marital closeness that have appeared throughout the marital career continue in the aged period. More than three times as many in the higher socioeconomic class named a spouse as confidant as in the lower socioeconomic class. The percentages are 28 percent in the higher group and eight percent in the lower-class group. Among men, however, the differences are even more pronounced—36 percent of men in the middle class as compared with two percent in the working class. In the latter group, persons were twice as likely to report a friend as confidant, and it is men who account for this difference..

On the basis of their analysis of detailed life histories of the interviewees, Lowenthal and Haven (1968: 29) concluded that the lesser importance of the spouse as confidant among men of the lower socioeconomic groups is connected with problems of gender-role socialization; working-class males considered close association with females a sign of male weakness. Thus the close relations characteristic of marital happiness in the aging period of the marital career appear to be less often present in working-class couples. The conjugal role segregation and vertical communication structures more characteristic of this class in earlier family life stages continues. Spouses express their feelings to outsiders with whom they do have shared concerns.

**Sexual Relations**
Contrary to customary beliefs, coitus can contribute to morale among the elderly. In the Stinnett, Carter, and Montgomery study (1972), referred to earlier, 7.8 percent of their sample rated sexual satisfaction the most important characteristic of a successful marriage. And Masters and Johnson (1966: 245) also found coital activities to continue in their samples of men and women over 60. As with the middle aged, regularity of sexual expression is important for satisfactory sexual relations. Women, particularly in the over-70 age period, are at a disadvantage in this respect. There is attrition in the opportunity for intercourse due to death of spouse or because of the spouse's ill health. Men's sexual responsiveness wanes over time. The man who is 60 years of age or older has a lower maintained level of sexual tension and reduced reactive intensity during intercourse. Thus he may lose interest in sex even if he and his wife do not experience the infirmities of old age that prevent coital activity. Wives, therefore, may be denied regular sexual expression even when interested. Masters and Johnson (1966: 263) report, however, that the male of 70, or even 80, who is in adequate health can perform adequately if his sexual interest is reawakened due

to some new "physiologic outlet or psychologic reason." A 93-year-old man interviewed in the Clark and Anderson study (1967: 274) of the aged in San Francisco may be permitted the last word on males' sexual abilities in old age. Mr. Ed Hart had outlived three wives, the last with whom in his early eighties he had enjoyed a platonic relation. Considering this, he said, "It's just deterioration, I presume. But it is certainly nothing to get upset about. This seems to be what happens to all male animals as they grow older—but you don't stop loving or living."

The importance of cultural factors as well as psychological factors in the aged's sexual activities is reflected in older men's being more positive about sex than older women despite the males' lesser sexual responsiveness (Feigenbaum, et al., 1966). Women of advanced ages, 62 to 96, grew up in the era when women generally were not supposed to enjoy sex. This early socialization, coupled with the ridicule and disapproval still too prevalent in society with respect to elderly persons' engaging in sexual activities, helps to account for women's lesser interest. More education and higher-class status was also associated with more positive attitudes toward sex among the 273 respondents.

Couples facing old age together have difficulty changing the separateness emphasized among position-oriented couples to a more interpersonally sensitive person-oriented relation. The limited linkages that exist between the level of family developmental task performance at one stage and the next are not easily modified. When the family developmental task of morale maintenance is poorly accomplished at previous stages, the problems that retirement brings add to these constraints in discouraging couples from experimenting with role changes and new roles.

Interestingly enough, it is the usually higher-status man who is at a disadvantage when aged. His centering of attention on instrumental activities outside the home becomes a disadvantage when such activities cease. If he is able to work out with his wife new activities relating to the house, we have seen, his morale will be high. But working-class men particularly do not find it easy to choose developmental tasks that will increase expressive roles nor are they skilled at communicating their discomforts to their wives, a first step in negotiating new conjugal role patterns. Unless they retain, or find new outside interests and contacts, men are increasingly dependent on their wives for association and care as friends on the job fall away and household chores remain a mystery. Women in contrast have cultivated the sociability skills and social networks of kin and friends that provide an alternate source of companionship to their husbands while still retaining household interests and skills. Thus the disproportionate number of widows probably presents fewer problems to society than would a disproportionate number of widowers.

## THE MARITAL CAREER IN PERSPECTIVE

Marriages may be made in heaven, as the popular saying goes, but their maintenance occurs in an earthly setting. The emotional euphoria with which most marriages start is eroded over time by establishing daily routines, by growing irritations from constant association, by competing attractions of jobs and children, and by coping with the multitudinous problems, both large and small, that family life in an industrialized society entails. Fortunate couples develop an intimate understanding unique to the relationship that replaces the raptures of the first period of the marital career.

Our scanning of the stages of marital existence from its formation to its dissolution has shown how important the couple relation is to personal morale in the later years of life. Yet we have also seen how what goes on before in the marital exchange sets limits on what can occur in later years. A lasting emotionally supportive relationship grows out of mutually satisfactory affection-giving communication, and power patterns. Such patterns enable the couple to accomplish their various family developmental tasks at particular stages without too much cost in terms of future rigidity.

In addition to the expectable temporal changes encompassed in the marital career, societal changes reflected in rising divorce rates are affecting marriages. Wives are pivotal persons both in the ongoing existence of the marriage and in the societal upheavals affecting marriages. The previous chapters have shown that women continue to center their life plan on family roles. An overwhelming proportion of women plan to marry, do marry, want children, give birth to them, and assume the major responsibility for their care. Women depend upon family relationships for much of their self-identity, which makes them particularly vulnerable to the vicissitudes of marriage. This vulnerability accounts for the repeated research finding that husbands are freer to establish patterns of marriage to which wives then adjust.

But this very interpersonal vulnerability of wives gives them a particular strength. There is less discontinuity over time in the role sequences of women because so many of them do center on family relationships. The skills, moreover, that women develop in nurturing relationships enable them to maintain the network of supportive social relationships essential for morale particularly in later years. Their whole style of relating to people emphasizes maintenance of good relationships even at the expense of momentary disadvantage. In power relations, for example, evidence suggests women seek egalitarian patterns rather than power at the expense of husbands (Lewis, 1972). As a consequence, unlike men, women do not have to shift gears, so to speak, to new activities and new ways of relating at retirement. Many of their skills and activities remain so meaningful throughout life that in a sense they never undergo the trauma of retirement.

Wives' roles not only strengthen an individual but point the direction that satisfying marital interaction will take. As we have seen, husbands are happier in their later years when they take on the supportive activities primarily associated with women. If they are empathic and interpersonally sensitive throughout marriage, husbands can also join their wives in anticipating change and develop new interaction patterns. Debilitating cleavages less often develop as husbands as well as wives work to maintain shared understandings. Thus, the fragile consensus linking husband and wife over time demands increasingly the lessening of traditional gender roles and the addition of supportive roles to the role repertoires of husbands.

## REFERENCES

Blood, Robert O. and Donald M. Wolfe, *Husbands and Wives: The Dynamics of Married Living.* New York: Free Press, 1960.

Centers, Richard, Bertram H. Raven, and Aroldo Rodrigues, "Conjugal Power Structure: A Re-examination," *American Sociological Review*, 1971, 36, 264–278.

Clark, Margaret and Barbara G. Anderson, *Culture and Aging.* Springfield, Ill.: Charles C Thomas, 1967.

Cooper, Barbara S. and Mary F. McGee, "Medical Care Outlays for Three Age Groups," *Social Security Bulletin*, 1971, 34, 3–14.

Crawford, Marion P., "Retirement and Disengagement," *Human Relations,* 1971, 24, 255–278.

Feigenbaum, Eliott, Marjorie F. Lowenthal, and Mella L. Trier, "Sexual Attitudes in the Elderly," Paper Presented at the Gerontological Society, New York, 1966.

Feldman, Harold, *Development of the Husband-Wife Relationship, A Research Report,* Mimeographed. Ithaca, New York: Cornell University, 1965.

Lewis, Robert A. "Satisfaction with Family Power over the Family Life Cycle." Paper presented before the Annual Meeting of the National Council on Family Relations 1972.

Lipman, Aaron, "Role Conceptions of Couples in Retirement," in Clark Tibbitts and Wilma Donahue, eds., *Social and Psychological Aspects of Aging.* New York: Columbia University Press, 1960, 475–485.

Lowenthal, Marjorie F. and Clayton Haven, "Interaction and Adaptation: Intimacy as a Critical Variable," *American Sociological Review*, 1968, 33, 20–30.

Masters, William H. and Virginia E. Johnson, *Human Sexual Response.* Boston: Little, Brown, 1966.

Pineo, P. C., "Disenchantment in the Later Years of Marriage," *Marriage and Family Living*, 1961, 23, 3–11.

Riley, Matilda White and Anne Foner, *Aging and Society I, An Inventory of Research Findings.* New York: Russell Sage, 1968.

Rollins, Boyd C. and Kenneth L. Cannon, "Marital Satisfaction over the Family Life Cycle: A Reevaluation," *Journal of Marriage and the Family*, 1974, 36, 271–283.

Spanier, Graham B., Robert A. Lewis, and Charles L. Cole, "Marital Adjustment over the Family Life Cycle: The Issue of Curvilinearity," *Journal of Marriage and the Family*, 1975, 37, 263–275.

Stinnett, Nick, Linda M. Carter, and James E. Montgomery, "Older Persons' Perceptions of Their Marriages," *Journal of Marriage and the Family*, 1972, 34, 665–670.

Streib, Gordon F. and C. J. Schneider, *Retirement in American Society.* Ithaca, New York: Cornell University Press, 1971.

Thompson, Gayle B., "Work Versus Leisure: An Investigation of Morale among Employed and Retired Men," *Journal of Gerontology*, 1973, 28, 339–344.

U.S. Bureau of the Census, *Current Population Reports*, Series P-20, No. 295, "Educational Attainment in the United States: March 1975," U.S. Government Printing Office, Washington, D.C., 1976a.

U.S. Bureau of the Census, *Current Population Reports*, Series P-20, No. 285, "Mobility of the Population of the United States: March 1970 to March 1975," U.S. Government Printing Office, Washington, D.C., 1975.

U.S. Bureau of the Census, *Current Population Reports*, Series P-20, No. 292, "Population Profile of the United States: 1975," U.S. Government Printing Office, Washington, D.C., 1976b.

U.S. Department of Agriculture, *Family Economics Review*, ARS-NE-36, "Spending on Medical Care," U.S. Department of Agriculture, Federal Building, Hyattsville, Maryland, 1976.

U.S. Department of Health, Education, and Welfare, *Facts About Older Americans, 1975*, Washington, D.C.: U.S. Government Printing Office, 1975a.

U.S. Department of Health, Education, and Welfare, *United States Life Tables: 1969–71*, No. (HRA) 75–1150, Vol. 1, No. 1, U.S. Government Printing Office, Washington, D.C., 1975b.

U.S. Senate, *Recession's Continuing Victim: The Older Worker*, Printed for the use of the Special Committee on Aging, Ninety-Fourth Congress, Second Session, 1976, Washington, D.C.: U.S. Government Printing Office, 1976.

# Parents and Children

# 11

# First acquaintance

With this chapter, we begin our examination of the parent-child relation as it continues over time. Parenthood marks a critical transition point that ushers in a new family stage. The first child's arrival results in the addition of parental roles to the role clusters of husband and wife. Intergenerational as well as cohort relationships are now present in the family unit with the attendant possibilities for misunderstandings owing to differences in historical time perspectives.

We have already seen the changes parental roles create in marital relations. The focus of this and the following chapters will be on the parent-child subsystems. During the years when children are present in the household, the progress of the oldest in his educational career serves to punctuate periods in the family's life span. To provide a basis for comparison, let us begin our discussion by looking at those couples who never have children.

## CHILD-FREE COUPLES

Although only six percent of the married women born in the 1930s and 1940s will not have children (Carter and Glick, 1970: 302), there is some suggestion that more

younger women and their husbands are choosing not to have children
Their number has increased tenfold since 1967, the same period when
evidence of overpopulation and environmental pollution have received
wide public notice. In 1967, one of 7 married women under 24 planned
to have no children, as compared with one out of 10 married wives in
1974 (U.O. Bureau of the Census, 1975).[1] Whether or not these women
included the approximately four percent of women in the childbearing
ages that a Rhode Island study showed were involuntarily childless, or
those whose husbands are sterile cannot be determined (Rao, 1974:
156).

The heavy costs of child rearing from the time the child arrives may
be a factor in the thinking of couples who choose not to have children.
At 1977 prices, the total, direct cost of clothing, housing, feeding, and
keeping a child healthy until the age of 18 is $36,261, and this sum is
based on a so-called "low-cost" living level. It becomes $53,605 at
the "moderate cost" level. If one adds four years of college, the total
expense is $44,156 at the low-cost level and $64,215 at the "moderate-
cost" level (Espenshade, 1977: 25, Table 15). Moreover, when one
estimates how much a first child can cost the mother who drops out
of the labor force in "lost" earnings, the additional expense of rearing
a child over his first 15 years of life ranges from $32,885 for women
with a high school education to $42,841 for college graduates.[2] Even
if women only spend their child's first four years at home, the "costs"
mount. They are $16,111 for the woman with a high school education,
and $20,990 for the college graduate (Espenshade, 1977: 26-27,
Table 16).

Few studies have been done specifically of child-free couples. What
evidence we do have suggests that these couples put heavy stress on
the inviolability of the marital relation (Veevers, 1973). The voluntarily
child-free wives married at least five years who talked to Veevers reported a strong commitment to the husband-wife dyad and to extrafamilial activities.[3] They feared the coming of children would threaten
the present marital interaction. Their satisfactory conjugal relationship,

---

[1] Whether this resolve will continue or not until the women are past childbearing age
is not possible to predict at this time.

[2] For an elementary school graduate, the cost is $26,562, and for the woman with five
or more years of college, it is $54,347 (Espenshade, 1977: 26–27, Table 16).

[3] We use the term "child-free" rather than the term "childless" to emphasize the
element of choice involved in the status of these couples.

in which joint role organization prevailed, would become segregated, they felt, if they had children. In their view, the egalitarianism they prized would also be threatened by children. None of the 52 women were interested in fulfilling the family development task of socialization that parenthood entails. They viewed the immaturity of children negatively, and they placed high value on being able to take on individual developmental tasks that would increase their own competencies. All but one of the women were either employed or attending a university, and they wished to continue their freedom to explore opportunities in the broader community.

A third of the women had entered marriage with a clear understanding that there would be no children. The other women had postponed having children for a future period when dyadic patterns had been established, but the day-to-day pleasures of the couple relation had prevented this future from ever arriving (Veevers, 1973).

The separation in persons' minds between their own and their relatives' childbearing and the problems brought on by world overpopulation are nowhere more apparent than in others' reactions to child–free couples. Instead of applauding their decision as a contribution to society's welfare, associates labeled these couples as selfish, immoral, and unhappy, and they viewed the women as unfulfilled and unfeminine. Thus while couples do not have to explain their decision to have children, those who are child-free must account for their decision not to procreate. For this reason, couples without children try to isolate themselves from couples with conflicting views. The child-free seek out single friends, or couples who are minimally involved with their children. In this way, the child-free try to maintain their life style from outside challenge (Veevers, 1975; Houseknecht, 1977).

## THE DECISION TO HAVE CHILDREN

Outsiders not only pressure young couples to have children but also to have them early in their marriage. When Maxwell and Montgomery (1969) queried 96 married women aged 21 to 81 concerning the responsibilities of young couples to become parents, they found that older women who had been married more than 15 years were more likely to feel couples should have children in the first two years of marriage. This finding suggests that parents and other persons in the parents' generation exert pressure on young couples to time their children's arrival early in marriage, the period when the couple may not yet have passed through the critical transition period of getting married.

The same small study also showed that a majority of women view the family in the traditional way as existing for the purpose of procreation. They believed that couples should center their attention on their children rather than on themselves. Consistent with this attitude, the women also felt that children are the indispensable indicators of marital love and strengthen that love, a belief not wholly consistent with the research reviewed earlier in Chapter 7 and Chapter 8. In addition, from these respondents' perspective, women remained unfulfilled without children (Maxwell and Montgomery, 1969: 344). These sentiments were found more often among lower-class than middle-class women, a finding we would expect, given the greater emphasis on parental than marital roles in the lower class.

Societal pressure exists and is effective because people customarily possess values that make the presence of children seem essential to family life. Hoffman and Hoffman (1973, 46–47) present the following values as instrumental to the childbearing decision:

1.  Children confirm, by their presence, adult status and give persons, particularly women, a recognized social identity.
2.  Children provide a means for continuation of the self, a kind of immortality.
3.  Children tie parents to the community through children's activities in school, public recreation programs, and the neighborhood.
4.  Children show, according to religious doctrine, that couples are moral beings, since they place other's welfare before their own and contribute to the continuity of the group.
5.  Children protect parents from loneliness in an impersonal world.
6.  Children supply novelty and fun to family life that keeps it interesting.
7.  Children with their attendant socialization requirements develop competencies in parents and give them a sense of accomplishment.
8.  Children provide scope to parents for demonstrating creative child rearing strategies.
9.  Children permit parents to exercise power over others, as well as to gain prestige, since parents usually receive more social approval than do childless persons.
10. Children give some parents a sense of vicarious achievement through their children's accomplishments.
11. Children can be of economic utility, especially to elderly parents who need financial aid or a place of residence.

The extent to which couples hold these values and want children, is shown by the practice of adoption. The childless are overly represented in the approximately four percent of United States women who adopt children, although in recent years, the number of women who have children already and adopt is increasing. In any case, adoptive mothers are found in all classes, races, and religions. Full time occupational responsibilities among white women does decrease the number who adopt, but this is not true for black women (Bonham, 1977: 305).

Once persons decide to have children through adoption or biological parenthood, critical changes in the role clusters of married couples occur. In the rest of the chapter, the discussion will cover parenthood as a critical role transition, and how persons learn to be parents.

## BECOMING PARENTS

Becoming parents may be a normal stage in the family life cycle, but the limited learning couples bring to their new roles creates worries that in extreme cases affect infant care. There is often a lack of formal or informal training for performing parental roles. The implicit socialization for such roles that the child experiences in taking the roles of his father and mother while interacting with them is absent when he or she is an infant. "Even the role-taking the older child engages in when interacting with his parents would seem to be more effective for acquiring general values rather than the specific skills of parenthood" (Hill and Aldous, 1969: 925). To learn the behaviors associated with parental roles, the individual needs actual role rehearsals. Yet many children, particularly only children and youngest children, may not have the opportunity for infant- and child-care responsibilities with siblings or other children and are therefore ignorant of what to expect in the way of infant behaviors.

As Rossi (1968: 35) points out, the pregnancy period itself is utilized by relatively few couples as anticipatory socialization for parental roles. Unless the couple already has children, the couple's preparation generally consists of obtaining the clothing and equipment the coming baby needs. Reading, seeking counsel from friends, discussing the situation with other couples, or all three constitute the usual sources of information on infants. Since there is usually no actual experience with infant care, the information sought may be inappropriate or irrelevant. Even couples active in prenatal courses such as the Lamaze training classes for natural childbirth feel unprepared for performing parental roles after the child's arrival (Wente and Crockenberg, 1976). The pregnancy period differs in this respect from the period prior to marriage when the couple is committed to one another. At that time man and woman can try out interaction patterns and in their role making explore attitudes and expectations concerning marital roles and family issues. They can also discover issues on which they disagree and how to handle conflict.

The suddenness of the arrival of parental responsibilities accentuates the problems of lack of learning (Rossi, 1968: 35). There is no equivalent to the honeymoon period in which parents and infant can become gradually acquainted. A demanding and helpless baby allows for no respite regardless of how unpleasant the care is or how inadequately parents give it.

Finally, Rossi notes (1968: 36) that the available child-care information is often inadequate. There is expert counsel on how to feed and clothe young children in order to make them healthy. When one seeks help, however, on what methods to use in rearing children so they can live reasonably comfortably in their families or cope with community temptations, general prescriptions outnumber specific suggestions.

Certainly, DeLissovoy's longitudinal study of high-school marriages (1973b), which we discussed earlier, presents a graphic illustration of the difficulties resulting from the absence of socialization for parental caretaking roles. When the couples had been married only three months, those without children believed they would have little difficulty in feeding children, getting them to mind, and clothing them. The seven couples with children, however, gave substantially less optimistic answers.

The 37 high-school-aged couples he was able to interview after 30 months of marriage had, by then, all had children; fourteen couples had two, and one couple was expecting a third. The decline in ratings on child-training competencies at this period for the couples who had had children in the interim suggested that the earlier optimistic estimates were unrealistic.

Parental knowledge of infant developmental norms and maternal attitudes toward child care both indicated how ignorance of parenting skills contributed to the reported difficulty the couples had in handling children. Couples had unrealistically high expectations concerning the early development of their children as shown in Table 11-1. These high expectations were combined with attitudes that generally were at the lower end of the rating continuum on acceptance of children and at the higher extreme of the continuum on control.

These attitudes and expectations were reflected in a general irritability, impatience, and proneness to use physical punishment, which

Table 11-1.
**Ages at Which Parents Expected Babies to Achieve Selected Patterns of Behavior**

| Areas of development | Approximate Norm in Weeks | Parents' Estimates in Weeks | |
| --- | --- | --- | --- |
| | | Mothers | Fathers |
| Social smile | (6) | 3 | 3 |
| Sit alone | (28) | 12 | 6 |
| Pull up to standing | (44) | 24 | 20 |
| First step alone | (60) | 40 | 40 |
| Toilet training (wetting) | a | 24 | 24 |
| Toilet training (bowel) | a | 26 | 24 |
| First word | (52) | 32 | 24 |
| Obedience training | b | 36 | 26 |
| Recognition of wrongdoing | b | 52 | 40 |

Source: revised version of DeLissovoy, 1973(a): 23.
a The norms range from two to two and-one-half years, with girls being trained faster.
b These norms vary according to the area of training. They are all over 52 weeks.

DeLissovoy (1973a) found to characterize the young couples' treatment of their children. Just five of the 37 mothers after 30 months of marriage spontaneously cuddled or played with their children. Moreover, despite DeLissovoy's attempt to minimize personal involvement in the research by not answering child-care questions, the "cruel acts" he witnessed made this resolve difficult to maintain. In two instances, he found it necessary to intervene to protect the infant (DeLissovoy, 1973a: 24–25).

The punitive behavior of these young parents—80 percent of the mothers used physical punishment as a means of controlling their young children—was exacerbated by the social and economic difficulties they faced. These difficulties soured their marriages and contributed to the stress of their performance of parental roles. But they, like most other parents, including middle-class families and college graduates, were ignorant of parenting skills. Physicians, usually through their nurses, told them only of formulas for feeding the infant and when new foods should be introduced. The couples' parents also gave little advice on how to nurture children aside from stressing the importance of early toilet training, being strict so the baby would "mind," and letting the child "cry it out" so it would not be spoiled. To other questions, they would respond, "You'll find out soon enough." Quite clearly people need more instruction with more realistic goals to handle children competently (DeLissovoy, 1973a: 24).

In contrast with these findings, data from the Feldman study (1971) of first-time parents demonstrate how being comfortable in parental roles continuing in the couple's marital satisfaction. When couples saw their six-month-old babies as bringing them closer together, they were apt to report being able to handle the child when he or she cried at one month of age. They also did not feel threatened if they could not stop the crying. And their feeding of the child depended on his or her needs rather than theirs, a sensitivity that may well have lessened child-care problems. Too often, when parenting proves difficult and the worried parents argue with each other, the performance of parenthood roles becomes an issue in marital conflict. Thus, sucess in parental roles can result in less strain for marital relations.

### Infant Characteristics and Parental Satisfaction

Maintaining infants physically and beginning to socialize them are not one-way processes from parents to children. From birth on, the characteristics of the child influence parental feelings and nurturance. In Russell's (1974) study, for example, each parent ranked his or her infant on a series of items detailing typical infant behaviors. Both father and mothers with "quiet" babies, who ate well, slept through the night, established routines easily, and were healthy, were less likely to see parenthood as crisis. In contrast, mothers, and particularly fathers, were more apt to report a high degree of crisis when they had active babies who cried a great deal, had feeding problems, slept less than most babies of comparable age, and had been seriously ill.

Meyerowitz (1967) also reports on data from Feldman's sample of first-time parents that the baby's characteristics at five months are related to the couple's reporting a high frequency of events like "laughing together." This euphoria was associated with the baby's requiring less care during the day. Laughing together was also related to the wife's feeling able to deal with her own and her husband's feelings for the previous two months, an indicator of her effective coping with parenting roles. This active influence of the supposedly passive infant on family life provides graphic support for the assumption of the family development framework that individuals not only are affected by their environment but also actively influence it.

## INTERGENERATIONAL RELATIONS AND THE NEW CHILD

The coming of children begins a new stage in the family life cycle for the couple through their taking on parental roles. The arrival also adds to the role clusters of *their* parents. These grandparental roles can substitute for the parental roles that women lose when their children leave home and for the occupational roles that men and women give up at retirement. We will discuss variations in perceptions of grandparent-hood and the performance of grandparental roles in Chapter 15. Here we will examine how grandparent-parent interaction affects parental relations with the infant.

Past family interaction influences mother-infant behavior. If women had good relations with their mothers, they tend to be better mothers, presumably because they identified with a positive role model. Again, we see how occurrences in earlier family stages—in this case when women were in their parental families—set limits on task accomplish-ment in the later stages when they, themselves, have children. In Moss, Ryder, and Robson's (1967) longitudinal study of middle-class newly-weds, for example, the degree of a mother's responsiveness to her infant who was generally born some 25 months after the marriage was related to *her* mother's warmth when she was growing up. The fre-quency of mother-daughter positive interactions, she reported, was related to the amount of nurturance, "holding and attending" behaviors the daughter gave her baby, even when the baby's fussy and crying behaviors were controlled for. Also, the more these women saw them-selves as different from their fathers at the earlier period, the more responsive they were to their infants. Since fathers in this generation were less involved in family matters, they were poor models for the needed child-care skills.

We know that the way parents accomplish the socialization task at one stage exercises constraints on the kinds of parent-child relations possible at the next stage. Less obvious, perhaps, but suggested by this research, is the linkage between the kind of parents fathers and mothers are and their children's behavior with their own children. Women and men whose socialization has ill-prepared them for parent-hood, both in attitude and skills, will tend to have more difficulty with infants. This difficulty has negative effects on the infant, whose dis-comfort adds to the parent's stress. The limited linkage between task performance levels at consecutive stages, which Magrabi and Marshall (1965) hypothesize, is thus supported.

The influence of parents on their children's own behaviors stems initially from the period when they were sharing the same residence. But when they are grown, children usually choose to continue close relations with their parents despite the boundaries of their own nuclear family units. These relations hold some element of tension. Children, now adults, seek to control the amount of influence parents will exer-cise while parents remember the period when their influence was wel-comed and even requested. The role sequences of adviser and counselor are cherished ones as they confer power on parents as well as give them an opportunity to assist their beloved children. What the parents perceive as assistance, however, the younger generation may perceive as interference. Some of the intergenerational misunderstandings that can occur under such circumstances appeared with the first-time parents Feldman studied over time. After their infant's arrival, the couples felt on a more equal basis with their parents, particularly with the same sex parent. But at the same time there was also much disagreement over child rearing (Meyerowitz and Feldman, 1966).

## THE JOYS OF PARENTHOOD

Up to this point, we have emphasized mainly the problems parenthood brings, the difficulties in learning parenting skills, the financial problems, and the arguments with grandparents that may result. There are gratifications, however, and Russell (1974) has listed some of these as well as the factors related to them. Consistent with the strain infants put on marital and intergenerational relations, she found her new parents were more likely to check the items describing the personal pleasures that babies bring than the items suggesting ways that the infants improve relations with spouse, parents, relatives, or neighbors. Thus parents were apt to check the following joys resulting from the baby: (1) "fun to play with and to be with"; (2) "fewer periods of boredom"; (3) "pride in baby's development"; (4) "feeling of fulfillment"; and (5) "a purpose for living." In contrast, they were less apt to check the following: (1) "new appreciation of my own parents"; (2) "more things to talk to spouse about"; (3) "feeling closer to spouse"; (4) "relationship with relatives closer"; and (5) "increased contact with neighbors" (Russell, 1974: 299).

One might hypothesize that those checking fewer pleasures are having more difficulties performing parental roles. Using such a criterion, the morphogeneses in family structure incumbent upon new parents appear to be less easy for the more affluent. For both men and women, the higher the education, the fewer the gratifications they checked. Occupational prestige was also negatively related to perceived gratification among men, but not among women (Russell, 1974: 298).[4]

---

[4] It may be, of course, as Russell (1974) points out, that the better off are more honest and that the less highly educated and advantageously employed are giving socially desirable and less candid responses.

The timing of the birth is clearly a factor. Enjoyment of the infant was more likely for those under 23 if they had been married for a longer period. Women over 23 were less happy the longer they had postponed parenthood. Younger women seem to need time to work out marital arrangements before facing the dislocation and rearrangement in ways of living that the new infant makes necessary. Older women, however, may lack the required patience and energy the infant demands, or they may have put off parenthood because they had negative feelings about it (Russell, 1974: 298).

The relation of identification with same sex parents and being able to perform parental roles appeared for both husbands and wives in the Russell study (1974). Placing "father" high on a list of important identities for men and placing "mother" high on the salient identities list for women was related to more gratification. Other indicators of role competence such as attending classes, reading books, or caring for children prior to parenthood—types of parental role rehearsal—also appeared among the happier fathers. They also were more apt to report wanting additional children, which suggests the present experience was proving to be a pleasant one (Russell, 1974: 298).

Finally, the state of the marital relation was also a factor in satisfaction with parenthood. High marital adjustment was associated with high infant gratification among men and women. Moreover, the continued importance of the couple relation is demonstrated by the higher-reported pleasure with the baby if the spouses saw the baby as contributing to strengthening their marriage.

## CLASS DIFFERENCES IN PARENTHOOD DIFFICULTIES

There appear to be several reasons for the negative association reported above between amount of education and occupational prestige (Jacoby, 1969: 224–225). Middle-class parents set higher standards for child rearing. They expect their children to achieve more in the way of education and occupation and, for that reason, perceive more possibilities for obtaining low rankings as parents. Middle-class men and women on the average come from smaller families. The higher standards they set for themselves as parents are, therefore, coupled with less apprenticeship experience in caring for younger children. Middle-class couples are also more concerned about their marital relation. They, therefore, may perceive the amount of time parental roles require as competitive with the maintaining of the marriage relation.

In addition, middle-class women are more apt to have been trained specifically for some occupation and to be committed to an occupational career through choice rather than necessity. Career women with children must constantly face the problem of obtaining adequate help or of finding competent day-care facilities. It is primarily on their shoulders that the responsibility falls for juggling socialization and physical maintenance task schedules so that they fit with occupational timetables. If women drop out from the job world for the years their children are young, their skills become outmoded, and they are replaced by persons, usually men, who can devote full time to getting ahead. The coming of children for the middle-class career woman can result, therefore, in an unwanted captivity by household affairs and the cutting off of opportunities to participate in an attractive occupation.

Working-class couples tend to be less prepared financially for parenthood than middle-class couples, but working- and lower-class women report the transition to parenthood as nonproblematical. The new roles in the wife-mother role cluster, they believe, serve as links to their husbands and not as barriers. Children, and not an occupation or a close marital relation, are their means for self-fulfillment. The least-educated women, the same survey results showed, were most likely to see no "problems or frustrations" in motherhood. If there were any, they knew "what you have to do," and that was to accept them as a part of being mothers (Lopata, 1971: 211). The working-class mother involved in the round of family life was living as she expected she would. She had no regrets for lost employment opportunities, since absorbing occupations were never a viable alternative to marriage and parenthood.

## PARENTHOOD AND WOMEN'S FAMILY RESPONSIBILITIES

Particularly for women, as we saw in Chapter 7, the coming of children creates an intensification of the family caretaking roles already present in their positional role cluster. At the same time, the world of many women suddenly narrows to the four walls of their dwellingplaces.

The isolation of nuclear families from kin and the absence of child-care facilities means that new mothers often feel an obligation to stay home to see that their helpless infants are adequately nurtured. Not until children show some capacity to care for themselves, or there are other adequate nurturing agents, do many women start reactivating extrafamilial roles. An increasing number of women, however, are continuing to work during the time they have infants and preschoolers. In 1976, 35 percent of these children in two-parent homes had mothers who were working full time, as compared with 46 percent of children 6 to 13, and 53 percent of children 14 to 17 years of age (U.S. Department of Labor, 1977).[5]

Women, even when working, continue to bear the brunt of physical maintenance, a task that requires considerable amounts of time. In the survey of families done by Walker (1971), which we referred to in Chapter 7, the physical maintenance task went from 9.1 hours for one child to 10.7 hours per day for two children. This increased to 11.4 hours with three children and 12.6 hours for families with four to six children (Walker, 1971: 3–4). Working wives whose youngest child was two to five years of age spent 1.9 hours on an average caring for the physical upkeep of family members each day, about half the amount of time infants required. Their husbands devoted 0.8 of an hour per day to such activities. Full-time housekeepers worked 2.4 hours a day on such tasks with preschoolers and their husbands 0.5 hours.

By the time the children were in school, families could devote less time to such care as children became more independent. Working-women were spending about an hour as a daily average on such tasks when the youngest child was 6 to 11 years of age, and their husbands were working 0.5 of an hour. The comparable figure for wives employed completely at home was 1.8 hours and for their husbands 0.4 hours. When the youngest child was 12 to 17 years of age, both groups of women were spending less than half an hour a day on these tasks, 0.4 hours to be exact, and their husbands 0.2 hours a day (Walker and Woodes, 1972: Table 1).[6] But regardless of the age of the child, or their

---

[5] The proportion of children having working mothers is much higher in father-absent families because of the economic reasons described in Chapter 4. For children under five years, it was 47.6 percent in 1976, 58 percent for children 6 to 13, and 65 percent for children 14 to 18 years of age (U.S. Department of Labor, 1977: Table 2).

[6] When there were no children, women who were not employed outside the home, or who worked less than 15 hours a week, spent an average of 5.7 hours a day on *all* household tasks. Their husbands contributed 1.4 hours per day. Women who worked 15 or more hours a week used 3.7 hours in such activities and their husbands helped 1.2 hours. With one child, the time for the wives who were non-employed or employed less than 15 hours a week rose to 7.4 hours, while their husbands spent 1.7 hours on the average a day on housekeeping duties. For the more heavily committed employed women, the time was 5.1 hours and for their husbands 1.4 hours (Walker, 1971: Table 2).

own job demands, women assume the main responsibility for seeing that the household runs smoothly (Aldous, 1969. 470, Table II).

The net result of these data is that employed women with young children constitute the priority in the least overworked persons in the United States. Their stay at home peers are not far behind and, in addition, experience a drastic narrowing of the life space within which to operate. Their marital power may go down—the evidence is not clear-cut on this point—but their expected contributions to the physical maintenance of the household, aside from breadwinning, certainly go up. The fact that there is not more discontent among mothers of young children is a tribute both to the strength of women's socialization to put family role demands first and to the lovable qualities of the children.

**Expenditure Patterns**
The addition of parental roles to the role clusters of husbands and wives also results in shifts in expenditure patterns. This topic very clearly relates to families' selective boundary maintenance in its transactions with outsiders. It also shows how these transactions are affected by internal family changes as well as transactions families maintain with the occupational world. Most childless couples enjoy a relatively high financial income owing to both spouses' choosing to engage in employment outside the home. As a consequence, young couples invest in the standard consumer package with the highest average purchase of durables of any family stage (Wells and Gubar, 1966: 362, Appendix I). They acquire cars, and they purchase durable and sensible furniture, refrigerators, and stoves.

This buying spree ends with the arrival of the first child, when the mother drops out of the labor market. Car purchases, for example, decrease and do not pick up until the youngest child is at least six years of age. But physical maintenance more than ever is a family developmental task at this stage.

The proportion of homebuyers is greatest among young couples with children, although the proportion of homeowners does not peak until the years when couples have no children under 18 (Wells and Gubar, 1966: 356).

The kinds of small purchases that characterize the couples with young children phase are what one might expect. Expenditures for soap powders and detergents go up despite the young child's often reported aversion to soap and water. Apparently mothers try to clothe themselves and their slightly soiled preschoolers in clean clothes, and parents are likely to buy washers and dryers at this period in order to do so. Expenditures for baby food, bland cereals, vitamins, and chest-rub and cough medicines are also high. And, to conclude on a somewhat happier note, parents are pushovers for salespersons whose merchandise includes dolls, wagons, sleds, and skates (Wells and Gubar, 1966: 362, Appendix I).

**Conflicting Parental and Occupational Demands**

The discrepancy between the family's growing demand for consumer goods and the young father's income is reflected in a drop in job morale. Wilensky (1961: 228) suggests that job satisfaction depends upon the balance that exists between occupational rewards (income and job status) and occupational expectations (consumer wants and job-status demands). This balance, Wilensky argues, is greatly affected by family career stage. At the newlywed stage, when there are two incomes, rewards are large relative to responsibilities and aspirations. But when the children come and the family loses one wage earner, an imbalance occurs. Family consumption needs skyrocket, but the peak in earnings is not often reached at this critical childbearing and child-rearing period when men are 25 to 35 years old. As a result, job morale declines until income rises, or until children leave home and debts are settled (Wilensky, 1961: 229).

An unpublished study of all nonsupervisory workers at an electric utility company, for example, shows this relation between family and occupational careers. Among the 6621 semiskilled and skilled blue-collar and white-collar clerks, job satisfaction was high for young bachelors and married men without dependents. It dropped after two to three years with the arrival of children, and the larger the family, the larger and longer the drop in job morale. There was a gradual recovery when men were 45 to 54, at which time income and job security are usually higher and family obligations declining with the departure of children. Workers whose wives were not employed outside the home experienced the drop in job morale earlier than those whose wives were in the labor force (Wilensky, 1961: 229, footnote 9).

The coming of children thus puts an understandable strain on the marital relation and brings the morale maintenance aspect of the family development task into sharp relief. Not only have couples with children become hostages to fate but also hostages to mortgage and loan companies. In addition to the problems of fatigue, upset routines, and houseboundness ensuing upon a child's arrival, they experience a drop in standard of living, decreased savings, and financial worries.

But why, if children are such a problem, do couples continue to have them? The list of reasons given in the first part of this chapter, plus the joys of parenthood new fathers and mothers expressed to

Russell (1974), provide as good a set of answers as any to this question. The well-being of children, those innundibuted appropriate into the world, however, must be taken into account in any balance sheet of parent child relations. Since today's contraceptive culture permits couples to choose when and how many children to have, the children who are born are more likely to be wanted than to be suffered as "mistakes," a clear gain for children. Yet the many couples who want children but who are ignorant of the problems and the privileges bestowed by parenthood can only be accounted a clear loss for children. Too many children continue to experience unhappy family lives while growing up owning to the ineptitude of parents. Parenthood, after all, is the last demanding occupation left to nonprofessionals.[7] Accordingly, the following chapters are designed to provide some information on positive parenting during the family lifetime in the light of what current research tells us.

# REFERENCES

Aldous, Joan, "Wives' Employment Status and Lower-Class Men as Husband-Fathers," *Journal of Marriage and the Family*, 1969, 31, 469–476.

Bonham, Gordon Scott, "Who Adopts: The Relationship of Adoption and Social-Demographic Characteristics of Women," *Journal of Marriage and the Family*, 1977, 39, 295–306.

Carter, Hugh and Paul C. Glick, *Marriage and Divorce: A Social and Economic Study*. Cambridge, Mass.: Harvard University Press, 1970.

DeLissovoy, Vladimir, "Child Care by Adolescent Parents," *Children Today*, 1973, 2, 22–25(a).

DeLissovoy, Vladimir, "High School Marriages: A Longitudinal Study," *Journal of Marriage and the Family*, 1973, 35, 245–255(b).

Espenshade, Thomas, J., "The Value and Cost of Children," Population Bulletin, Vol. 32, No. 1, (Population Reference Bureau, Inc., Washington, D.C., 1977).

Feldman, Harold, "The Effects of Children on the Family," in Andree Michel, ed., *Family Issues of Employed Women in Europe and America*. Leiden: E. J. Brill, 1971, 104–125.

Hill, Reuben and Joan Aldous, "Socialization for Marriage and Parenthood,"

[7] Lott (1973: 575) has noted perceptively that it is *"because* childbearing is necessarily a female-only activity . . . and because child rearing, too, has been primarily performed by women that both are accorded so little respect" (italics in original). Rejection of child rearing on feminist grounds indicates the movement's acceptance of the male-oriented values it is seeking to change.

in David A. Goslin, ed., *Handbook of Socialization Theory and Research.* Chicago: Rand McNally, 1969, 885–950.

Hoffman, Lois W. and Martin L. Hoffman, "The Value of Children to Parents," in J. T. Fawcett, ed., *Psychological Perspectives on Population.* New York: Basic Books, 1973, 19–76.

Houseknecht, Sharon K., "Reference Group Support for Voluntary Childlessness: Evidence for Conformity," *Journal of Marriage and the Family,* 1977, 39, 285–292.

Jacoby, Arthur P., "Transition to Parenthood: A Reassessment," *Journal of Marriage and the Family,* 1969, 31, 720–727.

Lopata, Helena, *Occupation: Housewife.* New York: Oxford University Press, 1971.

Lott, Bernice E., "Who Wants the Children? Some Relationships among Attitudes toward Children, Parents, and the Liberation of Women," *American Psychologist,* 1973, 28, 573–582.

Magrabi, Frances M. and William H. Marshall, "Family Developmental Tasks: A Research Model," *Journal of Marriage and the Family,* 1965, 27, 454–461.

Maxwell, Joseph W. and James E. Montgomery, "Societal Pressure Toward Early Parenthood," *Family Coordinator,* 1969, 18, 340–344.

Meyerowitz, Joseph H., "The Transition to Parenthood and Sources of Satisfaction," Paper presented at the 1967 Annual Meetings, American Sociological Association.

Meyerowitz, Joseph H. and Harold Feldman, "Transition to Parenthood," in Irving M. Cohen, ed., *Family Structure, Dynamics and Therapy*, New York: American Psychiatric Association, 1966, 78–84.

Moss, Howard A., Robert G. Ryder, and Kenneth S. Robson, "The Relationship Between Pre-Parental Variables Assessed at the Newlywed Stage and Later Maternal Behaviors," Paper presented at the 1967 Annual Meetings, Society for Research in Child Development.

Rao, S. L. N., "A Comparative Study of Childlessness and Never-Pregnant Status," *Journal of Marriage and the Family,* 1974, 36, 149–157.

Rossi, Alice S., "Transition to Parenthood," *Journal of Marriage and the Family,* 1968, 30, 26–39.

Russell, Candyce S., "Transition to Parenthood: Problems and Gratifications," *Journal of Marriage and the Family,* 1974, 36, 294–302.

U.S. Bureau of the Census, Current Population Reports, Series P-20, No. 277, "Fertility Expectations of American Women: June, 1974," U.S. Government Printing Office, Washington, D.C., 1975.

U.S. Department of Labor, Office of Information *News*, February 25, 1977.

Veevers, Jean E., "The Moral Careers of Voluntarily Childless Wives: Notes on the Defense of a Variant World View," *Family Coordinator,* 1975, 24, 473–487.

Veevers, Jean E., "Voluntarily Childless Women: An Exploratory Study," *Sociology and Social Research,* 1973, 57, 356–366.

Walker, Kathryn E., "ARS Summary Report of Time Used for Household Work," New York State College of Human Ecology. Ithaca: Cornell University, 1971.

Walker, Kathryn E. and M. Woodes, "Time Use for Care of Family Members," Use of Time Research Project Working Paper, Number 1, Department of Consumer Economics and Public Policy, Cornell University, September 21, 1972.

Wells, William D. and George Gubar, "Life Cycle Concept in Marketing Research," *Journal of Marketing Research*, 1966, 355–363.

Wente, Arel S. and Susan Crockenberg, "Transition to Fatherhood: Lamaze Preparation, Adjustment Difficulty and the Husband-Wife Relation," *Family Coordinator*, 1976, 25, 351–357.

Wilensky, Harold L., "Life Cycle, Work Situation, and Participation in Formal Associations," in Robert W. Kleemier, ed., *Aging and Leisure: Research Perspectives on Meaningful Use of Time.* New York: Oxford University Press, 1961, 213–242.

# 12

# The attachment period

To organize the voluminous material on child rearing of infants and preschoolers, we shall focus on certain behaviors, namely, those of control and affection, which are of central importance in the parent-child relation. The changes in their manifestation over time and the later consequences of these parent-child interactions will constitute the major portion of the discussion. The behaviors associated with control and affection influence the extent to which parents and children become attached to each other and socialization can occur.[1] Without love, children will not easily accept the learning tasks set by parents, and without control, the children will not know what they are to learn.

Not only do control and affection-giving behaviors influence parents' performance of the socialization task but also the task of maintenance of morale in the family. Parental support has much to do with children's feelings of self-worth, and this sense, coupled with parental control, can help children to learn behaviors that make interactions with others pleasurable for them and for others. A benign circle is created in which these children have the qualities that encourage nurturance and this nurturance encour-

---

[1] Socialization refers to the activities by which the individual acquires the knowledge, skills, and values that enable him to participate in the groups to which he belongs. Family members socialize each other into new ways throughout the family life cycle, particularly at transition periods to new stages.

ages the behaviors in children that contribute to their task-learning skills.

## THE INFANT AS ACTIVE AGENT IN SOCIALIZATION

Too often, children are viewed as the passive recipients of their parents' socialization attempts. But children socialize parents to become sensitive to their needs so that the influence is two-way. This two-way influence is consistent with the following assumptions in the family developmental framework: (1) an individual both initiates actions owing to maturation and social development and reacts to environmental pressures; (2) an individual in a social setting is the basic autonomous unit. The success of parental socialization, one of the major family developmental tasks when young children are present, depends on the willingness of children to learn family ways. For this to occur, parents have to be sensitive to children's signals that they are ready to learn. This learning readiness on the part of children underlies the concept of the individual developmental task. Unless an individual initiates the activity, she/he will not be ready to accomplish the task; hence the behavioral expectations of parents must be timed to coincide with the child's desire and ability to meet them if the socialization process is to succeed. The DeLissovoy research (1973) discussed in the previous chapter indicated how the lack of fit between parental demands and children's behaviors led to child abuse and parental unhappiness.

As early as infancy, children are disposed to learn societal ways, providing they have caretakers who respond to infant demands by cooperating to satisfy them rather than by rejecting or ignoring them. Take, for example, the interaction outcomes of 25 white, middle-class pairs of infants and mothers whom home visitors observed at three-week intervals during the children's first year of life. Their reports showed that maternal behaviors, like sensitivity, cooperation, and acceptance, which promote harmonious infant-mother relations were related to the infants' compliance to their mothers' prescriptions and proscriptions. These maternal qualities were associated to a lesser degree with the infants' self-control. Among these young children, however, only 20 percent indicated internalization of rules, and this degree of socialization was also associated with precocious cognitive development (Stayton, Hogan, and Ainsworth, 1971: 1062). These infants appeared to be disposed to comply with maternal control in a "responsive, accommodating social environment without training" (Stayton, Hogan, and Ainsworth, 1971: 1065).

According to this view of socialization, infants come to seek contact and social interaction and to grow attached to particular figures in their environment. This proximity-seeking attachment develops at about the same time as obedience and locomotor capacities. The juxtaposition of attachment, obedience, and greater mobility comes as caretakers have to control infants because their arena of action is expanding. That the maternal qualities encouraging infant obedience and attachment are related to internalized controls among a small proportion of intellectually advanced infants, suggests that these maternal qualities will also promote self-control in the second year (Stayton, Hogan, and Ainsworth, 1971: 1068).

Although women generally take on the major child-care responsibilities, whether or not they are working, fathers too are important in infant socialization. Among 54, five-to-six-month-old black infants from impoverished and lower middle-class backgrounds, for example, male infants whose fathers spent more time interacting with them, according to mothers' reports, were rated by home visitors as more alert, more responsible, and more active in eliciting stimuli in their environments than infants whose fathers did less with them (Pedersen, Rubenstein, and Yarrow, 1973).

There is even evidence that fathers and mothers behave differently toward infants and their actions have different effects on children (Lamb and Lamb, 1976). Mothers observed with seven-to-13-month-old infants held the infants more often for caretaking purposes and restricted their exploratory activities. Mothers' games were also more often conventional—pat-a-cake and the like—or they made use of toys in their attentions. In contrast, fathers held the infants more often to play with them or responded actively to the babies' wishes. The fathers' play tended to be more vigorous, involving physical activities; or it was of an unusual and unpredictable type, the type the babies liked most.

These fathers' behaviors seemed to be related to the dependency of their children. When the infants became one year of age, fathers began to pay less attention to their daughters, although the mothers interacted equally with their children regardless of their gender. At the same time, girls became more dependent than boys on contact with or in proximity to their parents (Lamb and Lamb, 1976: 382). The greater interest fathers often show in sons, which has been documented by other studies (Parke and O'Leary, 1976), encourages sons' acceptance of fathers' socializations attempts, but daughters often lack these distinctive contacts they need for their social development.

Another observational study, this time of 36 infants from "relatively poor" families, shows not only how children initiate interaction but how maternal behaviors contribute in children's competence (Clarke-Steward, 1070.1£). The black and white children, who were equally divided as to sex, were observed in their homes during seven visits from the time they were nine months old until they were eighteen months old. The conclusion of this longitudinal research was that the children's competence in cognitive language and in social development was significantly related to a mother's sensitivity to her child's cues and her ability to respond quickly and appropriately to them. A child's comprehension of language and talking were encouraged by the amount of verbal behavior a mother directed to her infant (Clarke-Steward, 1973: 92). The cognitive development of a child and the complexity of a child's play with objects, however, depended on how much time a mother spent talking to and playing with her child. It was not the number of interesting objects in the environment that was related to the child's speed in processing information, in recognizing the permanence of objects, or in performing on Bayley's scale of mental development. The mother's service as mediator between environmental objects and the child, her gauging of when their presentation would be most pleasing, was the critical factor in the child's speed in processing information (Clarke-Stewart, 1973: 71). This finding is important since not all families can afford many toys. Most, however, can afford to have at least one caretaker to respond to a child's action overtures. Their encouragement of the child's interest in the environment, even if it is comparatively bare, is what makes the difference in the child's ability to deal with his or her surroundings (Clarke-Stewart, 1973: 70).

There was, however, a complementarity in the child's attachment to his mother and her physical contacts with him. "The more often the child looked, smiled or vocalized to his mother, the more affectionate and attached to the child she became and the more responsive she was to his distress and demands" (Clarke-Stewart, 1973: 93). Thus the child by his affection giving was an active agent in the mother-child attachment.

## CHILDREN'S COMPETENCE AND RESPONSIVE CARETAKERS

The relation between responsive socializing agents and children's competence continues beyond the infant period. In a series of studies with young children of varying ages, Burton White (1972) supplies additional

documentation of the process. Through a complicated screening process, he and his associates did an in-depth study of the characteristics
of the 13 most competent and 13 least competent children by observing
extensively 400 three-, four-, and five-year-olds, who came from a
range of residential, social, and ethnic backgrounds.

They judged competency on the basis of a child's social and nonsocial abilities. As social abilities, they looked for a child's ability to
use adults as resources, to get and to maintain adult attention in
socially acceptable ways, and to express both affection and hostility to
peers and adults. They assessed nonsocial abilities as a child's ability
to plan and to carry out a sequence of activities; and they judged intellectual competence as taking the perspective of another, noting discrepancies, and dealing with abstractions in terms of rules, letters,
and numbers.

The differences in the two groups of children in innate motor and
sensory capacities seemed to be "generally quite modest" (White,
1972: 80), so White wanted to discover what factors in the environment
would explain the differences in developmental outcomes among these
children. On the basis of the home observations of 13 one-year-old and
20 two-year-old children, coupled with relevant data from his previous
research, White came to a number of conclusions.

His first was that during the first year of life, the infants seemed to
be very much alike and their families did not differ greatly in the ways
they treated them. But for the child's taking on individual developmental
tasks, particularly in the area of cognitive skills and accomplishing
them, the period from 10 to 18 months was crucial. This is the time when
a child's motor abilities increase her or his range of explorations. The
period when the child becomes mobile marks the period of transition
to the stage when he ceases to be an infant and becomes a preschool
child. This transition is marked by the development of speech and the
assertion of identity as well as proximity-seeking behavior toward the
persons to whom he is attached.

Although in a responsive environment a child becomes attached to
his or her caretakers and is aware of their expectations, as shown in
the previously discussed study of Stayton, Hogan, and Ainsworth (1971),
the child also creates difficulties for members of the family. Great curiosity is associated with poor coordination, lack of knowledge of dan-
gers, ignorance of the relative value of environmental objects, and
unawareness of the rights of others (White, 1972: 100).

The actions and reactions of the chief caretakers, usually the mothers, under these often trying circumstances, had much to do with
whether children learned to like to take on new developmental tasks,

tasks that would make them more competent. Mothers who were performing their parenting roles effectively and had competent children were reasonably satisfied and content with their lives and could enjoy their young children. They also gave their children a good deal of attention and consideration. Mothers who were less effective in terms of their children's competencies were unhappy and angry about their situations. They often avoided being with their young children, or they did not enjoy them when the children were present (White, 1972: 102).

These attitudes were reflected in the priorities women assigned to household roles. Mothers of competent children placed house-care roles second in priority to those of child care. They prepared the environment and themselves to encourage the child's cognitive, motor, and social development. The houses contained fewer precious possessions that children had to stay away from at the expense of their curiosity, motor development, and sense of control over their environment. Mothers of competent children also appeared to take greater risks with the safety of the children rather than to limit their exploration and thus their cognitive development (White, 1972: 103).

Women who socialized competent youngsters, however, did not have to spend a major part of their time in child care. Children were not blocked off by playpens or barriers from discovering their surroundings. Instead of valuable objects on low tables, there were inexpensive, small things that fitted easily into a child's hands and were visually interesting, like jar lids, tablespoons, and plastic containers, the sort that fill daily needs in every home regardless of income (White, 1972).

Let us summarize and draw conclusions from these several studies. In terms of what we know from the Clarke-Stewart study (1972), effective caretakers serve as guides and mediators for children's experiences in their environments. Although working at other things, caretakers are generally near. Children can go to them for help or for interpretation in initiating events. Usually, although not always, caretakers respond with aid, enthusiasm, or an idea that will further expand children's understanding and their verbal skills. During this time, children begin to establish an identity as persons with particular ways of initiating activities with others. The resulting change from happy, compliant one-year-olds to more negative, venturesome two-year-olds presents problems for all caretakers. But the less skillful seem to react to the demands and encounters that teach children who they are with too much punitiveness or too much acquiescence. Children may, accordingly, flee or cling. In the first case, they are losing their interpreters of the expanding world; in the second, they are cutting off their contact with it (Anonymous, 1973: 7).

The verbal responses of the skillful mother require only 10 to 30 seconds of her time but are focused on the child's interests. And it is this teaching "on the fly," to use White's term (1972: 101), coupled with a great deal of verbal communication at the child's initiative, that makes these women socializers of competent children.

From the description of these maternal behaviors and the home setting, it is clear why competent children can come from homes with a number of closely spaced children as well as from more affluent homes with fewer children close together in age. Skillful parenting behaviors are not dependent on high income or formal education levels, though they may be on high energy resources. White estimates 90 percent of child caretakers fall between the extremes of skillful and clumsy parental role performances. He believes that mothers can survive these stressful periods and become the kind of caretakers that produce competent children. They, too, through knowing which of their behaviors they should downplay and which they should emphasize, can better accomplish the socialization task (Anonymous, 1973).

## VARIETIES OF SOCIALIZATION TECHNIQUES AND CHILDREN'S COMPETENCE

Thus far, the discussion has centered largely on mothers' responsiveness to infants. Less consideration has been given to parental rule setting and rule enforcement. As children leave infancy and reach the age of three- and four-year-olds, parents become more active teachers in response to their children's search for knowledge about their surroundings. Parents also begin to expect more of children in the way of self-control. And the varying combinations of rule giving and support are associated with differential behaviors in children, as Baumrind (1972) found in a study of 150 four-year-olds, who were enrolled in a preschool. She made home observations and interviewed both parents. Baumrind found three types of parents that she characterized as authoritarian, authoritative, and permissive.

Authoritarian parents gave their children little discretion to behave at odds with rules. Communication was one-way, since the position-oriented parents believed children should accept the parental word on what was right and wrong. As a consequence, behavioral rules were inflexible and sometimes not clear; occasionally, rules had to be enforced with punishment.

Authoritative parents, in contrast, encouraged two-way communication patterns. They gave children reasons for a particular policy and encouraged them to express objections. In Bernstein's terms, such parents were person oriented and appeared to use an elaborated language code to give children an understanding of a perspective while encouraging them to conform their particular behavior. Parents firmly enforced the standards they set but also encouraged independence and individuality.

Permissive parents, in contrast, tended to set few standards for children to obey. They were acceptant of all behavior unless it led to physical harm. But many of these parents were unconcerned about their children or rejected them.

The behaviors the children from these families displayed while they were in nursery school over a three-to-five-month period specify our knowledge of what parental socialization techniques are associated with competence in children. Daughters of authoritarian parents were significantly less independent and dominant and somewhat less domineering, purposive, and achievement-oriented than daughters of authoritative parents. Sons of authoritarian parents as compared with sons of authoritative parents were more hostile, and resistive to others as well as less achievement-oriented.

There appeared to be no significant differences in children from permissive and authoritarian homes. But girls from permissive homes were less dominant, purposive and independent than girls from authoritative homes. Similarly, boys from permissive homes were less purposive, but they were also more hostile and resistive and less achievement oriented than boys from authoritative homes.

These results indicate the importance of a balance between control and support in socializing children for social competence. Parents can set standards and enforce them and still have independent, achieving children. However, they must provide enough nurturance and affection so children feel rewarded for taking on tasks; and they must be sensitive to their children's feelings and objections. Authoritarian parents appear not to balance their demands with enough love to make them palatable. Children are not attached enough to take on willingly the learning tasks their parents set. Permissive parents are warmer but too little involved to set standards the child is ready to master.

## GENDER DIFFERENCES AND PARENTAL PRACTICES

As early as the preschool years, there is evidence from longitudinal studies that parental practices affect children's future intellectual achievements. This is particularly true for girls who appear to need a little maternal "rejection" as children to become independent and self-confident adults (Hoffman, 1972: 146). Maternal "hostility" during the first three years, along with pressures for the child to do better than her age peers, were associated with daughters' intellectual mastery as adults. Such were the findings among the 69 persons in the Fels Institute sample who were studied from the time they were infants until they were adults. For boys, however, intellectual mastery as adults was related to low "hostility" and high maternal protectiveness during their first three years (Kagan and Moss, 1962: 221–222).

"Hostility" in this sample of normal families from middle- and working-class backgrounds, it should be noted, did not refer to the more severe forms of rejection found in homes of children with disabling social or emotional problems. Instead, it included a mother's criticism of a child's behavior, skills, and personality; expressions of preference for a sibling; and an openly critical attitude toward a child (Kagan and Moss, 1962: 205–206). Demanding mothers were themselves intellectually competent persons, and they were critical of their young daughters' task performances. They were not so critical, however, that their daughters' dislike kept them from using their mothers as role models.

Protective maternal behaviors with daughters from infancy to three years of age, in contrast, were correlated with their adult daughters displaying behaviors stereotypically ascribed to women. These women tended to react to stressful situations by withdrawing from them rather than by attempting to resolve the problems directly (Kagan and Moss, 1962: 214). Sons whose mothers were highly involved with them as infants took a different behavioral route. Protective mothers who coupled demands that their preschool and school-aged sons master various tasks with encouragement for them to do so had adult sons successfully involved in intellectual accomplishments (Kagan and Moss, 1962: 222).

These findings of the debilitating effects of restrictiveness without warmth on children's development are consistent with an argument of Bronfenbrenner (1961: 11–12) concerning the differential socialization of boys and girls. Based on a review of relevant research findings, he concluded that girls are undervalued and overattended while boys are overvalued and underattended. The result in his view, is timid, dependent girls and irresponsible, rebellious boys. To develop qualities of responsibility and independence in children, he argues that parents need to offer control and affection to boys but to be wary of high restrictiveness coupled with high affection giving to girls. As Baumrind (1972) also concluded, parents who want to socialize competent girls muot otroo their talking initiative, being assurative, and maintaining their individuality. At the same time parents need to set standards and expect girls to meet them. By focusing on task accomplishment and not on their love for or power over the girl, parents can strengthen her independence.

## INTERGENERATIONAL RELATIONS AND EFFECTIVE PARENTHOOD

In several previous places, the relations of the older generation to the new parents have been discussed. In the DeLissovoy interviews (1973) with high-school-aged parents, for example, we saw how the young people looked to their parents for help in developing child-rearing skills, but the young couples' search for knowledge resulted in little useful information. The Meyerowitz and Feldman findings (1966) presented the other side of the picture. The intergenerational tensions that existed appeared to be based on the young couples' resentment at their parents' unsought advice giving. The earlier discussion of the relation between the connectedness of social networks and the type of conjugal role organization (Bott, 1971), however, indicates that just as parental support contributes to competency in children so can it also contribute to the same effect in adults.

To gain some sense of why close ties to kin can ease the socialization problems of mothers, let us see what interviews with 41 middle-class women, all of whom had at least one preschool child and a varying number of children at other ages, can tell us (Abernethy, 1973). Highly competent mothers were judged to be those who gave the following kinds of responses: an "appreciation" of sibling personality differences; and an emphasis on the developmental approach to child rearing. Both characteristics seem to fit the "responsive" mothers described in the previous studies. These "high-competent" mothers also expressed "confidence" in their ability to deal with children. The contrasting group of women judged to be of low competence gave the following types of responses: "apprehension" over what children would be doing; a feeling of being overwhelmed by children's "demands for attention"; "uncertainty or passivity" in response to disciplinary problems; and "dependence on books for theories of childrearing" (Abernethy, 1973: 88).

Women with a tightly knit network whose relatives or friends saw each other independently reported feeling more comfortable in performing maternal roles. The closer they lived to network members and the more frequently they saw them, the higher their feelings of competence. This was particularly true when they saw their mothers often. These women apparently sought out their mothers and were pleased with their aid. It was not a case, as in previously reviewed findings, of parental help being ineffective or not wanted.

The emotional support and help with child-care duties that network members supplied appeared to explain the results. Since the task of socialization was more clearly defined for the mothers by prescriptions from the members, they less often had to "make" their roles of teacher, disciplinarian, affection giver, and counselor. Friends, kin, and particularly mothers, it appears, also provided the encouragement that enables women to keep trying out various behaviors when the members' prescriptions failed. Not being so intimately involved in the family's life, they remain more objective about child-care problems. And mothers being bound to daughters by ties of affection and former joint residence can be particularly sympathetic and capable of giving women a sense of self-esteem. By sharing some of the responsibilities when women are tired, network members also permit mothers to get their "second wind" to continue performing their roles.

Women in loosely knit networks, however, felt uncomfortable in performing their maternal roles. Their friends, lacking contact with one another, do not necessarily share a common perspective. Inquiries for advice may result in a variety of conflicting suggestions, giving those who seek advice little confidence in trying out the suggestions. In addition, since the values of a mother's friends differ, she receives less emotional support for her own efforts. The greater residential distance of friends and kin also cuts down on the physical help a mother in a loosely knit network can count on in emergencies. As a consequence, the cushion of encouragement and job substitutes that women with close-knit networks and nearby mothers can count on in their role-making attempts are lacking, and with this lack of support also goes a lack of competence (Abernethy, 1973).

## SOCIALIZATION IN ONE-PARENT FAMILIES

What difference does it make in the socialization of children when their parents are divorced? Until recently, social scientists could supply little information about parent-child relations in families where the husband-father position was vacant. Now, however, we can turn to the longitudinal study of divorced couples referred to in Chapter 8. These couples all had children, one of whom was a four-year-old child in a preschool. Interactions of each parent with the child in the preschool, as well as interview material and diary records over a two-year period after the divorce, were compared with similar data from married parents having children of the same gender, age, and birth order in the same preschool (Hetherington, Cox, and Cox, 1976).

The interdependence of the marital and parent-child subsystems in the family was clearly demonstrated in these truncated families. The marital conflict leading to the divorce and the critical role transition period in which the resulting family changes occur were reflected in socialization problems. When the ex-spouses disagreed in their attitudes about their children and felt ill will for each other, then the more frequent were the fathers' visits, the more disruptive were the children's behaviors and the more poorly the mother and their children got along together. The reverse of this situation occurred when the ex-spouses maintained some positive feelings for each other and there were few conflicts.

Social networks composed of parents and other relatives, and particularly of divorced friends, helped divorced mothers to be better parents. Support networks for fathers, in addition to relatives and married friends, included women with whom they were forming intimate relations. But none of these persons were so effective as a continuing positive relation with former spouses, and the continued involvement of fathers with their children in encouraging effective parenting for both fathers and mothers (Hetherington, Cox, and Cox, 1976: 426).

The stress peak in parent-child relations appeared to be one year after the divorce. Mothers were most salient for the children, since they were the parents who continued the family careers of the remaining truncated units. Fathers also had increasingly fewer contacts with their children over the two-year period. Both parents, however, for at least the first year, seemed to be so caught up in the problems of their divorced status that they withdrew from parenting roles. Thus they made fewer maturity demands of their children, showed them less affection, were less effective in communication, and exercised less control than couples still sharing a marital career.

Mothers issued more commands in an attempt to control their children while fathers, wanting their contacts to be as pleasant as possible, were indulgent. By the end of the two-year period after divorce, however, the use of negative sanctions by mothers was declining, and such use by fathers was increasing (Hetherington, Cox, and Cox, 1976: 425).

Two years later, parents were more active mothers and fathers.

Maternal affection-giving and communication behaviors were more effective, and mothers were able to give more explanations for the higher maturity standards they were setting. Fathers, too, were more consistent in their expectations, which were also higher, and were doing better in talking to their children about their expectations. But they were becoming less nurturant and more detached, apparently recognizing the boundaries of the family unit to which they were now an outsider (Hetherington, Cox, and Cox, 1976: 424).

Children's behaviors, in turn, were affected by the changing parental behaviors. Some divorced mothers characterized their relations with their children after one year of being divorced as a "declared war" or a "struggle for survival." Observation showed children were more compliant to fathers' than to mothers' commands, with girls more so than boys; but neither were so compliant with either parent as children in intact families (Hetherington, Cox, and Cox, 1976: 425). Thus ineffective parenting was associated with children's lesser acceptance of parental rules. Only two years after the divorce did mother-child relationships seem to be reestablishing themselves, as mothers were more comfortable in the divorced status, as fathers were becoming less important, and as the family unit, even though truncated, was obviously going to continue.

**Remarriage and Children**

That the same event may have different effects in the parent-child and marital subsystems is demonstrated by remarriage. The reinstitution of the husband-father position introduce generally a positive role transition for divorced women. The remarriage means reactivation of sexual and companionship roles important to women's morale. Some of the pressures from being an "around-the-clock" parent are relieved now that there is some other adult in the house to assume household task responsibilities. As a consequence, the longitudinal study of divorced parents showed the divorced who remarry tend to be as happy as intact couples (Hetherington, Cox, and Cox, 1976: 423).

In contrast with these positive results for mothers, the older a child is, the more difficult appears to be his or her adjustment to the new household member. Particularly when a child is reaching adolescence and must deal with his or her own sexual feelings, the stepparent's coming—a coming that indicates the parent's own sexual interest and activities—can lead to difficulties. This possibility is increased when a new husband attempts to take on father roles. Children see him as trying to displace their existing real father. Again, we see how marital and parental subsystems can be at cross purposes.

## SUMMARY

This chapter has dealt with parent child relations from infancy through the preschool family stages. The infancy period is critical for establishing the parent-child attachment that will make the child want to take on the various developmental tasks socialization requires. This attachment also makes the burdens of child nurturance more palatable to parents.

The consistency of the research findings reviewed is remarkable, given the number and variety of samples. The findings make clear that from infancy on a child is an active agent in the socialization process. His initiatives in smiling, vocalizing, and looking at his caretakers, for example, increase the amount of responsiveness to the infant's needs the caretaker shows (Clarke-Stewart, 1973). This responsiveness in turn is related to an infant's cognitive development as well as to his obedience (Stayton, Hogan, and Ainsworth, 1971). These indications of infant competence in dealing with physical surroundings and his caretakers carry over to the preschool period when caretakers continue to be responsive to a child's needs.

The timing of instruction and information giving by parents to coincide with a child's readiness to learn are optimal for a child's development (White, 1972). In addition, a balance between control and support in the socialization attempts of parents is necessary for a child's task accomplishment. Two-way communication structures and cloverleaf affection patterns are important in a child's accomplishing developmental tasks (Baumrind, 1972).

The active role a child plays in the socialization process also appears with respect to the kind of parents who perform their roles with a minimum of difficulty. Effective parenting that is sensitive to the learning readiness of a child is associated with activities that strengthen parental attachment to a child. Too much or too little parental standard setting, coupled with little positive or even negative support, produces hostile and unlovable children (Baumrind, 1972). Parents thus tend to have children who reflect their style of parenting.

## REFERENCES

Abernethy, Virginia, "Social Network and the Response to the Maternal Role," *International Journal of Sociology of the Family*, 1973, 3, 86–92.
Anonymous, "Growing Up Competent," *Carnegie Quarterly*, 1973, 21, 6–8.

Baumrind, Diana, "The Development of Instrumental Competence Through Socialization: Focus on Girls," in Anne Pick, ed., *Minnesota Symposia on Child Psychology*, VII. Minneapolis: University of Minnesota Press, 1972, 3–36.

Bott, Elizabeth, *Family and Social Network: Roles, Norms and External Relationships in Ordinary Urban Families.* New York: Free Press, 1971.

Bronfenbrenner, Urie, "The Changing American Child—A Speculative Analysis," *Journal of Social Issues*, 1961, 17, 6–18.

Clarke-Stewart, K. Allison, "Interaction Between Mothers and Their Young Children: Characteristics and Consequences," *Monograph of the Society for Research in Child Development*, 1973, 38, Serial no. 153.

DeLissovoy, Vladimir, "Child Care by Adolescent Parents," *Children Today,* 1973, 2, 22–25.

Hetherington, E. Mavis, Martha Cox, and Roger Cox, "Divorced Fathers" *Family Coordinator*, 1976, 25, 417–428.

Hoffman, Lois W., "Early Childhood Experiences and Women's Achievement Motivation," *Journal of Social Issues*, 28, 1972, 129–155.

Kagan, Jerome and Howard A. Moss, *Birth to Maturity.* New York: John Wiley, 1962.

Lamb, Michael E. and Jamie E. Lamb, "The Nature and Importance of the Father-Infant Relationship," *Family Coordinator*, 1976, 25, 379–388.

Meyerowitz, Joseph H. and Harold Feldman, "Transition to Parenthood," in Irving M. Cohen, ed., *Family Structure, Dynamics and Therapy.* New York: American Psychiatric Association, 1966, 78–84.

Parke, Ross D. and S. E. O'Leary, "Father-Mother-Infant Interaction in the Newborn Period: Some Findings, Some Observations and Some Unresolved Issues," in K. Riegel and J. Meacham, eds., *The Developing Individual in a Changing World*, Vol. II, Social and Environmental Issues. The Hague: Mouton, 1976.

Pedersen, Frank A., Judith Rubenstein, and Leon J. Yarrow, "Father Absence in Infancy," Paper presented before the 1973 Meeting of the Society for Research in Child Development.

Stayton, Donelda J., Robert Hogan, and Mary D. Salter Ainsworth, "Infant Obedience and Maternal Behavior: The Origins of Socialization Reconsidered," *Child Development*, 1971, 42, 1057–1069.

White, Burton, "Fundamental Early Environmental Influences on the Development of Competence," in Merle E. Meyer, ed., *Third Symposium on Learning: Cognitive Learning.* Bellingham, Washington: Western Washington State College, 1972, 79–105.

# 13

# Socialization in the context of school and work careers

So far, our discussion of socialization has focused on interactions within the family. By looking at the interdependence of its members, we have seen the effect of the broken marital relation on parents' transmitting rules to children and on their socializing children in a two-way intergenerational process. In this chapter we shift focus to the transactions between families and other societal organizations, transactions that affect socialization. School and work careers not only occupy significant portions of the time and interest of family members, but events in these careers, such as the oldest child's school progress and the ending of the occupational career, can be used to clearly differentiate periods in the family career.

There is little selective boundary maintenance in family members' participation in work and school organizations if by selective we mean freedom of choice. Economic necessity and legal requirements demand family transactions with occupational and educational organizations respectively, and those transactions affect family life. In this chapter, we will see how what goes on at school and on the job influences socialization, particularly in the family stage when primary-school children are present.

The social distance that families do manage to maintain from school and work place stems from the distinctive character of families. Family membership, as Litwak and Meyer point out (1966: 36), results from birth or choice usually on emotional grounds and lasts for lengthy periods. Most schools and places of employment are bureaucracies that operate with personnel selected on the basis of merit and with limited periods of membership. Family cohesiveness rests on deep attachment as well as on task accomplishment. Cohesiveness in school and work bureaucracies depends primarily on wage and working conditions, with positive feelings for the organization being less important.

Transactions between family and other organizations are carried out by "common messengers," persons who play roles in the family and in the other organizations (Litwack and Meyer, 1966). The student mediates the transactions of the two bodies, just as the family providers tie the family to the work place. Because the student's power position in the family is low, other family members share the responsibility for transactions with the schools. The variation in the social distance that families maintain from other organizations is evident with respect to schools and affects their transactions.

## FAMILIES AND SCHOOLS

As a formal socialization agency, the school is designed to teach a child the cognitive skills needed to get along in society. The family supposedly specializes in a child's social and emotional development. But contacts with teachers and peers also affect social development, just as family conversation and family interests affect cognitive development. Teachers are concerned with a child's acquiring social skills, internalizing moral values, and learning self-control; and the ideas a child gains from school associates affect his or her reception of parental rules and discipline. At the same time, interactions within the family affect a child's school career.

This spillover effect of school and family socialization is consciously fostered by school authorities when they seek the cooperation of parents to encourage a child's learning. The authorities then attempt to enlist parental support in getting children to conform to school demands. Parents too may enlist the aid of schools for socializing children in sensitive learning areas such as sex education. In these cases, school authorities and parents seek to lessen the social distance separating them.

## School Entry

When the oldest child enters school, the family experiences a period of role making before it establishes interaction patterns appropriate to the new stage. The experiences of 54 middle-class parents whose children were just entering kindergarten demonstrate just how much stress the period of transition can entail.[1] These 45 mothers and 9 fathers from 46 families met under the auspices of two suburban parent-teacher associations for a series of group meetings that began just prior to their child's entering kindergarten and continued for five to six weeks after school had started (Klein and Ross, 1958). The parents were divided into six groups to discuss family members' feelings and behaviors upon the child's entry into school, discussions that may have made specific those concerns and changes that other parents may take for granted. Because parents were invited to participate in a study of the "normal responses" of children to a period of transition, however, the sample was biased toward families experiencing minimal stress.

The critical role transition period of school entry appeared to be divided into roughly four periods during which family patterns broke down and were gradually redeveloped in new ways. In the first period before the child went off to school, both parents and children experienced concern because of heavy street traffic and possible bullying by older pupils. Parents were also afraid that teachers and other parents would be critical of how well they had accomplished their socialization task with the child (Klein and Ross, 1958: 66).

During this initial period children were reassured through school experiences involving anticipatory socialization. These experiences included the child's preschool participation and his contacts with older siblings or friends already in school. The schools themselves provided

---

[1] For some children, this critical role transition point occurs before the legal school-entry age of five or six. With one-third of all married women with husbands present who had children under six years of age now in the labor force (Bronfenbrenner, 1975), more young children are entering some sort of day-care arrangement. The effect of such arrangements on child and family alike have not been widely studied, perhaps because such a small proportion of preschool children—15 percent of the total child-care hours in 1975—are in formal child-care agencies. The rest are in baby-sitting arrangements with relatives—45 percent of child-care hours—or with nonrelatives—37 percent of child-care hours (Woolsey, 1977: 153, Table 2 citing *National Child Care Consumer Study*, 1975, II, Tables 8-1, 8-2). The few studies we do have suggest that children under four in full-time *group* day care may show anxious attachments or "defensive processes akin to detachment" (Ainsworth, 1973: 79; Emlen and Perry, 1974).

opportunities for children to meet the teacher or even to visit a kindergarten class (Klein and Ross, 1958: 65).

The second family transition period occurred after the child had gone off to school. During this time parents noted child behaviors that indicated tension resulting from the new experience. Children were fatigued, ate less sometimes, and had stomach upsets. They were irritable with siblings, friends, and parents; they were charged with hitting others, being uncooperative, and "talking back." They resumed such earlier behaviors as bedwetting, thumb-sucking, and increased dependence on their mothers. They also showed signs of being worried in their talkativeness or in their reticence, depending upon the characteristics of the children (Klein and Ross, 1958: 64).

Parents, too, were affected. Children were learning new skills and behaviors to a degree that proved surprising and occasionally disconcerting to their parents. Children began to show more independence, and rebelled at being watched or having a baby-sitter. They played farther from home and visited neighbors' homes more often. They also displayed more advanced behaviors such as doing more things for themselves, imitating older children, and helping with other sibs. They were concerned about their clothing and appearance, and this interest in self-identity carried over to greater awareness of their mothers as persons (Klein and Ross, 1958: 65).

These changed behaviors and parental reactions led to a period of parental criticism of the school and worry about the values their children were acquiring. During this time, parents expressed negative feelings toward the school and the teacher. They were annoyed at the child's seeing the teacher as an authority, and they felt inadequate as socialization agents in comparison with the teacher (Klein and Ross, 1958: 67). These feelings were complicated by the value conflicts parents experienced with respect to school situations. Although they wanted their children to learn to conform to group prescriptions, parents also wanted them to remain individuals. They worried about children's not fighting when attacked, yet they wanted them to avoid aggressiveness. And while parents viewed positively children's learning to get along with members of the opposite sex, they wondered if they would develop "premature" sex interests (Klein and Ross, 1958: 66).

The last phase of the transition period heralded the end of the role-making period and marked the establishment of new family interaction patterns. New family routines in getting the child off to school on time and in having sufficient sleep were now operating. Modifications in the family power structure gave the child freedom to display his new skills and to accept more self-responsibility for performance of some household tasks. Communication patterns reflecting the greater input of the child, due to his expanded contacts, began to develop. Parental affection giving remained important for the child who was taking on new tasks at home and at school to assure him that he was valued regardless of how well he was doing.

The child beginning his school career is making new roles within the constraints set by the tutelage of siblings, teachers, and parents. And yet, as we have seen, parents and siblings have to adjust their feelings and their behaviors to the skills and values the child develops as a consequence of his new status as pupil.

## CONTROL PATTERNS, COMMUNICATION, AND CHILDREN'S SCHOOL COMPETENCE

Lest it be thought that family transactions with school have consequences only for families, it is well to discuss how family interaction patterns affect children's performance in school. Research using Bernstein's concepts of position-oriented and person-oriented families is relevant here. You will remember from Chapter 2 that Bernstein made this distinction on the basis of differences in family power structures and language codes. In person-oriented families, children have some scope to "make" their roles. Parents are sensitive to the changing needs and abilities of their offspring owing to two-way communication patterns, and the family role assignment reflects changes (Cook-Gumperz, 1973: 14). Such families may also make use of an elaborated language code, which permits parents to specify their feelings and intentions in order to insure their intelligibility to the child (Cook-Gumperz, 1973: 10). Position-oriented families, in contrast, rely primarily in their speech on the common experience and values that family members share, and their language code is restricted in complexity and specificity.[2] Parents take less account of the different abilities of family members, since roles are allocated on the basis of established age and gender norms (Cook-Gumperz, 1973: 13–14).

These differences in family role organization and language codes

---

[2] All persons use elaborated and restricted speech codes. Persons of particular ethnic backgrounds sometimes appear inadequate in their language skills because they are observed in settings that are strange to them, they use nonstandard dialects, and they see no reason to "perform" for outside inquisitors (Cole and Bruner, 1971).

carry over to parent's performance of the rule-giver and disciplinarian roles. Bernstein contrasted the amount of discretion the child possesses in his compliance to parents' socialization attempts according to the type of control parents use and their language codes. He set up a four-fold category classification based on the positional/personal control distinction and the restricted/elaborated speech codes. Table 13-1 presents this classification. The figure shows that children have less discretion when their parents combine a restricted speech code with position-oriented controls. Such parents are more apt to give the child commands and administer physical punishment, two strategies Bernstein (1971: 156) labels as the imperative mode of control. Children have the most discretion, according to Bernstein, when their parents use an elaborated speech code to explain their rules or discipline.

Table 13-1.
**Parental Control Strategies and Speech Codes As Related to Children's Responses**

| Control Strategies | SPEECH CODES | |
| | Restricted | Elaborated |
| --- | --- | --- |
| Position-Oriented | *Parent*—Often uses imperative controls. *Child*—Can react only by obedience, rebellion, or withdrawal. Sensitive to who has power in a group. | *Parent*—Sometimes uses imperative controls. Explanation of rules in moral terms such as: "Good children wash their hands before dinner." *Child*—Sensitive to general rather than to specific qualities of individuals. Discretion in asking for reasons for rules. |
| Person-Oriented | *Parent*—Minor use of imperative controls. Attempts to explain discipline. Appeals to child's emotions: "You'll be happy if you stop doing that." *Child*—Some discretion to protest against parental controls. | *Parent*—Seldom uses imperative controls. Explanation of rules in terms of child's characteristics: "You can't watch TV, because you are just getting over a cold and need your rest." *Child*—Can question discipline. Sensitive to personal qualities of individuals. |

Source: Based on Cook-Gumperz, 1973; Bernstein, 1971.

They can tailor their explanations to the child's ability to understand.

Parents' control and communication patterns have an effect on children's school performance, beginning with how they prepare their children to enter the school career. When interviewers asked 160 black mothers and their four-year-old children from a broad range of socioeconomic backgrounds how they would prepare their children for school if the children were starting there for the first time the next day, relevant differences in preparation appeared. Women who used elaborated codes gave the following type of answer.

*First of all, I would remind her that she was going to school to learn, that her teacher would take my place, and that she would be expected to follow instructions. Also that her time was to be spent mostly in the classroom with other children, and that any questions or any problems that she might have she could consult with her teacher for assistance.*
*Anything else?*
*No, anything else would probably be confusing for her at her particular age. (Hess and Shipman, 1965: 877)*

These person-oriented women assured their children they would exercise some control over what happened to them in the classroom situation. Children also received information about what the situation was like and what they were to do. They were reassured concerning the new situation, since their mothers told them the teacher would take their place and would handle any problems that might arise.

This preparation can be contrasted with the kind of explanation, women using restricted codes gave. Here is a good example. " 'Well, John, it's time to go to school now. You must know how to behave. The first day at school you should be a good boy and should do just what the teacher tells you to do.' " (Hess and Shipman, 1965: 877)

These mothers emphasized the differential power positions of teacher and child. They gave the children little discretion to exercise control. They were to be obedient, and that was the only information they were given concerning the goal of the school. Mothers did not show them that there was some similarity between home and school situations. Thus these children began their school careers with little information about what the school setting was like or to whom to go if there were problems.

These communication differences carried over to the competency with which the mothers played the role of socializing agents. Their interactions with their children were observed in school-like situations in which the mothers were asked to show their children how to do several tasks. Mothers with elaborated language codes, outlined what was to be done. They also gave enough information that a child could go ahead on his own. If a child was about to make a mistake, his or her mother would warn that child of the need to avoid the mistake. A child was thus encouraged to exercise foresight, weigh the alternatives, and make his or her own decisions. Women who used restricted language codes were less clear and precise in their verbal instructions. A child did not know what to expect or how to perform. A mother would watch her child make a mistake and then punish the child. Because she would not alert the child to the consequences of acts, the child could not reflect on their linkage to previous acts. By emphasizing the rightness or wrongness of individual acts, these mothers failed to let children discover the overall meaning of the activity (Hess and Shipman, 1965: 884–885).

Children's success in the tasks their mothers were attempting to teach was related to maternal teaching style. Mothers who used elaborated codes included more abstract words in their instructions and used more complex sentence structures (Hess and Shipman, 1965: 876). Their children, in turn, used more general abstract cognitive responses and fewer nonverbal responses (Hess and Shipman, 1965: 879), tendencies that would aid them to learn in school.

These mother's skills, in turn, appeared to be related to their educational achievements. The higher the education of the mothers in the study, the more apt they were to give person-oriented explanations using an elaborated language code. The less highly educated mothers more often used the restricted language code. Thus parents' educational careers, which have much to do with the vocabularies they use, influence children's educational careers from as early as the children's preparation to enter the school setting.

As the studies by Hess and Shipman and others (Cook-Gumperz, 1973; Feshbach, 1973) suggest, children from families in which educational and financial resources are lacking tend to become used to limited learning since the environment in which they live allows little discretion and their mothers do not provide the necessary information to function competently. Unlike the middle-class children in the Klein and Ross study (1958) referred to earlier, they may be poorly prepared for what to expect in school and how to learn. Thus a study of seven-year-olds whose mothers used restricted speech to administer position-oriented rules and discipline did less well on school verbal intelligence tests than did their age peers whose mothers relied upon person-oriented control strategies implemented by elaborated speech (Cook-Gumperz, 1973).

## OCCUPATIONAL CAREERS AND FAMILY LIFE

The previous discussion showed that family differences in language use and socialization techniques affect children's school performances. At this point, we will examine how differences in work-life careers influence the qualities parents seek to develop in their children, qualities that also affect school performance. A series of studies by Melvin Kohn and his associates (1969) suggest that class differences exist in the behaviors that parents value and work to instill in children and that these differences are related to occupational experiences.

When asked to choose the characteristics they considered most important in children, working- and middle-class parents differed. Working-class parents tended to place highest priority on children's conformity, while middle-class parents more often placed it on children's self-direction. Specifically, working-class parents were more concerned with honesty, cleanliness, doing well in school, obedience, and neatness. Thus they would be anxious that their children conform to teachers' rules. In contrast middle-class parents, while concerned with honesty, cleanliness and the other traditional values, also gave their attention to children's self-control, curiosity, and consideration of others (Kohn, 1969: 21; and Kohn and Schooler, 1969: 662). They were more concerned that their children question teachers on knowledge issues rather than accept without question what they say.

These value differences carried over to parental behaviors. Working-class parents were more apt to discipline their children on the basis of the direct and immediate consequences of their children's acts and to penalize children for refusing to do what they were told. Middle-class parents were more prone to discipline children according to their interpretation of the children's intent. They were thus more likely to rebuke children who lost their tempers or got into fights while working-class parents were more apt to punish children who engaged in wild play that resulted in destruction (Kohn, 1969: 104–105).

After Kohn had traced the relation between parental values and the rules they set and the misbehaviors they disciplined, he then tried to explain why these value differences between the two classes existed. He concluded they had to do with the different occupational worlds the two classes experience and with the consequent differential preparations children receive for these worlds. In their transactions with their places of employment, middle-class persons are more often in positions that require self-direction. They are fairly free to set their own pace and to decide how to fulfill a relatively complex task. Con-

consequently, they see the necessity for children's being able to control themselves in the interest of task accomplishment. In contrast, working class persons less often exercise self-direction on the job. In their transactions with persons at work, they usually must conform to job routines set by supervisors who see they do conform. Consequently, they see conformity as essential to children's getting along (Kohn and Schooler, 1969: 676–677).

Education, too, plays a part, since the intellectual flexibility associated with higher education prepares persons for occupations requiring self-direction, which predisposes their holders to value self-direction rather than conformity (Kohn and Schooler, 1969: 677). Upon entering school, children are thus either conditioned by their parents' occupational and educational careers to go on to more advanced levels of education and training or to leave school early for the labor market.

**Occupational Careers and Fathers' Transmission of Values**

Not only does occupation influence socialization values and concomitantly, school competencies, but the effectiveness with which fathers play their occupational roles appears to affect their success as socialization agents. In the longitudinal study that assessed marital satisfaction over time, which we discussed in Chapter 8, there were data from men on satisfaction with their occupations and with their associated levels of living. This perceived occupational effectiveness after 20 years of marriage was related to similarity of values between parents and adolescents concerning the characteristics a youth of the same sex should have. The greater the fathers' perceived occupational effectiveness, the more successful he was in transmitting his values to his son. For daughters, there was some tendency for fathers who perceived themselves to be most effective to be somewhat less successful in socialization than slightly less effective fathers (Count van Manen, 1973: 13). Perhaps the effective men were so involved in their work transactions that they spent too little time with daughters to influence their particular values. And, because they felt sons to be more their own than their wives' responsibility to guide them, fathers might show a greater concern for sons. Along with their sons' admiration, this greater concern would explain the greater similarity of values between highly successful fathers and sons than between equally successful fathers and daughters.

## OCCUPATIONS, FAMILIES, AND SCHOOLS

After this discussion on the relation of occupations to parental social-ization values, it is easier to interpret and put in broader perspective earlier references to class differences in children's preparation to learn in the school setting.[3] The propensity of middle-class children to perform more competently in school than lower-class children is related to the greater harmony between parental expectations and goals and those of teachers. The kind of jobs middle-class parents and their associates are likely to hold require long periods of training. In addition to acquiring specialized training, this schooling enables them to operate on their own in their chosen occupations. Conse-quently, middle-class parents expect and encourage their children to learn in school. They effectively anticipate what children will need in the way of information to ease the tensions of entering school. Once children are in school, they support the authority of teachers and their demands upon the child. In addition, when a child is having difficul-ties with lessons, parents help, or they know where to turn to get help if they cannot give it themselves. They are also able to talk with a teacher directly if their child and his or her teacher are in serious conflict (Toby, 1956).

Lacking a history of doing well in school themselves, lower-class parents are less in sympathy with the goals of teachers. When their children have trouble learning or do not like the teacher, parents are less knowledgeable about how to handle the matter. In addition to being unable to help with a child's homework, they feel uncomfort-able about talking to the teacher, who is generally from a different class. A fear that education will make their children different can also minimize the pressure they exert for the child to do well in school. Thus their children perform less well in school and leave school earlier. Lacking specialized training, they obtain jobs similar to those of their parents, jobs that demand little self-direction. Their child-rearing values

---

[3] Reviews of class differences in family behaviors often raise questions among per-ceptive students as to why the "good guys," who seem to do things right, also tend to be middle class. Some of this association has to do with the fact that most re-searchers are middle class, and the way they structure their dependent variables is in terms of their class values. As researchers they themselves try to avoid such judg-ments. But the values of egalitarian marital relations, companionship between spouses, and the use of reasoning as a child-rearing technique are not restricted to middle-class persons. Thus readers who impose a value judgment on what is better or worse in the studies reviewed usually do so from a value perspective that is broadly accepted. And there is overlap in behaviors among classes (Erlanger, 1974).

are consequently affected. They are apt to replicate their parents' patterns of control and communication with their own offspring; hence the story is repeated. In their transactions with educational organizations, another generation of children undergoes schooling but is never vitally touched by a school career. Parental, occupational, and school careers are thus interdependent, the events in one limiting and reinforcing events in the others.

# REFERENCES

Ainsworth, Mary, D. S., "The Development of Infant-Mother Attachment," in Bettye M. Caldwell and Henry N. Ricciuti, eds., *Review of Child Development Research*, III. Chicago: University of Chicago Press, 1973, 1–94.

Bernstein, Basil, *Class, Codes and Control*. London: Routledge & Kegan Paul, 1971.

Bronfenbrenner, Urie, "The Challenge of Social Change to Public Policy and Developmental Research," Paper presented at the Meeting of the Society for Research on Child Development, 1975.

Cole, Michael and Jerome S. Bruner, "Cultural Differences and Inferences about Psychological Processes," *American Psychologist*, 1971, 26, 867–876.

Cook-Gumperz, Jenny, *Social Control and Socialization*. London: Routledge & Kegan Paul, 1973.

Count-van Manen, Gloria, "The Impact of 'Too Much' Parental Input Upon Child Socialization," Unpublished paper, 1973.

Emlen, Arthur C. and Joseph B. Perry, Jr., "Child-Care Arrangements" in Lois W. Hoffman and F. Ivan Nye, eds., *Working Mothers: An Evaluative Review of the Consequence for Wife, Husband and Child*. San Francisco: Jossey-Bass, 1974.

Erlanger, Howard S., "Class and Punishment in Childrearing," *American Sociological Review*, 1974, 39, 68–85.

Feshbach, Norma D., "Cross-Cultural Studies of Teaching Styles in Four Year-Olds and Their Mothers," in Anne D. Pick, ed., *Minnesota Symposia on Child Development*, VII. Minneapolis: University of Minnesota Press, 1973, 87–116.

Hess, Robert D. and Virginia C. Shipman, "Early Experience and the Socialization of Cognitive Modes in Children," *Child Development*, 1965, 36, 870–886.

Klein, Donald C. and Ann Ross, "Kindergarten Entry: A Study of Role Transition," in Morris Krugman, ed., *Orthopsychiatry and the School*. New York: American Orthopsychiatric Association, 1958, 60–69.

Kohn, Melvin L., *Class and Conformity*. Homewood, Ill.: Dorsey Press, 1969.

Kohn, Melvin L. and Carmi Schooler, "Class, Occupation, and Orientation," *American Sociological Review*, 1969, 34, 659–678.

Litwak, Eugene and Henry J. Meyer, "A Balance Theory of Coordination Between Bureaucratic Organizations and Community Primary Groups," *Administrative Science Quarterly*, 1966, 11 31–58.

Office of Child Development, Department of Health, Education and Welfare, *National Child Consumer Study*, II, 1975.

Toby, Jackson, "Orientation to Education as a factor in the Social Maladjustment of Lower-Class Children," *Social Forces*, 1956, 35, 259–266.

Woolsey, Suzanne H., "Pied Piper Politics and the Child Care Debate." *Daedalus*, 1977, 106, 127–146.

# 14

# Letting go

The mutual attachment that makes parents and children a viable unit is of primary importance in socialization. If parents are to succeed in this family development task, there must be enough parent-child attachment that children internalize parental expectations. Otherwise, children's conformity would depend upon the continuing presence of rule givers. There will be sufficient warmth under most circumstances for children to become attached to parents and to accept parental prescriptions. The nurturance given by an infant's caretakers in response to its initial dependency tends to assure mutual affection and to elicit positive behaviors as an infant develops. But once age and physical mobility enable a child to enter the world outside the home, parent-child ties loosen. The concern of this chapter is the process of letting go that both parents and children must go through in order for children to become independent adults.

## VARIATIONS IN TIMING OF LETTING GO

The period of the family life cycle ushered in by the oldest child's entering secondary school is usually the time when parents become conscious that their children will soon be leaving home to take on occupational and family responsibilities. Children, too, at that time begin demanding more power to make their own decisions. Their friendships with peers assume increasing importance as physiological changes graphically indicate that they are able to engage in adult sexual behavior.

This period when adolescents are pressing for more independence in anticipation of leaving the parental family unit has often been characterized as a stormy one from the perspective of the adolescent and as one of a "generation gap" between parents and children from the perspective of society. Both characterizations suggest that parent-child ties are not just loosened but are broken. Adolescents are seen as possessing attitudes and values that put them in conflict with their parents and other responsible adults. The process of preparing youth for adult status is, according to these views, a stressful one in which the changes sought by the youth run counter to the goals of his parents. Consequently, parents resist making changes and conflict results.

There is an increasing body of research, however, that suggests this family stage is not so conflict-ridden (Thurnher, Spence, and Lowenthal, 1974). Parents can anticipate their children's entering adult status and consciously prepare them for it. Paradoxically, by gradually letting go of their control over the adolescent, parents insure that the two generations remain attached. Parental control even under these circumstances, however, does not proceed at the same rate in all areas. Parents and children maintain some stable arrangements that ease their morphogenesis attempts in other areas. An early study of 686 students in the fourth to the tenth grades (Bowerman and Kinch, 1959) shows the determinants of the timing variation in the rate of parent-child separation.

The children, all of whom were from the state of Washington, reported on the comparative influence parents and peers of the same age exercised in three areas. The first, *identification*, had to do with whether the students believed parents or friends understood them better, and whether, as adults, they would rather be the kind of persons that either their parents or their friends were. The second area, *associations*, covered the students' preferences for spending evenings and weekends either with peers or with parents. The *normative* dimension dealt with the relative influence parents and peers had on the students' ideas of what was right and wrong, the importance of school, and

their final decision when either parents or friends wanted them to do
something of which the other group disapproved (Bowerman and
Kinch, 1959: 207). In terms of family development concepts, the identification area had to do with how well the family developmental task
of socialization had been fulfilled. The parental role sequence of play-
mate-companion was relevant to the associations area, while the role
sequence of rule giver related to normative decisions. Students were
classified as family or peer oriented in each area, depending on which
group received more of their choices. If they gave an equal number of
responses naming parents and friends, they were placed in the neutral
category.

Table 14-1 shows that the greatest shift in behavior that appeared
in this cross-sectional study had to do with the youths' sociability behavior and the least in the area of values. In the fourth grade, three-

TABLE 14-1
**Percentage of Children Classified as Having Family, Peer, or Neutral
Orientation, by Grade in School**

| Orientation | Grade in School | | | | | | |
|---|---|---|---|---|---|---|---|
| | 4th | 5th | 6th | 7th | 8th | 9th | 10th |
| Combined Orientation | | | | | | | |
| Family | 87.1 | 80.5 | 80.2 | 66.7 | 41.7 | 44.7 | 31.6 |
| Neutral | 6.9 | 12.2 | 11.2 | 9.3 | 18.3 | 22.4 | 20.2 |
| Peer | 5.9 | 7.3 | 8.6 | 24.1 | 40.0 | 32.9 | 48.1 |
| Normative Orientation | | | | | | | |
| Family | 82.2 | 64.6 | 69.8 | 51.9 | 33.0 | 42.4 | 30.4 |
| Neutral | 5.9 | 12.2 | 12.1 | 13.9 | 14.8 | 16.5 | 19.0 |
| Peer | 11.9 | 23.2 | 18.1 | 34.3 | 52.2 | 41.2 | 50.6 |
| Association Orientation | | | | | | | |
| Family | 75.2 | 65.9 | 62.1 | 51.9 | 20.9 | 21.2 | 15.2 |
| Neutral | 15.8 | 24.4 | 25.0 | 22.2 | 39.1 | 37.6 | 29.1 |
| Peer | 8.9 | 9.8 | 12.9 | 25.9 | 40.0 | 41.2 | 55.7 |
| Identification | | | | | | | |
| Family | 81.2 | 79.2 | 77.6 | 72.2 | 57.4 | 62.3 | 51.9 |
| Neutral | 13.8 | 18.3 | 18.1 | 18.5 | 24.3 | 24.7 | 21.5 |
| Peer | 5.0 | 2.4 | 4.3 | 9.2 | 18.2 | 13.0 | 26.6 |
| Number | 101 | 82 | 116 | 108 | 115 | 85 | 79 |

Source: Bowerman and Kinch, 1959: 208

fourths of the children chose their parents as persons with whom they preferred to do things, and just nine percent their peers. By tenth grade, only 15 percent of the youths preferred their parents, while 50 percent selected peers. With respect to identification, however over half (52 percent) of tenth graders reported their parents understood them better and provided a model they wished to emulate, as compared with 81 percent of fourth graders. The change in the area of normative decisions was in between the extremes of association and identification behaviors. The percentage choosing family over peers, when the two groups' values clashed, decreased from 82 to 30 percent as one went from the yougest to the oldest students. Peer choices increased over the same period from 12 to 51 percent.

These findings indicate that parents tend to lose companionship roles while retaining their roles as support givers and adult role models. They continue to exercise influence through their children's acceptance of parental values, though they share this influence with peers.

The shift in relative influence from parents to peers not only varies with respect to area but also is uneven over time. The variation in timing appears to be related to changes in the children's school careers. Students in the school district sampled moved to middle school in the sixth grade and then to high school for the ninth grade after they were well into adolescence. These school shifts resulted in new peer contacts and slowed the students' letting go of family ties. In the unfamiliar situations, youths turned back to parents for support and companionship, as shown in Table 14-1. Once they had reestablished friendships, however, they again continued their movement into predominantly peer social networks (Bowerman and Kinch, 1959: 208).

School exits coupled with school entries at more advanced levels signal to parents children's increasing maturity. These graduation points serve as occasions for parents to relax their control, as they anticipate the departure of children from home. Since children in the new setting initially are turning more to parents, the lack of child pressure for more independence makes it easier for parents to institute rational policies to prepare children to take care of themselves.

The increasing orientation of youths to outsiders accompanies the physiological changes of puberty. Girls, who mature earlier than boys, show a shift from family to peer influence about a year before boys. Their awareness of the development of adult sexual capacities leads them to put aside childish dependencies. Thus the combined scores on the three areas showed that girls changed from preferring parents overwhelmingly in the sixth grade to only a little over half in the seventh with a corresponding increase in peer orientation. Boys did not show comparable changes until the eight grade (Bowerman and Kinch, 1959: 209).

The degree to which parental influence continues is related to parental support behaviors. The lesser amount of time that parents of larger families have to give specific children appears to account for the heavy peer orientation of children from these backgrounds. From seventh grade on, youths from families where there were more than three children showed a greater shift to peer orientations in all areas for most comparisons (Bowerman and Kinch, 1959: 209).

To obtain specific data on how well parents were accomplishing the family developmental task of morale maintenance, students answered the following questions: (1) How well do you get along with members of your family? (2) Do you receive the attention from family members you think you should? (3) Do you talk over personal problems with family members? (4) Does the treatment you get from family members meet your expectations? The students also answered these same questions with respect to their friends. From their answers to these questions, it was possible to form groups of students. There was the group of the fortunate 148 students, who got along well with both families and peers; the 161 students who looked to their families but not to their peers for personal satisfaction; the 156 who reversed the peer-parent balance and found fulfillment with friends; and finally, the unhappy 221 who had neither friends nor families who met their morale needs (Bowerman and Kinch, 1959: 210).

How children felt they were treated in their families had more to do with whether they were largely influenced by peers than the behavior of peers. Although all groups shifted their orientation to peers in the higher grades, this was less true of those in close touch with parents. Thus over half of students in the tenth grade who had good relations with parents were oriented to them in values and decision making. This was true of only 16 percent of tenth grade students who did not get along well with parents. In the area of identification, 77 percent of the parent-oriented youths as compared with 32 percent of the peer-oriented youths retained parents as role models.

These findings, however, indicate that despite maintaining warm relations, parents and children are letting go. Even among tenth graders who looked to parents and not to peers for support, only 31 percent preferred parents to peers for companionship. Students of the same age who got along with peers but not parents could muster only seven percent with a similar preference (Bowerman and Kinch, 1959: 211).

Bronfenbrenner (1975) reports similar results from a more recent work. Children who are susceptible to peer influence come from homes where one or both parents are frequently absent. These children also describe their parents as less affectionate and less firm in discipline. Bronfenbrenner (1970: 90) concludes that "attachment to age-mates appears to be influenced more by a lack of attention and concern at home than by any positive attraction of the peer group itself."

There are adolescents, as indicated above, who are close neither to parents nor to peers. Longitudinal studies involving observations and interviews with mothers and children as the latter were growing up point to the limited linkages between socialization at one family stage and the next that affect peer and parent relations.[1] Punitiveness, irritibility, and anxiety, along with ignoring behaviors in mothers during the late primary years, were associated with adolescents' not getting along well with peers (Kagan and Moss, 1962: 323). Boys were cold and hostile and girls appeared discontented (Schaefer and Bayley, 1963: 84, 86). Thus maternal treatment that suggests children are unlovable affects these children in ways that make the maternal perceptions reality when children become adolescents.

But, in general, the so-called generation gap between parents and children has been overemphasized. Parent-child detachment does occur over time. The timing and the extent of detachment, however, depend on the kind of family relations youths have. Parents still remain influential as persons to be emulated and retain equal influence in decisions of what is right and wrong, provided the affection-giving patterns joining parents and youths are strong.

This conclusion is supported by what 52 high-school seniors and 54 parents whose youngest child was a senior in the same school had to say about the things they considered important (Thurnher, Spence, and Lowenthal, 1974). These parents and youths were randomly selected from a middle class area in a large Western city and, except for two pairs, were unrelated. The two generations showed a continuity of traditional values with differences appearing primarily in "behavioral style and the timing of and attitudes toward means of attaining them" (Thurnher, Spence, and Lowenthal, 1974: 318). The youths' appraisal of their parents and the parents' evaluation of their

---

[1] The Fels research was done with 44 boys and 45 girls from 63 different families who were studied from 1929 to 1954. The families were predominantly middle class although there were some families of farmers and laborers (Kagan and Moss, 1962: 10–11). The Berkeley Growth Study had a sample of 27 boys and 27 girls from a variety of socioeconomic backgrounds with the middle class predominating. They were studied from their births in 1928 or 1929 until they were 18 (Schaefer and Bayley, 1963: 10).

children were generally positive, and both groups placed heavy emphasis on two-way communication. There were also some women who had been socialized by their children and had accepted the self-realization values more common among the younger generation.

Mothers appeared to be more accepting of adolescent aspirations than fathers, which may account for the youths' feeling closer to mothers than fathers. This was true even though boys tended to be rather patronizing in their descriptions of their mothers. They perceived them as worriers, overanxious, and emotional while girls said they were warm, understanding, and considerate. Both, however, viewed fathers as hard-working but rather distant from family concerns (Thurnher, Spence, and Lowenthal, 1974: 316), making for the switch-board communication structure and satellite affection-giving patterns described in Chapter 3.

The parents and the youths did report some intergenerational conflict, but the disputes were not on fundamentals. They were on such matters as the use of the family car, the time to get home from dates, the proper length of hair, and the need to maintain some order in clothing and rooms (Thurnher, Spence, and Lowenthal, 1974: 317).

## PARENTAL INFLUENCE AND THE POWER AND AFFECTION STRUCTURES

Previous chapters on the parental career have demonstrated that competent parents socialize competent children and that the structures of power and affection have much to do with children's behaviors. But evidence also indicates that accomplishment of the individual task of moral development is related in parents and children with the family affection structure and, to a lesser extent, with the power structure influencing the level of accomplishment (Peterson, 1976). Forty-nine intact, four-person families in which the older child was 13 years old were observed while they discussed two moral dilemma stories and questions designed to elicit controversy.

Ratings of the interaction of these largely middle-class families showed a positive relation in the members' level of moral development according to Kohlberg's (1969) seven-stage classification. High levels in parents were associated with high levels in children, just as there was a family association in low level moral development.

When it came to the kinds of socialization patterns that appeared in families differing in level of moral development, principled adolescents as compared with youths in the conventional or preconventional stages received more support from their parents and, in turn, gave more support to their parents and to their younger siblings. The cloverleaf affection structure existing in those families was reflected in the kinds of control the fathers exercised. Among highly supportive fathers, adolescent moral development was higher if fathers depended largely on reasoning with little use of love withdrawal and only with medium amounts of orders and demands (Peterson, 1976). Thus, as we have seen, youths' feelings of being well treated and being able to tell their troubles to a family member are not only associated with their continued acceptance of parental values but also with their level of moral development.

Families' power patterns, in addition to affection-giving and communication structures, also have much to do with how well prepared youths are to realize these values as independent adults. A classic cross-sectional study, this time with seventh-through-twelfth graders living in Ohio and North Carolina, shows how power structures affect youths' training for independence. (Elder, 1962: 243).

The students filled out questionnaires in which they reported the kind of parent-child power structure that existed in their families in terms of how decisions affecting them were made, both by their mothers and by their fathers. The possible answers and the labels that Elder (1962: 244) assigned to the various power arrangements are as follows:

1.  *Autocratic*—My parent (father or mother) says what I must do.
2.  *Authoritarian*—My parent listens to me, but still makes the decisions.
3.  *Democratic*—My parent has the final say although I have a lot of opportunity to make my own decisions.
4.  *Equalitarian*—My parent's opinions and mine are equally important in decision making.
5.  *Permissive*—I can make my decisions but my parent would like me to take into account his/her opinion.
6.  *Laissez Faire*—I can do what I please regardless of my parent's opinion.
7.  *Ignoring*—My parent doesn't care what I do.

Parents varied, the findings showed, on the amount of power they allowed youths to have. Mothers gave children more decision-making discretion than did fathers. Thirty-five percent of the youths reported their fathers were in "autocratic" and "authoritarian" arrangements, the two most asymmetrical power structures. The comparable percentage for mothers was 22 percent. A larger percentage of mothers, 42 percent, as compared with 32 percent of fathers, were "permissive" or "equalitarian." Only a negligible proportion of students reported "laissez-faire" or "ignoring" parents (Elder, 1962: 245).

Age was clearly a factor in how much voice youths had in making decisions concerning themselves. Both parents, but mothers to a greater degree, allowed youths in grades 10 to 12 more power in decision making than they did youths in grades seven to nine. Only 18 percent of mothers and 33 percent of fathers of older sons were in the "autocratic" and "authoritarian" categories as compared with 29 percent of mothers and 37 percent of fathers of younger sons, with similar figures appearing for daughters.

Although class differences in dependency on peers or parents did not appear in the largely middle-class sample of Bowerman and Kinch (1959: 207), they did appear in the Elder study. Consistent with the greater emphasis on conformity among persons in lower-class occupations that Kohn (1969) found, lower-class parents tended more often to be authoritarian than middle-class parents. The latter were more likely to be "democratic," "equalitarian," and "permissive," power patterns that would prepare the adolescent to direct his own behavior, the quality middle-class parents tend to prefer to conformity.

The results on family size support the hypothesized tendency for larger families, in this study defined as those with more than two children, to have a more vertical power structure. This greater proportion of authoritarian and autocratic parents among larger families also held regardless of class (Elder, 1962: 253).

To this point, we have seen some of the factors, such as social class, age of child, size of family, and gender of parent, that appear to be related to how asymmetrical the parent-child power structure is. Let us now examine the adolescents' perception of the fairness of the arrangements. Youths in "democratic" structures tended to be most satisfied, and those in highly parent-dominated arrangements least satisfied. Four-fifths (85 percent) of students in "democratic" power structures were satisfied. Just over half the students reported the arrangements fair in "autocratic" structures (fathers 51 percent; mothers 55 percent), although the percentage increased to 59 percent for mothers and 75 percent for fathers in "authoritarian" patterns (Elder, 1962: 258).

There also appeared to be a relation between the power and affection-giving structures, as well as between the power structure and the youths' perception of its fairness. This relation appeared even though only a minority of adolescents perceived their parents as rejecting them. The percentage of youths who felt rejected was least for "democratic," "permissive," and "equalitarian" relations, where it was only about 10 percent. Over half the students in "laissez faire" or "ignoring" power patterns reported they had felt rejected. Among those in "autocratic" relations, it was over 40 percent, for both parents, 26 percent for mothers in "authoritarian" arrangements, and 18 percent for fathers in this sort of structure (Elder, 1962: 259). Note here, as with the fairness findings, adolescents perceived mothers in authoritarian relations more negatively than fathers, probably because of the gender stereotype that women are not supposed to be domineering.

The data do not indicate the causal direction of the relation between the parent-child power and affection structures. Whether their lack of warmth forces parents to be domineering if they wish to enforce conformity or whether their superior power position leads to lack of intergenerational affection cannot be determined.

The consequences of the various power structures for the adolescent's learning to be independent are clear. Dominating or ignoring parents are not giving their children the experience of making decisions under parental guidance. In addition, the negative parent-child relations associated with such power arrangements discourage intergenerational continuities in behaviors and values. Neglectful parents may never have been involved enough with their adolescents, so that the two generations have much to let go. Parents who monopolize decision-making power, on the other hand, appear not to want ever to let go. And their children, although resenting the power structure as unfair, are not prepared to be independent.

Such parents also serve as poor teachers of affection giving, although we have seen how essential this skill is if children as adults are to enjoy satisfactory marital and parent-child relations. The failure to prepare children to establish intimate relations with others is particularly a danger for adolescent boys. The stereotypic male characteristic of not displaying emotion is given positive sanction in many social groups. When fathers are cold, boys have little opportunity to escape internalizing this value with unfortunate consequences for themselves and their future wives and children. Girls and women, however, are supposed to show emotion according to gender stereotypes. Daughters of rejecting parents are apt to have contacts with women who are warm. These examples, coupled with positive societal evaluation of warm feminine behavior, can provide the socialization in affection giving girls lack at home.

## PARENTAL STRESS AND THE PERIOD OF LETTING GO

For youths and parents who are united by bonds of attachment, the process of letting go can be difficult. A delicate balance must be maintained between the youth's need to learn to do things for himself and his need for supportive guidance during the learning period. Adolescence can be characterized as a period of noncommitment. Fortunate youths are experimenting with a variety of personal appearance modes and a range of educational and occupational choices. In order to avoid premature commitment, however, they need to be able to exercise the option of returning to the dependent stance of their younger days. Then, reassured and refreshed by a period of reflection, they can set out again into the world beyond the family boundaries with a bit more confidence and a bit more independence than was true the previous time. These periodic advances and retreats of adolescents are hard on parents. The modifications in role sequence contents appropriate to interactions with mature adolescents are constantly having to be replaced by earlier behaviors suited to younger children.

McArthur (1962) once summarized the intermeshing of individual developmental tasks of adolescents and parents as follows. For youths, the tasks were to achieve emotional, and we would add, physical independence of parents; to learn to behave in socially responsible ways; and to develop more adult relations with peers of both sexes. For parents, the tasks were to assist youths to become adults possessing these qualities, while reestablishing marital bonds eroded by the wear of parent-child ties and fulfilling civic and social responsibilities (McArthur, 1962: 189–190).

These tasks serve to point up the difficulties adolescents and parents face. Both parties have to rework family interpersonal relations—parents with spouses, and adolescents with parents—while establishing or repairing extra-familial social networks. For adolescents, these networks are particularly crucial. From these contacts, they will eventually establish the dyadic relations that will replace their parental family in providing emotional support.

With the unmaking and remaking of relations attendant on letting go, it is not surprising to find that the period when children are adolescents is often viewed by parents as a difficult time. Interviews with a national sample, representative of white persons over 21 years old, and living in private households, showed how the problems of parents with adolescents compared with those of parents with younger children. Although fathers whose oldest children were adolescents were most apt to give negative or neutral responses to questions concerning life changes brought about by having children, they tied with fathers of primary-school children in the proportion reporting that their life was restricted because of having children this age. Almost three-fourths of them, 73 percent, along with three-fourths of fathers of school-aged children said they had problems with their children. The latter group of fathers, however, probably because of the greater dependence of their children, was more apt to feel seriously inadequate in the way they performed their parental roles, while fathers of adolescents only at times felt this way (Veroff and Feld, 1970: 383–384, Table 4-d).[2]

Where the two groups of men believed they were inadequate differed. Fathers of school-agers for whom the family developmental task of socialization loomed large, felt they were not competent as rule givers. About a third, 31 percent, as opposed to no fathers of adolescents, said they lacked patience and control over their tempers. The latter group, however, felt inadequate in the companionship role, as their children approached adulthood. Almost three-fourths, 73 percent, of the fathers of youths believed they did not spend enough time with their children. The comparable percentage for the fathers of school-aged children was 31 percent. But both groups tried to distance themselves from their children rather than actively involve themselves in parental role performances (Veroff and Feld, 1970: 383–384, Table 4-d).

When we turn to mothers of adolescents as compared with mothers of children of other ages, we find that they most often felt they were inadequate in their maternal role performances. While 28 percent of them felt inadequate "often" or "a lot of times," the next highest group of mothers, those with school-aged children, expressed these views just 17 percent of the time. Like fathers, the mothers of youths saw this inadequacy as related to companionship. And they (43 percent), along with mothers of school-aged children (38 percent), and their husbands did not actively involve themselves with their children (Veroff and Feld, 1970: 381–383, Table 4c,-d).

But mothers seemed to be most negative about parenthood before children went to school. This period is when they felt most restricted by parenthood and were most negative in their reports of the effects of having children. Over a third of them (35 percent) as compared with

[2] Nineteen percent of fathers of primary school-aged children as compared with 10 percent of fathers of adolescetns felt "often" or "a lot of times" inadequate. Thirty-five percent of the latter fathers, however, "sometimes" felt this way. The comparable percentage for fathers of school children was 26 (Veroff and Feld, 1970: 384, Table 4-d).

30 percent of other mothers felt tied down by their children. And about a fourth (26 percent) of the mothers of preschoolers, and 21 percent of mothers having adolescent children, made negative statements about their interactions with children.

Mothers' perception of having child-rearing problems, like that of fathers, was greatest during the years of heavy socialization responsibilities when children are in school. The ages of children once they were in school appeared to have little effect on mothers' child-rearing difficulties. Four-fifths of mothers of adolescents said they had problems, but this was also true of 86 percent of mothers of school children. Mothers of preschool children were somewhat less likely to report problems (71 percent), although, as reported above, they were the most unhappy with parenthood (Veroff and Feld, 1970: 381–383, Table 4c,-d).

It appears, then, that fathers do not see children as problematic until they start school. Mothers, however, with the main responsibility for child care report the negative aspects of children earlier, when children's nurturance needs tie them down. Since children tend to see authoritarian parents as rejecting and paternal power is more often authoritarian, fathers lack the cushion of mutual understanding that would ease the stress as children and youths demand more power to make decisions. But mothers also have difficulty adjusting to youths seeking greater independence.

These data also indicate why marital satisfaction is particularly low in the primary and secondary school years. Stresses in parent-child relations feed back on husband and wife relations making them less pleasant. And these stresses in part result from children's demands for greater freedom stemming from the school career. Thus the interdependence of the family members and their careers appears again in our coverage of the family career.

## PARENTAL STRESS AND EXTRAFAMILIAL TRANSACTIONS

Some family transactions with community groups are dependent on the stage of the family-life cycle. Examples of this type of transactions are those with the schools discussed earlier and those with voluntary organizations (Babchuck and Booth, 1969). Parental membership and participation in youth-serving groups are high when children are in the late primary grades and are adolescents. Parental interest in groups like the scouting organizations, or the Young Womens' Christian Associa-

tion and the Young Men's Hebrew Association, give parents a legitimate reason to have a voice in children's peer activities. Parents can
see for themselves what goes on in the programs sponsored by youth
groups as well as exercise some influence on what these activities are.

A second type of transaction ties families to the community over the
majority of their existence, but the need of families for these transactions peak at particular stages. A good example of such transactions
are those having to do with the occupational world. The need of families to have income in order to fulfill the physical maintenance task is
ever present. These needs, however, are at their height when children
are adolescents. The costs of educating youths or of outfitting a new
residential unit for youths preparing for adult status, often outstrip parental earning power. Parents, therefore, experience financial as well
as emotional stress during the period when adolescents are becoming
independent.

Oppenheimer (1974) has documented this so-called life-cycle
squeeze resulting from the discrepancy between paternal income and
the lengthening economic dependency of adolescents. The Bureau of
Labor Statistics has put together family budgets based on prevailing
consumption patterns of families in the U.S. To maintain a level of living
equivalent to that of a hypothetical family composed of an employed
husband 38, a wife not employed outside the home, a boy 13, and a
girl 8, the family income must not only increase with the number of
children, as Oppenheimer (1974: 229) points out, but also with the
children's ages. A childless couple needs an income only 49 percent
as large as that of the hypothetical family to enjoy an equivalent
consumer-comfort level. Where the household head is 35 to 44, with
two children younger than six, the income would have to be 80 percent
of the hypothetical family's, but this percentage increases to 113 percent when the eldest child is between 16 and 17 (Oppenheimer, 1974:
230). For families with three children, the ratio goes from 97 percent
to 128 percent, depending on whether the oldest child is under 6 or 18
years of age. According to these Bureau of Labor Statistics figures,
therefore, parents with three children in the family at the adolescent
stage of the life cycle must have an income more than 2.5 times as
large as that of a childless couple if they are to have a level of consumption similar to a couple without children (Oppenheimer, 1974:
231).

Although the demands of the family life cycle peak at the same time
for all parents, the point at which income from various occupations is
at its height differs. Low earnings generally characterize all persons

starting their work careers, regardless of occupation. This fact is a primary reason there are so many two-income families among young, childless couples. For higher-earning occupations, however, peak earnings come relatively late in the age of a worker, but the percentage increase over the initial starting salary is considerable. Thus, among the highest paid managers, U.S. Census data showed the peak median earnings came when men were 45 to 54 years of age. These earnings were 30 percent higher than the median earnings at ages 25 to 34 (Oppenheimer, 1974: 238). Moreover, because the peak comes relatively late, the deterioration of earnings for men 55 to 64 is not pronounced. For example, it was only two percent for the highest paid managers (Oppenheimer, 1974: 246).

Professionals, managers, and sales workers who are in the more highly paid occupations in which income ceilings are reached late in life will have therefore little difficulty in keeping up with or surpassing the level of living of their younger colleagues, even though they have heavier family responsibilities.

The situation is different for men in less well-paid occupations. Here median income peaks earlier, but at a lower level than the higher-income occupations. The deterioration in earnings for older men is also greater. As an example of this type of income history, men in middle-level occupations, such as craftsmen and foremen, reach their earnings peak when they are 25 to 34. At ages 45 to 54, however, median earnings are six percent below this peak and at 55 to 64 the income is 12 percent less (Oppenheimer, 1974: 236, Table 3). These men, therefore, face the heavy educational and support expenses of adolescents with incomes that are not much more, and sometimes even less, than those of their younger colleagues who have fewer family expenses. (See Table 14-2 for other examples.)

When there are adolescents at home, this life-cycle squeeze between men's earnings and family financial demands influences the upsurge in older women's employment outside the home. Of currently married women 35 to 39 years old whose only child was 12 to 17, for example, three-fifths (59.6 percent) were employed outside the home. Only two percent fewer women (57.8 percent) of the same age and marital status with two adolescents under 18 were working. For married women, husbands present, who were 40 to 44, 56.3 percent of those with one adolescent were employed. The comparable figure was 53.9 percent when women of this age had two adolescents under 18 years of age (U.S. Bureau of the Census, 1973: 155–156, Table 13). The number of teenage children and age of mothers had little influence on employ-

Table 14.2

## Median 1959 Earnings of White Males 18–64 Years Old by Age and Occupation Classified by Peak Median Earnings

| Occupation Classified by Peak Median Earnings[a] | Age | | | | |
|---|---|---|---|---|---|
| | 18–24 | 25–34 | 35–44 | 45–54 | 55–64 |
| **Professional and technical workers** | | | | | |
| 9+ | $3,062 | $7,125 | $10,135 | $10,596[b] | $9,125 |
| 7–9 | 2,759 | 6,353 | 7,554 | 7,719[b] | 7,328 |
| 5–7 | 2,210 | 5,092 | 6,491[b] | 6,087 | 6,036 |
| **Managers, officials, and proprietors** | | | | | |
| 9+ | —[c] | 6,886 | 8,962 | 9,500[b] | 9,286 |
| 7–9 | 3,528 | 6,146 | 7,735 | 7,657 | 7,896[b] |
| 5–7 | 3,583 | 5,776 | 6,133[b] | 6,125 | 5,417 |
| **Sales workers** | | | | | |
| 7–9 | 3,412 | 6,321 | 6,989 | 6,981 | 7,077[b] |
| 5–7 | 1,778 | 5,014 | 5,750[b] | 5,018 | 4,312 |
| **Clerical workers** | | | | | |
| 5–7 | 2,508 | 5,077 | 5,709[b] | 5,489 | 5,190 |
| 4–5 | 2,333 | 4,406 | 4,906[b] | 4,804 | 4,636 |
| **Craftsmen and foremen** | | | | | |
| 7–8 | —[c] | 6,000 | 7,348 | 7,440[b] | 7,154 |
| 5–7 | 3,283 | 5,579 | 6,028[b] | 5,675 | 5,291 |
| Under 5 | 2,468 | 4,801 | 5,080[b] | 4,406 | 3,630 |
| **Operatives** | | | | | |
| 5–7 | 2,977 | 4,870 | 5,284[b] | 5,190 | 4,781 |
| Under 5 | 2,605 | 4,537 | 4,995[b] | 4,689 | 4,135 |
| **Service workers** | | | | | |
| 5–6 | —[c] | 5,336 | 5,721[b] | 5,692 | 5,071 |
| Under 5 | 1,116 | 3,534 | 3,935[b] | 3,809 | 3,356 |
| **Laborers under 5** | 1,669 | 3,936 | 4,128[b] | 3,701 | 3,415 |
| **Total** | 2,465 | 5,256 | 5,901[b] | 5,544 | 4,009 |

Source: Derived from subsamples drawn from the original 1/1000 samples from the 1960 Census of Population and Housing, and adapted from Oppenheimer, 1974: 236, Table 3.

[a] To make the headings less cumbersome, the occupation-earnings headings were shortened so that peak median earnings were presented as 9+, 7–9, etc., rather than $9,000 or more, $7,000–8,999, etc.

[b] Peak median for occupation.

[c] Medians were not computed for sample sizes below 50.

Note: Excluded were men in the following categories: armed services, farm occupations, apprentices, occupation not reported, no occupation, and a small number of men in occupations that could not be readily classified in the 18 categories employed in the table. Men with zero or negative net earnings for 1959 were omitted.

ment when families are going through the financial deficit years when adolescents are present.[3]

The life cycle squeeze has tragic results for poor families. "Habitually living as they do under circumstances in which demands are greater than resources, they experience adolescence as a period not of temporary discrepancy, but of ever increasing deficits" (Aldous and Hill, 1969: 9). As a result, parents do not discourage adolescents from fending for themselves, whether or not they are ready for independence. And it is at this point in the family life cycle when the transmission of poverty to the next generation is most likely to occur.

By the time adolescents leave home, parents supposedly have socialized them to play adult occupational and spousal roles. For poor families, the necessary timing for independence is absent. Parents are unable to insure youths the educational credentials such as a high-school graduation that are a prerequisite to steady employment. They are even less able to assist adolescents who take on occupational and family responsibilities at the same time. These adolescents experience no period of noncommitment in which to experiment with educational and occupational alternatives. Such a period presupposes parental financial support that is nonexistent in financially pressed families. There is a career event pile-up. Instead of exercising choice, adolescents fall into low-paying jobs with little stability and no future in their occupational careers, and drift into marriages which initiate family careers with family responsibilities coming too soon and too fast. Thus "marriages involving persons who are under 19 years old are disproportionately found in groups with lower levels of education and among persons holding unskilled and semi-skilled jobs" (Aldous and Hill, 1968: 4). Premarital pregnancies, which are a factor in one-third to over one-half of all such young marriages, can mean the premature addition of parental roles, and further add to the financial pressures these couples experience. The DeLissovoy study (1973: a.b), which we discussed earlier, details graphically the consequences of early marriage and early parenthood in terms of low income, forced living with parents, marital conflict, and unsatisfactory parental role performance.

The lack of a moratorium period for adolescents and parents to

---

[3] Gendell (1975) points out that the presence and age of children as well as husbands' incomes affect the rate of women's employment, with maternal responsibility having the greater effect. When women have children under six, they are less apt to work regardless of husbands' incomes.

prepare for the adolescent's placement in the adult community leads to a continuance of poverty. The abrupt break of the youth's asserting independence from the parental family does not lead to a break from the conditions of poverty that characterized the parental family. Instead, the juxtaposition of the launching period of the parental family with the establishment stage of the newly married means that youths enter adult life not on their own terms but on whatever terms a grudging society is willing to give. Under these circumstances, parents transmit more of their weaknesses than of their competencies to the next generation.

A clear example of this in a noneconomic area is the intergenerational transmission of divorce. Children of divorced parents tend themselves more often to divorce. This parent-child similarity in marital outcomes is not necessarily due to the failure of parents to serve as adequate role models (Pope and Mueller, 1976). Instead, according to the reports of a national sample representative of ever-married white women under 45, it appeared to be related to high-risk mate selection in the children's generation. Even when religious affiliation, socio-economic status of fathers, and rural-urban residence were controlled, women from broken homes were less well educated, were more often pregnant at the time of marirage, and married at younger ages than women from intact homes. Moreover, the husbands of women who came from broken homes had lower status occupations and were more likely to have been married before (Mueller and Pope, 1977). Thus the intergenerational transmission of divorce like that of poverty seems to be related to poor timing of marital and parental careers in the younger generation.

# SUMMARY

While Chapter 12 indicated the kinds of parental behaviors associated with the development of various competencies in children as they are growing up, this chapter dealt with the process whereby parents socialize adolescents to become adults. The changes in power and sociability patterns that are associated with parents and youths letting go of their interdependencies do not necessarily lead to conflict or to generational differences in values and attitudes. Strong parent-child attachment eases the stress of establishing new patterns that will give youths more power to make their own decisions. Despite the lessening of time spent together with attendant parental supervision of adolescent activities, youths often look to parents as role models for adult behavior and accept their values with respect to fundamental issues of behavior.

When there is conflict, it appears to represent a continuation of unsatisfactory parent-child relations over the years. The constraints set by the level of prior task performances are not overcome. Neglectful, domineering parents lead children to turn to peers for the understanding and support lacking at home. Parents, however, who give adolescents little decision-making power ill-prepare them for independence.

Other adolescents who have adult status thrust upon them prematurely are not necessarily involved in conflicts with their parents. The latter, however, are unable to meet the financial obligations that the costly socialization of adolescents require. In these families, parents cannot select the sort of occupational and educational transactions that will benefit themselves and their children. Family boundaries are easily breached, and parents have as little control over their children's associates as they have over their own incomes.

To the extent, however, that parents are prepared to engage in anticipatory socialization of their adolescents for independence the process of letting go seems to be reasonably satisfactory. The mutual attachment both generations feel helps ease the discomfort that comes from the conscious recognition of the youth's coming departure from the family.

# REFERENCES

Aldous, Joan and Reuben Hill, "Breaking the Poverty Cycle: Strategic Points for Intervention," *Social Work*, 1969, 14, 3–12.

Babchuck, Nicholas and Alan Booth, "Voluntary Association Membership: A Longitudinal Analysis," *American Sociological Review*, 1969, 34, 31–45.

Bowerman, Charles E. and John W. Kinch, "Changes in Family and Peer Orientation of Children Between the Fourth and Tenth Grades," *Social Forces*, 1959, 37, 206–211. Copyright © The University of North Carolina Press.

Bronfenbrenner, Urie, "The Challenge of Social Change to Public Policy and Developmental Research," Paper presented at the Meeting of the Society for Research in Child Development, 1975.

DeLissovoy, Vladimir, "Child Care by Adolescent Parents," *Children Today,* 1973, 2, 22–25(a).

DeLissovoy, Vladimir, "High School Marriages: A Longitudinal Study," *Journal of Marriage and the Family*, 1973, 35, 245–255(b).

Elder, Jr., Glen H., "Structural Variations in the Child-Rearing Relationship," *Sociometry*, 1962, 25, 241–262.

Gendell, Murray, "Further Comment on V. K. Oppenheimer's 'The Life-Cycle

Squeeze. The Interaction of Men's Occupational and Family Life Cycles'," *Demography*, 1975, 12, 333–336.

Kagan, Jerome and Howard A. Moss, *Birth to Maturity*. New York: John Wiley, 1962.

Kohlberg, Lawrence, "Stage and Development: The Cognitive Development Approach to Socialization," in David A. Goslin, ed., *Handbook of Socialization Theory and Research*. Chicago: Rand McNally, 1969, 347–480.

Kohn, Melvin L., *Class and Conformity*. Homewood, Ill.: Dorsey Press, 1969.

McArthur, Arthur, "Developmental Tasks and Parent-Adolescent Conflict," *Marriage and Family Living*, 1962, 24, 189–191.

Mueller, Charles W. and Hallowell Pope, "Marital Instability: A Study of Its Transmission Between Generations," *Journal of Marriage and the Family*, 1977, 39, 83–93.

Oppenheimer, Valerie Kincade, "The Life-Cycle Squeeze: The Interaction of Men's Occupational and Family Life Cycles," *Demography*, 1974, 11, 227–245.

Peterson, Gail B., "Adolescent Moral Development as Related to Family Power, Family Support and Parental Moral Development, Unpublished doctoral dissertation, University of Minnesota, 1976.

Pope, Hallowell and Charles W. Mueller, "The Intergenerational Transmission of Marital Instability: Comparisons by Race and Sex," *Journal of Social Issues*, 1976, 32, 49–66.

Schaefer, Earl S. and Nancy Bayley, "Maternal Behavior, Child Behavior and Their Intercorrelations from Infancy through Adolescence" *Society for Research in Child Development Monograph*, 1963, Serial no. 87.

Thurnher, Madja, Donald Spence and Marjorie Fiske Lowenthal, "Value Confluence and Behavioral Conflict in Intergenerational Relations," *Journal of Marriage and the Family*, 1974, 36, 308–319.

U.S. Bureau of the Census, Census of the Population: 1970, Subject Final Report PC (2)-6A, *Employment Status and Work Experience*, U.S. Government Printing Office, Washington, D.C., 1973.

Veroff, Joseph and Sheila Feld, *Marriage and Work in America*. New York: Van Nostrand Reinhold, 1970.

# 15

# Separate residences

Parents do not cease to be parents just because their adult offspring establish their own separate households. Parent-child interactions customarily continue, even though parents quite clearly are not legitimate members of the new nuclear family unit. Parents continue to perceive children as in, though not necessarily of, the parental family. The previous chapter showed that parents and children can prepare to separate with a minimum of destructive conflict. Intergenerational conflict, however, can be accentuated when youths who have left home are attempting to assert their separate identities. This chapter will trace the relations of parents and children beginning with the tension-fraught days when children are setting up their own family units through the calmer phase when children bestow the status of grandparents upon their parents to the final stressful period when children must assume responsibility for elders who are in failing health.

## DRAWING APART

In the previous chapter, we saw that just as adolescents prefer to engage in sociability activities with friends rather than parents, so, too, do parents distance themselves from their maturing children. The completion of this drawing apart process is symbolized by the separate residence of the newlyweds, which represents the separate identity of the new family unit.

A recent study of persons facing various critical transition points referred to in the previous chapter, indicates how the individual's location in the family life cycle affects his perspective. The sample, which was generally representative of the population in the area served by the mental health personnel of the University of California School of Medicine, San Francisco, consisted of the following age groups: 50 high-school seniors, who were not married; 50 newlyweds, who were not yet parents; 50 parents whose last child, a senior in high school, would soon be leaving home; and 50 elderly persons who were within three years of retirement or whose husbands were within this period. Each group was equally divided as to gender, and none of the sample members were related, except for three parents of high-school seniors (Lurie, 1974: 262).

When asked about their feelings for their parents, newlyweds expressed the most ambivalent and negative feelings of all the age groups. High-school seniors still living at home expressed positive feelings about their fathers although they did not feel close to them. Newlyweds who had left home, however, reported negative feelings as well as a lack of closeness toward fathers. All the sample members were more positive toward their mothers than their fathers, a finding that again points up mothers' centrality in the family affection structure. But even with respect to mothers, high-school boys and newlywed women were more ambivalent in their feelings than any of the other age groups (Lurie, 1974: 262–263).

Complementary findings come from interviews with three-generation lineages consisting of intact couples at the grandparent, parent, and child generations who were linked by kinship bonds. While middle-aged parents spoke of their children as "family," the married children referred to their parents as "relatives" (Aldous, 1967). Another three-generation study also showed that parents tended to emphasize intergenerational similarities while the young maximized the differences (Bengtson and Kuypers, 1971). Some intergenerational hostility or ambivalence seems necessary for persons to establish their new identity as independent adults and as founders of new family units. Young people must prove both to themselves and to outsiders that they can perform competently without the aid of the parental family. This necessity continues into the stage when couples have their first child. As discussed in Chapter 11, new parents often express resentment at actions they interpret as interference, but their elders see as aid. Yet newlyweds often report better relations with parents after leaving home (Lurie, 1974: 264). When the family unit is established to the new couple's satisfaction, the couple can again dwell upon the feelings of attachment joining the generations. Somewhat the same shift to more positive evaluation of parents probably occurs when a couple feels more comfortable with their parental roles.

Bengtson and Kuypers (1971) use the concept of "developmental stake" to explain the tendency for parents to perceive similarities with their offspring and the continuities of intergenerational ties while adult children emphasize differences and establish intergenerational barriers. The older generation is concerned with its success in transmitting its values to children in the course of socialization. They wish to have "social heirs." Thus they minimize parent-child differences. The younger generation has a different developmental stake. They want to do more role making to establish their own values and strategies commensurate with changing technological, demographic, and political realities. Concerned as they are with creating the new rather than accepting the existing, the younger generation stresses differences and discontinuities.

**Parent-Married Child Interaction**
The boundaries of the newlyweds' family are not necessarily impermeable to parental influence. But whether the younger generation chooses to encourage the relation depends in part on the type of parent-child interaction that existed in the past. Early research of Sussman (1954) demonstrates the constraints previous family task accomplishment places on the stage when children leave home. In looking at the intergenerational patterns of 97 white, middle-class parents, he found their control strategies during the child-rearing family stages to be critical. Those parents who had discouraged the child's becoming independent still attempted to maintain control despite the child's marriage. The result was conflict, and the literal breaking of parent-child ties. In contrast, parents who prepared their children for adult status had less difficulty accepting the child's withdrawal into a different family unit. They and the newlyweds maintained contact (Sussman, 1954: 115–116).

Sussman found other factors to be associated with parent-newlywed contacts. These factors also appeared to stem from parent-child power patterns. They included the similarity of the background of the child's spouse to that of the parents, the absence of elopements, the presence of intergenerational assistance, and the proximity of the two genera tions' residences. By socializing children in such a way that they per- ceive parental control as just, parents are more apt to influence their child's choice of marital partners. The couple does not feel forced by parental disapproval to run away to be married. They do not have to move out of the area to avoid intergenerational conflict. This conclusion is supported by the findings we discussed in the previous chapter, namely, understanding parents continue to serve as role models and are influential in decisions of their adolescent offspring (Bowerman and Kinch, 1959), while adolescents are less apt to perceive highly controlling parents as fair (Elder, 1962).

It is ironic that parents who are not successful in letting go of their children seek to continue guiding their married children. Their fears that they have not prepared youths for independence lead them to give advice and counsel that is unwanted by married children.

This feeling of resentment at the demands of relatives is not restricted to the younger generation. Parents, too, even those who have nego- tiated the child-leaving period successfully may occasionally perceive their adult children as interfering. Having released their children, they may balk at having to reactivate parental roles of counselor and ad- viser. Such feelings may be particularly strong if they are attempting to develop extrafamilial roles or to reestablish marital roles. The attach- ment they feel for their adult children does not include taking on the responsibilities inherent in control. Being asked to play parental roles again not only suggests that they did not accomplish their task of socialization, but forces them to give up their expected freedom from parental responsibilities.

## Grandparent Roles

As Chapters 4 and 9 indicated, changes in longevity over the twentieth century have added a period after children leave home to the marital career. At this time when individuals are shedding many of their parent roles, they are also acquiring grandparent roles. To many parents, their children's children present an opportunity for strengthening intergen- erational attachments. To other parents, grandchildren are an unwel- come reminder that they are getting older. The ambivalence that some persons experience about becoming grandparents comes in part from demographic changes. Troll (1971: 278) points out that earlier mar- riage, earlier childbearing, and longer life means that "grandparenting has become a middle-aged rather than an old-aged phenomenon."

Women in their forties who are resuming occupational or associational activities are quite different from the rocking-chair grandparents typical of previous generations.

Neugarten and Weinstein (1964) found a number of different styles of grandparenting when they interviewed 70 middle-class couples who lived in the metropolitan area of Chicago. They all were within a close distance of married children who were in the child-rearing family stages. The grandmothers ranged in age from the early fifties to the mid-sixties. Their husbands were primarily in the age range of mid-fifties to the mid-sixties.

The couple's behavior toward their grandchildren seemed to fit into five different types. *Formal grandparents* carefully restricted their attention to providing special treats for their grandchildren and an occasional service as baby-sitter. They did not offer advice on child rearing and did not serve as surrogate parents. *Fun-seekers* played the role of companion to their grandchildren. Matters of authority were irrelevant. The different generations related as playmates with grandparents seeing their grandchildren as sources of personal enjoyment. *Surrogate parents* were found only among women who substituted for working mothers in child care. *The reservoir of family wisdom* was a grandfather style rarely found in this comparatively young sample. Lines of subordination of parents and their children were emphasized by the grandfather who dispensed special advice or demonstrated particular skills. The parents emphasized the vertical power structure, sometimes with resentment. *Distant figures* constituted the final grandparent style. These grandparents limited their contacts to birthdays and special occasions. They were remote figures insofar as the child's daily life was concerned (Neugarten and Weinstein, 1972: 202–203).

The age of the grandparents was related to the type of behavior toward grandchildren they displayed. Those under 65 were more apt to be fun-seekers or distant figures, depending on how involved they probably were in extrafamilial concerns. Those over 65 tended more often to play the formal grandparental role (Neugarten and Weinstein, 1964: 203). These styles also reflected what it meant to the respondents to be grandparents. About a fourth of the sample felt remote from their grandchildren and were little affected by them. These were people who had busy lives and found it difficult to picture themselves as grandparents. For some of the grandmothers who felt remote, beliefs that children had married too young or dislike of sons-in-law contributed to the lack of contact.

A feeling of biological renewal characterized the meaning of grandparenthood for two-fifths of the women. This sense of having a developmental stake in the new generation was expressed by only about a fourth of the men, probably because 46 of the 70 couples were grand-parents through the maternal line. Men tended to see biological con-tinuity as depending on the offspring of sons rather than of daughters. There were a few grandfathers who saw grandchildren as a means either for reactivating their teacher role or as a reason for providing financial aid to their children. In either case, these grandfathers saw grandchildren as benefitting from their years of experience.

Fun-seekers may have been those grandparents who viewed grand-children as a means for emotional fulfillment. They could enjoy them, because they had fewer occupational and family responsibilities than they did during the child-rearing years. Along with the formal grand-parents, they may also have viewed the child as a means for vicari-ously achieving what neither they nor their children had accomplished.[1]

Grandparents who choose to interact with their grandchildren, can make a real contribution to the latter's development. They can supply the unfailing warmth that promotes self-esteem in the younger genera-tion, but is difficult for harassed parents. Through their obvious attach-ment to grandchildren, grandparents can also indicate to worried parents that they are adequately performing their job of socialization. Grandparents too can gain from these cross-generation contacts. When not excessively prolonged or intense, the contacts can provide retired couples something to do and to talk about. Grandchildren can also socialize their elders into new ways.

Lack of two-way communication channels may account for the find-ing that as grandchildren and grandparents grow older, the two genera-tions appear to enjoy each other less. Thus Kahana and Kahana (1970) found white, four- and five-year-olds from middle-class families pre-fer indulgent grandparents who provide treats like Neugarten and Weinstein's formal grandparents. Eight- and nine-year-olds want grand-parents to be fun-seekers who play with them. But 11- and 12-year-olds are less interested in doing things with grandparents than in being indulged by them (Kahana and Kahana, 1970: 103). For their part, grandparents feel as they grow older that their older grandchildren do not want to bother with them. For this reason, they find younger grand-children more congenial. In addition, the longer they live, the more

---

[1] Neugarten and Weinstein (1964: 201–202) delimit the various meanings grandparent-hood had for their sample. The relation of the meanings to grandparenting styles is my interpretation.

grandparents prefer not to have to cope with the noise and high activity levels of children and youths (Clark, 1969).

### The Parental Generation as Kinkeepers

With today's couples having greater longevity, intergenerational relations often encompass at least three generations—the grandparents, the parents, and the married grandchildren. Parents who, as newlyweds, had erected family boundaries separating them from their parents in turn experience a similar exclusion from their children's family units. They, however, serve as kinkeepers for the generations and see that lineage ties are maintained through interaction and mutual help.

In the previously mentioned study of 79 three-generation lineages done by Hill and his associates (1970) in which the couples of each generation maintained their own residences, Macdonald (1964) examined the help exchange patterns of the three generations. He found that whether the help was in the areas of finances, household management, child care, or emotional gratification, parents were most often the givers. Only when the problem concerned care in time of illness did they receive as much as they gave. Grandparents were the heaviest receivers of aid in all areas except for finances and child care, areas in which married children received most assistance. Only in the area of sick care, did the latter give more help than their parents (see Table 15-1). Although families with higher incomes were more often "givers," the parental generation, regardless of income, tended to display more helping behavior than the other generations, just as the grandparental generation gave less (Macdonald, 1964: 163).

All three generations most often gave and received help from the other generations in the lineage rather than from other relatives. The proportion these intergenerational exchanges constituted of all such exchanges was greatest for the grandparents and least for the married grandchildren and was more true for help received than help given in all generations. Grandparents received 65 percent of all help from other generations and this was true for 53 percent of the help parents received and 44 percent of the assistance married children enjoyed. Grandparents (47 percent) and parents (44 percent) gave more of their assistance across the generations than did the children (28 percent). Perhaps because the latter had until fairly recently been living with sibs and were of an age to have more aunts and uncles living, they remained close enough to sibs, nieces and nephews, aunts and uncles, and cousins to devote a fourth of their help patterns to them. This was true for just nine percent of the grandparents' giving and 14 percent of the parents' assistance (Macdonald, 1964). Regardless of giving pat-

Table 15-1

Comparison of Help Received and Help Given by Generation for Chief Problem Areas[a]

| | Type of Crisis | | | | | | | | | |
|---|---|---|---|---|---|---|---|---|---|---|
| | Economic | | Emotional Gratification | | Household Management | | Child Care | | Illness | |
| Gener-ation | Gave % | Recvd % | Gave % | Recvd % | Gave % | Recvd % | Gave % | Recvd % | Gave % | Recvd % |
| Total | 100 | 100 | 100 | 100 | 100 | 100 | 100 | 100 | 100 | 100 |
| Grand-parents | 26 | 34 | 23 | 42 | 21 | 52 | 16 | 0 | 32 | 61 |
| Parents | 41 | 17 | 47 | 37 | 47 | 23 | 50 | 23 | 21 | 21 |
| Married Children | 34 | 49 | 31 | 21 | 33 | 25 | 34 | 78 | 47 | 18 |

Source: Hill, 1965: 125, Table 6-3.
[a] Percents may not total 100 due to rounding.

terns, however, it is apparent from this representative sample of three generation lineages living in the Minneapolis-St. Paul metropolitan areas of Minnesota that in times of crisis families turn first to immediate kin for help. They do not choose to expose their problems to outsiders unless family sources prove ineffective.

It is well to note, however, that despite lessened strength and finances, grandparents did give as well as receive. The relations they maintained with grandchildren, however, were less close than those they maintained with children. The generational barrier that exists between grandparents and grandchildren may be heightened by that of age. As previously noted in the discussion of grandparents' roles, grandparents feel unable as time goes on to fulfill the companion role to active grandchildren. They may then retreat into the distant figure style, since many lack the knowledge to serve in the reservoirs of wisdom style and others lack the strength or finances for the formal style. Thus, while seven-tenths of married children visited their parents at least weekly, and four-tenths of the members of the parent generation visited their parents that often, only one of 10 grandchildren maintained sociability contacts with grandparents at this level (Aldous, 1967: 242–243).

There are class differences in the kinds of assistance parents give their married children. Middle-class parents more often give financial

aid, while working-class parents give child-care or household management services (Adams, 1964; Aldous, 1967). The monetary aid that
middle-class parents give may provide a means for their exercising
influence, which the younger generation may resent as interference.
The incipient conflict inherent in such aid, along with the greater
number of opportunities to make friends that persons in middle-class
occupations enjoy, may explain the somewhat lesser visiting that
white-collar families did with kin in the three generation study (Aldous,
1967: 244). Since the three-generation lineages all lived in the same
general geographical area, this difference could not be explained by
the greater residential propinquity of kinsmen among the working
classes.

Gender differences in assistance and interaction also exist in ways
that seem to minimize intergenerational conflict. Most kinship studies
show that families possess closer relations with maternal kin (Troll,
1971: 269). Women appear to be able to cross the boundaries of families with diplomacy. Women maintain more sociability ties and mutual
assistance exchanges with relatives and are fonder of them. These findings are consistent with the greater extent to which girls are socialized
as they grow up to develop bonds of affection with their parental families. The independence of family that young men are supposed to
cultivate before establishing their own also is less emphasized in young
women. The greater mother-daughter attachment stands both in good
stead when young families need child-care help. Mothers constitute
less of a threat to the boundaries of their daughters' families. Their
household assistance when a new baby arrives, or help with child
care, strengthens daughters' performance of their wife-mother roles.
Through example, counsel, or provision of "time off" periods from family responsibilities, mothers can increase the competence of daughters
who are performing the same family roles mothers performed in years
past.[2]

We have seen above that the parent generation ministers to the
grandparental generation. Middle-aged children have the responsibility
of seeing that their parents are accomplishing the family development
tasks of physical and morale maintenance in a fashion that permits
them to maintain their separate residences. It is easier for mothers to
accept the household assistance of daughters whom they once taught

---

[2] The help a mother can give her daughter should not obscure the possible tensions
existing in her relation as mother-in-law to the daughter's husband. For a study of
in-law problems, see Duvall, 1954.

to perform these roles, just as it is easier for the daughters to accept a mother's help with child-care tasks. Just as grandparents may view the help of in-laws as interference, so may daughters-in-law resent having to give it. For these reasons, when older couples without single children must share a residence, they are most apt to move in with a married daughter (Riley and Foner, 1968: 171, Exhibit 7-13).


# THE LAST FAMILY STAGE: RETIREMENT BACK TO THE FAMILY

One of the most controversial theories in the gerontology area is that of disengagement. According to this theory, as persons age they experience "an inevitable mutual withdrawal" from others and others from them, which results in less interaction between the individual and his social networks (Cumming and Henry, 1961: 14). This process supposedly is functional for the individual who has high morale during his "inevitable" withdrawal from society, and functional for society since it permits younger persons to occupy the roles vacated by the elderly. Hochschild (1975: 562) has subjected this argument to fundamental criticism, particularly by pointing to the difficulty in disproving it, given the disagreement surrounding the operationalization of the disengagement concept.

Of greater concern to us, however, are her comments regarding the content of the argument. She points out that retirement, the signal for disengagement from the work career, has different meanings for different people depending upon their occupations. For persons in demanding and interesting positions, retirement means disengagement *from* an occupational career of prestige, money, and absorbing activities. Others see retirement as disengaging *back* to the warmth of family ties and willingly relinquish work, union, and church responsibilities. Another group of persons is retiring *toward* new developmental tasks using the time now available to cultivate interests beyond family and work.

As we saw in Chapter 10, those men who perceive "retirement" as *from* something will continue to see their identity in terms of the occupational career and thus have the most difficulty with morale. They do not become involved in couple or family activities; nor do they take on new church, club, or citizen roles. Fortunate, therefore, are those professionals like doctors, lawyers, or academicians who can continue their occupational activities on a consultant or part-time basis after retirement (Rowe, 1972). Even more fortunate are those persons who avoid judging their worth by the standards of the working world and where disengagement from it means reengagement in the family or in activities of their own choice. The important point is, however, that for none of these groups does retirement symbolize the inevitable process of disengagement.

Longitudinal data from the parents of children in the Guidance Study and the Berkeley Growth studies continued intermittently for 40 years provide more detailed information on the antecedents of various retirement outcomes (Maas and Kuypers, 1974). The 95 mothers and 47 fathers whom it was possible to interview at the time their children were 40 were interviewed intensively on their marriage, their relations with their children in the studies, and their work careers during the children's first eighteen years in the 1920s and 1930s. They were generally in their thirties at the time assessments were made of their early behaviors. In addition those chosen for the study "overrepresented . . . the middle and upper class" of the socioeconomic hierarchy despite having lived through the 1930s depression. As a group, the sample possessed continuing superior health. The parents' ages at the time of the follow-up interviews ranged from 60 to 82, with the average age for the women being 69 and for the men two years older (Maas and Kuypers, 1974: 4–6).

The effect on retirement outcomes of limited linkages between developmental task accomplishment in the marital career at earlier periods and the present is apparent in the data. Men who used retirement to take on new developmental tasks had relatively unsatisfactory marriages at the two periods. The continuing low levels of friendliness and companionship over the years suggests that this group may well represent the aged survivors of the "conflict-habituated" couples in the middle years of marriage described by Cuber and Haroff (1965) in Chapter 8. These men remain on affectionate terms with their children, but are only "distant figures" in their grandparenting styles. Hobbies and church activities supply the life focus, the continuing unsatisfactory marital career does not (Maas and Kuypers, 1974: 111–113).

The "unwell-disengaged" fathers also show the limited linkages between early adulthood accomplishments and old age. Maas and Kuypers (1974: 113–114) reported that these men are socially withdrawn from an early age. When young they appear to have been highly involved in their work and successful in terms of affluence and upward social mobility. This very success, as described in Chapter 8, seems to be associated with family rifts. In their "conflict-habituated" marriages (Cuber and Harroff, 1965), the men argue about religion and about expenditures and management of their incomes. They also have poor relations with their children. In old age, these men are still unhappy over how decisions are made in their marriages, the marital power structure is not egalitarian, and neither spouse can count on the other for assistance. Coupled with the dismal marriage situation of these men are their unhappy relations with their children. Their disapproval of the visiting patterns of their children and of the child-rearing practices used with their grandchildren is consistent with earlier strained relations. Thus retirement for these men represents disengagement *from* their only meaningful positional career. Their unhappy marital and parental careers, in conjunction with their history of ill health, leave them in old age disengaged from social networks and without the energy to develop compensatory leisure or organizational roles.

Another group of fathers are similar to this group in their successful occupational involvement and in their dissatisfaction with their marriages and with their children. These "remotely sociable men," to use the label of Maas and Kuypers, differ from the previous group, however, in their present possession of a number of acquaintances. In the past, they were also close to their children and not in conflict with their wives. What seems to have occurred over the years is that their occupational careers superseded family careers. A habit of viewing persons as being useful to goal accomplishment rather than as having intrinsic worth in their own right is an ethical outlook that seems to mark the impersonal contacts that constitute these men's lifelong social relationships (Maas and Kuypers, 1974: 117).

But what of the antecedents of the fathers who retired *back* to family concerns? As young adults, they were the group most expressive of their affection to family and friends. Their closeness to their wives, their mutual sexual adjustment indicated the positive quality of their marital relations. They were also good with their children, being open in communicating their sentiments, negative as well as positive. These ways of relating continue into old age, so that the men have a network of loving members with whom to be involved (Maas and Kuypers, 1974: 118).

Mothers show less continuity in patterns of behavior into old age than do fathers, probably because a sizable number of them suffer more disruption in their marital careers by death or divorce. Of the 95 women in the sample, 47 were still in their first marriages, 15 in second marriages, 28 widows, and 5 divorced. The "visiting" mothers, as Maas and Kuypers label one group, seem to be partners of the "unwell-disengaged" and "remotely sociable" men. In their early years these women are in conflict with their husbands over the husbands' occupational careers. Their marital satisfaction is low. In old age, these women become heavily involved in parenting roles and do a lot of informal entertaining of family and friends. Their marriages, however, are of little importance (Maas and Kuypers, 1974: 128).

Over the years, these women appear to have lost touch with their husbands owing to the latters' preoccupations with their occupational careers, but another group of women, the "uncentered" mothers, are disengaged from life because of the loss of their husbands. In early years, these women's homes and husbands were their reasons for being. Children and grandchildren, although often present, cannot substitute for dead husbands and lost houses (Maas and Kuypers, 1974: 125). More fortunate are the "husband-centered" mothers whose husbands are still living. Their early married years were happy ones, with close marital ties, similarity of interests, high sexual adjustment, and an absence of conflict. They also were interested in their children. In old age, however, they do not see their children often, nor are they involved in grandparenting roles. Their concerns are focused entirely on their husbands, with attendant high potential sorrow if the husbands die first (Maas and Kuypers, 1974: 129).

Another group of women who are highly dependent upon their marital careers for life's meaning are the "disabled-disengaged" mothers. Like their male counterparts, the "unwell-disengaged" fathers, they were concerned about their health in early life and got along poorly with spouses and children. But, unlike the males who could turn to occupational careers for solace, these women became more dependent on their spouses over the years. Communications, which was open, remains so, and the couples do most things together. Relationships with their children, who are more often sons with their lesser concern for relatives, remain strained (Maas and Kuypers, 1974: 127).

It would be misleading, however, to leave the impression that aging women are dependent solely upon parental or marital careers for satisfactory lives. Some women whose marriages were unhappy, or who lost their husbands when they were in their fifties, manage to find in occupational careers a means to accomplish new developmental tasks. They are able to make new friends while maintaining close ties with their children. If still working, they enjoy the job, and if not, their lives are enriched with sociability activities (Maas and Kuypers, 1974: 120). Others are heavily involved in citizenship and voluntary organizational roles, often in leadership positions. Their early years of marriage were conflictual, and in old age fall to secondary importance. Relationships with their children, which were problematic in the early years, now become more positive. These women also maintain informal ties with their grandchildren, perhaps playing the role of fun-seekers (Maas and Kuypers, 1974: 122).

These longitudinal data indicate how the early marital and parental careers cast their shadows on existence in old age, for both women and men. In general, the elderly whose lives center on marital or parental roles achieve satisfactory family relationships in early life. If not, old age represents an opportunity to maintain friendships as well as to try out leisure activities or community roles for the able and to lapse into lives revolving around health routines for the disabled

### Contacts Across the Generations

Couples who have pruned community commitments to center their energies on family affairs are generally concerned that children keep in close contact. That morale maintenance rather than physical maintenance is critical to older couples is shown in the conversation of 718 retired men living with their wives whose children have all left home. While 84 percent said children should visit and 93 percent believed children should keep in close touch, just 60 percent felt children should help when parents are ill, and only 49 percent said children should give financial aid (Streib, 1958: Table 4).

Contrary to popular opinion, the need of the grandparental generation for personal contacts is met.[3] A large scale study of old people (Shanas et al., 1968) showed 84 percent of the respondents had seen at least one of their children within the previous week and 90 percent within the last month. At the retirement stage, couples often move so they are near at least one child. As a result, only about 15 percent of aged parents live more than a short ride from some child. About half live within walking distance or a short ride, and the remainder are in the same dwelling with an adult offspring (Schorr, 1966).

Children are then usually near enough to give warm support to parents, support they can direct to encourage the elderly to try out new roles. Foote (1956) has urged spouses to assist each other to take on new interests so that they will be matched in their development of abilities. This same perspective can be generalized from the marital to the lineage relation. Adults can urge aging parents to take on new interests that are consistent with health and finances and that will keep living worthwhile. In addition to urging such new departures, adults

---

[3] The myth of the isolated old person, Shanas (1963) has argued, is due to the aged, particularly the childless, who do not have kin contacts and to professional workers, who are most likely to see such old persons.

can make them possible through arranging transportation to amusement or political gatherings or by doing the necessary shopping for sewing and woodworking supplies. At these times, children can repay some of the sacrifices of personal desires and plans which parents willingly accept while rearing offspring.

The role making that occurs when the middle-aged must assume caretaking responsibilities for their parents can be stressful for both generations. Yet the trauma inherent in the situation is eased if children can accomplish the developmental task of "filial maturity" (Blenkner, 1965). By filial maturity, Blenkner means that children assume a more mature filial position in which they expect to be depended on more and are, therefore, more dependable. The drawing apart that characterizes the period when youths are leaving home is replaced by the attachments of adults to their parents as individuals. They now recognize their parents as products of life histories that began long before they were conceived. They can accept in their parents limitations and needs as well as strengths and competencies. They realize that, besides being responsible for their existence, parents are human beings with all the attendant possibilities for glory and failure. Middle-aged children who can accomplish this task are anticipating their own old age and beginning to socialize themselves for it. In this process they identify with parents just as they did when preparing, years ago, for adulthood (Blenkner, 1965: 58).

# REFERENCES

Adams, Bert N., "Structural Factors Affecting Parental Aid to Married Children," *Journal of Marriage and the Family*, 1964, 26, 327–331.

Aldous, Joan, "Intergenerational Visiting Patterns: Variation in Boundary Maintenance as an Explanation," *Family Process*, 1967, 6, 235–251.

Bengtson, Vern L. and Joseph A. Kuypers, "Generational Differences and the Developmental Stake," *Aging and Human Development*, 1971, 2, 249–259.

Blenkner, Margaret, "Social Work and Family Relationships in Later Life with Some Thoughts on Filial Maturity," in Ethel Shanas and Gordon F. Streib, eds., *Social Structure and the Family: Generation Relations*. Englewood Cliffs, N.J.: Prentice-Hall, 1965, 46–59.

Bowerman, Charles E. and John W. Kinch, "Changes in Family and Peer Orientation of Children Between the Fourth and Tenth Grades," *Social Forces*, 1959, 37, 206–211.

Clark, Margaret, "Cultural Values and Dependency in Later Life," in Richard Kalish, ed., *The Dependencies of Old People.* Ann Arbor, Mich.: Institute for Gerontology, 1969.

Cuber, John F. and Peggy B. Harroff, *The Significant Americans.* New York: Appleton-Century-Crofts, 1965.

Cumming, Elaine and William Henry, *Growing Old.* New York: Basic Books, 1961.

Duvall, Evelyn M., *In-Laws: Pro and Con.* New York: Association Press Book, 1954.

Elder, Jr., Glen H., "Structural Variations in the Child-Rearing Relationship, *Sociometry,* 1962, 25, 241–262.

Foote, Nelson, "Matching of Husbands and Wives in Phases of Development," *Transaction of Third World Congress of Sociology,* IV, 1956, 24–34.

Hill, Reuben, "Decision Making and the Family Life Cycle," in Shanas and Streib, *op. cit.* 1965, 113–139.

Hill, Reuben, Nelson Foote, Joan Aldous, Robert Carlson, and Robert Mc-Donald, *Family Development in Three Generations.* Cambridge, Mass.: Schenkman, 1970.

Hochschild, Arlie, R., "Disengagement Theory: A Critique and Proposal," *American Sociological Review,* 1975, 40, 553–569.

Kahana, Boaz and Eva Kahana, "Grandparenthood from the Perspective of the Developing Grandchild," *Developmental Psychology,* 1970, 3, 98–105.

Lurie, Elinor E., "Sex and Stage Differences in Perceptions of Marital and Family Relationships," *Journal of Marriage and the Family,* 1974, 36, 260 260.

Maas, Henry D. and Joseph A. Kuypers, *From Thirty to Seventy: A Forty Year Longitudinal Study of Adult Life Style and Personality.* San Francisco, Jossey-Bass, 1974.

Macdonald, Robert, "Intergenerational Family Helping Patterns," Unpublished doctoral dissertation. University of Minnesota, 1964.

Neugarten, Bernice and Karol Weinstein, "The Changing American Grandparent," *Journal of Marriage and the Family,* 1964, 26, 199–204.

Riley, Matilda White and Anne Foner, *Aging and Society,* I. New York: Russell Sage, 1968.

Rowe, Alan R., "The Retirement of Academic Scientists," *Journal of Gerontology,* 1972, 27, 113–118.

Schorr, Alvin L., "On Selfish Children and Lonely Parents," *The Public Interest,* 1966, 4, 491–495.

Shanas, Ethel, "The Unmarried Old Person in the United States: Living Arrangements and Care in Illness, Myth and Fact," Paper prepared for the International Social Science Research Seminar in Gerontology, Markaryd, Sweden, August, 1963, cited by Blenkner, *op. cit.,* 49.

Shanas, Ethel and Gordon F. Streib, *Social Structure and the Family: Generational Relations.* Englewood Cliffs, N.J.: Prentice-Hall, 1965.

Shanas, Ethel, Peter Townsend, Dorothy Wedderburn, Henning Friis, Poul Milho, and Jan Stehouwer, *Older People in Three Industrial Societies.* New York: Atherton Press, 1968.

Streib, Gordon F., "Family Patterns in Retirement," *Journal of Social Issues,* 1958, 14, 46–60.

Sussman, Marvin B., "Family Continuity: Selective Factors Which Affect Relationships Between Families at Generational Levels," *Marriage and Family Living,* 1954, 16,112–120.

Troll, Lillian E., "The Family of Later Life: A Decade Review," *Journal of Marriage and Family Living,* 33, 1971, 263–290.

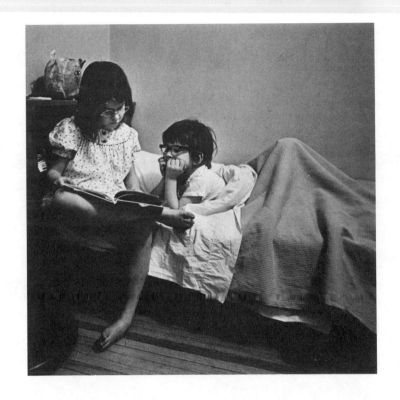

# 16

# The Sibling Career

# Sibing relations:
# A matter of choice

The focus on the sibling subsystem in this chapter returns us to an analysis of cohort as opposed to lineage relations. Like spouses, siblings are generally close enough in age to be concerned with the same life-course events, whether attending school or getting married, and to have a common perspective on the various events in historical time that they are living through (Bengston and Black, 1973). In contrast, parent-child relations constitute intercohort transactions. Although parents and children are part of a common line of descent, their age differences mean that they view the same event, whether life-course or historical, from a different generational perspective. Parents, for example, who grew up in a period of normatively prescribed sexual behavior may be in violent disagreement with children who are engaging in courtship role making in a period of changing sexual norms. Sibs can be more understanding since they have the same role concerns and are acquiring their values from similar experiences.

In fast-changing societies, cohorts either supplement or substitute for lineages as socializing units. This chapter will show how socialization occurs in the sibling subsystem. Older siblings demonstrate to younger brothers and sisters that family boundaries can be crossed and provide models of how to deal with extrafamilial agencies and people. They serve as pioneers for younger siblings to follow in their ever-expanding world outside the family (Bank and Kahn, 1975).

The demarcation of family stages using events in the firstborn's life cycle is particularly appropriate for the sibling relation. Critical role transition points for elder brothers or sisters not only affect sibling interaction but can be lived through vicariously by younger family members and used for purposes of anticipatory socialization.

The present chapter will analyze the changing nature of sibling relations according to the various stages in family development. We shall see how this relation, beginning as an obligatory tie based on birth to the same parents and life in the same household, becomes a voluntary one. Friendship replaces kinship as a basis of sibling solidarity. Since changes in the sibling subsystem occur within the context of other family subsystems, we shall be particularly concerned with the interrelation of the parent-child and the sibling relation.

**A caveat:**   Although this chapter documents the importance of sibling relations, we do not as yet have the needed knowledge to understand siblinghood. Family scholars have concentrated their attention on the marital and parent-child subsystems of the family at the expense of the sibling relation. This neglect is understandable if not acceptable when one considers the problems involved in studying sibling interactions. It is very difficult to separate sibling influences from influences originating in the number of children in a family; their age and gender composition; and the influences from parents, peers, and social class. To add to their difficulties, researchers studying siblings, like parents themselves, are not always certain when the sibling complement is complete (Irish, 1964). Husbands and wives can change their mind or make mistakes, as did one couple who, after buying a motor launch and christening it "The Five of Us," added a rowboat named "And One More." For these reasons, when possible, we shall note convergent findings from several studies. In such cases we will have greater confidence that the findings are not the artifacts of small, unrepresentative samples.

## THE BEGINNING OF THE SIBLING RELATION: COMPETITION FOR ATTENTION

For a sibling subsystem to exist, there has to be more than one child in a family. In the United States, there are few families with only one child. One analysis of family composition showed that of families with heads 35 to 44 years old having children under 18 years of age, 71.7 percent had more than one child (U.S. Bureau of the Census, 1975: 5, Table E). And among adults whose families of orientation are largely complete, the percentage having siblings is even higher. Adams (1968: 94) found in his representative sample of white persons in a southern community, Greensboro, North Carolina, that 87 percent of his 799 respondents had siblings. Thus most people have siblings present when they are growing up and must develop some sort of interaction patterns with them. During the family stages when children are not yet in school, the parent-child relation can threaten the development of solidarity within the sibling subsystem, just as we have previously seen it can also threaten marital solidarity. Because of their dependence upon a caretaker for nurturance, children find themselves in competition for the mother's attention. In addition, the behavior of a mother may encourage sibling rivalry even before the birth of another child. (There is a conspicuous absence of studies on how a father's behavior to a young child is affected by the arrival of additional children.)

Baldwin's early longitudinal study of changes in maternal treatment of children when a younger child is born suggests why rivalry occupies such a prominent place in the sibling literature. He examined the observational records of 46 mother-child pairs in which the Fels parent behavior rating scales were used. Observers recorded the mother's treatment of her child during the year preceding her next pregnancy, in the year of pregnancy, and for a year after the pregnancy. Although the age and gender of the siblings were obviously uncontrolled factors, we have in this study the advantage of observational reports covering an important change in the plurality patterns of a family.

Baldwin found that the amount of warmth mothers showed their first children, as indicated by such variables as affection giving and approval, dropped significantly with the arrival of another child as did the amount of contact they had with the older child or children. At the same time, there was an increase in maternal restrictiveness and severity of penalties with these older children.

Despite his small sample, it was possible for Baldwin to control for ordinal position. He compared the treatment of mothers having their second child (13 cases) with the other mothers having children of higher birth orders. He found the former mothers showed a significantly greater decline in the clarity of their policy toward their firstborn children during their pregnancies and after it, accompanied by a significantly greater rise in disciplinary friction. He concluded that these shifts in maternal behavior "were consistent with the hypothesis that more extreme shifts in parent behavior are to be observed when the second child is born than during other pregnancies" (Baldwin, 1947: 36).

A question Baldwin was unable to answer to his own satisfaction from the data was whether the overall changes in maternal behavior were due to children's becoming subject to older age norms or to their "displacement by younger siblings" (Baldwin, 1947: 36). He had found the same differences in a previous comparison of maternal treatment of three- and nine-year-olds, with mothers of the older group being more demanding and less warm.

In any case, the coming of another sib seems to herald higher maternal expectations for children and pressures upon them to take on individual developmental tasks while maternal encouragement diminishes. Such treatment may well make children resent the family newcomer whose presence seems to be associated with changes in mothers' behaviors.

Baldwin's small study suggests that factors affecting sibling sentiment stem from maternal treatment. It is well to remember here, however, as elsewhere in our discussion that children elicit behavior as well as react to it. Thus Sutton-Smith and Rosenberg (1970: 15), two psychologists who have systematically done research on siblings, point out that firstborns have some physiological characteristics that affect their treatment. They tend to be smaller infants than later borns, but they grow at a faster rate. After they reach the age of two, firstborns tend to be larger in weight and height than secondborns when they reach the same age, until they attain adulthood. As a result, parents may feel that firstborns are able to reach higher goals than their sibs.

Whether it is due to their physical characteristics or parental inexperience, firstborns, research shows, are reared in special ways. Lasko (1954), for example, did a longitudinal study of which the results were consistent with those of Baldwin. Forty mothers from predominantly middle-class backgrounds were observed with their firstborns and secondborns. Since there were repeated observations by researchers visiting the homes every six months, the mothers' behavior toward the children could be rated on the Fels parent behavior rating scales when each child was at the same chronological age. The mothers, it appeared, attempted to accelerate their firstborns' intellectual and verbal development. After the age of two and until they entered school, first-borns were held to a higher set of expectations by their mothers, who treated them less warmly than younger sibs at the same ages. First-borns, accordingly, along with a decrease in the amount of interaction they had with their mothers, found it less pleasant. Continued maternal attempts to accelerate the development of their oldest children, were associated with disciplinary difficulties at all levels.

Mothers, however, were stricter and more arbitrary in their rules with their younger children. This was especially true with children who were secondborns in families in which there were no younger children. They were treated "much more restrictedly and coercively" at school-entering ages than secondborns who were middle children of the same age (Lasko, 1954: 126). Lasko also found that mothers were somewhat warmer with their youngest children and attempted to accelerate their development less than they had when middle children were the same age. These lower expectations, however, were combined with greater restrictiveness.

The evidence suggests that regardless of birth order children experience maternal discrimination when they compare themselves with their brothers and sisters. There is a tendency for firstborns to be subject to continued high expectations from mothers although the arrival of other children is associated with a loss of maternal attention and warmth. Middle children, who never enjoyed the undivided attention of their parents, have to meet high maternal demands, although not so high as those for firstborns. Mothers give more affection to middle children than to oldest children but less than to youngest children at comparable ages. The youngest children also do not have to meet the higher maternal expectations placed on their elder siblings. Mothers, however, appear to couple greater solicitousness with more restrictiveness. Thus siblings appear to have grievances against each other as well as their mother because of her differential treatment.

## SOCIALIZATION WITHIN THE SIBLING SUBSYSTEM

### The Family With School-Aged Children

The previous section has indicated how the differential treatment of siblings by mothers can foster rivalry among children during the family development stages of childbearing and of preschool children present. As families enter the stage when the oldest child goes off to school, however, the sibling subsystem becomes more active.[1] It is at this point of greater independence that older children may establish coalitions to oppose maternal discrimination.

We have already seen that mothers have lower expectations for each successive child. This may be a consequence of mothers being educated by their older children to be more realistic in their expectations (Sutton-Smith and Rosenberg, 1970). Socialization within the sibling subsystem can be even more effective. As members of the same cohort, siblings are close enough in age that they have fairly recently played or will play roles having similar content to those of their sibs. Their understanding of one another's role clusters is increased by the amount of time siblings spend together in a variety of household settings and in a variety of activities. Moreover, because sibling roles are not so scripted by norms as those in the mother-child subsystem, siblings engage in more role making. The range of behaviors they can try out on each other is greater, and the resultant interaction patterns more agreeable to the parties concerned than those the vertical parent-child relation permit.

**Discipline.**   Parents recognize the advantage siblings possess as socializing agents and may co-opt older siblings to serve as parental surrogates. On the basis of questionnaires, interviews, and family histories from persons representing 100 families with at least six children, Bossard and Boll (1956) found that siblings made very effective disciplinarians. While 44 percent of the 100 respondents objected to their parents' discipline, only 11 percent objected when a sibling was the disciplinarian. Siblings less often used physical punishment, but they were more apt to know what would really constitute acceptable discipline for an unruly sib. Besides fitting punishment to the child, sib disciplinarians were in a better position to judge what constitutes intentional rather than inadvertent misbehavior.

**Power.**   In establishing power patterns within the sibling subsystem, children socialize each other into the various strategies that can be used to obtain one's goal over opposition. In jockeying for a favorable position in the power hierarchy, older siblings learn to model their behavior on that displayed by their mothers in the parent-child system.

---

[1] Bank and Kahn (1975: 319) have reported, for example, that four-and six-year-old brothers in a sample of middle-class families spend more than twice as much time alone together as with their parents.

Younger siblings, too, make use of the parent-child subsystem. They appeal to parents to equalize their lesser power in the sibling relation. Both age groups try out various techniques until they find those that are most effective in sibling interaction. In the process of role making, they are learning to deal with peers.

In one study, ninety, second-year college students from middle-class backgrounds supplied information on how their sibs tried to influence them (Sutton-Smith and Rosenberg, 1970: 44). The students were equally divided among the eight, two-child family positions—two boys, two girls, an older boy and younger girl, etc. Firstborns, subject to their mothers' high expectations, perceived themselves as bossy and were so perceived by their younger siblings. The more dependent laterborns, interacting with their bossy elders, rated themselves (and were so rated by firstborns) as appealing outside the sibling subsystem to parents as well as to these same older sibs for sympathy and aid.

When younger, the oldest sibs tended to use their superior physical force to obtain their ends. With increasing age, they followed their parents' example and gave rewards or deprived their younger brothers and sisters of privileges. The latter responded by stubborness, anger, or attacks on their older tormentors in the form of harassment and pestering. These same findings appeared in a sample of 95 fifth and sixth graders in an Ohio school predominantly from middle-class homes and also members of two-child families (Sutton-Smith and Rosenberg, 1970: 44 and 57). Thus we have some validation at two age levels for the kind of power strategies that sibs use.

The data from these children suggest that when strategies based on physical force are predominant in sibling role making, there will be a great deal of quarreling. Boys with younger brothers, or with older sisters, are particularly likely to use "beating up, wrestling or chasing" to get their way, since they are customarily stronger. These tactics appear to have an effect, for their siblings report themselves and are described by their younger brothers as "getting angry, shouting and yelling" (Sutton-Smith and Rosenberg, 1970: 45). It is also in these dyads that one finds the most quarreling (Sutton-Smith and Rosenberg, 1970: 53). Presumably, in these sibling subsystems, as opposed to two sisters or an older brother and a sister, the power structure appears unstable. The disadvantaged partner is, therefore, always trying to overthrow it.

**Gender role learning.** It is apparent from the above descriptions that younger siblings do not give in meekly to their domineering older siblings but engage in a good deal of struggle and protest. In this process, they develop an awareness of who they are and an ability to get along with their peers. They learn to play the companion role effectively enough that at least during primary school years, younger siblings are more popular with peers than are older siblings (Sutton-Smith and Rosenberg, 1970: 64).

Siblings as members of the same cohort tend to interact as relative equals in contrast to the clear hierarchy of power that exists in the parent-child subsystem. Their mutual socialization can compete with and even hold the advantage over that of parents. A case in point exists in the area of gender role learning. Long before many parents were consciously discouraging traditional role typing by gender in their children, researchers found a blurring of gender roles in cross-sex sibling subsystems.

Brim (1958) looked at information from a sample of 384, six-year-old children in which admirable controls were established to uncover ordinal position effects in sibling relations. The sample is worth describing in some detail, because it indicates how many controls must be instituted in sibling research and suggests why adequate sibling research is costly. Helen Koch (1954), who collected the data, sampled middle-class children from Chicago, all of whom had only one sibling. She designed her research so that there were 48 children in each of the eight possible group of sibling positions in two-child families. She had 48 girls, for example, who had older brothers, 48 who had older sisters, 48 who had younger brothers, and 48 who had younger sisters. Moreover, as if this sample design were not complicated enough, she divided each sibling grouping in three according to how much younger or older the siblings were—zero to two years, more than two years to four years, and more than four years.

Brim (1958) believed that the sibling power structure would be reflected in the area of gender role learning. Younger siblings, he hypothesized, would more often be socialized by their elder siblings, even if these elders were of the opposite rather than the same sex. To test this hypothesis, he examined the ratings Koch had asked the six-year-olds' teachers to make of their pupils' behavior. Today, we would object to the arbitrary fashion in which he and his judges separated into male and female categories the traits on which the teachers made ratings. Traits like "tenacity," "aggressiveness," and "procrastinating" were judged to be masculine. Such traits as "kindness," "affectionateness," and "jealousy" were labeled feminine. The teachers, who made the ratings, were also affected by gender role stereotypes. Girls were rated higher on "masculine" traits than were boys who showed the same degree of these traits. In like fashion, boys were rated higher on "feminine" traits than girls who displayed the same degree of these traits (Brim, 1958: 13).

Of more interest to us, however, were Brim's findings that behavior ratings of children with cross-sex brothers and sisters showed more overlap with traits assigned to the opposite sex than ratings of children with same-sex siblings. This was true whether the sib was older or younger, and regardless of the age differential. As Brim hypothesized, however, the more powerful firstborns appeared to serve more often as socializing agents than did secondborns. Younger sibs took on the cross-sex characteristics of their older sibs more often than the reverse process occurred.

This unplanned sibling gender-role socialization may place the sibling subsystem at odds with the conscious socialization attempts of some parents, but there may also be struggles within the sibling subsystem that prevent such socialization from occurring. Boys who had two sisters as compared with one in a sample of 214 small town children did not show similar gender role blurring (Sutton-Smith and Rosenberg, 1970: 34). Their sisters' behavior in such cases seemed to serve as a countermodel of how not to behave for boys seeking to establish their own identities.

### The Family with Adolescents

As children reach adolescence and begin to cope with the developmental tasks of establishing intimate heterosexual relations while lessening emotional dependence upon parents, the sibling relation can assume particular importance. We have just seen that gender-role learning occurs within the sibling subsystem. Concomitantly, sibs also learn from each other how to get along with peers of the opposite gender.

Adolescents of the same sex can serve as models for their younger siblings, supplying cues and even explicit advice on skills that enhance one's attractiveness to the opposite sex (Hill and Aldous, 1969: Bossard and Boll, 1956). Older sibs of the opposite sex can also assist individuals to feel at ease with opposite-sex peers. In an observational study of 53 boys and 52 girls from two- and three-child families who attended a primary school, researchers could determine with whom the children chose to interact. They found that secondborns with cross-sex siblings, more often interacted with cross-sex peers. Gender of siblings was not associated with peer interaction of firstborns. To a lesser extent, the same phenomenon appeared only among girls in three-child families (Sutton-Smith and Rosenberg, 1970: 29). This study suggests that interaction with older sibs of the opposite sex gives children sufficient confidence to engage in more interaction with cross-sex peers, interactions that should quicken adolescent task accomplishment.

Having been so recently in the same learner position as their younger siblings, older siblings serve as constant reminders that adolescent tasks can be mastered as well as supplying up-to-date information on their content. In any competition with the parent-child subsystem for superior influence in socialization on how to get along with peers, the sibling subsystem is liable to win out. Older adolescents, too, gain something from the sibling relation in addition to the enhanced self-respect that comes from playing the roles of adviser and confidant. Although the teasing and pestering for information that younger siblings display along with their admiration can prove tedious, these same siblings can serve as allies and alternate sources of support in parent-adolescent struggles. Younger siblings are aware of, and may be old enough to share, the values and concerns of older youths. They may also see their own self-interest is involved in helping their elder siblings to establish precedents of increasing independence from parental supervision. Some information on the formation of sibling coalitions against parents for this purpose is reported in Bossard and Boll's study of large families. Such coalitions were present in 60 of 75 families for which Bossard and Boll (1956: 189) possessed relevant information.

**Affection structure.** For siblings to form coalitions against parents, there must exist some understanding among them. Data analyzed by Bowerman and Dobash (1974) show that the affection structure in a majority of cases is strong enough in sibling subsystems to support the formation of alliances against the parent-child system. In the sample of 7100, white, seventh to twelfth graders living in urban areas who supplied information on parent-child power relations reported in Chapter 14 (Elder, 1962), 65 percent of the students felt close to their siblings. Two-thirds of these respondents reported being "quite close" and the others said "extremely close." Just 10 percent were "not particularly" close and three percent "not at all close" to their siblings. The remainder were "somewhat close."

Affection among siblings varies by age and gender. As youths get into the tenth to twelfth grades of high school and start looking beyond the family for close relations, their affection for siblings whether these siblings are older or younger tends to decline. The only exceptions are boys or girls with older sisters. Same-sex siblings feel closer than cross-sex siblings, and females tend to feel closer to siblings of either sex. There is also some indication, contrary to popular belief, that sibilngs in two-child families are closer to each other regardless of age and sex than siblings in larger families (Bowerman and Dobash, 1974: 51, Table 2).

These findings suggest, although the data are cross-sectional and not longitudinal, that sibling ties become more a matter of choice than of obligation as youths become older. The expansion of the world of peers with whom they have contact is associated with a narrowing of sibling ties. This does not necessarily mean that sibling solidarity is weakened. The principle of least interest operates here (Waller and Hill, 1951). Younger adolescents who continue to look to older siblings for guidance work to preserve the relation. More importantly, when older siblings do maintain close relations with younger siblings, it is a matter of choice. And this choice, as with friendships, is based on similarity of interests. Same-sex siblings are closer.

By the time children reach adolescence, therefore, siblings may serve as mediators within the family and between the family and the broader community. For younger siblings, the older siblings provide role models of heterosexual behaviors among peers. For older siblings, the younger siblings provide support and understanding that can ease parent-adolescent conflicts. The sibling subsystem, therefore, despite its conflicts with the parent-child subsystem can serve to keep adolescents oriented to their families even as it prepares them to leave these families.

## SIBLING RELATIONS ACROSS FAMILY BOUNDARIES

The voluntary nature of the sibling affection structure that develops in adolescence becomes of increasing importance as siblings leave the parental household to form their own family units. During the establishment period and with the increasing responsibilities that childbearing brings, young married couples may find the voluntary nature of sibling ties a blessing. Just as the sibling subsystem can compete with the parent-child subsystem for the allegiance of its members, so too can it compete with the marital subsystem of the siblings. In a study of in-law relations, wives reported difficulties with sisters-in-law ranked second only to those with mothers-in-law (Duvall, 1954: 221–243).[2] The relative

---

[2] The strength of the incest taboo indicates how strong cross-sex sibling relations can at times become. Middleton (1962) reports that in Egypt from around 30 B.C. to 324 A.D., brother-sister marriages occurred among other groups than royalty. They occurred among the well-to-do in order to preserve intact the family property.

separateness that even the closest siblings experience after their respective marriages serves to maintain the boundaries of the new family units.

The factors that explain sibling solidarity after each has left the parental family appear to be those that explain any voluntary interpersonal commitment. Similarity of interests as indicated by age closeness and same gender status is one. Another factor is residential proximity, which easily permits siblings to keep in touch with each other's changing interests. A third factor is the presence of common obligations such as aging parents. The absence of invidious comparisons would be a fourth factor.

Adams' study (1968) of sibling relations among a representative sample of 799 families in Greensboro, North Carolina, tells us much about the operation of these factors in sibling contacts among adults. Data came from wives and husbands with siblings who had been married less than 20 years and were still in their first marriages. These respondents emphasized the voluntary nature of sibling contacts. When asked about their contacts with siblings, less than one third of the 697 felt obligated to remain in touch. Seventy percent said they did so because they enjoyed the contacts.

Residential proximity was the most important factor in continued sibling contacts. Blue-collar siblings saw each other more often than white-collar sibs. Their manual occupations permitted them to be more residentially stable than white-collar people, who work with ideas and people. Sisters with family concerns in common maintained contact even across geographical barriers through letters. Brothers and cross-sex siblings lost touch when they lived at a distance from one another (Adams, 1968: 103).

Age closeness like gender was of lesser importance than proximity in keeping siblings together. When respondents had more than one sibling to choose among, 27 percent of the 518 respondents chose the sibling closest in age as their favorite. A slightly higher number, 29 percent, chose another sibling, and 44 percent had no particular favorite (Adams, 1968: 127). Gender similarities may have overriden age similarities in accounting for the higher number of disparate age favorites among siblings, although Adams does not give us the necessary information to make this judgment.

Sibling contacts were particularly likely to continue if they occurred within the context of the more obligatory parental contacts (Adams, 1968: 127). Holidays, birthdays, and other family ritual occasions, along with parental emergencies, can bring siblings together and signify their solidarity. Because of the obligatory nature of such meetings, spouses may feel less competition from the sibling subsystem than if siblings convene without such an excuse.

Spouses are not alone in feeling resentment toward siblings of their marriage partners. Sibling solidarity can disappear when one sibling has made good and another has not. Where occupations compete with families for men's commitment, invidious intersibling comparisons along with different occupational interests may have something to do with the lesser contact brothers maintain as compared with sisters.

The emphasis among many persons in the United States on a middle-class style of life in which children go to college and there is money for annual vacations and a suitable display of worldly goods presupposes a certain level of occupational achievement. Persons who hold white-collar jobs are considered to be more successful in terms of maintaining such a life style than those holding blue-collar jobs.

One of the reference groups individuals can use for purposes of determining their relative achievement is siblings. Adams (1967: 366) has hypothesized that individuals are more likely to idealize and feel affection for middle-class siblings who have "made good" rather than for working-class siblings. But where there are disparities in social status, brothers are likely to make comparisons to the disadvantage of the less successful. As a consequence, even when such siblings live near each other, they are less likely to interact.

Adams (1967) examined possible intergenerational changes between white-collar and blue-collar occupations of his male respondents and their fathers' occupations and the occupations of husbands of female respondents as compared with those of the respondents' fathers. As he hypothesized, affection and idealization tended to be more common if the sibling was white collar, whether the sibling dyad consisted of brothers, sisters, or a brother and a sister. Blue-collar men with white-collar brothers, however, showed the least idealization of the more successful brothers and were least fond of them, probably because they had suffered from their own and others' disparaging comparison of them with the white-collar brothers. Higher status persons, regardless of gender, are likely to be critical of less successful sibs. Adams (1967: 373) reports the perceptive remark of a young middle-class wife concerning the nonreciprocal nature of affection between her and a sister. " 'Her husband,' she said 'hasn't been what a husband should be. . . . I'm not close to her, but if you asked her she'd say I'm her favorite sister.' " Feelings thus affect the frequency of sibling contacts. Cross-class siblings meet together less often than blue-collar siblings, but more often than white-collar siblings who are separated by geographical distance.

Given the voluntary nature of the sibling bond, the competing interests of own families, and the possibilities that exist for invidious comparisons, it is a tribute to the strength of sibling bonds that there exists a fair amount of mutual assistance among siblings. These exchanges are less than exchanges within lineages. About four-fifths of Adams' respondents (79 percent) were engaged in mutual assistant patterns with parents or children (Adams, 1968: 53, Table III-5). Such transactions with siblings involved 20 percent of his respondents (Adams, 1968: 129). Sibling assistance, however, is greater than occurs with other kin or among friends (Adams, 1968: 145, Table V-4; Hill, 1968).

After parents die, siblings lack this common concern to create occasions for meetings. The limitations on current role playing set by previous role performance is apparent in sibling relations. When siblings do not share common interests, the loss of parents can mean the breaking of sibling ties. Thus Rosenberg and Anspach (1973) with a random sample of white working-class adults, 45 to 79 years of age, found older persons less likely to keep up relations with siblings. While 67.9 percent of the 302 persons under 55 years of age maintained contact with siblings in the area, just 52 percent of the 532 older persons did so (Rosenberg and Anspach, 1973: 110, reformulation of Table 2). This is particularly true when the settling of the financial affairs of parents brings sibling rivalries to a peak. An exception occurs when older sisters, especially in larger families, continue in their role of parental surrogate and mediate such disputes. They also can perform other kinkeeping functions by making their homes the center for holiday celebrations of siblings and their families and by encouraging brothers and sisters to keep in touch with family "newsletters."

## SIBLING RELATIONS IN OLD AGE

As noted above, a number of researchers have found that the sibling role companion sequence is less important during the busy years when siblings are caught up in the affairs of their own families but in the aging period sibling relations may take on renewed meaning. Sibling ties for the elderly have the advantage that they do not continually have to be reaffirmed. After the role transitions of children leaving home and of occupational retirement, persons can reestablish close relations despite the passage of years with only sporadic contact. Research by Cumming and Schneider (1961) shows the importance of sibling solidarity as people grow older. From a Kansas City, Kansas, sample of 220 persons who were representative of persons in that city between the ages of 50 and 80, they interviewed intensively 15 representative individuals. The sibling bond among these respondents ran a close second in importance to the parent-child bond, and for women with sisters it seems at least to equal the spousal relation in significance. For these persons, who grew up around the turn of the century, sibling solidarity was second only to the mother-child bond as a source of affection. In that era, apparently, fathers more often played the holes of disciplinarian and rule giver, and their superior position in the family power structure was associated with a peripheral position in the affection structure.

These aging persons felt affection for their children, and obligation to their parents who were still living, but they enjoyed their sibs for reasons of sociability. Since parents had often died or, if living, had become senile, and since their children were busy with their own families, morale among men and women in this small sample was higher when they had siblings living nearby.

Similar findings appeared in a sample of 435 persons over 60 years of age who were fairly representative of persons in this age group in the San Francisco Bay Area. Only 38 percent had living spouses, and 39 percent were without children, but 93 percent had living siblings. As a consequence, the sibling relation was the most common kinship tie that these elderly people maintained. They tried to maintain contact with brothers and sisters and were particularly touched by their deaths (Clark and Anderson, 1967: 295). They made an effort now that they were no longer preoccupied with jobs and children to see sibs, even though they were separated by great distances. The need to visit sibs while they were living also provided an excuse for the elderly to break away from routines required by previous family and work responsibilities. Visits to distant sibs made travelling less expensive and supplied travel points around which to plan lengthy trips (Clark and Anderson, 1967: 296). Siblings, according to these people, could also provide comfort and support when relations with children were strained. In such cases, brothers and sisters were the first persons whom the elderly mentioned as capable of providing a home in case of need and of not making the recipient feel a burden.

Sibling rivalry and jealousy of the more successful, however, did not disappear with age. Limited linkage of roles from earlier stages occurred. Mr. Booth, one of the 203 persons, 60 years of age and over, Peter Townsend studied in a working-class section of London, expressed the continuation of old rancors. With respect to his sisters he said, " 'We don't bother about any of them. . . Two of my sisters have got a bit of money but they wouldn't give you anything. They'd help the church rather than their own' " (Townsend, 1957: 99). In these circumstances, siblings remain separated even in old age.

But in this residentially stable sample, most siblings remained in touch, "Nearly one-fifth of those with siblings saw at least one every day," and another one-fourth had weekly visits with a sib (Townsend, 1957: 103). Visiting patterns of the past continued, since brothers maintained fewer contacts with siblings than did sisters.

### Sibling Ties as Substitutes

Some persons, notably the single and the childless, are particularly dependent upon sibling ties. They are joined by the divorced and widowed whose relations with their own children are poor. Women also keep in closer touch with siblings than men. In Townsend's London study (1957: 103), the childless saw a third of their brothers and one-half of their sisters at least weekly. In this area, where there was little residential mobility to separate kin, women with children visited a third of their sisters and 15 percent of their brothers, weekly or oftener. Men with children, however, had contact with only three percent of their brothers and nine percent of their sisters this often. The more recent study of a random sample of working-class persons in Philadelphia, Pennsylvania, which we referred to earlier, produced similar results. The 360 persons who were divorced, separated, or widowed were more apt to visit siblings in the area than were the 500 married couples interviewed (Rosenberg and Anspach, 1973: 111).

Unmarried siblings may try to live near each other or continue to share the family home after parents die. Married siblings, particularly women, appear to be especially solicitous of the unmarried by providing the assistance and solace children are supposed to give. The childless, however, whether married or single can provide, because of the lack of family responsibilities, things for siblings and their families that other relatives beset by their own family duties lack the time and funds to do (Townsend, 1957: 105). Thus the bachelor uncle or married aunt without children, in addition to assuming the burden of seeing parents through their last illnesses, may provide funds for nieces' and nephews' educations or help out with siblings' house payments.

## THE SIBLING SUBSYSTEM IN PERSPECTIVE

Sibling relations deserve more attention from family scholars than they have so far received. Such relations are obligatory when children are growing up in the same household. The long hours siblings spend together are occasions for socialization that may counter the more conscious socialization efforts of parents. But sibling socialization also supplements socialization in the parent-child subsystem, with consequences that take on particular importance as siblings enter adolescence. This transitional period between childhood dependence and adult independence can be less stressful when older siblings serve as behavioral models for sociability relations outside the family, and when younger siblings provide support in parent-adolescent conflicts within the family.

As adolescents mature in a family, sibling relations gradually take on the quality of other extrafamilial cohort relations. The time is particularly favorable for a change from obligatory to voluntary relations to occur. Also, the old rivalries for parental attention lose their force as youths turn their attention to peers.

A concern with the parents who gave them a common identity, however, makes for continued sibling contacts after each has established his own residence. Shared interests and geographical proximity encourage sibling solidarity despite its possible competition with the marital subsystem of the siblings.

Sibling relations that have remained close over the years provide an additional source of companionship in the aging years. At that time, their voluntary nature gives sibling contacts the sociability qualities of friendship; at the same time, the blood tie provides an additional quality of dependability that friendship relations lack. Fortunate, indeed, are older adults who are caught up in a network of warm support made larger by the presence of siblings.

# REFERENCES

Adams, Bert N., *Kinship in an Urban Setting.* Chicago: Markham, 1968.

Adams, Bert N., "Occupational Position, Mobility and the Kin of Orientation," *American Sociological Review,* 1967, 31, 364–377.

Baldwin, Alfred L., "Changes in Parent Behavior during Pregnancy," *Child Development,* 1947, 18, 29–39.

Bank, Stephen and Michael D. Kahn, "Sisterhood-Brotherhood is Powerful: Sibling Subsystems and Family Therapy," *Family Process,* 1975, 14, 311–337.

Bengston, V. L. and K. Dean Black, "Intergenerational Relations and Continuities in Socialization," in W. Schaie and P. Baltes, eds., *Life Span Development Psychology: Personality and Socialization.* New York: Academic Press, 1973.

Bossard, James H. S. and Eleanor Boll, *The Large Family System.* Philadelphia: University of Pennsylvania Press, 1956.

Bowerman, Charles E. and Rebecca M. Dobash, "Structural Variations in Sibling Affect," *Journal of Marriage and the Family*, 1974, 35, 48–54.

Brim, Orville G., "Family Role Structure and Sex Role Learning by Children: A Further Analysis of Helen Koch's Data," *Sociometry*, 1958, 21, 1–16.

Clark, Margaret and Barbara Anderson, *Culture and Aging*. Springfield, Ill.: Charles C Thomas, 1967.

Cumming, Elaine and David M. Schneider, "Sibling Solidarity: A Property of American Kinship," *American Anthropologist*, 1961, 63, 198–207.

Duvall, Evelyn, M., *In-Laws Pro and Con*. New York: Associates Press, 1954.

Elder, Jr., Glen H., "Structural Variations in the Child-Rearing Relationship," *Sociometry*, 1962, 25, 241–262.

Hill, Reuben, "Decision Making and Family Life Cycle," in Bernice Neugarten, ed., *Middle Age and Aging*. Chicago: University of Chicago Press, 1968, 286–295.

Hill, Reuben and Joan Aldous, "Socialization for Marriage and Parenthood," in David A. Goslin, ed., *Handbook of Socialization Theory and Research*. Chicago: Rand McNally, 1969, 885–950.

Irish, Donald P., "Sibling Interaction: A Neglected Aspect in Family Life Research," *Social Forces*, 1964, 42, 279–288.

Koch, Helen, "The Relation of Primary Mental Abilities in Five- and Six-Year-Olds to Sex of Child and Characteristics of Siblings," *Child Development*, 1954, 25, 209–223.

Lasko, Joan K., "Parent Behavior toward First and Second Children," *Genetic Psychological Monographs*, 1954, 49, 97–137.

Middleton, Russell, "Brother-Sister and Father-Daughter Marriage in Ancient Egypt," *American Sociological Review*, 1962, 27, 603–611.

Rosenberg, George L. and Donald F. Anspach, "Sibling Solidarity in the Working Class," *Journal of Marriage and the Family*, 1973, 35, 108–113.

Sutton-Smith, Brian and B. G. Rosenberg, *The Sibling*. New York: Holt, Rinehart and Winston, 1970.

Townsend, Peter, *The Family Life of Old People*. London: Routledge & Kegan Paul, 1957.

U.S. Bureau of the Census, Current Population Reports, Series P-20, No. 291, "Household and Family Characteristics: March 1975," U.S. Government Printing Office, Washington, D.C., 1976.

Waller, Willard and Reuben Hill, *The Family: A Dynamic Interpretation*. New York: Dryden Press, 1951.

# 17

**Overview**

# Challenges and new directions

"Not another book on the family!" a colleague of mine groaned when I announced my intention of writing this book. I believed then, and I continue to believe, that I was writing about the family from a different perspective, a perspective that makes this more than just another book on the family. Others have used similar conceptual filters, but I have tried to go beyond their work and to make a contribution of my own (cf., Duvall, 1971; and Rodgers, 1973). This chapter will provide an opportunity for me to summarize what I consider important in my interpretation of the family development framework. I will also discuss the framework in the light of methodological considerations and some of the criticisms scholars have made of it, concluding with suggestions on fruitful areas for future work and their probable relevance for practitioners.

## A Summing Up
We have seen the changes that the passage of time brings to three different family subsystems—the marital, the parent-child, and the sibling. To simplify the analysis, we have discussed each subsystem separately. It was impossible in these discussions, however, not to observe the

phenomenon of the interdependencies among the subsystems. In the analysis of the marital career, we showed in Chapter 7 that marital satisfaction is profoundly affected by the addition of parental roles to family positions. In like fashion, the departure of children from the home to start their own marital careers has pronounced effects on spousal roles in the postparental phase (see Chapter 9). The arrival of grandchildren activates grandparent roles in the cluster of family roles (see Chapter 15). And how experiences in the preexisting parent-child subsystem carry over and affect the new parent-child subsystem is seen in Chapter 11. The interdependence of the parent-child subsystem and the sibling subsystems, as well as the changes in the relationships among siblings when they marry, became apparent in Chapter 16.

Just as the family subsystems impinge upon one another, so too do the individual's various careers in his or her family position. The relationships established by past marriages continue to have effects. In addition to marital roles, the individual plays parental roles or responds as an adult "child" to others playing such roles. And sibling roles that may have been crowded out during the busy child-rearing years are waiting to be reactivated in the postparental and aging periods.

One of the recurring themes underlying relationships in the family subsystems is the importance of the affection structure. The marital career is initiated because of the love a man and a woman feel for each other, and its continuance in an era of easy divorce largely depends upon the bond of affection. In like fashion, parents and children who have lived through the stages of cohabitation stay in frequent contact through affection more than obligation. And sibling ties that continue despite the competing demands of marital and parental careers are based on love. This warmth that keeps family members in close touch over the years can take the form of shared activities, shared confidences, or shared routines; but in any case the presence of the intimate relation is something family members treasure, try to preserve, and search actively to replace if family ties are broken.

The addition of marital, sibling, or parental roles to a family position, however, creates critical role transition periods while the individual works out an accommodation among new and old roles. We have seen the family morphogenesis that occurs as the child takes on the developmental tasks associated with entering new careers. The role making he engages in with other members to establish the specific content of the various roles leads to new interaction patterns.

The uneasy coexistence of the several competing roles within the individual's family position over time depends also upon his or her role obligations in extrafamilial settings. We have taken particular note of the interdependence of occupational and educational careers and family role performances. The timing of marriages (Chapter 6) is affected by occupational income, and the loss of occupational roles (Chapter 10) ushers in the final phase of marital companionship. In addition, Chapter 13 shows how the values fathers seek to inculcate in their children stem from their occupations.

Since the relations of family and extrafamilial roles is one of interdependence, family roles affect role performance outside the family and vice-versa. The influence family roles have on occupational behaviors was shown in the material contained in Chapter 11 on the association of men's lower job satisfaction and the simultaneous peaking of family and occupational demands on his time. Chapter 14 indicated that women's reentry into the labor market after dropping out during the childbearing period coincides with the gap between the heavy financial costs of educating adolescents and the capacity of men's incomes to meet these costs. These costs, however, will never arise if youths fail to receive the parental encouragement that will lead them to incorporate the quest for knowledge in an extended educational career as a developmental task (see Chapter 13). Thus family socialization affects school behavior.

## Research Designs

To document these interdependencies of family subsystems, positional careers, and extrafamilial careers, we have drawn upon a variety of researches. Many of these researches have been cross-sectional in nature, so that the dynamics of temporal change have been absent. The issue of marital satisfaction is a case in point. The longitudinal research of Burgess and associates described in Chapter 8 showed us not only how occupational involvement of husbands and wives can affect marital satisfaction but also how marital satisfaction in one cohort of middle-class couples can change over the years. But such research is costly in terms of time and money, both for investigators and the families they study. In addition, changes in values and differences in the historical events that families live through both make it difficult to determine how far longitudinal findings from one set of families can be generalized to families living in other times under other circumstances (Rollins, 1975).

We, therefore, have had to depend largely on cross-sectional research to give us some idea of what happens to marital satisfaction when couples go beyond the middle years of marriage, the point where the research of Burgess stopped. Results from cross-sectional studies on marital satisfaction over the years are not always in agreement

(Spanier, Lewis, and Cole, 1975). The Blood and Wolfe (1960) findings suggest a continuing decline, while other investigators with smaller, less representative samples find some indication of an upturn in the later years (Rollins and Cannon, 1974).

As divorce becomes increasingly an acceptable solution to marital unhappiness, unhappy couples part, leaving only relatively happy couples to be sampled beyond the initial years of marriage (Miller, 1975).[1] Definitive answers to questions of changes in family behavior over the years, whether the dimensions are marital satisfaction or power structure, must thus wait for the results of long-term longitudinal research utilizing more adequate data collecting instruments and for larger more representative samples from different time periods.

Feldman's study of the effects on couples' interaction patterns of the coming of children described in Chapter 7, presents a welcome alternative to cross-sectional and traditional longitudinal studies for some family development issues. This *segmented longitudinal panel with controls*, as Hill (1964) labels the design, focuses on specific critical role transition points. The investigator studies families as they go through such a transition period, and by comparing these families with a control group of comparable families who have not experienced this change, he can distinguish transition effects from family longevity effects. At the same time these segmental longitudinal studies are short-term in nature and so manageable in terms of the financial outlay and personal effort by investigators and sample families alike.

The findings concerning patterns of intergenerational helping, which were reported in Chapter 15, presents still another alternative to conventional longitudinal research for collecting data on family development. This strategy consists of sampling three-generation family lineages, reconstructing past changes through retrospective interviews, and following the families for a limited time period to observe current change. Hill and his associates (1970) were the first to use this technique. Having three generations of married couples of which each generation maintains its own residence enables the investigator to analyze family careers at different historical periods. The disadvantages of this design lie in its dependence on respondents' memories for information

---

[1] As it becomes possible even for conventional people to admit to marital discord and other family problems, more honest answers may also become socially desirable. Such a development would certainly ease the researcher's task in investigating marital satisfaction. At present, many couples tend to be reluctant to admit that marital discord exists when outsiders question them.

of past family events, and in the absence of controls for intragenerational age differences. Some couples in the grandchildren generation, for example, can overlap in age and in the critical transitions being experienced with other couples in the parental generation. Families in both generations may be welcoming new arrivals or saying farewell to children leaving home to enter college or work life. Data analyses based on generational comparisons obscure these differences in family event experiences (Elder, 1975).

## New Yields from Cohort Analyses

One source of excellent longitudinal data that is not weakened by questions of sample size and representativeness is information drawn from the United States Census concerning the family careers of persons born at the same time. Although the investigator using census data is limited in what she or he can study by the kind of questions the census people ask, some of the most provocative studies appearing in previous chapters, such as the Oppenheimer (1974) research summarized in Chapter 14 on the variation in timing of peak earnings among men in different occupations, are based on these data.

A good example of such cohort analysis is the research of Peter Uhlenberg (1974) in which he traces the marital and parental careers of women born at 10-year intervals from the period 1890–1894 to the period 1930–1934. This research provides a useful summary of changes in family careers in the twentieth century, thereby reminding us of the historical backdrop against which family development occurs. Uhlenberg was able to determine changes in the proportion of women conforming to the modal family career, which includes marriage, having children, and rearing those children with a husband present. Women who fail to conform to this conventional pattern may have died young, never married, been childless after marriage, or experienced the dissolution of their marriages when children were present.

Uhlenberg found that an increasing proportion of white women experienced this "preferred" life course with each succeeding decade. As Table 17-1 indicates, more than three times as many women born in the early 1890s died before reaching the age of 15 as did women born in the early 1930s. As compared with the youngest cohort of women, over twice as many women born in the early years who survived to be 50 years old never married, and of those who did marry, over four times as many remained childless. The youngest cohort, however, was more likely to experience marital dissolution due to divorce and separation.

The data also suggest that the conventional life course has reached a turning point with women born in 1940–1944. More of these women

Table 17-1

**Distribution of White Females in the U.S. By Type of Life Cycle Experienced, Birth Cohorts from 1890–94 to 1930–34**

| | The Number Out of 1000 Surviving to Age 15 Who Experience Each Type of Life Cycle | | | | |
|---|---|---|---|---|---|
| Birth Cohort | Total | Early Death | Spinster | Childless | Unstable Marriage— with Children | Preferred |
| 1890–94[I] | 1000 | 170 | 80 | 185 | 140 | 425 |
| 1900–04 | 1000 | 125 | 75 | 155 | 170 | 475 |
| 1910–14 | 1000 | 90 | 60 | 145 | 185 | 520 |
| 1920–24 | 1000 | 60 | 50 | 85 | 200 | 605 |
| 1930–34 | 1000 | 50 | 45 | 55 | 205 | 645 |
| | The Number Out of 1000 Surviving to Age 50 Who Experience Each Type of Life Cycle | | | | |
| 1890–94[I] | 1000 | | 100 | 225 | 165 | 510 |
| 1900–04 | 1000 | | 85 | 180 | 195 | 540 |
| 1910–14 | 1000 | | 65 | 160 | 200 | 575 |
| 1920–24 | 1000 | | 50 | 90 | 215 | 645 |
| 1930–34 | 1000 | | 45 | 55 | 215 | 685 |

Source: U.S. Bureau of the Census: 1944, Tables 1, 7, 13; 1955, Table 16; 1971a, Table 7; 1971b, Table 1; 1972a, Table 1; 1972b, Table 5. U.S. Department of Health, Education, and Welfare, NCHS: 1972a, Table 5-5; 1972b, Tables 1-4 as appearing in Uhlenberg, 1974: 286.

[I] Data, other than deaths, are for "native whites."

are never marrying as compared with the cohort born a decade earlier, as Table 17-2 indicates, and if younger women marry, they are more likely to remain childless or experience divorce. Thus, estimates for all women born in the 1950s suggest that seven percent will never marry and of those who do, some four percent will remain childless while one-third will divorce (Glick, 1977).

Nonwhite women in every birth cohort, when compared with white women, are less apt to experience the modal positional career. Table 17-3 shows that mortality rates, even as recently as 1930–1934, were still twice as high for black women as those for white women. An increase in the number of women living to experience marriage and childbirth, moreover, would be compensated for by the recent increase in women not marrying and, if marrying, remaining childless or breaking off the marriage (see Table 17-2).

These analyses based on census data do two things. They supply us

Table 17-2

**Comparison of Life Cycle Patterns at Ages 25–29 for Birth Cohorts of 1930–34 and 1940–44, White and Negro, U.S.**

| | Characteristics of Females Aged 25–29 | | |
| | | Ever-Married | |
| Birth Cohort | Single % | Childless % | Married once, Spouse present % |
| --- | --- | --- | --- |
| White | | | |
| 1930–34 | 9.7 | 12.3 | 85.6 |
| 1940–44 | 10.9 | 15.0 | 81.1 |
| Negro | | | |
| 1930–34 | 15.8 | 14.5 | 66.4 |
| 1940–44 | 21.3 | 8.5 | 63.6 |

Source: U.S. Bureau of the Census; 1971b, Table 1; 1972a, Table 1 as appearing in Uhlenberg, 1974: 288.

with individual cohort histories and reliable information on changes in the family careers of women born before the end of the last century to the end of World War II. They also suggest the difference in family milieus between children of white and nonwhite women with concomitant differences in socialization. In 1976, 47.5 percent of black children under three years of age were living with both parents and were children of the household head. Over one-third (35 percent) of them were living with their mothers only, while 15.8 percent were living with neither parent. Among white children under three years of age in the same year, however, 89.3 percent were living with both parents, one of whom was the household head, 8.9 percent were living with their mothers, and 1.3 percent with neither parent (U.S. Bureau of the Census, 1977: 28, Table 4; cf., Uhlenberg, 1974: 290).

In addition to demonstrating the use of census data as a strategy for conducting longitudinal type research, the findings of the Uhlenberg research point up a criticism often made of the family development framework. Because the proportion of women who are departing from the conventional pattern of marriage—that is, childbearing and remaining with the children's father during the child-rearing years—is increasing, family observers are questioning the usefulness of the family stages as presently demarcated (Trost, 1973). As demonstrated in Chapter 4, however, it is possible to develop criteria appropriate for analyzing temporal changes in the family careers of the multi-marrieds and those whose marital careers have ended before their parental careers.

Table 17-3
**Distribution of Nonwhite Females in the U.S. by Type of Life Cycle Experienced, Birth Cohorts from 1890–94 to 1930–34**

| | | | | | Unstable | |
| Birth | | Early | | | Marriage— | |
| Cohort | Total | Death | Spinster | Childless | with Children | Preferred |
|---|---|---|---|---|---|---|
| | | The Number Out of 1000 Surviving to Age 15 Who Experience Each Type of Life Cycle | | | | |
| 1890–94[I] | 1000 | 390 | 30 | 125 | 275 | 180 |
| 1900–04 | 1000 | 335 | 35 | 180 | 260 | 190 |
| 1910–14 | 1000 | 250 | 45 | 190 | 265 | 250 |
| 1920–24[I] | 1000 | 175 | 55 | 155 | 320 | 295 |
| 1930–34[I] | 1000 | 100 | 80 | 70 | 400 | 350 |
| | | The Number Out of 1000 Surviving to Age 50 Who Experience Each Type of Life Cycle | | | | |
| 1890–94[I] | 1000 | | 50 | 210 | 450 | 290 |
| 1900–04 | 1000 | | 50 | 265 | 395 | 290 |
| 1910–14 | 1000 | | 55 | 255 | 355 | 335 |
| 1920–24[I] | 1000 | | 70 | 185 | 385 | 360 |
| 1930–34[I] | 1000 | | 90 | 75 | 445 | 390 |

Source: U.S. Bureau of the Census: 1944, Tables 65, 76; 1955, Table 32; 1964, Table 17; 1971a, Table 7; 1971b, Table 1; 1972a; Table 1; 1972b, Table 5. U.S. Department of Health, Education, and Welfare, NCHS: 1972a, Table 5-5; 1972b, Tables 5-8 as appearing in Uhlenberg, 1974: 289.
[I] Data, other than deaths, are for Negro females.

Feldman and Feldman (1975), for example, have described four "subcareers"—what we call careers—that together constitute the family positions individuals fill. Persons can be categorized according to their location in a career based on sexual experience, a marital career, a parent-child career, and an adult-parent career. According to this category system, a person could be married (marital career), engaging in an affair with a fellow employee (sexual experience career), playing maternal roles to a four-year-old son (parent-child career) and interacting with her or his own parents (adult-parent career). The Feldmans (1975: 281) have argued that what we would label as critical role transition points occur when one or more of these careers intersect. They give the examples of the addition of the marital career to the sexual career experience of cohabitation, or the intersection of the parent-child career with the marital career when the first child is born. These are transitions present in the stages discussed in Chapters 6 and 7. The ending of the individual marital career in divorce and the continuance of the sexual career with a new lover, culminating in reentry into the marital career with a different partner, constitutes a stage demarcated in the one-parent classification covered in Chapters 4, and 8.

## Individual and Family Perspectives

Elder (1975) also writes of multiple careers but in the context of a fundamental critique of the stage concept. According to him, tinkering with the criteria for demarcating family stages, even if this tinkering is based on research, will not help. In his view, family stages tend to be artificial entities encompassing too wide a range of parental ages to encourage research on the intersection of the multiple career lines that adults follow. In arguing the absence of the systemic character of the family stage concept, Elder refers to the individual's life course. He sees family stages as being too simplistic to allow for differances in the timing of lifetime events in work life or residential histories as well as in family life. Promotions, demotions, or residential moves, all con-stitute career changes that affect the adult along with changes in the role sequences in his family position. The synchronization of these multiple career lines, Elder declares, requires a more episodic ap-proach than family stage analysis permits.

Reuben Hill (1975) has pointed out, however, that Elder in his critique is taking a concept out of its context. He should be examining the more encompassing conceptual framework of family development rather than singling out the concept of stages for criticism. These stages or categories are, after all, only guides for dividing family careers into manageable units, according to the scholar's purpose, which the panoply of family development concepts then permits us to analyze in detail.

We would also add that life-course analysis of individuals is at a different level of conceptualization than family study. The focus of the family development framework is on a particular group of affiliated indi-viduals. Critical events in the various careers of these individuals, whether in the family, in work life, or in school life, have repercussions on other family members. But somehow or other, in trying to enlighten ourselves with respect to family behavior, we must grasp the implica-tions for family existence of the intermeshing of the multiple careers, not just those of one individual but those of all individuals in specific family units. Perhaps this aim is too grandiose, but in this book we have sought to shed light on the convergence of the positional careers of family members within the context of occupational and educational roles. The concept of stage has proved useful in highlighting the critical role transitions of marrying, of having children, of adjusting to their leaving home and of retiring from an occupation—all events that herald changes in the multiple careers of several family members.

Family stages may well provide too clumsy a category system to cope with individual life-course changes. They can be made more useful in answering questions concerning families, however, particularly when the criteria for stage demarcation are tailored to the family groups in question, whether one parent families or families formed by remarriages. These criteria necessarily will take into account the multiple career lines of the life courses of individuals. But only critical role transitions of individuals that coincide with those of other family members or create qualitative differences in family functioning will serve to define family stages.

## New Directions

It is appropriate to conclude this short assessment of some of the criticisms of the family development framework with a consideration of fruitful research and theoretical activities in the light of the material covered in this book. The framework, itself, is still in the process of development, and where and how it develops depends upon the efforts scholars devote to it. One of the first priorities may well be to change its character from that of a conceptual framework to that of a theory. To begin to do this, more of the propositions containing family development concepts that are implicit in the preceding chapters need to be made explicit and tested using appropriate longitudinal research designs.

Some of these potential propositions have to do with the concept of limited linkage. It incorporates the assumption that family behavior is the result of past experience incorporated in the present together with the members' goals and expectations for the future. Propositions specifying what family task behaviors at one period set limits on behaviors at the next are important to family members, practitioners, and policy makers alike.

For example, further research may provide support for the proposition that the level of morale maintenance prior to a critical role transition is related positively to morale maintenance in the next period. If, however, destructive conflict-management patterns between spouses, or between parents and children, can be modified through practitioner-helped family training in communication skills, low morale maintenance at one period may not exercise a dampening influence on the next (Miller, Corrales, and Wackman, 1975). On the other hand, we also need to know for our "family survival" kit whether effective conflict-management patterns, once established, can withstand the problematics of subsequent periods. Empirical tests of propositions embodying this idea clearly benefit troubled families in danger of breaking up.

Policy makers aware of the train of woes throughout the family career brought on by low finances in the establishment period, which we have referred to throughout this book, are also concerned with the limited-linkage phenomenon. Their interest lies in determining the most efficacious timing for outside income supplementation to institute a more benign sequence of limited linkages (Aldous and Hill, 1969).

Another area where work will contribute both to the shift of family development from framework to theory, as well as to applied concerns, is that of structure modification as incorporated in the feedback concept. With individuals increasing their demands for a higher quality of family life, researchers need to look at the process whereby families compare where they are with where they wish to be and decide whether changes in goals or achievements must be made. The kinds of goals persons are seeking and the conditions of their attainment, when publicized in marriage preparation courses or by family counselors, encourage more realistic appraisals of what is possible in family life.

Changing family interaction patterns to meet family goals, an alternative strategy for dealing with a mismatch between goals and achievements, can be extremely difficult. One of the characteristics of families that makes the institution so strong is the interactional structures that members can depend on despite changes in their outside careers. Pressure to change these routines, therefore, can run into stiff opposition, particularly if the pressures come from low-power members or even from significant outsiders. Research on innovating families and the intrafamilial and extrafamilial factors that ease family morphogenesis is well worth pursuing as a part of the interest in the feedback process.

Finally, a sustained effort to establish an optimal timetable for family events could tie together work on limited linkages and feedback processes. Such a timetable cannot insure that all couples following it will have family careers terminated by death rather than by divorce. It will, however, incorporate what we know concerning the timing of family events as it appears optimal for majority groups of families.

Take marriage as an example. It used to be that policy makers were very concerned that divorce was not easily available. At the present time, however, policy makers and ordinary citizens alike see marriages that are easily entered into as the problem. Too early marriages—marriages involving teen-agers—are disproportionately represented in the divorce courts. Older couples tend to be better prepared financially and to be able to exercise more control over the timing of the first child, a second event in the family career timetable that can contribute to marital difficulties when it comes too close to the wedding.

We do not know very much about whether there is a "too-late" timing period for marriages nor whether there is an optimal time for remarriages and for giving birth within them. These are additional research issues of interest to family development scholars and to lay persons.

## PRACTITIONERS AND THE FAMILY DEVELOPMENT FRAMEWORK

Special note needs to be taken that the family development approach is particularly congenial to the concerns of practitioners like social workers, ministers, counselors, doctors, nurses, and teachers who must deal with families or their members. It points up periods when problems peak due to a dearth of resources. Tables 6-1, 6-2, and 6-3 provide a useful summary of the balance sheet for particular stages. Resources of money, emotions, and time can be in short supply when role transitions close out family stages and introduce new ones, with their attendant changes in interaction patterns. Practitioners aware that clients are in such periods are alerted to possible problems not covered in conventional symptom sheets.

The emphasis in the family development framework on timing can also prove useful to practitioners who are aware of optimal family career schedules and who are able to help families compensate for timing failures. Thus programs to encourage responsible parenthood for the already pregnant adolescent can focus on parenting skills, prenatal and postnatal care of mother and child, and day care while women are completing educations or taking jobs. But for adolescents not yet having to face the responsibilities of parenthood, practitioners can institute sex education and family-life programs that discourage unwanted pregnancies while emphasizing the competencies required for entering into marital and parental careers. Such programs point up the need to avoid career event pileups that juxtapose the beginnings of marital and parental careers with a consequent forcing of premature educational exits and occupational entrances. At the same time, they indicate to women the high probability of spending their adult years in the work force, often as the heads of families broken by divorce.

There is increasing evidence that practitioners can also help families to develop interaction patterns that better serve their own family career goals. Members can be taught to become conscious of their actions in the short behavioral sequences pointed up in the concern of the family development framework with interaction structures. Communication strategies that wind down conflicts or that encourage discussion of sensitive issues can be taught (Miller, Corrales, and Wackman, 1975). When parents and children can talk to one another with few reserves, parents can accept and prepare their children better for adult responsibilities. Again, practitioners can assist in this process by offering parents the instruction and self-insight they need to socialize children in such areas as sexual behavior, where parents all too often feel inadequate but resent other agencies taking on the task (Scales and Everly, 1977).

In dealing with events outside the family that impinge on family processes, the family development framework emphasizes the status of practitioners as outsiders with whom family members interact with varying degrees of willingness. Accordingly, practitioners will see themselves in their transactions with families as admitted more or less on sufferance. They must win their way if their ministrations are to be successful.

At the same time, practitioners' attempts to gain the perspective of the members involved in family problems gives them a unique advantage. As outsiders, they can provide relatively unbiased feedback on what family members are doing right and on what they are doing wrong in coping with the situation that brought them to a practitioner's attention. Since families usually seek out practitioners for professional help, they are prepared to listen to the counsel and perhaps to institute the changes the practitioner recommends. Families may even come to accept the social workers, or even the law enforcement officers, whose services are imposed rather than sought out, if these representatives of the broader community can demonstrate how their assistance fits in with family goals.

The overall task of practitioners is to work themselves out of a job. They can prepare families to cope with the expectable role and career transitions they will experience over time. By teaching families how to find help in the large medical, educational, or social welfare bureaucracies, practitioners can contribute to the beliefs of families in their own problem-solving skills even when they must turn to outside professionals for counsel.

## A Final Comment

While writing this book I have felt myself to be at many times a bit like a juggler trying to keep a number of balls in the air. In my case, it was trying to keep track of the changes in the family subsystem I was examining at the time while allowing a necessary margin for its interaction with the other family subsystems. In some analyses, as with those involving adults and their parents or adult siblings, my thinking was complicated by the presence of relationships among nuclear family members who were simultaneously in different family units.

Although I am committed sufficiently to the family development framework to write a book about it, I have had no illusions that it is intellectually or practically complete. Yet in describing the work that is left to be done on the framework, I am not displeased with what I have been able to achieve in this formulation.

With its emphasis on the interplay of the careers of family members throughout the family cycle, it gives a dynamic picture of family behavior lacking in other perspectives. Moreover, because of the framework's focus on change, it is as difficult to ignore extrafamilial sources as it is intrafamilial instigators of change. At the same time, consideration of family structures and family tasks indicates the continuities that supply the background for the family's ongoing processes.

# REFERENCES

Aldous, Joan and Reuben Hill, "Breaking the Poverty Cycle: Strategic Points for Intervention," Social Work, 1969, 14, 3–12.

Blood, Robert, O. Jr. and Donald M. Wolfe, Husbands and Wives: The Dynamics of Married Living. Glencoe, Ill.: Free Press, 1960.

Duvall, Evelyn, Family Development. Philadelphia: J. P. Lippincott, 1971.

Elder, Glen H., "Age Differentiation and the Life Course," in Alex Inkeles, James Coleman and Neil Smelser, eds., Annual Review of Sociology, I. Palo Alto, Cal.: Annual Reviews, 1975, 175–190.

Feldman, Harold and Margaret Feldman, "The Family Life Cycle: Some Suggestions for Recycling," Journal of Marriage and the Family, 1975, 37, 277–284.

Glick, Paul, C., "Updating the Life Cycle of the Family," Journal of Marriage and the Family, 1976, 39, 5–13.

Hill, Reuben, "Methodological Issues in Family Development Research," Family Process, 1964, 3, 186–205.

Hill, Reuben, Personal Communication, 1975.

Hill, Reuben, Nelson Foote, Joan Aldous, Robert Carlson, and Robert McDonald, Family Development in Three Generations. Cambridge, Mass.: Schenkman, 1970.

Miller, Brent, "Studying the Quality of Marriage Cross-Sectionally," Journal of Marriage and the Family, 1975, 37, 11–12.

Miller, Sherod, Ramon Corrales, and Daniel B. Wackman, "Recent Progress in Understanding and Facilitating Marital Communication," *Family Coordinator*, 1975, 24, 143–152.

Oppenheimer, Valerie Kincade, "The Life-Cycle Squeeze: The interaction of Men's Occupation and Family Life Cycles," *Demography*, 1974, 11, 227–245.

Rodgers, Roy, *Family Interaction and Transaction: The Developmental Approach*. Englewood Cliffs, N.J.: Prentice-Hall, 1973.

Rollins, Boyd, C., "Response to Miller about Cross-Sectional Family Life Cycle Research," *Journal of Marriage and the Family*, 1975, 37, 259–260.

Rollins, Boyd C. and Kenneth L. Cannon, "Marital Satisfaction over the Family Life Cycle: A Reevaluation," *Journal of Marriage and the Family*, 1974, 36, 271–283.

Scales, Peter and Kathleen Everly, "A Community Sex Education Program for Parents," *Family Coordinator*, 1977, 26, 31–36.

Spanier, Graham B., Robert A. Lewis, and Charles L. Cole, "Marital Adjustment over the Family Life Cycle: The Issue of Curvilinearity," *Journal of Marriage and the Family*, 1975, 37, 265–275.

Trost, Jan, "The Family Life Cycle: A Problematic Concept," Paper presented at the Thirteenth International Seminar on Family Research, International Sociological Association, 1973.

Uhlenberg, Peter, "Cohort Variations in Family Life Cycle Experiences of U.S. Females," *Journal of Marriage and the Family*, 1974, 36, 284–292. Copyright 1974 by National Council on Family Relations.

U.S. Bureau of the Census, *Current Population Reports Series P-20*, No. 306, "Marital Status and Living Arrangements: March, 1976," U.S. Government Printing Office, Washington, D.C., 1977.

# Appendix A

## Glossary of Terms Used in the Family Development Framework*

**achieved roles**—roles that are acquired by the individual's own efforts.

**anticipatory norms**—norms that encourage families to prepare for change, e.g., preparing for parenthood.

**anticipatory socialization**—socialization that prepares the individual for roles he/she will have to perform in the future, also referred to as **role rehearsal.**

**ascribed (or ascriptive) roles**—roles that are assigned by virtue of some characteristic the actor possesses, and over which he/she has no control, such as age or sex.

**cohort**—a group of individuals born in the same time period whose timing of critical transition points in their family careers can often be determined through archival records such as U.S. Census data.

**concept**—an idea that refers to the common elements found in a number of different events.

**conceptual clarity**—one criterion of a concept's usefulness. It concerns how clearly defined are the limits of the phenomena the concept demarcates.

**conceptual framework**—a group of related concepts that, taken together, form a coherent picture of the subject matter with which the concepts are concerned.

**conceptual scope**—one criterion of a concept's usefulness. It concerns the range of phenomena to which the concept refers.

**conjugal role organization**—the division of household tasks between husbands and wives.

    1. *joint conjugal role organization*—tasks are interchangeable between husband and wife or performed jointly.

    2. *segregated conjugal role organization*—tasks are divided between husband and wife, usually according to traditional gender task assignment with little overlap. (Elizabeth Bott, *Family and Social Network: Roles, Norms, and External Relationships in Ordinary Urban Families.* New York: Free Press, 1971.)

**critical role transition point (or period)**—an interval in the life of the individual that marks normal discontinuities in career behaviors, e.g., beginning the marital career, becoming a parent, retiring from an occupation.

**expressive vs. instrumental roles**

    1. *expressive roles*—roles that contain norms regulating behaviors

* Compiled by Stephen R. Jorgensen and Joan Aldous.

concerned with providing emotional support for others through mediating disputes, being affectionate, and nurturant.

2. *instrumental roles*—roles that contain norms concerned with organizing and directing the activities of others that have to do with task performance.

**family career**—consists of the individual members' positional careers over time. The concept suggests the interdependencies of the family that tie the members' role clusters into a family role complex, as well as the expectable changes these interdependencies entail, from the time the family is formed until its dissolution; also referred to as **family life cycle.**

**family development framework**—the set of concepts that focus on expectable changes in families, from the time a couple begins cohabiting until the dissolution of the family due to death of one of the spouses or their separation and divorce.

**family developmental (or development) task**—any of the functions of the family specified according to the family career stage in which the family is.

These functions include the following:

1. physical maintenance of family members
2. socialization of family members for roles in the family and other groups
3. maintenance of family members' motivation to perform family and other roles
4. maintenance of social control within the family and between family members and outsiders
5. addition of family members through adoption or reproduction and their release when mature.

See also **individual development task.**

**feedback process**—transmissions of information from outsiders and family members that may result in a "mismatch" between the information and family values or goals.

1. *negative feedback*—the family attempts to bring members into conformity with existing behavior patterns and values that will lead to deviance reduction and homeostasis.

2. *positive feedback*—the family encourages changes from previous behavior patterns and values that will lead to increased deviation and morphogenesis.

**hypothesis**—a proposition translated into operational terms so that the specified relationship among variables can be empirically tested.

**individual developmental (or development) task**—a task that arises at or about a certain period in the life of a family or individual, unsuccessful achievement of which may lead to the individual's unhappiness, his/her difficulty with later tasks, and disapproval by society. (Modified from Robert J. Havighurst, *Human Development and Education*. New York: Longmans Green, 1953, 2.) See also **family development task.**

**interaction structure**—patterns implicitly growing out of role relations between and among all family members.

    1. *power*—family relationships based on the relative probabilities of family members being able to act despite the opposition of others.

    2. *communication*—the channels by which information, feelings, and casual observations are transmitted among family members.

    3. *affection*—family relationships based on interpersonal intimacy varying on a closeness-distance dimension.

**interdependency of positions**—a property of the family as a social system, such that the interactions of members affect other members not originally involved.

**joint family**—a family consisting of more than one nuclear family sharing a common residence, e.g., two brothers and their respective wives and children, or parents, their children, and their children's children.

**limited linkage**—the constraints task achievement in previous stages places on behaviors in the current stage.

**morphogenesis**—the process by which the family establishes new behaviors and explores alternate goals so that there is a clear divergence from older ways and values.

**norms**—behavioral expectations that set off one role from another; the socially and culturally defined "ought to's" of behavior that accompany a social role.

**nuclear family**—is a family consisting of the husband, wife, and their children sharing a common residence.

**organismic fallacy**—the assumption that the family has a life apart from the lives of its members.

**person-** versus **position-oriented families**

    1. *person-oriented families*—families whose power structures entail roles allocated on the basis of personal qualities and not on the basis of age and gender; communication channels are two-way, from parents to children and children to parents.

    2. *position-oriented families*—families whose power structures entail roles allocated according to the age and gender of the member and not on the basis of his/her individual characteristics; communication channels are one-way, from parents to children. (Basil Bernstein, *Class, Codes and Control.* London: Routledge & Kegan Paul, 1971.)

**plurality pattern**—number of possible interpersonal relationships in the family at any point in time based on the number of its members. The number of dyadic relations in a family can be determined by the following formula in which *y* stands for the number of family members.

$$\frac{y^2 - y}{2}$$

**position**—the elements of a social system to which are assigned certain roles. In the family, the positions consist of husband-father, wife-mother, daughter-sister, and son-brother.

**positional career**—the progression of changing roles, role sequences, and role clusters belonging to a position viewed over time, which can include educational and occupational as well as marital, parental, sibling, and child careers.

**proposition**—a statement that links two or more aspects of phenomena demarcated by concepts.

**research**—the means for systematically collecting and analyzing information about some subject, such as the family, in order to describe it, to list hypotheses concerning it or to apply the information to modify the subject under investigation.

*cross-sectional research*—research in which the information is collected at one point in time.

*longitudinal research*—research in which the sample of persons from whom information is collected are followed over a period of time with several data collecting periods.

**restricted** versus **elaborated language codes**

1. *language code*—the principle that regulates the selection and organization of speech events.

2. *restricted language code*—a sort of oral shorthand in which a change in pitch or slight gesture serves to call up in the auditor the shared experience that gives meaning to the communication.

3. *elaborated language code*—a code that utilizes a wide range of vocabulary and different kinds of sentence structures. (Bernstein, *Ibid.*)

**role**—consistent behavior appropriate to a particular situation that has developed through the individual's interactions with others and is influenced by their sanctions and relevant preexisting norms.

**role cluster**—the total complement of roles and their associated norms that make up a social position at one particular time.

**role complex**—the total complement of positions, roles, and their associated norms that define a socal system such as the family at one particular time.

**role differentiation**—the division of roles into different types, such as instrumental and expressive roles.

**role making**—interaction patterns are improvised by the actors with whatever patterning that occurs resulting from habituation rather than initial normative prescriptions. The actors are creating normative expectations within the family group itself.

**role reciprocity**—an exchange relationship that implies sanctions will be employed if one actor's rights are not fulfilled by another person performing his duties. The aggrieved party can stop fulfilling the duties that constitute the other's rights until this other party performs his/her duties.

**role sequence**—the behavioral changes in the content of a role over time.

**selective boundary maintenance**—a property of the family as a social system. The family develops certain characteristics possessed by all members which identify them as part of the family unit and distinguish them from nonmembers, e.g., certain phrases, pet names, rituals. The family maintains its contacts selectively in such a way that it maintains its identity.

**social network**—the face-to-face, close associates of an individual.

1. *close-knit social network*—the associates in the individual's social network are mutually acquainted and see one another when the individual is not present.

2. *loose-knit social network*—the associates in the individual's social network do not know each other or, if acquainted, know each other only slightly (Bott, *ibid*.).

**social system**—a set of positions directly or indirectly related in a causal network so that each position is related to at least some others in a more or less stable way over any particular time period.

**stage**—divisions within the family career that are different enough from one another to constitute separate periods.

**status**—a social position defined by the varying sets of rights and duties assigned to it.

**structural patterns**—customary and enduring interaction patterns between social positions, such as power and communication structures.

**structure-modifying group**—a property of the family social system. Despite continuity and stability in many areas of behavior, the family must be adaptive in its interaction patterns owing to demands for change from members and outsiders; also referred to as *family morphogenesis.*

**subsystem**—interchanges between system positions such as husband and wife, parent and child, or among siblings that set the members apart to a varying extent from the broader family unit's influence.

**systemic concept**—one criterion of a concept's usefulness. It concerns the concept's fruitfulness in pointing out additional characteristics shared by the phenomena in addition to those the concept labels. For example, the concept, husband, groups together individuals who, besides sharing a particular marital status, often engage in similar role behaviors, such as breadwinner and household maintenance specialist.

**task performance group**—a property of the family as a social system. Family members must perform certain socially defined tasks that enable them to maintain their daily activities, and that enable the family to continue as a group, e.g., physical maintenance, social control, motivation, and morale maintenance.

**theory**—a set of related propositions, some of which have been derived from others, and some of which have been empirically confirmed.

# CHAPTER OPENING PHOTO CREDITS

Chapter One          Ron Sherman/Nancy Palmer
Chapter Two          Hella Hammid/Rapho-Photo Researchers
Chapter Three        Erika/Photo Researchers
Chapter Four         Mimi Forsyth/Monkmeyer
Chapter Five         Kathy Bendo
Chapter Six           Kathy Bendo
Chapter Seven        Photri-Photo Research
Chapter Eight         Mary Stuart Lang
Chapter Nine         David Bellak/Jeroboam
Chapter Ten           Victor Friedman/Rapho-Photo Researchers
Chapter Eleven      Chester Higgins/Photo Researchers
Chapter Twelve      David A. Krathwohl/Stock, Boston
Chapter Thirteen    Bill Anderson/Monkmeyer
Chapter Fourteen    Mary Stuart Lang
Chapter Fifteen      Ira Kirschenbaum/Stock, Boston
Chapter Sixteen     Paul Sequeira/Photo Researchers
Chapter Seventeen  Mary Stuart Lang

# Author Index

# Subject Index